Reading Comprehension Instruction

Reading Comprehension Instruction

Issues and Strategies

KATHERINE MARIA

York Press/Parkton, Maryland

This book was manufactured in the United States of America. Typography by Brushwood Graphics, Inc., Baltimore, Maryland. Printing and binding by McNaughton & Gunn, Inc., Ann Arbor, Michigan. Cover design by Joseph Dieter, Jr.

Library of Congress Catalog Card Number 90-70057
ISBN 0-912752-20-3

CONTENTS

FOREWORD

As Dr. Maria makes clear in the early chapters of this book, much has been learned in recent years about reading comprehension. New discoveries have given us a new appreciation of the complexity of the reading process—of its interactive, interrelated, and thus holistic nature. Naturally, as new discoveries become better known, recommendations for their use in new instructional thrusts soon appear in the literature on reading instruction. Thus, because we have learned that many stories have a predictable structure, we are urged to teach story grammar. Because we understand that good readers may implicitly ask themselves questions as they read, we are urged to teach students about self-questioning techniques. Because we have learned that students who know a lot about a topic understand a lot of what they read about it, we are urged to devote instructional time to developing the students' background before they read a selection.

A new discovery is often followed by proposals for testing students on their knowledge of whatever language structure or process has been found to be important in comprehending written language. Thus, we have been urged to test students on their knowledge of story structure, on their use of self-questioning, and on their background for what they read.

The new discoveries offer great promise for more effective teaching of reading. But these same discoveries also pose a potential danger: Educators, in an effort to teach the cognitive processes and the implicit knowledge of language structures that are the substance of many of the discoveries, may try to systematize these processes and knowledges into a set of skills (although they may not call them that). Thus, the discoveries, even though they have revealed more of the complex, interactive nature of reading, may fuel a new wave of skills-based instruction, in which the "skills" would be cognitive processes or verbalized knowledge of language structures.

Perhaps this danger arises because it is easier to prepare materials, lessons, and tests based on an array of named "skills" or abilities than to deal flexibly with the needs of particular students in a particular classroom. But using a preselected array of materials and lessons to teach reading comprehension is like carrying out a political campaign by preselecting an array of statements and tactics and using them without regard to the issues and situations that arise.

The challenge, then, is to learn how to use the new instructional possibilities at times and in ways that will help the students who need them at particular times and in particular circumstances.

To meet this challenge, the teacher needs a guide that will show how the new instructional possibilities can work in classrooms—as ways of learning about the instructional needs of the students and as ways of responding to those needs. In this book, Katherine Maria provides this kind of help. By discussing the theoretical and research bases of many instructional techniques, by evaluating those techniques and suggesting modifications for particular situations, and by illustrating instructional techniques using classroom examples, she makes the new discoveries in reading comprehension come alive as a range of strategies that the teacher can use flexibly to help each child read better. This relevance to the job of teaching makes the book uniquely useful, not only as a guide for classroom teachers, but as a text for courses in developmental or remedial reading.

Katherine Maria brings to the writing of this book an unusual background. While she is a thorough scholar, immersed in the new developments in the field, she has also remained a teacher, both of children and of other teachers. She not only knows, she can do. She is gifted in working with children, and in this book she shares her gift.

Walter H. MacGinitie

PREFACE

This book is the result of one teacher's search for ways to help children understand what they read. Ten years ago I was a Title I remedial reading teacher working with children in grades one through six. I had been teaching these children for about six years, and although I was not completely successful with all children, I was confident that I was helping them recognize words. I had no systematic approach, however, about how to help them when they did not understand what they were reading. I knew that I was not teaching comprehension; I was only testing for comprehension, as were the teachers in Durkin's study (1978–1979). I discovered on my own what Durkin discovered in another research study (1981), namely, that there was no help for me in the teachers' manuals of basal readers. One book, Russell Stauffer's *Directing Reading Maturity as a Cognitive Process* (1969), seemed to offer some answers, but they were not enough.

Looking for more answers, I enrolled in Teachers College, Columbia University. Cognitive psychologists were exploring the nature of the reading process, and study after study was beginning to throw light on how we understand what we read. Through a combination of luck and good advice, I became the student of a very special teacher, Walter MacGinitie. He didn't give me all the answers. He was wise enough to know that he didn't have them all. He made me aware of something far more valuable: where and how to look for ways to help children understand what they read. This book is dedicated to him in gratitude. The search is by no means over, and I trust that I am wise enough to know that it can never be over. My hope is that this book will inspire the search in other teachers like myself.

The first section of the book (Chapters 1 through 4) discusses the components of comprehension instruction: the reading process, the reader, the text, the school environment, and the teacher as a particularly influential component of that environment. Chapter 2 includes a discussion of reading disability from a perspective that considers extrinsic as well as intrinsic factors and suggests that reading comprehension problems are often the result of an interaction of both types of factors. Chapter 4 discusses how comprehension instruction can be implemented. It presents several models of comprehension instruction and describes the strengths and weaknesses of each model.

The second section (Chapters 5 through 8) discusses the *what* of comprehension instruction: factors to be considered and techniques to be used before, during, and after reading. The third section (Chapters 9 and 10) relates comprehension instruction to a total language arts program including listening, speaking and writing, as well as reading, and considers the relationship between comprehension instruction and comprehension assessment. The techniques discussed in these later sections are suitable for all children since they, like adults, experience difficulty understanding certain texts in certain situations.

ACKNOWLEDGMENTS

I am very grateful to Allison Kelly, Rosemarie Armetta, and the Chapter I children and teachers in Yonkers and in District 3 in New York City. They were a constant source of inspiration as were my graduate students whose questions and comments clarified my thinking. I am particularly grateful to those Chapter I children who were my students in demonstration lessons and the teachers who contributed activities and lessons to this book: Nanci Autieri, Jackie Bernstein, Carene Domato, Harriet Hirsch, Debbie Kiely, Priscilla Tortorella, and Barbara Zucrow. I want to express my appreciation to Mary Alice Fitzgerald and Lois Dreyer who read portions of my manuscript and offered valuable comments. I would also like to thank Walter MacGinitie for reading Chapter 10 and giving me the benefit of his expert advice. To Evelyn Blustein, my dear friend and colleague, I owe a special debt of thanks. She read every word of the manuscript, and agonized over the problems with me so much so that she had a few sleepless nights on my behalf. Her advice was and is a never-failing source of support.

Finally, I am grateful to my family—my grandchildren, Jessica, Christopher, Michael, and Daniel for understanding when I was too busy to play with them and my sons, Michael and Christopher, and their wives, Jennifer and Kathie, for understanding when I was too busy to babysit. To my daughter Anne, I offer my special thanks for helping me keep my priorities straight and providing me with the perspective of a classroom teacher. To my husband Mike above all, my deep thanks for all the hours he spent alone without complaint and all the times he said just the right words that enabled me to do one more rewrite.

COMPONENTS OF THE READING COMPREHENSION PROCESS

CHAPTER

1

THE READING PROCESS

Reading comprehension instruction, as defined in this book, means help-ing children to understand written text. In most cases, the children will be reading the text themselves. Therefore, the first issue we need to consider is the nature of the reading process.

Reading is different things to different people. For some teachers and the-orists, reading is a composite skill like bicycle riding that is made up of many different subskills. Bicycle riding uses subskills like pedaling and steering. Sub-skills in reading include skills such as knowing the sounds of the short vowels and using context as an aid to word recognition. By instruction and practice with each of the subskills, children acquire the automatic skill of reading.

Reading subskills must be integrated, and the composite skill, i.e., read-ing, must be practiced in order to achieve fluency, just as bicycle riding must be practiced in order to achieve proficiency and ease. However, as Anderson et al. pointed out in *Becoming a Nation of Readers* (1985), for the most part this read-ing practice does not occur. Seventy percent of the children's time in primary schools is spent completing worksheets which require only "a perfunctory level of reading" (p. 75). "The amount of time children spend reading in the average classroom is small. An estimate of silent reading time in the typical primary school class is seven or eight minutes per day, or less than 10% of the total time devoted to reading" (p. 7).

Many people, including some teachers, believe that reading is syn-onymous with decoding, the process by which words are recognized. Thus for them, the subskills of reading include word recognition skills only. For some within this group, reading may even be synonymous with phonics. According to them, if a child understands and uses the sound/symbol system of English, then the child can read. They believe that recognizing words by sight is not really reading. Comprehension is not seen as a part of the reading process, but rather as a more generalized cognitive process.

One of the reasons there was so little attention paid to comprehension instruction during the sixties and seventies was the prevailing view (Devine 1986) that if children were taught word recognition, comprehension would follow automatically. Comprehension was considered a product of the reading process. As Durkin (1978–1979) pointed out, comprehension was assessed; it was not taught. When children did not understand what they read, their failure was attributed to lack of intelligence rather than lack of instruction. This was not the view, however, of the earliest reading theorists.

Men like Huey (1908) and Thorndike (1917) emphasized reading as a meaning-acquisition process, i.e., reading as comprehension. Thorndike's description (1917) of understanding a paragraph, reprinted in 1973, sounds modern in its characterization of reading as a constructive, holistic process.

> Reading is a very elaborate procedure, involving a weighing of each of many elements in a sentence, their organization in the proper relations one to another, the selection of certain of their connotations and the rejection of others, and the cooperation of many forces to determine final responses. In fact . . . the act of answering simple questions about a simple paragraph . . . includes all the features characteristic of typical reasoning (Edward L. Thorndike 1917, p. 323, reprinted in Robert L. Thorndike 1973, p. 137).

From the beginning of the century until the sixties and seventies, a behavioristic theory of learning was the dominant theory in psychology. Reading theories based on this view of learning did not emphasize comprehension. Comprehension was considered to be an automatic outcome of word recognition or decoding and not a subject for special study or emphasis. However, when psychology turned to the information-processing model of learning in the sixties, the process of comprehension became a very natural object of study for reading researchers, psycholinguists, and cognitive psychologists working in a variety of areas: artificial intelligence, information processing, discourse analysis, text analysis, and memory, as well as reading.

We do not claim to understand the reading process at the present time, but we certainly know more about it now than ever before. The knowledge we have gained about the comprehension process based on the explosion of research in the past twenty years has changed the definition of reading held by most experts. With this new knowledge, we have come full circle so that the focus is once again on the process rather than the product of reading. The reading process is now viewed as one which involves comprehension and decoding as integrally related. This process in which the reader actively searches for meaning is characterized as: (1) interactive, (2) constructive, and (3) holistic.

READING AS AN INTERACTIVE PROCESS

One model of the reading process, the interactive model (Rumelhart 1977), is a model of the reading process as it takes place in the mature reader. The definition of reading outlined in this model blurs the distinction between decoding and comprehension since each is seen as interacting with the other. In Rumelhart's model, the reader processes factors like letter features and sounds (referred to as bottom-up factors) *at the same time* as factors like his or her knowledge of the topic of the text and the situation in which it is read (referred to as top-down factors). This interactive model, therefore, suggests that reading involves simultaneous parallel processing of both bottom-up and top-down factors. The model proposes that the weight given to particular factors, whether top-down or bottom-up, will depend on characteristics of the reader (such as decoding ability), the text (such as familiarity of topic), and the context or environment in which the reading takes place. Thus, the importance of top-down and bottom-up factors will differ from reader to reader, text to text, and situation to situation.

The bottom-up model (Gough 1972) and the top-down model (Goodman 1976), focused on word recognition aspects of the reading process, emphasizing either decoding or knowledge as the starting points in a serial linear process. These earlier models have generally been revised to include the idea of parallel processing so that in a certain sense all the models have become interactive (Samuels and Kamil 1984). Thus today there is general agreement that reading is an interactive process in the sense that it involves processing of bottom-up and top-down factors at the same time.

Today those who subscribe to both the top-down or bottom-up models of the reading process accept the idea of parallel processing, but focus on the importance of factors at a particular level rather than on the situational nature of the process. They continue to argue that either knowledge or decoding factors are the most important in the process. Bottom-up theories offer support for a heavy emphasis on phonics, while top-down theories underlie the whole language approach in which "decoding follows reading" (Poeten 1988). This disagreement over the primacy of bottom-up or top-down factors has dominated the area of early reading instruction.

While the models discussed thus far have generally focused on reading as a word recognition process, several theorists have tried to explain the interaction of comprehension and decoding factors. They have focused on reader-to-reader differences, attempting to explain how the reading process might differ for readers with different abilities. The LaBerge and Samuels model (1974) suggests that the way in which attention is deployed is one difference between novice and fluent readers. This model assumes that readers have a limited attention capacity. Because of this, novice readers, for whom the decoding process is not automatic, must switch their attention back and forth between decoding and comprehension. As readers become more fluent and the decoding process becomes more automatic, more attention is available for comprehension.

Chall (1983) implies that there are other differences between the early reading process and the mature reading process. Although she does not develop a formal model of the reading process, she does suggest a stage theory of reading as it takes place in instructional situations in school. She postulates that the reading process differs as the reader moves through a series of stages from nonreader to mature reader. In the pre-reading stage, top-down factors, such as knowledge and context, are more important. In the beginning reading stage, bottom-up decoding factors assume greater importance and in the later stages top-down factors become more important again. Part of the reason for the difference in the process at each stage is the reader's level of decoding ability and language ability, and part is the types of texts and tasks given to the reader. At the beginning stages, the reader is learning to read. In the later stages, the reader is reading to learn.

Stanovich (1980) offers a more formal model of the reading process which elaborates on the idea that the weight given to bottom-up and top-down factors differs from reader to reader. His model is called the interactive compensatory model. The key concept of his theory is that "a process at any level can compensate for deficiencies at any other level" (p. 36) so that "a deficit in any knowledge source results in a heavier reliance on other knowledge sources, regardless of their level in the processing hierarchy" (p. 63). For example, children who have difficulty with word recognition may overrely on their world knowledge of the topic, resulting in a distorted understanding of the text (Maria and MacGinitie 1982). Stanovich's model also explains how text factors may affect the nature of the reading process. If a text deals with a topic about which children are unfamiliar, they may have to pay more attention to phonic and syntactic cues.

Although all the models discussed thus far do recognize comprehension as an integral part of the reading process, they do not attempt to explain how comprehension occurs. Another interactive model (Kintsch 1979) attempts to explain the comprehension process. Comprehension of text is viewed as taking place in cycles. The model of processing begins with an input cycle consisting of a number of propositions. (Propositions are the semantic representations of the surface information in the text.) Each proposition consists of a predicate (a verb or relation) and one or more arguments (nouns or other propositions) (Kintsch and van Dijk 1978). The verb or relation connects the arguments so that they represent a single idea. A sentence usually contains several propositions.

Sentence boundaries often determine the number of propositions included in the input cycle. If a sentence is too long, however, it will be processed clause-by-clause (Jarvella 1971). Each proposition processed must be connected to those already processed. Therefore, propositions processed later are matched on the basis of relevance with propositions processed earlier and retained in short-term memory. More stringent criteria for relevance are applied at each succeeding cycle. If no match is found, a search for a match is made in long-term memory. If no match is found in long-term memory, either an inference is made or comprehension breaks down.

Since word recognition is not considered in this model, the processes just described are considered bottom-up factors. Like Rumelhart, Kintsch insists on the importance of both top-down and bottom-up processes. Kintsch's more recent work (1986) specifies top-down factors in greater detail and distinguishes between comprehension as recall and comprehension as learning from text. Kintsch suggests that one aspect of top-down processing involves "the establishment of a coherent representation of the meaning of the text both at the local and global levels" (1986, p. 89). This *textbase* is sufficient for recall and is necessary but not sufficient for learning. Integration of text with the comprehender's knowledge system involves making inferences, a term Kintsch uses synonymously with learning. This integration process involves the updating or construction of a *situation model* of the text, a mental representation of the situation described by the text. Construction of these two internal models involves factors such as the reader's goals for reading, world knowledge, and knowledge about text structure. These factors interact to affect processing at all levels and, as in Rumelhart's model, processing at one level affects processing at another level with information moving top down and bottom up.

Reading authorities who discuss comprehension and comprehension instruction often use the term "interactive" in a different sense than when they discuss formal models of the reading process. They focus on the interaction of the reader with the text in the reading process. Cooper (1986), for example, states that "the interaction between the reader and the text is the foundation of comprehension" (p.3). He goes on to explain that in order to comprehend a text, the reader must be able to relate the ideas in the text to his own ideas. Wilson and Gambrell (1988) similarly define reading comprehension as "the process of using one's own prior experiences and text cues to infer the author's intended meaning" (p.12). As *Building a Nation of Readers* (Anderson et al. 1985) points out, this view of reading as an interaction between the reader and the text implies that reading is a constructive process.

READING AS A CONSTRUCTIVE PROCESS.

We used to view text as a fixed object containing meaning. The reader's job was to *get* the meaning from the text. However, when we define comprehension as an interaction between the reader and the text, we move away from the idea of the reader getting meaning from the text. The reader is no longer passive and receptive but active and constructive in the communication process between reader and writer. The writer constructs a message, and the reader reconstructs that message based on his ability and prior knowledge. Thus, both reading and writing involve planning, construction of meaning, and revision (Tierney and Pearson 1983). It is important to note that readers construct meaning based on information they gather from the text. When theorists say that reading is a constructive process, they do not mean that the reader makes up the text as in "pseudo-reading" in which young children may make up what the book says based on the pictures and previous readings by adults (Chall 1983).

This new view of the reading process is the result of research, particularly in the area of artificial intelligence (Shank 1982), which has made it clear that no text is ever fully explicit. Text is now viewed as a "blueprint for meaning, a set of tracks or clues that the reader builds as he builds a model of what the text means" (Pearson 1985, p. 726).

As Wilson and Gambrell's (1988) definition of comprehension suggests, we have discovered that comprehension always involves inference. Since inference is based on the reader's experience and since each reader's experience is unique, each person's understanding of a particular text will also be unique. For example, the sentence "The dog bit the man" may seem to be totally obvious in its meaning, or capable of being literally understood. Yet research suggests that each reader will have a slightly different understanding of *dog* based on the dogs he has experienced directly or indirectly (Anderson and Pearson 1984). The sentence will make sense to the reader if he or she knows that it is not uncommon for dogs to bite men. If the reader does not know about dogs biting men, he or she can use linguistic ability to determine that the dog is doing the biting. The reader knows this because of the syntactic arrangement of the words in the sentence. Yet without some knowledge of how dogs bite, the reader may infer a different type of biting from the type the author expects the reader to understand. The reader may also have a different understanding of *bit* depending, to some extent, on whether or not he or she was ever bitten by a dog. And again the reader's understanding of *man* will depend on what some theorists call the reader's "instantiation" of the concept of man. He or she will understand *man* based on the men he or she has had contact with either directly or indirectly. If this possibility for variation in understanding is true for such a short, simple text, one that would generally be characterized as involving "literal comprehension," imagine the possibilities for variation in longer texts that, even on the surface, are obviously much more "inferential."

This view of reading as a constructive process can be quite disconcerting to a teacher. If there is the possibility for such variation, how can we be sure that anyone ever understands any text? Devine (1986) suggests that comprehension is rarely completely successful in terms of complete one-to-one correspondence between the writer's and the reader's ideas. This is due partly to the fact that once a text is written, it exists as a permanent entity independent of the writer. It may take on a meaning of its own, independent from that intended by the writer. Shakespeare's plays, for example, have meant different things to readers in different centuries. However, if a text is well written, it is a good representation of the ideas in the writer's mind. Usually enough overlap exists between the writer's and the reader's experiences to allow for considerable comprehension and communication. As Devine (1986) points out "most people in a society share the same language system and often the same ways of organizing discourse" (p. 65). The wider the gap, however, between the experiences of the writer and the reader, and/or the writer's use of language and the reader's language competence, the less the reader's "text in the head" will match the text itself and the less likely it is that communication will occur. Children may have neither the experiences nor the language competence assumed by the author of a particular text. Through comprehension instruction, the teacher bridges the gap between child and text.

READING AS A HOLISTIC PROCESS

When we say that reading is an interactive process, we are also implying that it is a holistic process. No theorist ever put it any better than a fifth-grade boy who was a subject in an informal study I conducted several years ago. I interviewed him about how he understood a text that he was reading. The text, *A City without Roads* (Rauch and Clements 1974), described the city of Venice. All the children I interviewed had trouble understanding the text at first. They found the topic strange and the language in the text confusing. This boy, like many of the other good readers, could not tolerate the confusion. He reread lines in the text puzzling over what a gondola was. His response to me when I asked him how he had found the answer is a great definition of reading which I have adopted as my own, "It wasn't any one thing. It was everything put together."

The important thing to remember is that breaking down reading into its parts is not really reading. Any teacher who has taught phonics, for example, knows there is a giant leap between learning the phonic elements and using them effectively in fluent reading. However, recognizing the complex, interactive, constructive, holistic nature of the reading process poses problems for teachers. How does one teach such a complex process?

Although recently the whole-language movement has attacked the idea of breaking down the reading process, most teachers today still view reading as a series of discrete skills. They also recognize that comprehension instruction is an integral part of reading instruction probably because the basal readers also espouse this point of view, and basal readers are used in most of American classrooms. Basal readers have their own lists of "specific" comprehension skills, such as recognizing cause and effect and getting the main idea. Comprehension instruction organized in this way focuses on individual skills rather than on the holistic process. Lists of comprehension skills are presented along with lists of phonic and other word recognition skills, suggesting that comprehension skills are analogous to word recognition skills.

Some materials even suggest that these comprehension skills can be taught and mastered in the same way that a child can master the short *a* sound. The child is given pretests and post-tests on the main idea, for example. If the child reaches the criterion level, the skill of "main idea" is checked off. However, if we think about it, we can see that comprehension skills are not skills that can be checked off as they are mastered. Recognizing the main idea and determining cause and effect are reading processes that continue throughout one's life, processes that are used in understanding more difficult, more abstract, and more varied texts.

Cooper (1986) and Nix (1981) have suggested that these traditional comprehension skills are not really very specific. For example, there are many cases in which getting the main idea involves recognizing cause and effect. These skills are just different ways of focusing the reader's attention on the text. Comprehension instruction is more complex than teaching a set of discrete skills.

READING AS A LANGUAGE PROCESS

It has always been recognized that reading is a language process. In the past, theorists placed much emphasis on the differences between oral and written language processes. The most obvious difference between reading and oral language is the visual nature of reading. In the sixties and seventies theorists (e.g., Gibson and Levin 1975) focused on this difference. This theoretical emphasis, in turn, led to much instructional attention to the visual aspects of the reading process. Children were given readiness activities using matching shapes and letters. Children were often classified as "perceptually handicapped" and those who failed to meet expectations in reading were given exercises in areas like visual tracking and visual memory to help improve their reading.

These instructional methods were largely unsuccessful (Hammill and Bartel 1975), so theorists began to emphasize the auditory nature of the reading process. In an extensive review of the research on causes of reading disability, Vellutino (1979) suggested that reading problems were largely language problems, citing studies such as Vogel (1975) to indicate that children had difficulty in reading because they also had difficulty with oral language. This view of reading disability focuses on the similarities between oral langauge and reading. Others (e.g., Gough and Hillinger 1980) have pointed out that there is a profound difference between learning to speak and learning to read. Although some children do learn to read without instruction, most have to be *taught* how to read.

Mattingly (1972) and Liberman et al. (1980) have suggested that one difference between reading and oral language is that reading requires "linguistic awareness," i.e., an awareness of language as an entity in itself. Young children use oral language effectively as a means of communication without consciously thinking about language and how it works. However, in its early stages reading requires translating written materials into oral representations. This involves conscious awareness of language at many different levels, e.g., knowledge about language phonemes and syntax (Menyuk and Flood 1981).

Researchers like Ehri (1979), Perfetti, Beck, and Hughes (1981), and Stanovich (1986) have suggested that in early reading "phonemic awareness" is particularly important. In order to read, children need to be aware of the phonemes as separate entities; that is, they need to know what phonemes are in a word and where they occur. This "phonemic awareness" is difficult to acquire because, contrary to common belief, we do not hear individual phonemes in a word (Liberman et al. 1967). When we say the word *cat*, our mouths form the /c/ at the same time as our throats form the vowel /a/ so that the sounds cannot be separated. The individual phonemes must be abstracted from the sound stream, a difficult cognitive task. Thus, a number of reading experts (e.g., Camp, Winburg, and Zinna 1981) believe that since reading is different from oral language, reading instruction should be direct, proceeding in careful steps using a bottom-up approach.

Top-down theorists like Goodman (1976) and Smith (1978) disagree vehemently with this approach to early reading. The whole language movement, the most recent manifestation of the top-down approach, emphasizes the similarities rather than the differences between reading and oral language. Whole language theorists view reading as a process that occurs naturally in a literate society and believe that children begin to acquire knowledge about print at birth. They believe that because reading is a naturally occurring process, children should learn how to read in the same way they learn how to talk. Cambourne (1984) describes seven conditions under which children learn to talk and suggests that these same conditions affect children's ability to read.

1. *Immersion*. Young children learning to talk are immersed in oral language. Adults speak to babies constantly from birth, treating them as though they understand. Children learning how to read should be surrounded by print in the same way. Classrooms should be literate environments.

2. *Demonstration*. Just as adults provide models of good oral language for children learning to talk, adults should provide good models of reading through activities like reading aloud and Sustained Silent Reading (SSR).

3. *Expectation*. Except in special cases, children are expected to be successful in learning how to talk. That same expectation of success should be conveyed to children who are learning how to read. Too often reading is treated as a difficult mysterious process. Learning to use oral language is a far more difficult task.

4. *Responsibility*. Although children's early words and sentences encode the same sorts of meaning (Ferguson 1989), children who are learning how to talk don't all learn in the same way. For example, children vary in their preference for nouns or other words (Bates, Bretherton, and Snyder 1988). Children learning to read should not be expected to learn to read in the same way, mastering the same skills at the same time.

5. *Approximation*. Young children learning to talk are praised not reprimanded for approximations like "Gama" for "Grandma." Miscues or approximations in reading should be evaluated in terms of their approximation to meaning. Reading "home" is a better miscue for "house" than reading "horse" because it is closer in meaning.

6. *Employment*. Young children learning to talk use language often even though they are not totally competent in it. Children learning to read should read often with each other, with the teacher, and with tapes.

7. *Feedback*. Adults correct the meaning but not the form of young children's oral language. Adults model the correct form. Teachers should focus on meaning in reading while providing corrective feedback with regard to form.

Although whole language theory emphasizes reading as meaning, instructional applications of the theory have focused largely on early reading and methods of teaching word recognition. We turn now to a discussion of similarities and differences between oral and written language which are more directly related to comprehension. Thus far in comparing how oral and written language are processed we have considered oral language as primarily auditory and written language as primarily visual. However, both oral and written language are composed of form, content, and function. They can be compared within each of these categories.

Form consists of phonology, syntax, and structure. Certainly, oral and written language share the same phonology and syntax to some degree. But, as discussed earlier in this section, the form in which phonology is presented is different and requires higher order processing in written language than in oral. While some experts (Chafe and Danielewicz 1987; Tannen 1982) suggest that writing tends to be more syntactically complex, Halliday (1987) suggests that oral language syntax is more complex. All agree, however, that the syntax of written language differs from that of oral language. In written language, the use of words that signal relationships between sentences and paragraphs, and thus hold the text together, is more extensive and complex. These words, labeled cohesive ties or markers by Halliday and Hasan (1976), include pronouns, conjunctions, time words like *then* or *later*, place terms like *here* and *there*, and many others. Written language, particularly expository text—text whose primary purpose is to inform—tends to be more formal than oral language with a different type of structure. It is important to note, however, that there is variation within both oral and written language. An informal letter may require less planning and organization than a formally prepared speech. Because of the permanent nature of written language, its organization may be more easily perceived.

Certainly, at times, oral and written language are concerned with similar content. This similarity is the basis of the instructional method called language experience, the idea that written language is speech written down. Narratives or stories based on an oral language tradition are found in both oral and written forms and are often very similar. However, written text, especially written expository text, differs from oral language in the type of information it communicates. The common sense knowledge communicated by oral language is tied to actions and to particular and concrete events. The knowledge communicated by written language may typically be more abstract, general, and logical (Olson 1977).

There is also less redundancy in written language than in oral language. Speakers tend to repeat themselves and to use more words than they would use to communicate the same message in writing (Wilkinson 1971). Putting the same idea in a slightly different way, Halliday (1980, 1987) suggests that oral and written language differ in the amount of lexical density found in the two forms. (Lexical density is defined as the number of content words per clause or sentence). It appears that lexical density increases as a result of the amount of monitoring that goes into the production of a discourse. Written text, which is "edited" more than spoken discourse, therefore has greater lexical density.

The main function of both oral and written language is communication. Halliday (1975) suggests that within this main purpose, there are seven kinds of language as categorized according to function.

1. Instrumental language—language for getting things, for satisfying needs.
2. Regulatory language—language for controlling others.

3. Interactional language—language for maintaining personal relationships.
4. Personal language—language for expressing personality or individuality.
5. Imaginative language—language for creating a world of one's own.
6. Informative language—language for conveying information, for communicating something about the experienced world.
7. Heuristic language—language for finding things out, for wondering, for hypothesizing.

Both oral and written language can serve all the described functions. Written language can serve these functions in a special way allowing us to communicate over space and time without the necessity for face-to-face interaction. Modern technology, to some degree, has blurred some of the distinctions between oral and written language. But, in general, oral language involves a shared non-linguistic context, i.e., the participants are in the same situation. Thus oral language is supported by other cues to meaning such as body language, gesture, and eye contact. There is also a high degree of interaction between participants in the language event. These characteristics of oral language make it particularly suited for the more personal and social kinds of language functions (instrumental language, regulatory language, interactional language, and personal language). Oral language in its purest form is conversation that involves continuing interaction between at least two people who are face to face. Telephone conversations have a high degree of interaction but not the shared context, while a teacher's classroom lecture has the shared context but not the same degree of interaction. Although reading is an interactive process, it certainly does not involve the same degree of interaction as oral conversation in which the participants take turns communicating and in which each utterance is a response to a previous utterance by the other participant.

Because of its permanent nature, written language is usually constructed without a particular reader in mind. In written language, the author and the reader do not share non-linguistic context. According to Cazden (1972), "Written text is the final point on the developmental dimension towards independence from non-linguistic context" (p.199). This lack of shared non-linguistic context makes comprehension of written language more difficult, but the permanent nature of written language is an aid to comprehension. If written language is not initially understood, it can be reread, thought about, and puzzled over with less burden on memory than oral language. Written language, therefore, is particularly suited for the more intellectual functions of language (imaginative language, informative language, and heuristic language).

In summary, reading is a language process similar to listening, speaking, and writing. Thus, whole language approaches, like the language experience method, can serve as important bridges between the child's oral language competence and his ability to comprehend written language. However, since written language is more difficult to comprehend because of its syntax, organization, abstract concepts, and the lack of direct interaction between reader and author, instruction in reading comprehension is necessary.

WHAT IS READING COMPREHENSION?

In this chapter, I have summarized the theories and research that have led to a new definition of reading—reading as a process involving both word recognition and comprehension. Since the focus of this book is reading comprehension, the definition of reading given here will also focus on comprehension while acknowledging the mutually beneficial interaction of word recognition and comprehension.

Reading comprehension is the holistic process of constructing meaning from written text through the interaction of (1) the knowledge the reader brings to the text, i.e., word recognition ability, world knowledge, and knowledge of linguistic conventions; (2) the reader's interpretation of the language that the writer used in constructing the text; and (3) the situation in which the text is read.

Since this newer way of looking at reading comprehension defines it as a process rather than a product, many authorities (e.g., Collins and Smith 1982) now suggest that in reading comprehension instruction children should be taught how best to engage in this process. Providing lists of specific skills was an attempt to break down the complexity of the process so that it could be taught. The traditional skills lists may be inappropriate, but the idea that the process must be broken down in some way in order to teach it is still valid, especially when dealing with children who have difficulty with the process.

One way of breaking down the comprehension process is to consider it in terms of the three components identified in the above definition: factors in the reader, the text, and the environment that interact to affect comprehension. Table I contains a tentative list of these factors, tentative because it makes no pretense of being exhaustive, and probably never can be, given the complexity of the process.

Table I

FACTORS AFFECTING THE READING PROCESS

Reader	Text
1. Decoding ability	1. Readability level
2. World knowledge	2. Content and topic

3. Linguistic knowledge:
    Vocabulary
    Sentence structure
    Narrative and expository schema
	3. Language used:
	    Vocabulary
	    Sentence Structure
	    Text coherence and structure

4. Metacomprehension:
    Knowledge about reading and different reading tasks
    Knowledge about oneself as a reader
    Knowledge about and use of reading strategies—comprehension monitoring
	4. Texts and their purposes:
	    Basal readers
	    Content area texts
	    Trade books

5. Interest and motivation	

Teacher
1. Management skill
2. Classroom climate
3. Teaching skill

The list, however, is a starting point based on current views of the comprehension process and serves as a framework for the rest of the book. The next three chapters will focus on the three components of the reading process: the reader, text, and school environment (particularly the teacher), suggesting ways in which differences among these components can affect the reading comprehension process.

Subsequent chapters will consider factors from each of the three components as they interact with each other (see table I). Particularly, these chapters will focus on how the teacher can serve as a bridge between the reader and text by the use of certain instructional techniques.

2

THE READER

Traditionally, the first component of the reading process, the reader, has received the most attention from parents, researchers, and teachers, particularly in those cases where the process breaks down and the child has difficulty with reading. In such cases, where a child is not reading as well as his or her peers, i.e., below grade level, he or she is often labeled a poor or disabled reader and causes of the reading problem are attributed to some defect in the child. For parents, this may mean berating the child for laziness. Others such as the children's peers or other lay people who characterize poor readers in this way may believe the child is not bright, often convincing the children themselves that they lack intelligence.

Today educators have adopted a more sophisticated definition of reading disability than simply reading below grade level by adding a consideration of the child's level of intelligence. Reading-disabled children are defined as those who are reading significantly below their potential. Potential usually is determined by performance on an intelligence test (McCormick 1987). Thus children with below average intelligence are not expected to read as well as their peers, while children with above average intelligence are expected to read at a higher level than their average peers (and are considered reading disabled if they are reading at grade level.) When intelligence is used as a factor in defining reading disability, the population of reading disabled children forms a typical bell-shaped curve with most reading disabled children of average intelligence and small approximately equal groups of children with high and low intelligence (McCormick 1987). It should be noted that one problem with this definition is that measures of intelligence are flawed. A child's performance on an IQ test is not really a measure of innate potential but more a measure of what the child has learned. Although this newer definition of reading disability acknowledges the relationship between level of intelligence and reading, it also recognizes the importance of other variables, e.g., neurological condition, socioeconomic status, educational opportunities, emotional state, attitude, and motivation. It also recognizes that these variables interact so that a child's reading problem usually cannot be attributed to only one of these variables.

Over the years, a great deal of research attention has been devoted to the search for the causes of reading disability. Most research has focused on the search for intrinsic causes, particularly in children whose reading failure could not be easily explained by obvious physical or sensory difficulties or lack of intelligence. Physicians were among the first to consider neurological causes. In the late nineteenth and early twentieth centuries Kussmaul (cited in Weiderholt 1974) identified "word blindness" in adults with normal sight, speech, and intellect and Hinshelwood (1917) described "congenital word blindness" in children. In 1928 Samuel Orton proposed a theory of reading disability which suggested that reading-disabled children had not established dominance of one side of the brain: these children did not prefer one side of the body for hand, eye, ear, and foot use. Orton believed that when neither side of the brain was dominant, children perceived words or letters appropriately on one side of the brain and as mirror images on the other side of the brain. This condition, which Orton calls strephosymbolia (twisted symbols), makes reading very difficult because children sometimes respond to the appropriate image and sometimes to the mirror image. When they respond to the mirror image, they make reversals of letters and words, perceiving b as d and was as saw. Later research (e.g., Balow and Balow 1964; Belmont and Birch 1965; Benton and McCann 1969; Capobianco 1967; Coleman and Deutsch 1964; Gates and Bennett 1933; Silver and Hagin 1960 cited in McCormick 1987) has discredited mixed cerebral dominance as the cause of most common forms of reading disability. Yet some professionals continue to attribute all degrees and kinds of reading failure to this cause.

The growth of the learning disabilities field has given greater prominence to a position that attributes reading problems to neurological dysfunction. In this field a reading disability is considered to be one form of a learning disability. However, in practice, reading is the academic area in which most learning disabilities are manifested (Connor 1983; Fleischner and Marzola 1988; Torgesen 1975) so that the terms *reading disability* and *learning disability* are often used synonymously. Johnson and Myklebust's (1967) definition of learning disability refers to neurological causation directly (" . . . we refer to children as having a psychoneurological learning disability, meaning that behavior has been disturbed as a result of a dysfunction of the brain" p.8). The federal definition of learning disabilities that guides current funding implies neurological causation by excluding other causes. It states that the term learning disabilities "does not include children who have learning problems which are primarily the result of visual, hearing or motor handicaps, of mental retardation, of emotional disturbance, or of environmental, cultural or economic disadvantage" (Federal Register 1977).

The new definition of learning disabilities proposed by the National Joint

Committee on Learning Disabilities once again refers to neurological causation directly. This definition has been endorsed by a large number of organizations concerned with the learning problems of children and adults but has not yet been adopted by the federal government. It reads as follows:

> Learning disabilities is a generic term that refers to a heterogeneous group of disorders manifested by significant difficulties in the acquisition and use of listening, speaking, reading, writing, reasoning or mathematical abilities. These disorders are intrinsic to the individual and presumed to be central nervous dysfunctions. Even though a learning disability may occur concomitantly with other handicapping conditions (e.g., sensory impairment, mental retardation, social and emotional disturbance) or environmental influences (e.g., cultural differences, insufficient/inappropriate instruction, psychogenic factors), it is not the direct result of those conditions or influences (National Joint Committee for Learning Disabilities 1981).

This definition, like the one commonly used by reading educators, acknowledges the principle of multiple causation, i.e., other factors may be affecting the child's performance in addition to the learning disability. However, the learning disability itself, which may be manifested as a reading disability, is attributed to neurological causes. As noted at the outset of this chapter, neurological causes are not the only causes of reading disability as it is defined by those in the field of reading. Other causes of reading failure are also postulated: in the thirties, forties, and early fifties popularization of Freudian psychology led to an emphasis on emotional disturbance as a cause of reading failure and to attention to motivation as a factor in reading problems. Since the sixties, attention also has focused on cultural "disadvantage" as a cause of reading problems. Yet regardless of whether intrinsic or extrinsic causes are suggested as the cause of the defect, reading failure is seen as resulting from a defect in the child.

The main reason for the continuation of the idea of a reading problem as due to a defect in the reader is probably the persistence of the medical model with which the study of reading began. The search for causes of reading disability resulting from the use of a medical model is important in helping us to determine how reading failure can be prevented. It has also had some good practical results. Programs providing supplementary reading instruction for "disadvantaged" children and learning-disabled children have been funded by the federal and state governments, and many children have been helped by these programs. On the other hand, discussion of causes does not help teaching practice. Research has not supported matching particular types of instruction with specific causes. For example, instruction designed to remediate deficits in basic processes like perception, attention, and memory did not improve the reading performance of learning-disabled children (Hammill and Bartel 1975). The labeling of children fostered by the search for causation has perpetuated the idea of blaming the child for reading failure rather than focusing attention on ways of adjusting instruction so that it is more effective.

Wixson and Lipson (1984) point out that the current interactive model of the reading process is not applied in cases of reading disability. They suggest that different models of the reading process are used to guide instructional decisions for able and disabled readers.

> When an able reader fails to successfully complete a particular reading task, we typically view this failure as the result of some aspect of the task, and alter the task accordingly. However, when a disabled reader fails, we presume that the failure reflects some internal disorder and initiate what Sarason and Doris (1979) call 'the search for pathology' (Wixson and Lipson 1984, p. 132).

The focus on reading disability as a defect in the child can sometimes serve as a welcome excuse that shifts the blame for the child's poor reading performance from the school to the child. For example, when reading failure is viewed as a necessary result of economic deprivation, teachers of children who are economically deprived may lower their expectations for these children since they can do nothing to correct the economic deprivation and the social problems which result.

However, the trend today is to attribute reading failure to intrinsic neurological causes rather than extrinsic economic causes. The number of "disadvantaged" children served by the Chapter I program has declined by 42% from 1966 to 1985 while the number of children identified as learning disabled has increased by 119% (McGill-Franzen 1987). Since reading is a cognitive process, there is always the possibility that neurological causes may contribute to a child's failure to meet our expectations in reading. Moreover, research has demonstrated the existence of a small group of people who are truly dyslexic, i.e., unable to learn to read because of neurological defects or differences. However, today all degrees and types of reading problems are attributed to neurological causes. Because a learning disability is unrelated to intelligence or to emotional problems and because of the publicity surrounding famous and successful learning disabled people, parents seem less threatened by the label of learning disabled than they are by other labels in special education. Having a child labeled learning disabled may be even more acceptable to some of them than considering their child "average." In several cases in my experience parents welcomed the diagnosis of a reading problem as a learning disability. Several years ago I overheard a young mother explaining to a colleague how relieved she was to find out that her eight year old daughter had a learning disability. She had been concerned that her child's poor performance in school might be related to the mother's frequent absences from home because of business trips. The diagnosis of a learning disability had relieved the mother of guilt. Her child was in a special program, and she could get on with her career.

Another reason for the persistance of the view of reading failure as due to a defect in the child is the fact that labeling children as handicapped or "disadvantaged" is politically necessary if children are to participate in programs that provide them with special reading instruction in small groups. (In practice, availability of funds often determines student placement, and distinctions between children whose reading failure is attributed to neurological causes and those whose reading failure is attributed to economic causes are not always clear.) Teachers with children labeled dyslexic or learning disabled may lower their expectations for these children and fail to provide them with reading instruction because they consider that instruction the responsibility of specialists.

Wixson and Lipson (1984) suggest that the reading performance of all children including those who fail to meet our expectations in reading should be viewed in the context of the interactive model of reading rather than in the context of a medical model. They point out that "While we are quick to accept the fact that variability in performance is a normal part of the process for able readers, we rarely allow for this possibility in evaluating the performance of less able readers" (p. 132). Viewing a child's failure to meet expectations in reading within the context of an interactive model eliminates the search for the cause of the defect and refocuses our attention on children's reading performance, how they read different texts in different situations, and which set of conditions is most likely to faciltate learning. The teacher's job is to determine those conditions under which the child can succeed and provide instruction that will increase the kinds of texts and situations that the child can deal with successfully.

It cannot be denied that some children fail to meet our expectations in reading with many different texts and in many different situations. Deciding what to call this group of children was one of the most difficult tasks I had in writing this book. I knew I did not want to call them *disabled readers* or *less able readers* or *poor readers* because all these terms are based on the medical model and suggest a defect in the child. I wanted a term that would suggest the special vulnerability of these children but would focus on the special responsibility we should feel toward them. I considered using the term *at-risk readers* suggested by Vacca (1988), but decided against it because describing these children as at risk for failure is not quite accurate; many of them are failing daily. Another problem with using the term *at-risk readers* is that the term is often used to refer only to minority children and children from a low socioeconomic level. I wanted a term that could be used to refer to all children who are failing to meet our expectations in reading regardless of their socioeconomic level.

I finally decided on the term *remedial readers* for want of any newer, more appropriate term. I chose this term because it suggests that while the group of children so labeled needs special attention, the group can be taught to read. The word *remedial* suggests a responsibility for teachers rather than a defect in the child. One problem with using the term *remedial readers* is that it has traditionally been used in classifying readers according to the setting in which they should receive instruction. Reading educators (Brown 1982; Harris and Sipay 1985) often classify children as (1) developmental readers: children who generally meet our expectations in reading and can be served by regular classroom instruction, (2) corrective readers: children who fail to meet our expectations in reading but whose problems are not very severe so that they can be served by the classroom teacher, and (3) remedial readers: children who fail to meet our expectations in reading and who need special reading instruction. I am not using the term *remedial readers* in its traditional sense here. I am using it to refer to all children who are failing to meet our expectations in reading, children commonly referred to as poor readers or disabled readers. The term *remedial* is used to suggest that the way in which we teach these children may need to be somewhat different from the way in which we teach average performing children. It is not used to suggest where the instruction should take place.

The table presented in Chapter 1, based on the interactive model of reading, allows us to consider all children including remedial readers in the context of the many factors that can affect their reading comprehension performance.

DECODING
The first factor listed in table I is decoding. Because decoding problems are obvious difficulties for many remedial readers, research and practice with these children have focused on reading as word recognition. Poor comprehension has often been attributed to poor decoding. It is true that if a child is unable to recognize any of the words in a particular text, he or she will not be able to understand that text. However, using poor decoding as the sole explanation for poor comprehension is not consistent with the interactive model of reading. This view is also not consistent with the results of a large number of studies comparing the listening and reading comprehension skills of good and remedial readers. The listening comprehension skills of remedial readers have often been found to be as poor as their reading comprehension (e.g., Berger 1978). When their listening comprehension is compared to the listening comprehension of good readers, some studies have found that the listening comprehension of the good readers is significantly better (e.g., Berger 1978; Guthrie 1973; Smiley et al. 1977). Since listening comprehension is traditionally assessed in a particular kind of listening situation, i.e., listening to written text read aloud, it seems more appropriate to describe the comprehension difficulties of the remedial readers in these studies as problems in the comprehension of written language, and to recognize that there are different levels of comprehension ability as well as different levels of decoding ability.

The interactive model views reading as a process in which word recognition and comprehension are integrally related. While there is evidence to suggest that the reader's level of decoding affects comprehension (e.g., Golinkoff 1975–1976) and vice versa (e.g., Goodman 1976), this evidence does not demonstrate that either factor is completely dependent on the other.

Today, most reading instruction for remedial readers emphasizes direct instruction of basic decoding skills usually to the exclusion of any comprehension instruction (Hayes and Jenkins 1986). There is evidence to suggest that direct instruction in decoding is sometimes successful with remedial readers, resulting in better comprehension. But in most cases, comprehension scores of remedial readers remain low (Brown, Palincsar, and Armbruster 1984). If comprehension is a low priority, and there is little or no systematic comprehension instruction for remedial readers, then the most likely result will be a failure to meet expectations in comprehension. Many reading authorities (e.g., Tharp

1982; Brown, Palincsar, and Armbruster 1984) urge that remedial readers should receive more direct comprehension instruction.

One of the reasons remedial readers receive so little comprehension instruction may be that many of their teachers believe comprehension instruction is only appropriate after word recognition fluency has been achieved. This was brought home to me recently when several teachers and I tried to select a text from among several trade books for a group of third grade remedial readers for whom we were planning a demonstration lesson in comprehension. I suggested several books from those available, but the teachers turned down every one, saying that they contained too many words the children would be unable to recognize. Deferring to their knowledge of the children, I kept suggesting simpler books. My final suggestion was *The Best Nest* by P. D. Eastman (1968), a Random House Beginner Book. My reason for suggesting this book was that, although it was a simple, predictable story, it contained information for the children to learn, i.e., places where birds build nests and materials birds use. In other words, comprehension instruction was appropriate for this text because there was something in the text to learn and understand. I pointed out to the teachers that texts at the very early reading level are not always appropriate for comprehension instruction. These texts are so simple that there is really no need for comprehension instruction. There would certainly be no point in using a text that read like "Nat the cat sat on a mat." The teachers, however, remained adamant in their belief that *The Best Nest* was too difficult. They were very concerned about the presence of words like *everybody*, *mattress*, and *stuffing* which they insisted the children would be unable to read. I suggested that it is not neccessary for children to be able to decode every single word in a text in order to understand it. Moreover, children may not recognize words in isolation, or even in context in certain texts, yet may recognize them in texts where other factors such as world knowledge and interest are strong. In this particular book, pictures gave clues to many of the words, e.g., *mattress* and *stuffing*.

It soon became clear to me that the teachers and I had different views based on our different theories of reading. The teachers apparently subscribed to a bottom-up theory of reading, believing that higher order processes like comprehension could not be successful without success first in prerequisite lower processes. I prevailed upon the teachers to let me try using *The Best Nest* with the children, reaching a compromise that allowed me to introduce several of the words in sentences before we began to read the book. The children were able to recognize all the words introduced in context. In fact, there were only two miscues in the children's reading of the 64 pages in the book. The lesson was very successful in terms of comprehension. Children learned the information about birds and their nests, adding this information to a semantic map containing information about birds that we constructed prior to reading. It was obvious to the teachers that these remedial readers enjoyed the focus on the ideas in the book. In other words, they enjoyed thinking and learning; they enjoyed real reading. I hope the teachers who watched the lesson began to rethink their theory of reading.

In summary, decoding is one of the many factors affecting the readers' comprehension. Remedial readers may benefit from instruction in decoding, but should receive comprehension instruction also.[1] Comprehension instruction does not have to wait until children attain perfect word recognition fluency. In fact, comprehension instruction may aid word recognition fluency.

WORLD KNOWLEDGE

The relationship between world knowledge (also referred to in the literature as background knowledge and prior knowledge) and reading comprehension has long been recognized. It seems obvious that knowledge about the topic of a text should aid comprehension of the text. Indeed, extensive research in the past twenty years using varied materials, subjects, and methods of providing prior knowledge demonstrates its extreme importance and its specific effects on reading comprehension. Bransford and Johnson (1972) used a specially constructed passage in a research study. Read the excerpt below and see if you can understand it.

> The procedure is quite simple. First you arrange things into different groups. Of course, one pile may be sufficient depending on how much there is to do. If you have to go somewhere else due to a lack of facilities, that is the next step. Otherwise, you are pretty well set. It is important not to overdo things (p. 722).

If you had not read the passage before, you probably had great difficulty understanding it. Bransford and Johnson demonstrated that high school students who could read and understand all the words in the passage were unable to understand or recall it without the title "Washing Clothes" which supplied the necessary background knowledge. Other studies using ambiguous passages showed that subjects with different perspectives (Anderson et al. 1977; Goetz et al. 1983; Pichert and Anderson 1977) or with different background knowledge (Brown et al. 1977) remembered only the information in the text that was important to their point of view. Pearson, Hansen, and Gordon (1979) found that children with knowledge of a text's topic were better at answering questions about it, especially implicit questions, than were children with little knowledge of the topic.

All of this research was inspired by a theory of knowledge, known as schema theory, applied to the reading process. Schema theory forms the theoretical base for the interactive model of the reading process proposed by Rumelhart (1977). As Anderson and Pearson (1984) point out, it is schema theory that helps us see how old knowledge interacts with new knowledge in

---

1. However, since the focus of this book is comprehension instruction, instruction in decoding or word recognition will not be discussed here. There are many other books that focus on reading as word recognition and include excellent suggestions for instruction. Two of these books are *Reading Process and Practice* by Constance Weaver (1988) and *Dyslexia: Theory and Practice of Remedial Instruction* by Diana Clark (1988).

the process of comprehension. This interaction *is* comprehension. Schema theory also supports the idea that reading is an active constructive process as discussed in Chapter 1. This theory will be discussed in more detail in Chapter 5. Here the point to be made is that schema theory has highlighted the importance of background knowledge and the problems that inadequate background knowledge can cause in reading.

So-called "disadvantaged" children, that is children with a low socio-economic status (SES), are often assumed to be lacking appropriate background knowledge. Many authors of children's texts write about experiences that are more commonplace for middle-class children. Because "disadvantaged" children do not share these experiences, they often have lower reading comprehension. Children learning English as a second language (ESL students) and children with limited English proficiency (LEP students) are often low SES children, although not necessarily. Even if they do not have a low socio-economic status, they come from cultures with different customs and values from native speakers of English and lack background knowledge assumed to be common by many authors.

It is important not to forget the interactive model of reading when we consider these children and their different background knowledge. Low SES, ESL, and LEP children lack background knowledge that is necessary for particular texts. Yet we often act as if they have a general knowledge deficiency rather than a lack of knowledge in certain areas. Because low SES children's reading is so far below our expectations, those of us who work with them tend to focus on what they don't know rather than on trying to determine what they do know. In some instances low SES children may have more knowledge than middle-class children. For example, Yando, Seitz, and Zigler (1979) found that disadvantaged children showed more spontaneous and flexible approaches to problem solving than did middle-class children.

Middle-class children classified as learning disabled are more likely to have appropriate background knowledge for many school texts. After all, by definition, children classified as learning disabled have a discrepancy between potential and achievement. Potential is determined by an IQ test, which is largely a measure of background knowledge. However, categorizing background knowledge dichotomously (present or not present) or even in terms of degree (more or less) is far too simplistic. The role of background knowledge in comprehension and learning is much more complex. Any child, but particularly middle class children classified as learning disabled, may have the necessary background knowledge but may fail to call it up and use it as an aid to comprehending a text (Anderson et al. 1985).

Pearson and Spiro (1980) describe readers who rely too much on bottom-up processing so that they are only able to answer explicit questions. They do not make use of their background knowledge to answer inferential questions.

Any child may have a rich fund of knowledge and yet lack the particular kind of knowledge needed for a specific text (Bransford 1984). Another problem is that many children have misconceptions about certain topics. These misconceptions cause greater interference with comprehension than does a deficiency in knowledge about the topic (Maria and MacGinitie 1987). The important point is that in all groups of children, even middle-class children with very similar backgrounds, variation in background knowledge is to be expected (Maria and MacGinitie 1987).

Although schema theory focuses attention on background knowledge, reading does not involve one factor only. Remember the definition from Chapter 1: Reading is everything put together.

Maria and MacGinitie (1982) and Pearson and Spiro (1981) believe overreliance on background knowledge can interfere with comprehension just as lack of or failure to use background knowledge can. Children who rely too much on prior knowledge use a few words in the text to call up related background knowledge, but they are not much constrained by the information in the text.

In a text that is consistent with prior knowledge, this type of strategy will often be successful. Texts used in the early grades tend to be consistent with middle-class children's prior knowledge. These texts and the questions teachers ask about them may be structured so as to encourage and reinforce overreliance on prior knowledge (MacGinitie 1979). Use of this strategy by remedial readers may also compensate for deficiencies in decoding or memory. Thus, it would seem that such a strategy might be particularly appealing to middle-class children classified as learning disabled.

Readers who rely too much on prior knowledge make inferences that add to the information supplied by the text. Again, with texts that are consistent with children's background knowledge, these inferences are beneficial. At other times, the substantial amount of inferencing appears to interfere with understanding the text as seen in the recall of the text below.

Text:
The dolphin loves to swim and play in the ocean. It dives way down under the waves and comes back up again. It can swim underwater for long distances. If it is washed up on the beach, it cannot move because it has no legs. It just flips its tail helplessly. But in the water, that tail makes the dolphin a good fast swimmer. Dolphins are mammals like lions or tigers. They are water mammals, though, and you must look for them in the sea and not in the jungle (Meyers and Zinar 1979).
Recall:
Dolphins are big, and they swim in the ocean. They can jump high in the air, and go deep in the water and stay underwater for a long time. They have flippers and not legs so they can't walk, but the flippers are good for underwater because you can make them go up and down and swim faster. They're like lions and tigers because they're all water animals. (Why?) Lions, tigers and dolphins. (What is a water animal?) An animal that likes water to swim and drink.

This recall contains much added inferential information that is correct: dolphins are big; they can jump high in the air; they have flippers that they can move up and down. However, attributing the dolphin's fast swimming to its flippers rather than its tail is incorrect in terms of information explicitly stated in the text. We may suspect that this child has transformed the verb *flips* into the noun *flippers*. Attributing the problem to a decoding difficulty is impossible since, in this case, the story was read to the child.

Schema theory and the interactive model of reading have focused our attention on the importance of world knowledge in reading comprehension. Lack of appropriate world knowledge may cause reading failure, especially in low SES and ESL children. Other children may have the necessary knowledge but may fail to use it. Both the variation in children's backgrounds and the fact that particular texts often require specific background knowledge suggest that a deficiency in world knowledge is always a possibility in any reading situation.

However, we must not forget that overreliance on prior knowledge can also interfere with comprehension. Durkin (1985) warns us that "the profession has gone from one lop-sided position in which the text was all that counted to another in which world knowledge is winning everyone's attention" (p. xviii). The interactive model of reading suggests that successful reading requires balancing background knowledge with other factors such as decoding and linguistic knowledge. In many cases it may be necessary to provide some background knowledge before reading a text. However, if all the information is provided before reading, there is no sense in reading. Children should be expected to learn new information by reading text.

LINGUISTIC KNOWLEDGE

Knowledge about language is part of the knowledge we acquire about the world. In fact, many philosophers, anthropologists, and linguists believe that culture and language are inseparable. Language expresses culture as well as limits what can be expressed in a culture (Whorf 1956).

However, since reading is a language process, the reader's knowledge about language in general and about written language in particular—knowledge about vocabulary, syntax, text structure, and structural cue words such as conjunctions—have a strong effect on reading comprehension. So for convenience sake, linguistic knowledge will be considered as a factor separate from world knowledge.

Schema theory suggests that we cannot read with understanding unless we already have some knowledge of the topic. However, we do learn new ideas by reading. It seems likely that we do this by using our linguistic knowledge to make up for our inadequate or incorrect world knowledge. An example of this is found in a study I conducted with fifth and sixth grade readers (Maria and MacGinitie 1987). These children, who had incorrect prior knowledge about several topics, read expository texts presenting new information that corrected their misconceptions. Texts that presented the misconception and then refuted it using a contrasting text structure—using *but* or *however*—were easier to comprehend than texts that did not mention the misconception. Statement of misconception and inclusion of cue words to the contrast structure were related to comprehension of the new contradictory information. This finding suggests a relationship between using linguistic cue words and learning new information. Kimmel and MacGinitie (1984) and Meyer, Brandt, and Bluth (1980) also found that use of linguistic cues was related to accuracy of recall of expository texts.

Many authorities today, particularly in the field of learning disabilities (e.g., Lerner 1985; Rubin and Liberman 1983), believe that most children who fail to meet expectations in reading have underlying problems with language. There are two types of language problems: language differences and language disorders.

LANGUAGE DIFFERENCES

A language difference means that the child's oral language is different in some way, due to environmental rather than intrinsic factors, from the language he is learning to read. The most obvious groups of poor readers with a language difference are ESL and LEP children. A typical LEP student will have an active vocabulary of about 800 English words after a year in an English-speaking school setting, while the average native speaker enters school with an expressive vocabulary of 1,500 to 2,500 words and a receptive vocabulary that may contain as many as 20,000 words (de Cordova 1989). School reading materials assume extensive prior language knowledge not only of typical school vocabulary but also of vocabulary and idioms that are learned in other social settings.

Several researchers have focused on phonology and syntax differences between dialects (e.g., Black English) and standard English to determine whether this is the reason for the disproportionate amount of reading failure in children whose language is different from standard English (Baratz and Shuy 1969; Goodman 1973; Goodman and Goodman 1978; Wolfram 1973). There is general consensus that these superficial differences are not the causes of reading failure in this population (Finn 1985). For example, in a study of the miscues made by dialect speakers and ESL children in second, fourth, and sixth grades, Goodman and Goodman (1978 cited in Weaver 1988) found that the miscues of these children are also superficial, e.g., the most common miscue is the absence of grammatical inflections on the ends of word. They conclude that these miscues do not interfere with comprehension.

Most teachers do not accept miscues that may be dialect appropriate. The reading problems children with language differences experience may be based partly on the fact that use of dialects and certain foreign languages in the United States are associated with low social status (Entwistle 1979). When a language difference is not associated with social class, reading problems do not result. Lambert et al. (1969, 1970, 1972) cited in Entwistle (1979) demonstrated that in Canada, English-speaking children placed in schools where French was spoken almost exclusively and where almost all instruction was in French read very well in both languages.

The musical "My Fair Lady" popularized the idea that language is a cue to social class. Research indicates that teachers use language cues to distinguish middle-class and lower-class children (St. John 1970; Stein 1971). These language cues then affect teachers' expectations of reading readiness before reading instruction has even begun (Rist 1970; Williams, Whitehead, and Miller 1971; Crowl and MacGinitie 1974). Once children are labeled as poor readers, the label tends to stick. Allington's (1984) study of first graders documents one way in which remedial readers receive reading instruction which differs from that received by good readers. In this study, the average good reader read three times as many words as the average remedial reader. Nagy and Anderson (1984) have suggested that these "staggering individual differences" persist throughout the school years with the differences increasing as the children get older. Thus a low SES child who is labeled a poor reader because of language differences may fulfill these low expectations because he or she is not given enough opportunity to read. Stanovich (1986) calls this ever increasing gap between good and poor readers the Matthew effect. The Matthew effect in reading is an application of the principle that those who start out at a disadvantage will get worse, while those who start out with an advantage get better.

Differences in reading between middle class and low SES children cannot be totally attributed to teacher expectations. There seem to be some language differences that may place low SES students at a disadvantage. Research has shown that low SES populations use implicit context-dependent language more than middle-class speakers (Bernstein 1964; Bruck and Tucker 1974; Dunn 1980; Hess and Shipman 1968; Smitherman 1980; Williams and Naremore 1969 cited in Finn 1985). In implicit context-dependent language, meaning is implied because the speaker assumes that listeners share the knowledge necessary to infer the meaning. Finn (1985) gives the example of a football player whose team has just won a game and who turns to his teammate and says "How about that?" In order to understand the meaning of that sentence you have to be there. Characterizing language as context-dependent means language that cannot be understood unless the listener is present and understands the situation.

In explicit context-independent language the speaker is more precise about meaning because the topic is not related to the immediate situation and the speaker does not assume the same degree of shared knowledge. As discussed in Chapter 1, written language is the most context-independent way of using language. Since low SES children have little experience with explicit context-independent speech, in which adults talk to them about events in which they have not participated, we might expect that they would have less facility with written language which is more explicit and context-independent than speech (Finn 1985).

Since language differences are often associated with lower social status, it is hard to separate these two factors. It is likely that language differences interact with lack of background knowledge and with teacher expectations to affect comprehension.

LANGUAGE DISORDERS

The second kind of language problem associated with reading difficulty is a language disorder. The cause of a language disorder is presumed to be intrinsic since a diagnosis is made only after the child has been exposed to standard English in a rich language environment (Lerner l985). A language disorder can occur as a language delay or a language deficit. The child with a language delay either may not talk at all or talk very little at an age when language should normally develop. A child with a language deficit talks, but has problems understanding or expressing oral language (Lerner 1985). Note that this definition like the definition of learning disabilities discussed earlier is at variance with the principle of multiple causation; it is possible for a child to have a language difference *and* a language disorder.

Language disorders are presumed to be the bases of most cases of learning disability, particularly in reading (Lerner 1985; Menyuk and Flood 1981). However, the nature of the oral language problem may vary. Children labeled reading-disabled have been shown to have a general lack of linguistic awareness (Downing 1980; Menyuk and Flood 1981). Others have difficulty with oral syntax (Vogel 1974) or a lack of morphological knowledge (Wiig, Semel, and Crouse 1973). (Morphological knowledge is knowledge of the rules for forming words with units of meaning such as prefixes, suffixes, and root words.) Some children have oral naming difficulties (Denckla and Rudel 1976; Wolf 1984) and problems with sentence imitation and grammatical completion (Newcomer and Magee 1977). In short, "deficiencies in language—in all conceivable aspects" have been identifed as related to failure to meet expectations in reading (Stanovich 1986, p. 385).

It is easy to see why all theorists have claimed a relationship between oral language and reading. Linguistic knowledge provides us with one of the most powerful cuing systems in reading. As Clay (1969) points out, children who lack this knowledge cannot use context for prediction and correction of errors in reading " . . . the very complexity that provides rich cue sources for the child who is able to discover the regularities of the code may present confusion to the child with limited language skill" (Clay 1969, p. 55).

WRITTEN LANGUAGE PROBLEMS

As discussed in Chapter 1, written language differs from oral language in content, vocabulary, syntax, structure, and use. It is not surprising that children may have no overt problems with oral language and still experience problems which relate to a lack of knowledge associated with written language (Maria and MacGinitie 1982; Menyuk and Flood 1981). Menyuk and Flood have extended the concept of language disorder to include the area of written language comprehension, suggesting ways a language problem might interfere with reading comprehension.

First, a child might have a language delay, yet experience no problems with reading in the early grades when written language is very similar to oral

29

language. However, as texts become more complex in the later grades, the child falls below expectations in reading. The child may not distinguish between the vocabulary and syntax used in oral language and written expository text, and may have trouble with the greater roles that structural cue words play in comprehending this type of text. Second, a child might have linguistic knowledge necessary for understanding written language but have difficulty in bringing it to conscious awareness, a situation analogous to the child who has background knowledge appropriate for a particular text but fails to call it up as an aid to comprehension.

Menyuk and Flood's hypothesis attributes written language problems to intrinsic causes. But extrinsic causes such as the relationship between the value placed on reading in the home and children's reading achievement (Heath 1983; Swaby 1989) also are likely. Children who are not exposed to written language until they come to school, whose parents do not read to them, may find reading more difficult than children who come from homes where books are valued and the parents read aloud to their children. We tend to think of lower-class homes as lacking this exposure to literacy, but in a society where both mother and father have demanding full-time jobs, middle-class parents may have neither the time nor the inclination to read to their children. We are a television society. The average television set is on for seven hours and two minutes a day (Television Bureau of Advertising 1984). Children from ages three to ten watch television an average of 30 hours a week (Waters 1977). And as Trelease (1985) has pointed out, watching television is very different from reading. It fosters a short attention span and provides a larger dose of the implicit context-dependent language that is unlike school language or written language. There is little time left for children to read to themselves or for parents to read aloud to them, so that for most children the only exposure to written language is what they receive in school. And as was discussed previously, all children, but especially remedial readers, do very little connected reading in school.

There are signs of change. Jim Trelease's *Read Aloud Handbook* (1985), urging parents to read to their children and suggesting ways to enrich the reading through discussion, is a national bestseller that has been reprinted fourteen times. *Becoming a Nation of Readers* (Anderson et al. 1985) highlighted the following three recommendations:

1. The single most important activity for building the knowledge required for eventual success in reading is reading aloud to children (p. 23).
2. There is no substitute for a teacher who reads children good stories. It whets the appetite of children for reading, and provides a model of skillful oral reading. It is a practice that should continue throughout the grades (p. 51). (It is important to note that through this process children who are unable to read fluently themselves are exposed to the vocabulary, syntax, and structure of written language.)
3. Children of every age and ability ought to be doing more extended silent reading (p. 54).

The whole language movement, which has been steadily gaining in popularity, emphasizes connected reading of trade books, teachers' reading aloud at all age levels, and responses to literature.

In summary, children who do not have oral language problems may have problems in comprehending written language due to an intrinsic language disorder or lack of exposure to written language. And, of course, an interaction of intrinsic and extrinsic causes is always possible. More specific problems with written language related to children's knowledge of vocabulary, language within and between sentences, and text structure will be discussed in Chapters 6 and 7.

METACOMPREHENSION
As noted in Chapter 1, the field of cognitive psychology is responsible for much of our knowledge about reading comprehension. Cognitive psychology includes the study of memory, attention, and information processing as well as comprehension. But it also studies metacognition, an individual's knowledge of and use of these processes. In reading, the study of metacognitive abilities has centered on the process of reading comprehension. While the term *metacognition* has also been used in the reading field, it seems more precise to use the term *metacomprehension* to refer to (1) the reader's knowledge about reading and different reading tasks, (2) the reader's knowledge about himself as a reader, and (3) the reader's knowledge about and use of reading strategies.

KNOWLEDGE ABOUT READING AND READING TASKS
Research has shown that good readers and remedial readers have different understandings about what reading is. Several interviews with children, which asked them about the purpose of reading (Forrest and Waller 1979; Garner and Kraus 1981–1982; Myers and Paris 1978; Paris and Myers 1981; Wixson et al. 1984), have provided evidence that " . . . poorer readers have little awareness that they must attempt to make sense of text; they focus on reading as a decoding process, rather than as a meaning-getting process" (Baker and Brown 1984, p. 358). Garner and Kraus (1981–1982) have suggested two reasons for this finding: (1) much emphasis is placed on decoding in school reading instruction and (2) good readers who are fluent in decoding will experience reading for meaning while remedial readers are forced to focus on decoding and, thus, may never experience what reading really is.

Children who view reading as decoding will have the same purpose (getting the words right) no matter what the reading task. Even a reader who understands that reading should focus on meaning, may not understand that different reading tasks have different purposes. When Forrest and Waller (1979) asked third and sixth-graders to read for fun, to make up a title, to skim, and to study, remedial readers were less likely than good readers to adjust their reading strategies to the different purposes. Wixson et al. (1984) developed the Reading Comprehension Interview which assesses children's knowledge about different reading situations using different materials, i.e., basal readers and content area textbooks. They give the example of one remedial reader whose only strategy was rereading no matter what the reading task or the reading material. Good readers are flexible. They recognize the different purposes for reading and the need for different strategies appropriate to these different purposes (Anderson et al. 1985). Smith (1967) found that good readers in high school read differently depending upon whether they are reading for details or general impressions. Remedial readers use the same reading behaviors in both cases.

READERS' KNOWLEDGE ABOUT THEMSELVES AS READERS

Readers' knowledge about themselves as readers, i.e., understanding their own strengths and weaknesses related to reading, also has an effect on comprehension. Throughout this chapter, it has been pointed out that people who come in contact with remedial readers, that is, teachers, peers, and sometimes parents, may have very low expectations for them. This and their own feelings of failure in reading often result in remedial readers having very poor opinions of themselves as readers (Butkowsky and Willows 1980).

It has been found that remedial readers believe their success and failure are due to external factors like task difficulty and luck, and not the result of effort on their part (Hiebert 1983; Hill and Hill 1982; Pearl, Bryan, and Donohue 1980). Therefore, even in situations where they are capable of success, they may believe that success will not be possible (Harris and Sipay 1985). Often their belief is correct. Remedial readers frequently are given material to read that is much too difficult for them, and placed in situations where it is impossible for them to succeed. Johnston and Winograd (1985) point out that the phenomenon of learned helplessness in which effort is seen as useless can be a valuable psychological defense for one constantly experiencing failure. When I taught remedial readers, I was always amazed at how well many of them understood the nature of their reading problems. But they didn't know what to do about it, and many of them had lost trust in the ability of teachers to help them.

One aspect of knowledge of oneself as a reader that has begun to be explored is reading style. Carbo (1981) has developed a self-report instrument, the *Reading Style Inventory,* that seeks to determine environmental, emotional, sociological, physical, and psychological factors that affect reading achievement. The child is asked questions such as whether he or she reads better:

> with music, talking, or silence? (environmental)
> with reading work checked by peers, adults, or self?
> (emotional)
> with five or six students, with the teacher, alone?
> (sociological)
> when permitted to move around? (physical).

From other questions on the inventory, it is determined whether the child's learning style is global, analytic, or both and whether the child would benefit from teaching with a particular modality or with a multisensory approach.

Based on the responses, the child is then matched with a particular method of reading instruction. Research studies by Carbo and her associates (Carbo 1987; Carbo, Dunn, and Dunn 1986; LaShell 1986) suggest that this match increases reading achievement. However, the reading methods suggested focus on word recognition rather than comprehension. As more and more instructional techniques are developed for comprehension instruction, research should be undertaken to determine whether these techniques should also be matched with reading style.

Carbo's work has been criticized because she recommends asking young and remedial readers about their metacognitive knowledge. Research cited previously demonstrates that these two groups are deficient in this area; however, in the area of metacognition, research has centered on children's task knowledge rather than on their self knowledge. As Socrates pointed out, getting to know oneself is the task of a lifetime. Children, undoubtedly, get to know themselves better as they get older, yet how can we be sure that what we perceive about a child is more valid than that child's perception of himself. Is it not the child's perception that influences his performance? *Reading Recovery* (Clay 1985), a program that provides intensive remediation based on remedial readers' learning styles, is one of the few remedial programs with documented success in reading (Walp and Walmsley 1989).

COMPREHENSION MONITORING:
READERS' KNOWLEDGE ABOUT AND USE OF READING STRATEGIES

What is a strategy? Most authorities agree with the definition given by Paris (1978) that a strategy is an intentional, deliberate self-selection of a means to an end. The idea of intentionality is what makes a strategy different from a skill. Strategies are not different actions, necessarily; they are simply not automatic. The goal in teaching a strategy is to have the strategy internalized so that it will become automatic. Even the most skillful reader among us makes use of strategies when comprehension problems arise (Paris, Lipson, and Wixson 1983). But strategies are particularly important for children, especially remedial readers, because they are engaged in initial learning in many fields and experience comprehension problems more than adults.

The first idea about reading strategies that needs to be considered is knowing when they are needed. Older skillful readers seem to stop periodically to check their understanding, alert to what Anderson (1980) refers to as the "click" of comprehension or the "clunk" of a comprehension problem. Remedial readers, it would seem, do not monitor their comprehension as well as do good readers. For example, Forrest and Waller (1979) found that remedial readers in the sixth grade were not good at rating the accuracy of their answers to comprehension questions. My own experience, supported by the experience of many teachers to whom I have spoken, is that one of the biggest problems in comprehension instruction is making children aware that they do not understand something; they think they do understand.

Certain readers may not be able to monitor their comprehension because of the way in which they process text. The problems experienced by top-down readers who rely too much on their prior knowledge and bottom-up readers who fail to go beyond the details to the total meaning of a text have already been discussed. Baker (1985) and Markham (1981) have suggested that readers with this latter problem are not able to monitor their comprehension because they do not "access appropriate memory representations and then combine and compare propositions as they read" (Garner 1987, p. 46). Because of this they do not notice intersentence inconsistencies (Garner 1987).

Even when remedial readers are aware of a comprehension problem, they may not know how to fix it. Rereading is one of the easiest comprehension strategies to use. Although Olshavsky (1976–1977) found that junior high school remedial readers did not differ from good readers in suggesting the use of rereading as a fix-up strategy, Garner and Kraus (1981–1982) found that they were not likely to suggest using this strategy.

Another strategy used by adult fluent readers is to ignore the comprehension problem temporarily, reading on to seek further clarification. Knowledge about this strategy seems to develop late (DiVesta, Hayward, and Orlando 1979). Baker and Brown (1984) suggest this may be because children attribute problems in understanding to failures in themselves. This explanation is easily acceptable when we consider the low opinions of themselves that remedial readers often hold.

Paris, Lipson, and Wixson (1983) have referred to metacognitive awareness of available strategies as declarative knowledge. They point out that readers also need procedural knowledge, knowledge about how to use the strategies. It appears that good readers often acquire the ability to use these kinds of strategies through experience. On the other hand, many remedial readers have no understanding of how to make use of strategies to solve comprehension problems even when they are aware of the usefulness of the strategy. For example, Garner, Wagoner, and Smith (1983) found that remedial readers were more likely than good readers to view rereading as the process of rereading the entire text rather than reading appropriate parts to find the answer to a particular question. Gillet and Temple (1986) suggest that a typical strategy used by remedial readers is to start in reading and when confronted by problems to get fidgety and distracted, lose their place in the text, and give up.

The research discussed up to now suggests that remedial readers may not use effective comprehension strategies spontaneously because (1) they are not aware of their lack of understanding; (2) even when they are aware of a comprehension problem, they do not know what strategies are available to them; and (3) even when they are aware of strategies, they do not know how to use them correctly.

However, we cannot be sure that comprehension failures are due to lack of awareness or knowledge about strategies. Training studies have shown that even when remedial readers can detect comprehension problems and have been taught how to use comprehension strategies, they often fail to use these strategies independently in the same situation or transfer their use to new but similiar situations (Brown and Campione 1978). Paris, Lipson, and Wixson (1983) have pointed out that effective comprehension instruction must also provide readers with conditional knowledge, i.e., knowledge about when and why various strategies should be used. This type of knowledge relates to understanding different purposes for reading, and is particularly important for remedial readers who often lack awareness of these different purposes.

Brown and Palincsar (1982) agree that there is need for informed training in strategies but also suggest the need for self-control training. Training in comprehension strategies should include help in controlling the strategies, as well as help with skills such as planning, checking, and monitoring.

Some theorists (Baron 1978; Campione and Brown 1978; Sternberg 1980, 1982, 1985) have suggested that metacognitive awareness and use of available strategies is a critical aspect of intelligence. Yet research has shown that these strategies can be taught. Effective training in metacomprehension, an integral part of the comprehension instruction discussed in more detail in Chapters 4 through 9, will include developing better awareness of comprehension problems. Declarative, procedural, and conditional knowledge about comprehension strategies, and help in overseeing the strategies are also important in instruction.

MOTIVATION AND INTEREST

As every teacher knows, motivation is a factor that strongly affects reading achievement. Bettelheim and Zelan (1981) remind us that children must want to read in addition to having the ability, or they will not be successful.

Since learning to read is a social process, a strong factor in children's motivation to read is the influence of their parents, teachers, and peers. Because parents are the strongest influences on their children, low parental expectations can have a particularly important effect on children's motivation to read regardless of the child's social class. Lower-class parents have educational aspirations for their children that are as high as middle-class parents (e.g., Brook et al. 1974 cited in Wigfield and Asher 1984); however, they often do not expect their children to achieve these aspirations (e.g., Resnick and Robinson 1975 cited in Wigfield and Asher 1984). These lower parental expectations may interact with social class influences on background knowledge and linguistic knowledge, contributing to the lower reading level of disadvantaged children.

When teachers have low expectations for children, they give them less praise and fewer classroom privileges (Brophy and Good 1970). This is likely to have a negative effect on the children's achievement motivation (Wigfield and Asher 1984), as is the different instruction mentioned earlier.

Motivation is also affected by children's desire to conform to peer group standards, a tendency that seems to increase through the elementary school years (Constanzo and Shaw 1966; McDonnell 1963 cited in Wigfield and Asher 1984). Since many lower SES children do not seem to value academic achievement to the same degree as do middle-class children, lower SES children may be motivated to do poorly in school in order to conform to their peer group, especially during adolescence.

The section on metacomprehension focused on the necessity for knowledge about and use of effective comprehension strategies. However, successful comprehension will not be achieved just because children *can* use effective strategies; they must also *want* to use them. Low expectations and repeated failures in reading can translate into readers' low expectations of themselves. This, in turn, results in learned helplessness so that they stop trying to learn.

Factors such as the children's willingness to take risks and the amount of time and effort required by a particular strategy affect children's motivation to use these strategies. As Paris, Cross, and Lipson (1984) point out "It is unlikely that children will adopt and use actions as strategies if they do not understand the value or reasons for doing so" (p. 1241).

Interest is another strong factor that affects a child's motivation and his reading achievement. Wixson and Lipson (1984) remind us that interest can have a positive effect on remedial readers. As every teacher knows, children can often comprehend texts considered too difficult for them when those texts are related to their interests. Reading aloud to remedial readers about topics of particular interest has a positive motivational influence on them.

In order to discuss decoding, background knowledge, linguistic knowledge, metacomprehension, and motivation in some depth, they have been considered separately. This should not cause us to lose sight of the fact that these factors do not exist separately. Moreover, the focus on the reader as one component of the process should not cause us to lose sight of the fact that factors in the reader will interact with factors in the text and the reading situation to affect comprehension. These other two components will be discussed more fully in the next two chapters; however, several scenarios from my experiences suggest how they may interact to produce success or failure in reading.

1.   The oral language characteristics of a low SES child cue low teacher expectations. These low expectations interact with the child's lack of experience with written language to produce the child's perception of himself as a poor reader. He was making a good start at decoding, but as the texts get more removed from his experience, his lack of appropriate background knowledge is more and more of a problem. He gives up trying and reads less. Less reading only compounds the problem—the Matthew effect.

2.   A middle-class child with a rich background of experience comes from a home where there are many books. His parents read aloud to him, and he looks forward to coming to school and reading himself. But he has problems with oral language. They are not serious enough to be noticed, particularly in conversation. His main problem is with word retrieval, so he cannot learn the names of the letters of the alphabet. Since knowing the names of the letters of the alphabet is highly correlated with reading ability, the school recommends that the child be retained in kindergarten. He will not be taught to read until he learns the names of the letters. His

father, who had similar problems as a child refuses to have the child retained. The parents work very hard at reducing their own anxiety and that of the child. They hire a special tutor for the summer who teaches the child to read. The child's experience with reading letters and learning their sounds helps him learn their names. The child is placed in a learning disability resource room. The classroom teacher and the resource room teacher work together to support the child, and by the middle grades resource room instruction is no longer necessary. Using his rich fund of background knowledge, the child learns to compensate for his difficulties.

3. Another low SES child enters a program in which her background knowledge is valued. She is exposed to rich experiences in oral language and in written language. Her teacher reads aloud to her class consistently and often. There are many books in the classroom. She is encouraged to use them, and the teacher makes sure that there are books of interest to her. Decoding is a bit of a struggle for her but she persists because she has a perception of herself as a reader. The more she reads, the better she gets. As the texts get more and more removed from her experience, she often does not have the appropriate background knowledge. Aware of this, the teacher provides support, connecting the content of the text to her experience through pre-reading activities.

CHAPTER
3

THE TEXT

In this chapter we turn to a consideration of the second main component in reading comprehension, i.e., the text, and factors in texts that may affect comprehension. In discussing these topics I will pay particular attention to the reading comprehension of children in school settings.

There are three main categories of texts that children use in school: (1) basal readers, (2) content area textbooks, and (3) trade books or children's literature. In addition, children who receive supplementary reading instruction often use texts like the *Merrill Linguistic Reader* or *Primary Phonics* (Mazar 1986), primarily designed to teach phonics. Since these latter types of texts focus on word recognition rather than comprehension, they will not be discussed here.

BASAL READERS
In the elementary grades children usually read in a basal reader. A survey of 10,000 elementary teachers, showed that 94% of these teachers relied on a basal reader for reading instruction (Educational Product Information Exchange 1977). As every teacher knows, basal readers are anthologies of different kinds of texts: narratives, expository texts, poems, and even plays. These readers, available at every grade level, claim to be comprehensive, i.e., they contain everything the teacher needs to teach reading, both word recognition and comprehension. The primary purpose of the basal reader is to teach children *how* to read, to teach the process of reading. The texts in the readers, *what* is to be read, are chosen by basal reader editors with this purpose in mind.

The Report Card on Basal Readers, the report prepared by the Reading Commission of the National Council of Teachers of English (Goodman et al. 1988), provides a history of the use of basal readers in schools. Texts designed to teach reading were used in schools in the eighteenth century, but the idea of a controlled vocabulary, so central to present day basal readers, was not introduced until the mid 1800s. In the 1920s many new components were added to the basal reader system: workpads, colored pictures, and teachers' manuals with instructions on how to teach reading. These manuals were based on the principles of behavior espoused by psychologists at that time and provided a scientific basis for reading instruction. In addition, they made financial sense. For a relatively modest expense, they provided the means by which a poorly educated teaching staff could teach all children to read. All that was necessary was to follow the instructions in the manuals.

Basal readers have changed over the years. "Not only have the readers become more realistic and colorful, the teachers' manuals more explicit and elaborate, and the seatwork more plentiful and varied, but new components (such as scope and sequence charts and tests) have been added to the 'basal reading system.' " (Goodman et al. 1988, p. 22). The texts now make more use of children's literature and there are more expository texts, although narratives still outnumber the expository texts (Flood and Lapp 1987). Stories in today's basal readers also provide more balance with regard to sex roles and ethnic groups. Publishers claim that the type of reading instruction provided by basal readers has changed over the years, taking into account new knowledge in the reading field and translating this knowledge into practical information for teachers.

Over the years, basal readers have been criticized for many things from the types of texts used to the types of questions suggested for teachers. Recently, criticism has centered on the way the basal readers claim to teach comprehension (e.g., Durkin 1981; Beck, Omanson, and McKeown 1981). Nevertheless, until the present time, reading experts have generally supported and encouraged their use; and administrators have, in many cases, even dictated their use as a means of ensuring reading instruction based on scientific principles. Although teachers have often complained about the inflexible way administrators have dictated the use of the basals, in general, teachers, seeing themselves as managers of the basal systems, also support their use. In one study (Shannon 1983) 485 teachers were asked how they would teach reading if administrators did not force them to use basal readers; 84% indicated that they would continue to use basals, albeit more than one set.

Basal systems provide structure and materials particularly important to new inexperienced teachers who feel they need that security. Administrators also feel more secure when teachers make use of basal readers in reading instruction because they know that children in different classes are receiving a common core of instruction.

Recently, adherents of the whole language movement, including teachers, have begun to attack basal readers as the source of the problems in today's reading instruction. Goodman et al. (1988) dispute publishers' claims that reading instruction in basal readers has been updated to conform to contemporary research. The report contends that changes in the types of reading instruction offered by the basal readers are only superficial. It contends that although basal readers update the language of teachers manuals to conform to new understanding of the reading process, they still espouse a passive view of learning based on behavioral psychology and a bottom-up reductionist view of the process. "They remain locked into the notion that the learning of reading can happen skill by skill and word by word and that learning is the direct result of teaching" (Goodman et al. 1988, pp. 124–5). As discussed in Chapter 1, most teachers also espouse a view of reading as a skill that must be taught part by part. Goodman et al. theorize that teachers hold this view because they have internalized the rhetoric of the basal reader system.

One of the main problems with basal reader systems is that they claim to be a complete reading program, yet they do not provide the opportunity for teachers to integrate reading instruction with other areas of the curriculum nor for children to select materials to read. Thus they do not provide the experiences necessary for a total reading program. Teachers should use basal readers judiciously, deciding which recommended activities to use with their children and when alternate types of activities are more appropriate. If teachers use basal readers as professionals who have control over the materials rather than as managers who are controlled by them, basal reader systems can be valuable instructional tools. However, teachers must supplement basal reader instruction with content area reading instruction and with opportunities for children to hear and read a wide variety of children's literature. Another problem with basal readers is that they are quite expensive.

Using the Association of American Publishers as a source, Goodman et al. (1988) reported that in 1985 one third of a billion dollars was spent for basal readers, accounting for 35 to 40% of the money spent for elementary school textbooks. About 80% of this money is spent on programs similar in format and published by six major publishers with similar philosophies of instruction (Educational Product Informational Exchange 1977). The success of the basal reader systems has meant that schools have little or no money left over for other types of texts, particularly children's literature. Basal readers often are the only texts used in reading instruction because they are available and convenient.

CONTENT AREA TEXTBOOKS

Another text commonly available in classrooms is the content area textbook. Content area texts, such as social studies or science texts, are designed to teach the content of a discipline not the reading process. They are important in reading instruction because they provide the opportunity for functional reading instruction, the application of reading skills, and strategies for learning. Although functional reading should be a component of reading instruction at all levels, it is particularly important in the later stages of reading instruction—in the upper elementary, middle school and high school years—when children should be using reading for learning. Teaching reading through the content areas has been recognized as an important part of a total reading program since the 1920s. Recent research in comprehension has greatly increased interest in this area.

Despite enthusiasm on the part of reading experts and researchers, functional reading instruction using content area texts is not common practice in classrooms for two reasons: (1) teachers' misconceptions about reading instruction in the content areas and (2) problems with the content and structure of textbooks. Due to pressures from outside and within the schools, teachers responsible for teaching a content area often see their goal as completing a curriculum program that stretches the limits of their time. The emphasis on testing and departmentalization of instruction at the upper grade levels supports this view. Several reading experts (Readence, Bean, and Baldwin 1985; Vacca and Vacca 1986) suggest that teachers responsible for teaching content resist the suggestion that "every teacher should be a teacher of reading" because of misconceptions about what is meant by this statement.

Teacher misconceptions include the idea that:

1. Teaching reading means teaching phonics and other skills that are not directly related to content area instruction.
2. The processes involved in comprehending content area texts are identical to those used in reading the narratives found in basal readers.
3. Most students have learned to read in the lower grades. Those who have deficiencies in skills necessary for success in subject matter reading should be served by remedial reading classes.
4. Most students have the prior knowledge necessary for understanding the important information in content area textbooks (Readence, Bean, and Baldwin 1985).

Note that most of these misconceptions are based on the idea of reading as a skill that can be taught part by part. It is easy to see that content area teachers in a departmentalized situation would treat the idea of teaching reading as an unnecessary burden that should not be part of their job. Assigning independent reading in textbooks with no purpose and no subsequent discussion of what is read is common practice (Rieck 1977). Even elementary teachers who teach reading and other subjects to the same students in a self-contained class often view reading instruction as restricted to work with basal readers. Readence, Bean, and Baldwin (1985) and Vacca and Vacca (1986) suggest that if content area reading instruction were defined as teaching children to learn from text, content area teachers would more readily view reading instruction as part of their job.

There are many problems in the content and structure of currently available textbooks. These problems, which will be discussed in detail later in this chapter, are another reason many teachers do not consider textbook reading an important part of content area instruction. These teachers believe that content can be learned more easily and efficiently through their oral presentations than through reading. Some teachers are very open about their refusal to use any textbooks in their instruction. Others, like the teachers in the Rieck (1977) study, say that they require reading; however, since their tests are based only on the material covered in class presentations and discussions, they give a message to their students that reading is not really important. In accomplishing the short term goal of covering the curriculum, teachers ignore the long term goal of enabling students to become independent learners. To fail to teach children how to use text to gain information is to render them illiterate in an advanced technological society like ours.

TRADE BOOKS—CHILDREN'S LITERATURE

The two terms *trade books* and *children's literature* are often used interchangeably to mean books written for children that are designed for enjoyment, whether it is the enjoyment of the beautiful language of a poem or the enjoyment of learning about the mysteries of the universe. There are more trade books available for children today than ever before; there is fiction—folktales, mysteries, sports stories, realistic fiction, science fiction—and non-fiction—biographies, how-to books, science books, histories.

Of course, just as with books published for adults, not all of these books are of top quality. Some authorities (e.g., Sutherland and Arbuthnot 1986) feel the term children's literature should be restricted to children's books that meet high literary and artistic standards. As in all literature, these standards tend to be subjective; one person's classic may be another's junk. Moreover, as adults we do not always read the highest quality literature. Sometimes we like to curl up with any currently popular mystery or romance. The same opportunity should be offered to children. Searfoss (1987) notes that children's choices in books are not always the same as those of the critics. He recommends that classroom libraries should have three categories of books:

1. Page turners—books loved by children but not selected by critics, books like *How to Eat Fried Worms* (Rockwell 1973), books by Dr. Seuss, or books of riddles and jokes.
2. Kid grabbers—books chosen by both children and critics, books in which the reader becomes very attached to a character, for example, the books by Judy Blume and Betsy Byars.
3. Good books—books rated outstanding by critics which may require teacher assistance for children to fully comprehend and appreciate, books like *The Stranger* by Chris Van Allsburg (1986) or *The Bridge to Terabithia* by Katherine Paterson (1977).

Hornsby, Sukarna, and Parry (1986) suggest that a book should be considered "real literature" if it is memorable and if children want to read it again and again. Page turners, the first category of books suggested by Searfoss, would meet this criterion of Hornsby et al., but might not meet their second suggested criterion, i.e., real literature "adds to the quality of one's life, it arouses feelings, stimulates thought and develops insight" (p. 8).

Because reading programs have centered on the basal reader, children's literature tends to be seen by teachers as recreational reading, "something to do when your work is finished." Thus remedial readers particularly have little opportunity to read children's literature. These readers rarely finish their work in time.

Establishing classroom libraries has always been encouraged, but the high cost of the basal readers often does not leave enough money to buy books to stock them. Several recent studies (Fielding, Wilson, and Anderson 1984; Morrow 1987), which provided funds for stocking classroom libraries with an ample supply of books, found that recreational reading improved the reading achievement and attitudes toward reading of remedial low SES readers and middle-class average readers. (The term recreational reading is somewhat misleading since independent reading of children's literature, just like reading content area textbooks, allows for functional reading, i.e., practice with the reading process.)

In the 1950s and early 1960s the individualized reading movement proposed using children's literature rather than the basal reader as the focus of reading instruction. In individualized reading programs children selected books they wished to read and met with the teacher in individual conferences to discuss their books. Small group skill instruction and whole group sharing were also an important part of the true individualized reading program (Veatch 1978), but these aspects were often missing from programs that characterized themselves as individualized. Because the individualized program had less structure than the basal program, it required much more preparation and management on the part of the teacher. Teachers also needed to be familiar with the large number of books in the classroom.

Some teachers rebelled against this extra expenditure of effort. Administrators often distorted the programs by mandating so much management and record keeping that there was no time for teaching. Commercial programs such as the Random House Individualized Reading Program (Cochran et al. 1970) attempted to provide structure for the teacher but fostered distortion of the basic tenets of individualized reading. In these programs books were chosen for the children and follow-up activities consisted of comprehension questions like those provided in the basals. Research (Johnson 1965; Safford 1960; Thompson 1975; Vite 1961) about the efficacy of individualized reading programs was inconclusive, generally supporting the idea that the success of such programs depended on the skill and enthusiasm of the teachers (Tierney, Readence, and Dishner 1985). Thus in the 1970s there was a return to reliance on basals and most individualized programs were abandoned.

In the 1980s the whole language movement has called for a return to the use of children's literature as the focus of an instructional program that connects the teaching of reading and writing. Like the proponents of individualized reading, the proponents of whole language instruction suggest that children should have much more choice in what they read. They also propose that instruction should take place in individualized conferences, small groups, and with the whole class. In whole language instruction, however, there is more emphasis on group discussion than there was in individualized reading programs, with children working in small groups and in pairs to help one another and receive help from the teacher.

The whole language movement provides a theoretical base for the use of children's literature which was not available when individualized reading was first used. Whole language theory suggests that since children learn to talk by using language for specific purposes, they will best learn to read and write not by learning separate reading and writing skills, but by using reading and writing for specific purposes (see discussion of Cambourne's conditions for learning in Chapter 1). Reading literature by authors that they have chosen gives children a purpose for reading as well as provides them with models for writing.

Like individualized reading, whole language instruction is less structured than the basal reading systems. It has, therefore, encountered some of the same problems as individualized reading, i.e., teacher resistance to the extra demands and administrator concern about control and management. As with any educational innovation that calls for the overturn of previous practices, some adherents of the movement have become fanatic, refusing to see value in any point of view but their own. A bandwagon effect has occurred with school districts rushing to change their instruction to fit in with the latest ideas. As a result, some teachers characterize themselves as whole language teachers because they are using big books (books with print large enough for the whole class to see) instead of basals. Some administrators have removed basal readers from classrooms with no transition period for teacher training and change. However, many whole language teacher support groups, which include teachers and administrators, are attempting to deepen their understanding of the reading process. Recently, several commercial programs such as *Bridges* I and II (Shafer 1988, 1990); and *Impressions* (Booth, Phenix, and Pauli 1988) attempt to provide a whole language perspective within a structure that is more like the basal system as an aid to transition.

Children's literature has been the focus of reading instruction in Australia, New Zealand, and Canada for some years. In the United States, at least one state, California, has made money available for the purchase of children's literature, and the California Reading Initiative calls for a reading program based on children's literature.

We turn now to a discussion of the factors that may affect comprehension in these three types of texts, relating them to reader factors as discussed in Chapter 2.

READABILITY LEVEL

One of the concerns that led to the development of basal readers was the problem of matching children with books that were at an appropriate level of difficulty in word recognition and comprehension. In the 1920s standardized tests were developed to measure children's reading ability objectively, and readability formulas were developed to provide an objective measure of text difficulty. Early formulas were difficult to use, but by the 1940s, formulas had been simplified. These simple formulas were found to be just as predictive as the more complex ones, so that readability formulas began to be more widely used.

Readability systems have been proposed based on factors such as organization (Templeton and Mowrey 1985), usage patterns of nouns and cohesive ties (Binkley 1988), and combinations of text and reader factors (Zakaluk and Samuels 1988). These systems are complex, and earlier attempts to deal with the same types of factors quantitatively were unsuccessful. Today the readability level of a text is usually determined by two factors related to style: word length and sentence length. For example, to determine the readability level of a text using the Raygor formula, one counts the number of words with six or more letters and the number of sentences in three or more 100 word passages. In the Fry formula the number of syllables is the measure of word length.

Readability formulas "state that, in general, on the average, the two inputs of sentence length and word difficulty accurately predict how easily a given passage will be understood by the average reader" (Fry 1989, p. 295). They are predictors of how difficult a text will be for typical readers using a variety of measures, e.g., multiple choice questions (Fry 1969; Harris and Jacobson 1976; Keenan 1982), cloze passages (Bormuth 1966; Entin and Klare 1978) and oral reading errors (Paolo 1977). Phrases in Fry's statement, however, like in general, on the average, and average reader should caution us against applying the formulas rigidly in individual cases. Questions about the validity of the formulas also suggest that they should be applied with caution. The formulas predict the difficulty of a text based on its similarity to some criterion of difficulty, either text passages like the McCall Crabbs Standard Test Lessons in Reading (1925) that have been assigned a grade level difficulty, or text passages whose grade level difficulty is based on the percent of deletions correctly identified in a cloze version of the text. In addition to questions regarding the validity of assigned levels and the cloze procedure (Carver 1977–1978; Kintsch and Vipond 1979; Kintsch and Yarbrough 1982; Stevens 1980), a major question relates to the fact that criterion passages are all short (Entin and Klare 1978). Factors other than word and sentence length cannot be easily observed in such short passages, so that short passages may make word length and sentence length seem more predictive than they really are (Klare 1984). Moreover, since different formulas are based on different criteria, readability levels on the same text will vary depending on the formula used. The level of text difficulty, then, is not precise, and the validity of the formulas is based ultimately on the validity of the criterion used.

Because readability formulas yield a number or a grade level, parents and teachers tend to consider them scientific and precise. Anyone who has ever tried to compute the readability of a text, however, knows that the process is far from precise. The Raygor and Fry formulas suggest using three 100 word passages randomly chosen from the beginning, middle, and end of the text. When rating long pieces of prose, great variation is often found in the readability of the three passages. In that case, it is suggested that additional passages be computed. Deciding how many passages to use is left up to the individual. The readability level is often the average of a wide variety of levels found within the book.

Once one has an average number of long words and an average number of sentences, one finds the appropriate point of intersection on a graph. Here too the process is not precise. The point on the graph may be at the line separating Grade 6 from Grade 7; the individual must decide whether to assign grade level 6 or 7 to the text. The fact that readability levels are expressed in terms of grade levels causes other problems. Klare (1984) points out that "A grade level score for an individual based upon a typical reading test means that he or she reads as well as some normative group. Such a score does not mean that the individual cannot read with understanding below or even quite far above that level under proper conditions. It is that score, however, which readability formulas attempt to predict" (p. 718). Grade level scores on standardized tests are often misinterpreted. This caused the International Reading Association to ask that the use of grade-level scores on standardized tests be abandoned (Reading Research Quarterly 1981). Grade level readability scores are just as subject to misinterpretation as grade level test scores.

Despite their lack of precision, readability formulas have been accepted as precise. Administrators and legislators dictate the use of materials that are on grade level or that match the reading level attained by the child. Some teachers, like the teachers described in Chapter 2 who considered *The Best Nest* to be too difficult for their students, have internalized the factors measured by the formulas and restrict remedial readers to reading texts with short words and sentences.

Basal readers are based on the concept of graded texts matched to the child's reading level. Placement tests, an integral part of the basal system, determine the child's level and he or she is then placed in the appropriate reader. Some ludicrous situations can result. I will never forget the little girl who came to me one September crying, "Second grade—*Dog Next Door*; third grade—*Dog Next Door*; now fourth grade—*Dog Next Door*. No more *Dog Next Door!*" Her distress over receiving the same basal reader for three years is quite understandable, not just because it is boring but because keeping her in the same book indicates to her that she has not improved. Children, too, internalize the rigid application of reading level. If they are reading the green book, they believe they are smart. If they are reading the red book, they think they are stupid. I was able to have this remedial reader placed in another basal at the same level for classroom reading instruction, but moving her up a level was considered unthinkable by her classroom teacher.

Reacting against the rigid application of readability formulas, Cadenhead (1987) has declared,

> Teachers must be freed from the slavish adherence to basal programs and encouraged to make decisions about children's performance. Competent teachers are sensitive to the relative difficulty of reading materials for children; they do not need to restrict themselves to the use of strictly graded materials. These same teachers can encourage children to read materials of varying difficulty rather than

lead the children through programs based on a theme of 'control' rather than challenge (p. 441).

Cadenhead suggests that using children's literature for reading instruction is one way to avoid the problem of reading-level placement. Since trade books vary so much in style and subject matter, specialists in children's literature, such as librarians who are familiar with the books and with children's preferences, are better predictors of the level of difficulty than are readability formulas (Davison 1988).

As mentioned previously, readability formulas only measure factors of writing style. These factors—word length and sentence length—are only reflections of difficulty; they are not the cause of the difficulty. Not all long words are harder to decode than short words. Children remember a word like *elephant* better than a word like *who*. On the other hand, long words tend to be used less frequently and are more abstract and technical than short words. Long complex sentences are not necessarily a factor of style only; they can also be indicators of a heavy concept load. It is often not the style of writing that is the source of text difficulty, but the heavy concept load (Kintsch and Miller 1984), the reader's lack of experience with the words and concepts, and his or her lack of prior knowledge. These factors, however, cannot be directly measured by readability formulas.

Failure to recognize that word length and sentence length reflect difficulty rather than cause difficulty has resulted in writing and revising basal readers and content area texts to fit the formulas. As will be discussed more fully later in this chapter, these revisions are often more difficult than the original text and result in a badly written text. Thus, the practice of writing and revising texts according to readability formulas has been condemned in a joint statement by the International Reading Association and the National Council of Teachers of English (*Language Arts* December, 1984).

Chapter 2 presented an interactive view of reading disability (Wixson and Lipson 1984), and suggested that a child's reading ability varies with the text used and the task demanded. Text difficulty also interacts with other factors such as the world knowledge of the reader. Like reading ability, text difficulty is a relative term: "It is meaningless to say a text is difficult; it is difficult for someone. Whether a text is difficult depends on the reader as well as on the text" (MacGinitie 1984, p. 142). Yet readability formulas consider only the text.

Anderson et al. (1985) and Klare (1985, 1988) suggest that readability formulas should be used as rough checks or screening devices for tentative matching of children and materials. The tentative nature of the match must be emphasized because factors such as the reader's prior knowledge, interest, and motivation should also be considered. Other experts like Cadenhead (1987) and Goodman et al. (1988) prefer the use of teacher or child judgment rather than readability formulas. Whatever view one takes, the main principle in matching readers with texts should be flexibility.

CONTENT AND TOPIC

In Chapter 2, I pointed out that the prior knowledge of the reader is one of the most important factors in comprehension, and that there is great variation in children's prior knowledge. The prior knowledge of the reader and the content of the text interact to produce comprehension.

Developers of basal readers attempt to handle the problem of prior knowledge in the early levels by providing simple stories about situations with which children are familiar. There is good reason for using stories; human beings have been characterized as "story telling animals." Children readily acquire an understanding of story structure so that stories are easier to read and comprehend than expository prose (Anderson et al. 1985). Since stories center on problems in human interactions, their themes may be more familiar to children and, therefore, easier to understand even at the later levels.

Stories in many basal readers differ from those found in trade books. Stories in trade books have more conflict and more information about the protagonist's point of view (Bruce 1984). Conflict makes for interesting stories, but basal readers are developed for a mass market where special-interest groups may object to including certain ideas in stories. Stories written for basal readers, therefore, tend to have little conflict, and if selections from children's literature are adapted for use in the basal, conflict may be softened. For example, Goodman et al. (1988) describe how the theme of sibling rivalry and the hostile feelings of three siblings are censored in the basal excerpt (Holt, Level 8, Grade 1) of *The One in the Middle Is a Green Kangaroo* by Judy Blume (1981).

When Goodman et al. (1988) analyzed the types of texts used in two popular basal systems (Ginn and Holt), they found that at the first-grade level, 40 to 90% of the stories were synthetic, i.e., written to fit the requirements of skill instruction, and 14 to 25% of the texts were adaptations from trade books. Holt had more authentic texts (texts from children's literature that were unchanged) than Ginn, both at the early levels and at the later levels (Grades 3 and 5). In both series, however, there was far more use of adapted or synthetic text (60 to 100%) than of authentic text. The main reason for the basals' use of synthetic or adapted texts at all levels is the need for a controlled vocabulary. Demands for ethnic and gender balance also motivate writing and revising. Basal reader developers, like the man in the folktale, *The Man and the Donkey*, try to avoid offending anyone, and so may end up offending the reader who wants a good story.

It should not be forgotten that text content also interacts with children's interests and motivation. Bettelheim and Zelan (1981) and Veatch (1985) suggest some reading problems may result from the fact that while children might be able to read the bland stories in the basal readers, they might not want to read them. Veatch (1985) suggests that basal reader lessons need to contain instructions for teachers on how to motivate children to read the stories, for without the teachers' urging, children would never choose to read them.

While children enjoy good stories, they also enjoy reading informative expository prose. Anderson et al. (1985) suggest that more expository prose is needed in basal readers to prepare children for reading content area textbooks. The type of expository prose found in basal readers and trade books for children is often a hybrid containing elements of both narrative and expository prose. The purpose of this type of text is to teach some area of content, e.g., how turtles reproduce, but the content is presented in the guise of a story about a particular turtle. Although text of this type should help children make the transition from narrative to expository prose, it may instead confuse them. The effects of this type of prose is a good subject for future research.

Another criticism of basal reader content is directed against its "magazine" style. Osborn, Jones, and Stein (1985) suggest that the format of short, non-related material may actually interfere with retention of information and vocabulary. Basal reader systems have attempted to counteract this criticism by organizing units of texts based on similar themes.

Some of the newer basal readers have made changes in response to these criticisms. They have become anthologies of children's literature in which the language and content of the original text are unchanged. These anthologies are less expensive for school systems to purchase than trade books.

The main criticism leveled against the material contained in current content area textbooks is that it consists of lists of facts whose significance within the social studies or science discipline, for example, is not made clear. Armbruster (1984) points out that students will comprehend and retain information about the building of the transcontinental railroad better if the motivations and goals for building it are made clear. Yet close analysis of several textbooks (Armbruster 1984) indicates that most of them do not contain explanations of motives and goals. Content area texts should move students through higher levels of concepts and vocabulary, and clarify the significance of facts. However, prepared lists of topics to be covered, presented to publishers by school districts, as well as the constraints of easy vocabulary and short simple sentences imposed by the use of readability formulas, often result in texts that "mention" information on too many subjects with too little depth.

At times, even texts that attempt to supply content in an appropriate and logical structure include irrelevant facts. For example, a section on the causes of the American Revolution in a seventh-grade American history text (Wilder, Ludlum, and Brown 1981) is interrupted with the information that the Battle of Bunker Hill was actually fought on Breed's Hill. It has been demonstrated that seductive details like this interfere with comprehension and learning (Hidi and Baird 1983).

Because of the wide variety of content currently available in children's literature, it has been recommended that children's literature serve as a supplement and even as an alternative to the textbook in content area instruction. Informational books are available on many topics in science and social studies. Because they focus on a single topic, they can cover the topic in greater depth. For example, historical fiction like *My Brother Sam is Dead* (Collier and Collier 1974) can make the significance of the conflicts between Tories and Rebels in the American Revolution quite clear to students. On the other hand, since textbooks offer a breadth of knowledge about a discipline, it would seem that the ideal content area reading program should provide for reading of both textbooks and children's literature.

LANGUAGE USED: VOCABULARY, SENTENCE STRUCTURE, TEXT COHERENCE, STRUCTURE, AND GENRE

Just as the content and topic of the text interact with the prior knowledge and interests of the reader, so, too, the language of the text interacts with the language ability of the reader. Authors writing for children try to tailor their language to the abilities of their readers; but in writing basal reader texts and content area texts, authors have been placed under constraints that substantially affect the language they use. Since basal reading systems are based on the idea that reading is a process of learning to read words, the vocabulary used is introduced carefully with frequent exposure to specific words. This may result in the placement of particular words in unnatural situations in order to provide practice. This may actually make word recognition and comprehension more difficult, for when language is unnatural and contrived, it is less predictable (Goodman et al. 1988).

Writing basal reader and content area texts to fit readability formulas results in the necessity for short words. The need for a controlled vocabulary and the demands of readability formulas preclude the inclusion of technical vocabulary, which may be one of the reasons why so few expository selections are found in basal readers. A second result of this writing-to-formula is the elimination of many words with idiosyncratic or stylistic connotations (Davison 1984) which simplifies the writing style of both basal and content area texts to the point of being boring.

Writing the texts to fit the readability formulas also results in the use of short sentences. For example, hearing that I am a reading specialist, a salesman for a set of new science texts told me that his company's consultant edited the texts so that all the sentences were short, and no sentence was allowed to overlap from one page to another. This attempt to make text more comprehensible, again, may actually result in text that is more difficult. Pearson (1974–1975) and Davison (1984) demonstrated that while eliminating words that explicitly signal relationships may result in shorter sentences, these sentences can be more difficult to understand because they require the reader to make inferences. Davison gives the following example to illustrate this point.

Original:
If given a chance before another fire comes, the tree will heal its own wounds by growing bark over the burned part.
Adaptation:
If given a chance before another fire comes, the tree will heal its own wounds. It will grow bark over the burned part (p. 135).

The removal of the *by* and the *ing* makes it necessary for the reader to infer that growing bark is *how* the tree heals itself. A reader who did not know much about trees might not relate the two sentences.

Words like conjunctions, pronouns, and adverbs can signal relationships between sentences as well as within sentences. Making these relationships clear and explicit is one way in which text can be made more locally coherent (cohesive). This local coherence, the text structure and content, and even the graphics all contribute to global coherence—the integration of high level important ideas in the text. The more coherent a text is at both the local and the global level, the easier it is to understand (Armbruster 1984). Armbruster refers to the type of text that is well organized and readable as *considerate*. Concept load and degree of explicitness of relationships between ideas, headings, adjunct questions, introductions, and chapter outlines all contribute to making a text considerate. Writing to a formula may only make the text more inconsiderate. Inconsiderate text requires the reader to provide the coherence and structure.

Inconsiderate content area texts are quite common; their content consists of lists of facts whose significance is unclear which also makes their structure illogical and/or unclear. Basal reader stories with unclear and unpredictable structure should also be classified as inconsiderate because they too are hard to understand.

Teachers should try to select considerate texts with language and structure appropriate for the children they teach. However, appropriate language is not necessarily easy to read and understand. Children need to be taught to understand written language and even inconsiderate text. One of the main reasons children find language construction difficult is that they lack experience with it, and allowing them less experience will only make it more difficult (MacGinitie 1984). If children are not exposed to long words, long sentences, difficult constructions and structures, and new genres, they will never learn to understand them.

TEXTS AND THEIR PURPOSES

The three types of texts discussed in this chapter, i.e., basal readers, content area texts, and children's literature, differ in their purposes. Basal readers are designed to teach word recognition and comprehension; and content area textbooks are designed to teach social studies, science, and other disciplines. New whole language editions of basal readers are attempting to include authentic texts with more interesting content and language. Many of them have become anthologies of children's literature. The purpose of children's literature is to tell a good story or give information in an interesting way. Since authors of children's literature need not focus so much on readability and controlled vocabulary, they can concentrate on good writing. Children need to be exposed to good writing, for it is good writing that makes us want to read. Basal readers and content area textbooks need to focus more on good writing rather than writing to fit readability formulas.

CHAPTER

4

THE TEACHER AND THE SCHOOL ENVIRONMENT

Reading comprehension involves an interaction of the reader, the text, and the situation in which the text is read. Chapters 2 and 3 discussed the first two components of the interaction. In this chapter we will discuss the school reading environment with special emphasis on one of the most important factors in that situation—the teacher.

It is the teacher more than the method or the type of materials that determines the success or failure of a reading program (Bond and Dykstra 1967). Early research studies that attempted to identify the personality characteristics of effective teachers were unsuccessful (Artley 1969 cited in Duffy 1982). More recent research has attempted to determine which teacher behaviors are associated with high student achievement. Much of this research has been ethnographic or "naturalistic" research, in which researchers look at classrooms and schools in the same way that anthropologists look at cultures, i.e., as participant-observers. This research has shown that classrooms are very complex places with teachers juggling many demands and pressures simultaneously (Duffy 1982). The first of these is the demand for maintaining good social relations in the classroom, while at the same time effectively teaching to large groups of children with various levels of ability. The second is the need for activity flow. Unless things keep moving, the entire complex system breaks down and the teacher loses control of the students. The third is the limitations placed on teachers from outside the classroom that hamper their instructional options. Chapter 3 discusses how the administrative dictates and materials used in reading instruction affect the way that teachers teach reading. If reading comprehension instruction is to improve, all of these problems must be confronted (Duffy 1982).

The factors discussed in this chapter have been limited to those aspects of teachers' skills that help them deal with the problems within the classroom—management, creation of an appropriate classroom climate, and teaching. In-depth discussion of factors from outside the classroom that constrain comprehension instruction is beyond the scope of this book. However, constraints arise from outside factors (e.g., scheduling, class size, etc.). Although I am separating the factors for purposes of convenience and clarity of discussion, remember that they are not really separate.

One factor that directly affects reading instruction for remedial readers is the way instruction is organized for them. As previously noted, federal guidelines require that many remedial readers have two teachers—a classroom teacher and a special teacher (either a remedial reading teacher or a learning disabilities resource room teacher). These special teachers usually have fewer problems with group dynamics and activity flow than classroom teachers because they deal with smaller groups. However, very often the children instructed by the special teachers have problems in behavior and attention.

MANAGEMENT SKILL
Guideline 1: Allot more time for connected "real" reading and for comprehension instruction.

Research findings concur with common sense in demonstrating that the amount of time spent on reading instruction is related to children's achievement. One of the most important things effective teachers of reading do is to allocate sufficient time for reading. In general, studies show that reading instruction in elementary schools averages about 30% of the school day, but there are great variations. Some teachers spend as little as 35 minutes a day on reading instruction (Rosenshine and Stevens 1984). Anderson et al. (1985) suggest that this is not enough. When working with remedial readers, it is especially critical to allot sufficient time for reading instruction.

In many schools, classroom teachers believe that the special teacher should have primary responsibility for the reading instruction of remedial readers. They may believe that these children are too far below grade level to be accommodated by regular classroom instruction and that they lack the expertise necessary for special instruction. However, if the only reading instruction remedial readers receive is that offered in the special programs, they may end up having less time allocated to reading instruction than that allocated to average readers. This is especially true for children in resource rooms where teachers are often responsible for areas of instruction other than reading (Allington and McGill-Franzen 1989; Haynes and Jenkins 1986). Hill and Kimbrough (1981) and Allington and McGill-Franzen (1989) found that special reading instruction often replaces rather than supplements classroom reading instruction. Haynes and Jenkins (1986) found that remedial readers classified as learning disabled and assigned to resource rooms had no more reading instruction than average readers who remained in the classroom. This situation is another example of how the Matthew effect (Stanovich 1988), discussed in Chapter 2, operates to widen the gap between children who meet our expectations in reading and those who do not. It is critical that classroom teachers and special teachers work together to provide more instructional time for remedial readers.

Even if enough time is allocated for reading instruction, very little time is allocated for comprehension instruction (Durkin 1978–1979). This is especially true in special reading classes and resource rooms where instruction focuses on phonics even more than in regular classes (Brown, Palincsar, and Armbruster 1984).

Finding more time for comprehension instruction may seem impossible for teachers who are already overburdened. Moreover, outside pressures like testing and schedules imposed by administrators may constrain teachers' options. Yet there are some steps a teacher can take.

Changing the focus of all reading instruction to reflect the interactive view of the reading process and the close relationship between word recognition and comprehension is the first step. There should be less emphasis on discrete elements and greater emphasis on the reading process as a construction of meaning. One way of focusing on meaning is to question children regarding whether a miscue makes sense in the context of the sentence or the entire text. For example, a child who reads a sentence as "The boy went in the horse" can be asked to read the sentence again and then asked if it makes sense. If the child does not see the problem, he or she can be asked whether boys can go into horses. The techniques presented later in this book—techniques which employ activities such as holding interactive discussions, connecting text information to prior knowledge, and summarizing—offer other ways of emphasizing reading for meaning.

Decoding instruction is necessary for young children and many remedial readers. Direct instruction in phonics may be an important component of this instruction for some children, in some situations, or it may be necessary because of particular testing demands. However, children should realize that phonics is but one of many tools they need to help them understand text. Remedial readers have particular difficulty in making these kinds of connections for themselves.

Secondly, there should be greater emphasis on teaching children how to learn from content area texts. Content concepts and reading comprehension strategies can be taught simultaneously (Jones et al. 1987), increasing substantially the amount of time allocated to reading comprehension instruction.

Teachers are justified in resisting the suggestion that they should do more within a given period of time. Thus, a third suggestion is for teachers to examine all aspects of their present reading programs, identifying those elements most necessary for the instruction of particular children and those that can be eliminated. For example, is teaching all those phonic rules really a good idea at this time? Will asking children to break words they already know into syllables help them recognize other words? Do these children need to have vocabulary introduced before *this* story?

Many reading experts suggest that teachers should reduce the amount of

time spent on workbook pages and skill sheets. In a classroom that is traditionally organized into three fairly homogeneous groups for reading instruction, workbook pages can aid activity flow. They may keep two groups of children busy while the teacher is working with the third. From the point of view
of instruction, however, many of these paper and pencil tasks are of doubtful
value (Anderson et al. 1985). Activities and/or worksheets that focus on comprehension, application, and/or reading for different purposes may be a better
use of time. Different classroom organizational patterns, to be discussed later,
can make these activities easier to use.

Teachers must be quite clear about their own theories of reading in order
to make decisions about what to teach. They must also have confidence in
their knowledge of the children they teach and willingness to take responsibility for professional decisions rather than abrogating that responsibility to
publishers of reading materials.

Guideline 2: Increase comprehension instruction time by improving classroom management.

Time allocated to comprehension instruction must be used efficiently so that
none is wasted on classroom management. Using time efficiently means having
well organized routines for gathering materials, making transitions between
activities, and providing help with assignments. Teachers who are good classroom managers set up rules and routines at the beginning of the school year,
and take care that the children understand the purposes of these rules and
routines. They arrange their classrooms so that all the children are in view and
that high traffic areas, like that around the pencil sharpener, are in uncrowded
locations. (A chapter by Evertson [1987] and a book by Camp [1982] are particularly recommended for their practical suggestions in this area.)

When instructional programs that focus on comprehension and functional reading use a variety of materials they require more management skill on
the part of the teacher. For example, teachers in these kinds of programs need
to give careful thought to how furniture is arranged in their classrooms so that
children can work alone, in small groups, and in pairs. They also need to establish routines and rules for organizing, selecting, and using library books.

Chapter I and LD resource room teachers need to pay particular attention
to management considerations within their classrooms because the time that
they have with the children is so short. Resource room and Chapter I programs
usually are "pull out" programs in which children move to different rooms for
remedial reading instruction. This can create management problems for the
special teachers and the classroom teachers; moving from one room to another
disrupts activity flow. Children must be settled down when they come and prepared when they go. One way of dealing with the problem is for classroom
teachers and special reading teachers to work together, establishing routines
that minimize the disruptions of moving from room to room. If a Chapter I
teacher is not a good manager, his or her 45-minute reading period may have
only 20 minutes of instruction.

Another problem with "pull out" programs is that there is often no communication between the two reading teachers so that many children participate in two isolated and completely different reading programs. Allington (Allington, Boxer, and Broikou 1987; Allington and Johnston 1989) describes the burden that this division of instruction places on the child who experiences a problem with reading. Allington urges that there should be "congruence" between classroom and supplementary reading instruction. Although many efforts are underway to increase communication between classroom teachers and special reading teachers, the situation is still far from ideal.

"Push-in" programs where the special reading teacher comes into the classroom to work with the children are popular attempts to achieve congruence between remedial and classroom instruction and minimize disruption caused by movement from one class to another. However, having two teachers working in the same room will not necessarily result in coordination of instruction, and push-in programs do not allow remedial teachers to work with children from several different classes at the same time (Walp and Walmsley 1989). Teachers and children who are not used to sharing a room may find it distracting. Push-in programs require tact and diplomacy on the part of both the special teacher and the classroom teacher; special teachers cannot claim to be experts who show the classroom teachers how to teach reading, and classroom teachers cannot treat the special teachers as interlopers on their turf. Support of administrators and preparation of teachers is necessary before implementing such programs.

Guideline 3: Keep children's attention by maintaining an appropriate pace of instruction. Longer wait times after asking questions are an important part of maintaining this appropriate pace.

Instructional time is not used effectively unless children attend to the instruction, or to use the research term, achieve a high rate of "engaged time." Great variations in the amount of engaged time, ranging from 50 to 90% of time allocated, has been found in classrooms (Berliner 1987a). Teacher behaviors related to the amount of engaged time in all academic areas (Kounin 1970) are:

1. With-itness—the teachers communicate to the children that they are aware of what is going on in all parts of the classroom
2. Overlapping—the teachers are able to do more than one thing at a time. They can teach one group while keeping an eye on the others
3. Smoothness—teachers can move from one activity to another without disruption; minor management problems are handled quickly without disrupting instruction or attention
4. Momentum—teachers keep the activity flow going at a quick pace
5. Alerting—teachers attempt to keep all students attentive even when only one student is responding
6. Accountability—teachers monitor all students' responses giving corrective feedback if necessary

It is easy to see why teachers need a high level of energy! A number of research studies other than Kounin's have indicated that teacher momentum or a fast pace of instruction in word recognition (Barr 1973–1974); mathematics (Good, Grouws, and Beckerman 1978); and science (Arlin and Westbury 1976) aids student achievement. Usually, when a teacher's pace of instruction is fast, more content is covered and there is more opportunity to learn. The Barr, Dreeben, and Wiratchi study cited by Barr (1982) found that even though low-ability students mastered a smaller percentage of the content than students with average and high ability, "mastery levels are fairly constant for ability groups, so that those children who cover more material learn proportionately more" (Barr 1982, p. 376). Administrators and parents often are concerned about the amount of material teachers present; they may urge teachers to move at a faster pace in order to cover more content. Moving too slowly will cause students and even the teacher to get bored. Teacher momentum is important.

On the other hand, speeding up instruction can sometimes do more harm than good, especially when working with remedial readers. Early studies found that increasing the pace of instruction for remedial readers may diminish rather than aid their learning (Gates and Russell 1938). Barr herself (1982) points out that it is *incorrect* to interpret her findings in word recognition as indicating that the easiest way to increase achievement is to increase the pace of instruction. Barr (1982) and Anderson et al. (1985) both point out that the pace of instruction is limited by the ability level of the students, the difficulty of materials, and the amount of allocated and engaged reading time.

Rosenshine and Stevens (1984) suggest that covering more content seems to relate more to improvement of word recognition than to comprehension because word recognition instruction usually involves instruction in explicit items and rules. Moreover, research findings related to "wait time" suggest that slowing down the pace of instruction a bit is a good idea in any teaching that involves higher order thinking skills. "Wait-time" is usually defined as the amount of time a teacher waits between asking a good higher-order question and calling on students. Many studies (Swift and Gooding 1983) have found that when teachers wait 3 seconds instead of their usual 0.8 second after asking a high level question, the following things happen:

1. More students respond, and there are more unsolicited responses.
2. Responses are longer, more appropriate, more complex, and at a higher cognitive level.
3. Alternative explanations increase (Berliner 1987a).

The image of the teacher as a racer who moves instruction briskly along should be replaced with the image of the teacher as a conductor with the class as the orchestra (Morine-Dershimer and Beyerbach 1987). The teacher can feel out the appropriate "tempo" by noting how the students respond. To put it another way, the pace of instruction must be associated with a high rate of engaged time and student success.

Guideline 4: Use a small group organization pattern as much as possible during all phases of instruction. Whole class instruction can also be used in the initial presentation phase.

Berliner (1987a) reminds us that getting children's attention is not sufficient for effective instruction; the children must also experience a high rate of success. High success rates are related both to achievement and to academic self-concept (Rosenshine and Stevens 1984), particularly for young children (Berliner 1987a; Rosenshine and Stevens 1984) and for remedial readers (Rosenshine 1987). Anderson et al. (1985) suggest that a high rate of success in reading means that children can read 95% of the words aloud and answer 80% of the teacher's questions.

The way teachers group students during all stages of instruction—initial presentation, guided practice, independent practice, and application—affects their rate of attention and their rate of success. Initial presentation and guided practice in reading instruction take place in small groups in just about every primary classroom and many middle-grade classrooms in the United States (Anderson et al. 1985). Brophy and Good (1986) suggest that this organizational pattern is appropriate for beginning reading instruction; teachers need to hear students read aloud so that they can monitor progress and diagnose and correct consistent errors. They suggest more use of entire class instruction when reading instruction focuses on comprehension rather than on decoding.

There are two reasons for disputing this recommendation. First, using small group instruction makes it easier to keep the attention of the children. They all have a chance to respond to the teacher's questions, allowing the teacher more opportunity to ensure a high success rate through monitoring and corrective feedback. This is important in comprehension instruction because it involves higher-order thinking skills and use of complex strategies. Second, pre-reading and during-reading techniques designed to improve comprehension instruction (presented later in this book) include interactive discussion as an important component. Interactive discussion is necessary when comprehension is taught as a constructive process. It is important for children to listen to and react to other interpretations of the same text so they can evaluate their own interpretations and be ready to defend or change them. Comprehension must be taught in groups, and small groups are better since they allow participation by all members.

Whole class instruction makes efficient use of teacher time during the initial presentation stage; it is easier for the teacher to prepare; and it provides variety. Consistently grouping children in the same way becomes so boring that it affects achievement. In whole class instruction the teacher is directly involved with all the students, which helps to keep the level of attention high, though in a large group the teacher must pay more attention to activity flow and must move at a rather brisk pace. Whole class instruction is more effective when followed by guided practice in small groups.

One disadvantage of small group instruction is that the teacher is usually involved in instructing one small group. The other groups of children must work independently and the teacher cannot give all his or her attention to monitoring their work in order to ensure a high rate of engaged time and of success. Yet "expert" teachers (experienced teachers who have been identified as especially effective by their peers and supervisors) seem to be able to process several sources of specialized information simultaneously (Brandt 1986). They exhibit the with-itness and overlapping behaviors identified by Kounin (1970) so that they are able to monitor students' independent work while instructing others.

Teachers using an individualized organizational pattern—providing instruction in small groups or in individual conferences as children need it—monitor children's independent work effectively by categorizing them into primary, secondary, and minimum attention categories. Assignment to these categories depends on factors such as whether a child (1) needs to be introduced to a new skill, (2) has just started learning something new, or (3) has just received primary attention and is comfortable with what he or she is doing (Kierstead 1986).

Monitoring the work of remedial readers is particularly important. Kierstead (1986) points out that effective teachers assign children to categories of attention on the basis of ability. Therefore a remedial reader would seldom be in the minimum attention category. It is easy to envision a teacher overwhelmed by the demands on his or her attention with a number of remedial readers. No matter how expert the teacher, he or she cannot be everywhere at once. More and more teachers are realizing that well-organized practice in small groups can be much more effective than individual practice. Cooperative learning groups, to be discussed in detail later, are one way of getting more able students to assist the teacher in monitoring the independent work of remedial readers.

Remedial readers are ostensibly placed in Chapter I and LD resource room programs to provide more opportunity for individual instruction. In practice, individual instruction in these programs may mean that children work alone on the same task (Cazden 1988; Haynes and Jenkins 1986; McGill-Franzen and Allington 1989), so that there is actually less direct instruction than if the child remained in his or her own classroom. Even in small groups in special reading programs, the independent work of remedial readers is hard to monitor; therefore, small group instruction in which interactions between teachers and students are "personalized" or adjusted to fit the needs of individual students is probably a better way of achieving true individual instruction.

Remedial readers should be carefully prepared before engaging in independent activities. The activities should relate to the focus of instruction and have an appropriate level of difficulty. A high rate of success in children's independent work should be achieved as a result of effort and thought (Brophy and Good 1986). Activities that integrate material already learned with new material are appropriate; but children should not continue to practice what they have already learned for the sole purpose of experiencing a high rate of success.

Guideline 5: *Use heterogeneous groups during the practice and application phases of comprehension instruction. Cooperative learning groups are particularly recommended.*

Reading group assignment in most classrooms is based on ability. Usually there are three formal groups: high, medium, and low, because more than three groups may be unmanageable (Finn 1985). Grouping by ability presumably makes it easier for the teacher to meet individual needs because the assumption is often made that those who are grouped together by ability will have similar problems. However, Finn (1985) points out that if ability grouping is based on test scores, homogeneity is really a myth. Children may achieve the same test scores for different reasons. For example one child may have poor comprehension because of poor decoding skills, while another may have poor comprehension due to lack of background knowledge.

There is evidence that when children are grouped by ability, those in the low group receive a different type of reading instruction that may work to their disadvantage (Allington 1983; Anderson et al. 1985; Eder 1981). Children in low groups do less reading in context and more oral reading than silent reading. When children in low ability reading groups read orally, the teacher corrects them more often than children in high reading groups. Children in low reading groups, then, tend to rely on the teacher and do not learn to self correct (Allington 1983). Just as in the Chapter I and LD resource room programs, emphasis in low reading groups is on decoding rather than comprehension. When teachers ask a comprehension question of children in low reading groups, it is usually a factual question. This different type of instruction affects children's achievement as well as their self-image.

Allington (1988) has noted that some teachers define children in their classes according to their reading group placement. Unfortunately, like the little girl who was stuck with the *Dog Next Door* for three years, many children also begin to define themselves in terms of their reading group placement. Placement in the low reading group gives them low status with the other children.

These instructional and social problems together with the new emphasis on reading as an active search for meaning has caused many reading experts to suggest the use of heterogeneous grouping in reading instruction. Finn (1985) and Robinson and Good (1987) propose the use of mixed ability groups based on children's interests. Researchers like Graves (1984) and Hansen (1984) who have had success with a workshop approach to the writing process suggest a similar approach to the reading process. They use heterogeneous groups in which children discuss individual trade books they have read. Each child is always reading three books: an easy book, a book of medium difficulty, and a challenging book. Children tell something that they remember from one of their books and something the book reminds them of, or as the children describe it "a rememberer and a reminder." Strickland (1988) describes successful heterogeneous reading groups in which a member of the group selects a story to be read from the basal reader and records the time each member of the group finishes. The members of the group then meet to discuss the story. Skill instruction is not abandoned in these meaning and process-oriented classrooms, but it differs from that found in traditional classrooms because children seek instruction from and give instruction to one another. The children learn from the teacher only those skills that they cannot teach themselves (Hansen 1985).

The biggest success story in the use of heterogeneous grouping is seen in the technique known as cooperative learning. This structured technique is often very successful not only for remedial readers, but for average readers, and even for good readers (Johnson et al. 1984; Slavin 1988). Many teachers may be hesitant to use a method in which children help one another learn because research indicates teacher-directed instruction is more effective than children working alone. However, when teachers use cooperative learning, they direct the initial presentation of material, either in whole class or small group instruction. Children then meet in peer-directed groups for guided practice.

These cooperative learning groups differ from traditional peer-directed groups in several ways. First, children are assigned to groups by the teacher and each child is assigned a role that is appropriate for a particular task. Second, assignments are structured so that children must work together to reach a goal. For example, children might be given the task of comparing two fables with regard to their structure and themes. All the children would receive copies of the fables and the questions, but one child might read them aloud for the group, another might summarize the group's responses, a third might record the responses, and a fourth might ensure that everyone participates in the discussion. Third, children are individually evaluated but children are also rewarded in terms of how well the group performs. The teacher teaches group process skills along with the content and continually monitors the group for problems. Simply putting children into small groups to work together is not nearly so successful (Slavin 1988).

Although children are assigned to Chapter I and LD resource room programs because they are remedial readers, there is variation within these groups too. An organizational pattern using heterogeneous groups can be used with these readers as well. Students who are remedial readers but who are better than others in their low reading group can be paired or grouped with children who are having more difficulty with a particular task. Likewise, cooperative learning groups can be used in homogeneous classes; but, they will be more effective when the groups are truly heterogeneous. Implementing a program of cooperative learning requires the support of administrators, colleagues, and parents. Parents of high-ability children may offer strong opposition. Teachers should move into the program slowly, perhaps at first using cooperative learning only for certain selected activities and preparing everyone for the changes involved. (For teachers interested in finding out more about cooperative learning, *Circles of Learning* [Johnson et al. 1984] is recommended.)

CREATING AN APPROPRIATE CLASSROOM CLIMATE

Teachers who follow the general management guidelines suggested for improving comprehension instruction will find that their classroom climate must change. Allotting more time for reading and comprehension instruction, improving classroom management, pacing instruction more appropriately, and changing classroom organizational patterns are some ways of communicating to children that (1) classrooms are places where they learn and that getting meaning from the texts that they read is a very important part of that learning; (2) the teacher expects that every child in the class will be successful in understanding and learning from text; and (3) he or she expects the children to take responsibility for that learning. In addition teachers must create this climate through everything they say and do.

Guideline 6: Create a classroom climate with an academic focus on clear thinking rather than on getting the one right answer.

The effective teachers described by Gabrys (1979) and Rosenshine and Stevens (1984) maintain a strong academic focus. The teachers are task oriented and businesslike, modeling this behavior for the children so that the climate of the classroom also becomes task oriented. In addition to using time efficiently they make their academic goals clear and move toward them with systematic well-developed lessons and few digressions. They ensure that all students participate in the lessons and they make precise use of student input. They assign homework regularly, give weekly and monthly tests, and emphasize the marking and grading of student's work. They encourage self-sufficiency in students, holding them accountable for both classroom work and homework.

Academic focus is particularly important for remedial readers. Because they have experienced so much failure in reading, many remedial readers seek to avoid tasks at which they might fail. They can be quite ingenious in the ways they seek to distract the teacher from the task at hand. Some teachers may be overly sympathetic and inadvertently collaborate in avoiding the reading task, or they may give remedial readers tasks that fail to challenge them. Although all teachers, and particularly Chapter I and LD resource room teachers, serve many roles such as counselor and surrogate parent, their role as teacher is the priority. Teachers can create the warm, calm, and relaxed atmosphere particularly needed by remedial readers, while maintaining a structured, organized academic climate. Rosenshine and Stevens (1984) note that observational studies of hundreds of elementary classrooms did not report one instance of a task-oriented teacher who was also cold and humorless.

Academic focus is necessary for effective comprehension instruction but academic focus alone is not sufficient. There must also be a focus on reading for meaning and a recognition that interpretations of a text will differ because reading comprehension is a constructive process. There must be a structure, but it cannot be one in which the teacher asks questions to get only one correct answer. In order for comprehension instruction to be effective there must be a climate of acceptance and respect for answers that have intellectual integrity but differ from the standard expected answer. For example, in one lesson I gave, children read the title *The Cow Who Fell in the Canal*. I asked how they thought the cow would fall in the canal. One child said it would be an accident of some kind because the title said the cow *fell* in the canal. Another child said the cow would jump into the canal on purpose. When asked to support his answer, he replied that perhaps the cow pretended to fall in the canal because she wanted to leave the boring place. The child mentioned that he had seen other children pretend to fall down.

The pre-reading lesson had activated the children's experiences about boredom and ways of counteracting it, so the child's answer was understandable and showed that he was using his own experience to make predictions. He could have been right, although in this case he was not; the cow fell into the canal accidentally. I accepted all answers and the children read the text to determine whose prediction was confirmed.

A climate of risk taking encourages children to make predictions and ask questions about what they are reading—both necessary strategies for effective comprehension. The classroom climate must be one in which children discuss their interpretations of text and feel free to disagree; in this open-minded atmosphere students and teachers can change their ideas because of the evidence provided by others in a discussion. In such a climate the ultimate sin is for either the teacher or the other children to humiliate a child for his or her comment or response.

In comprehension instruction the academic focus is on the nature of student's thinking. Thus the teacher often probes the child's thinking regardless of whether the answer to a question is the expected one. Teachers should not accept silly and irrelevant answers, but Niles and Harris (1981) point out that probing a child's thinking often makes clear that the student was on the right track but did not express his or her thoughts clearly. On the other hand, children may give right answers for the wrong reasons and must realize their mistakes. Probing the children's thinking means changing old habits; remedial readers having experienced failure previously will be particularly fearful of taking the risk of failing again. Teachers who are used to one right answer will find it hard to accept diversity. Although they may not tell a child, their facial expressions and their body language may convey how they feel about the answer. Teachers will need to be aware of these aspects of their behavior. Children who are used to having only wrong answers questioned will at first resent the teacher questioning their correct answers. The purpose of this questioning must be made clear to the students.

Guideline 7: *Create a literate environment in the classroom.*
The importance of comprehending written text is conveyed to the children not only through direct instruction but through a literate classroom environment. Searfoss and Readence (1985) suggest that classrooms for beginning readers who are just learning to decode should be print laboratories full of all kinds of texts and opportunities for children to explore the many uses of reading and writing. They suggest that "Classrooms should provide an environment that says to children 'It is safe to practice here; there is exciting reading here, so

dive in and read'" (p.23). As the focus of reading instruction shifts more and more away from decoding and toward comprehension, the literate environment remains important. Classrooms should have trade books to read and enjoy, and teachers should schedule reading and discussion time.

Content area instruction should involve reading to obtain information. The teacher should resist the temptation to provide content area information orally to the children. Having taught the children strategies, the teacher can provide tasks in which children must read in textbooks, trade books, and reference books in order to obtain the desired information. Perhaps most importantly, teachers in this kind of literate environment are models of literacy, conveying their enthusiasm through the reading and writing they do themselves: when they read aloud to the children, when they read silently during the sustained silent reading period, when they write comments in their own reading journals about what they have been reading, and when they react in writing to comments that the children have written in their reading journals, turning the experience into a written dialogue between child and teacher. (Use of reading journals will be discussed in Chapter 9.)

Guideline 8: *Convey the expectation that all the children in the class (including the remedial readers) will be successful in learning how to understand written text.*

Earlier chapters demonstrated the importance of high teacher expectations for remedial readers. But, it is not enough for the teacher to have high expectations; he or she must convey those expectations to the children. Several general teaching guidelines suggested earlier in this chapter can have the effect of conveying higher teacher expectations. Allotting more time for connected reading and comprehension instruction for remedial readers will change the focus of instruction and convey to the children that they must comprehend a text. Pacing the instruction appropriately and spending more time with students who are experiencing difficulty can show that the teacher believes they will be successful with more instruction. Giving children more time to answer questions can convey that the teacher expects them to know the answer. Placing remedial readers in heterogeneous groups can show them that the teacher believes they are capable of working effectively with other children in the class. Probing their thinking and asking them to come up with questions and predictions about the text can show them that their thinking is worthwhile, that they have something to contribute.

I have used the word *can* rather than *will* above because these actions on the part of the teacher may be interpreted differently by the students. Children who are used to being passed over if they do not have a quick answer for a question may view the teachers' provision of extra "wait time" as an attempt to put them on the spot, possibly humiliating them in front of their peers. In other words, the teacher's actions are often ambiguous (Winne and Marx 1987; Good 1987). Effective actions are those correctly interpreted. Teachers can make their actions less ambiguous by explaining the reasons for them. For example, a teacher can explain that people who have studied the way children answer questions have found that if children are given a little extra time to think, they can often come up with good answers to the teacher's question.

In addition to explaining the reasons for their behavior, teachers need to convey directly their expectations of success. This is extremely important, for without an expectation of success, children do not become the active readers necessary for successful comprehension.

Guideline 9: Make the children aware that the goal of comprehension instruction is to make them independent learners.
No matter how proficient a teacher is, he or she cannot do the learning for a child. Children must take responsibility for their own learning; in reading a text they must be active constructors of meaning. In comprehension instruction teachers provide children with the strategies by which they can become active learners.

Children who fail to meet our expectations in reading are often passive learners. They have experienced failure so many times that they have given up trying and may even resist learning. When dealing with children like this, I always try to keep in mind what one of the most difficult children I ever taught told me: "I would rather have you think I am bad than that I am stupid." Many remedial readers must feel this way but do not express it!

Children who are passive or resistant to learning need much teacher support and direction at first. The support allows remedial readers to experience success while being challenged, fulfilling teachers' and children's expectations of success. All models of comprehension instruction to be discussed in the next section provide for extensive teacher support when a strategy is initially introduced. Teacher explanation and modeling of the strategy provide support and direction. For example, in teaching children how to answer inferential questions, Gordon and Pearson (1983) follow the explicit comprehension instruction model of Pearson and Gallagher (1983) outlined in figure 1 (see page 66). They break the task into four elements: asking the question, answering it, finding evidence in the text for the answer, and giving the reasoning. At the first stage of instruction, the teacher might demonstrate all four elements of the task using the excerpt below.

> Ralph sat in an old wooden rocking chair. He rocked harder and harder. Suddenly he found himself sitting on the floor (Raphael 1982, p. 187).

The teacher asks the inferential question, "Why did Ralph find himself sitting on the floor?" and responds, "He was rocking too hard in a rocking chair." The teacher then provides evidence for the answer, namely that "It says he was sitting in a rocking chair and he rocked harder and harder," and explains the reasoning that led to the answer: "I know that if you rock too hard in a rocking chair it is likely to tip over."

In the next stage the teacher gradually releases responsibility to the children by placing them in charge of certain aspects of the task. She asks the question and answers it, but asks the children to provide the evidence and the reasoning that led to the answer. Next, she asks the question and provides the

A MODEL OF EXPLICIT INSTRUCTION

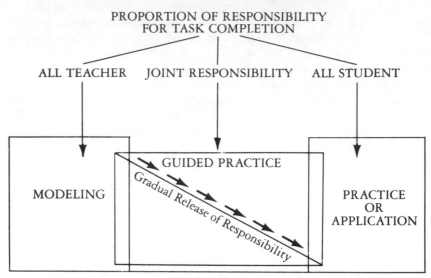

Figure 1. Explicit instruction model. Reprinted, with permission, from P. D. Pearson and M. C. Gallagher. *The Instruction of Reading Comprehension.* Contemporary Educational Psychology (1983).

evidence for the answer, asking the children to provide the answer and the reasoning. Finally, she asks the question and the children give the answer, providing the evidence and the reasoning. The ultimate goal is for the children to ask their own questions while independently reading for information and enjoyment.

Remedial readers may need to assume the responsibility more gradually than other students, but responsibility can and must be released. Discussing how children can use strategies on their own should be a part of every teacher-directed lesson. Providing them with opportunities to apply their use of the strategies with many different kinds of texts in many different situations and to share and fine tune their use of the strategies in discussion with other children is an integral part of comprehension instruction.

TEACHING SKILL
THE COMPREHENSION CURRICULUM
Guideline 10: Teach process and content.
Duffy (1982) points out that comprehension instruction is different from instruction in other content areas in that

> Research findings have not been translated into curriculum guidelines . . . teachers do not know what elements, operations, experiences, strategies, skills or attitudes should be the content of comprehension instruction (p. 367).

Comprehension instruction differs from other content areas in that the focus of its curriculum is the reading process rather than a specific body of content. Traditional instructional methods, such as the directed reading lesson in the basal readers focus on the content of the text. Questions and discussion center on what the text says. These traditional methods rely on practice, by which children "infer the existence of a language system and subconsciously use it to comprehend" (Roehler, Duffy, and Meloth 1984, p. 81). MacGinitie (1984) points out that when children do not understand what they have read, teachers usually explain the content rather than explaining to children how they can use cues in the text to understand the content. As we have seen in Chapter 3, many content area teachers take this approach because they believe their priority is social studies or mathematics rather than reading. It is even more disturbing when teachers who believe they are teaching children to comprehend a text fail to provide any process instruction. Of course, process cannot be separated from content; there cannot be a curriculum that focuses only on process.

> Reading curricula should stress interpretation but it should also include teaching children how to comprehend interpretations. . . . If we do not teach children comprehension strategies, then the better students will develop them on their own, and the worse readers will find reading very frustrating (Collins and Smith 1982).

What is needed is a better balance between instruction in process and content, what Roehler, Duffy, and Meloth (1984) refer to as a process-into-content emphasis.

MODELS OF COMPREHENSION INSTRUCTION
THE DISCOVERY LEARNING MODEL

Reading authorities today generally agree that both process and content should be part of comprehension instruction, but they differ on how to provide this instruction. Chapter 1 suggests that, although the specific skills approach is inappropriate, it is necessary to break down the process in some way in order to teach it. Proponents of the first model of comprehension instruction—the indirect or discovery learning model (Beach and Appleman 1984; Goodman 1984; Harste and Mikulecky 1984)—are opposed to breaking down the process in any way. Tierney and Cunningham (1984) worry that "To date our comprehension instruction has tended to emphasize the systematic, sequential and piecemeal at the expense of the aesthetic, experiential, vicarious and the wonder of reading" (p. 634). The experts who hold this view believe that the process should be taught indirectly: not by practicing specific skills but by extensive reading of many kinds of texts for different purposes. They believe that comprehension instruction should be discovery learning for several reasons.

The first reason involves the ill-structured nature of comprehension instruction. Since comprehension of written text involves subjectivity and reasoning, comprehension instruction is not considered to be a well-structured domain like mathematics. Frederiksen (1984) suggests that in ill-structured domains explicit instruction in strategies is much more complex, and opportunities to learn through practice, feedback, and discussion might be more appropriate. The second reason has to do with the fact that good comprehenders are active constructors of meaning. Proponents of discovery learning believe that explicit instruction of strategies does not allow children to learn a more active approach to problem solving (Frederiksen 1984).

It is true that many children discover how to comprehend text without explicit instruction. Through their own reading, they develop strategies that are quite successful. They may not need explicit instruction in comprehension. To be forced to use another strategy when they are already successful with one of their own may actually be harmful, as in the old adage, "If it ain't broke, don't fix it." On the other hand, direct instruction may be helpful as an alternative to developing strategies of their own through a painful process of trial and error. Doyle (1983) suggests that novices in all fields need direct instruction, while indirect instruction is more appropriate when the basic knowledge structures and skills of the domain have been acquired. Lundeberg (1987) raises a very important question: "Can we assume that students will learn all that we want them to learn through discovery learning?" The results of her own study and those of many other studies of comprehension instruction suggest that the answer to this question is "No." Lundeberg found that direct strategy instruction improved the performance of experienced law students in the ill-structured domain of case analysis. Studies by Palincsar and Brown (1984) and Hansen and Hubbard (1984), to name a few, found that children who failed to meet expectations in reading profited from instruction that showed them how to use a particular kind of strategy. Remedial readers do not develop successful strategies spontaneously (Rohwer 1971); they are hampered by many factors such as strongly held misconceptions (Larkin 1983; Maria and MacGinitie 1987); inappropriate strategies (Larkin 1983); and lack of flexibility (Brown 1980). Although the goal of comprehension instruction for all readers is to make them independent learners, remedial readers will need a substantial amount of teacher-directed instruction.

Guideline 11: Make teacher-directed instruction a component of comprehension instruction for remedial readers.

THE DIRECT INSTRUCTION MODEL

A second model of comprehension instruction is the type of direct-reading instruction exemplified by the DISTAR reading program. This program provides carefully sequenced, carefully scripted, highly structured lessons that break the reading process into small elements. The design of instruction is emphasized, not the teacher's role in communicating the curriculum. The teacher's job is to follow the script. This type of direct instruction is not teacher-directed, but program-directed instruction. This model is not recommended as a model for comprehension instruction for the following reasons:

1. It takes a bottom-up specific skills approach to both decoding and comprehension instruction.
2. It is based on a behaviorist theory of learning in which the learners are passive and the teacher controls instruction completely. Specific phonic

objectives, i.e., the short *a* sound, may be effectively taught to some children through this approach, but higher-level thinking skills such as making inferences cannot be programmed.

3. It focuses on content with little attention to process.

Other proponents of direct instruction emphasize the teacher's role. As discussed in the earlier sections of this chapter, Rosenshine (1979) and Berliner (1981) describe direct instruction in all content areas as involving teacher behaviors such as providing academic focus, ensuring high pupil engagement, and ensuring a high success rate. As Jones (1986) points out, however, focusing on these teacher behaviors involves viewing the teacher as manager and executive rather than as teacher.

THE MEDIATED INSTRUCTION MODEL

Instruction that is initially teacher directed but that gradually releases responsibility to the children has been termed *mediated instruction* (Duffy and Roehler 1986; Gavelek 1984; Jones 1986).

Mediated instruction is based on Vygotsky's (1978) theory of learning which states that social interaction plays a major role in fostering learning and is an impetus to cognitive growth. Vygotsky suggests that with the support of a more experienced learner, a child may participate in strategic activity without understanding it completely. With teacher support, the child gradually internalizes and comes to understand the strategies that he or she has performed in the interaction.

The teacher's job is to determine the child's zone of proximal development, i.e.,

. . . the distance between the actual developmental level as determined by independent problem solving and the level of potential development as determined through problem solving under adult guidance or in collaboration with more capable peers (Vygotsky 1978, p. 76).

The teacher then mediates between the child and those tasks that are beyond his or her level of independent competence, providing supportive instruction characterized by:

1. Intentionality—There is an overall purpose that is made clear to the students.
2. Appropriateness—Initial tasks can be solved with help. Tasks are neither too easy nor too hard but are in the zone of proximal development.
3. Structure—Modeling and questioning by the teacher help to structure the task for the student.
4. Collaboration—The teacher and students work together. The teacher is a coach rather than an all-knowing authority.
5. Internalization—The external scaffolding is gradually withdrawn and techniques are internalized by the students (Applebee and Langer 1983).

While discovery learning emphasizes the role of the learner and direct instruction emphasizes the role of the teacher, mediated instruction emphasizes the interaction between the learner and the teacher. The three models to be presented next—the text-based model, the explicit instruction model, and the combined model—are similar in that they are variations of the mediated instruction model. They differ in their starting point for instruction and in the types of texts they use.

THE TEXT-BASED MODEL

The text-based model (MacGinitie 1984) might be characterized as having a content-into-process emphasis. In this model the starting point is the text and the primary goal of instruction in this model is understanding a particular text. The teacher focuses questions and discussion on important concepts in the text. Process instruction is also provided as the teacher demonstrates the clues from the text and the process that he or she uses in making sense of it.

Ideally, in using this model, the teacher controls text selection and chooses each text because its topic will be of interest to the children. Another reason for selecting a particular text is that it relates directly to the content of the curriculum and contains material the children need to learn. The text should be a considerate one, well written and carefully organized. However, since teachers are not always free to select the texts they use in comprehension instruction, one may be selected because it is the next text in the basal reader or part of the social studies series. The basal reader story may be a bland, uninteresting story and the content area text may lack a logical structure, having instead lists of facts loosely related to a theme. If this is the case, the teacher may have to build interest and supply structure.

In using the text-based model the teacher reads the text very carefully and considers the following questions:

1. What phrases, sentences, or paragraphs might some students not understand?
2. What clues in the written context lead to the teacher's own understanding?
3. How might a student find those clues and so understand what the text says?

In asking these questions the teacher considers text and student factors that may interfere with comprehension. Teachers' knowledge of the children they teach and of the text should guide them in the selection of one or two concepts that will become the focus of pre-reading, during-reading, and after-reading activities. No one is better able to select the focus than the teacher because no one else has as much knowledge about the children, what they know, and what they need to learn.

The text-based model treats comprehension as a holistic process, focusing on helping children understand a particular text. Because it considers how factors in the text interact with factors in the children to affect understanding of a text, this model seems particularly suited to pre-reading comprehension instruction.

One objection to focusing on the problems posed by one text is that there is no evidence that improving comprehension of individual texts will improve overall comprehension. Lessons that show children how to understand particular texts should facilitate comprehension of subsequent texts more than lessons that make no attempt to show them how to understand (Beck, Omanson, and McKeown 1981). However, as discussed previously, comprehension instruction should emphasize process as well as content. When modeling strategies that can be used to solve comprehension problems posed by particular texts, teachers should point out their usefulness and provide practice in using them with other texts. The goal of this model, like the goal of explicit instruction, is to shift responsibility from the teacher to the children. The only real difference is the starting point for planning instruction.

THE EXPLICIT INSTRUCTION MODEL

The explicit instruction model, sometimes referred to as direct instruction, begins with a particular skill to be taught. It is defined by Baumann (1983):

> In direct instruction, the teacher, in a face to face, reasonably formal manner, tells, shows, models, demonstrates, teaches the skill to be learned. The key word here is teacher who is in command of the learning situation and leads the lesson, as opposed to having instruction "directed" by a worksheet, kit, learning center, or workbook (p. 287).

Elsewhere Baumann (1988) points out that this type of direct instruction should provide for the gradual movement from full teacher responsibility to shared teacher-pupil responsibility to full pupil responsibility. Thus Baumann's definition of direct instruction seems identical to Pearson and Gallagher's (1983) model of explicit comprehension instruction described in the previous section.

In the explicit model of comprehension instruction the goal of instruction is the same as in traditional skills instruction, i.e., the acquisition of instructionally relevant automatic skills. This model differs from traditional skills instruction, however, because the child is shown how to acquire the skill; there is a process-into-content emphasis. The teacher demonstrates the use of a strategy, and through practice the children internalize the strategy so that its use becomes automatic and they have acquired a skill. Over a period of time, children acquire a large repertoire of these skills, i.e., understanding pronoun referents (Baumann 1986); summarizing (Day 1980); and answering inferential questions (Gordon and Pearson 1983). In this model texts are chosen because they provide opportunities to learn the skill that is the focus of instruction. Children move from short, simple texts to longer, more complex ones.

Although explicit instruction teaches children how to acquire skills, it may retain the fallacy of the more traditional skills approach which treats comprehension as a set of discrete skills rather than as a holistic process. Another concern about the model relates to how one chooses which instructionally relevant skill to teach. At present, there is no consistent body of evidence to support the identification of a discrete list of skills that should be taught in reading comprehension programs (Cooper 1986). In fact, Cooper suggests that because each reader's comprehension process is somewhat different, it is un-

71

likely that a body of research will ever support conclusively any given set of comprehension skills as the essential skills to teach. Such a view seems rather radical, however. Intuitively, it seems there must be a core of skills that can be used by different readers for a wide variety of reading tasks.

THE COMBINED MODEL

The combined model draws upon the strengths of both text-based and explicit instruction. It has a process-into-content emphasis in that skills and strategies are taught, but teaching is closely tied to reading texts designed to provide information or enjoyment rather than texts designed to teach a specific skill or strategy. The technique that best exemplifies this model is reciprocal teaching developed by Palincsar and Brown (1984). In this technique four strategies are taught: question generating, summarizing, predicting, and clarifying. These particular strategies were chosen because research indicates that they are used spontaneously by good readers.

Thus the objection to the explicit instruction model raised by Cooper (1986) is addressed in this combined technique. As in the explicit-instruction model, the starting point is the teaching of strategies, although very little time is spent on teaching each separate strategy. Palincsar (1986) suggests introducing the strategies separately, one on each of four successive days. Then the strategies are immediately combined and modeled by the teacher with the primary goal of instruction the comprehension of a content area text. Again, as in the explicit comprehension model, the responsibility is gradually released to the children as they and the teacher engage in a dialogue. At first the discussion is teacher directed with the teacher modeling the strategies. Children then take turns taking on the role of teacher. Research has shown that after children have had some experience with the technique they often engage in dialogue with one another. The teacher continues to provide feedback as needed. (This technique is described more fully in Chapter 8.)

Guideline 12: Use a mediated instruction model in comprehension instruction, providing support for the children as they work toward independence.

A combined approach that teaches strategies in the context of reading texts for learning content or enjoying a story is the generally recommended variation of this model. At times the text-based model may be appropriate, particularly for pre-reading instruction, and at other times, the explicit instruction model may be needed in order to provide practice with specific strategies.

TOOLS FOR COMPREHENSION INSTRUCTION

Guideline 13: In providing mediated instruction use a variety of tools: questioning, explanation, modeling, and dialogue or discussion.

Each of these tools has something unique to contribute to instruction. The first two have been used extensively by teachers; yet there are less traditional ways they can be used in comprehension instruction. Modeling and dialogue have not been used as much in reading instruction, but they too play a role in effective comprehension instruction.

QUESTIONING
Guideline 14: Ask questions about process and content.
Make sure content questions relate to important information in the text.
In traditional reading instruction teachers ask the questions. Although questions are the means by which they assess comprehension, teachers have always considered them to be instructional tools also. However, the instructional effect of teachers' questions is generally indirect; the questions focus children's attention on what they are expected to learn from a text (Reynolds and Anderson 1982; Wixson 1983), but do not provide assistance with the learning.

The recognition that teachers' questions are usually literal detail questions and that these questions affect the way children read (Guszak 1967) led to the development of several taxonomies of questions (e.g., Barrett 1976; Sanders 1966). These taxonomies use information available in the text to categorize questions according to the level of the child's anticipated response. Barrett (1976), for example, categorized questions as literal, inferential, evaluation, and appreciation. Barrett suggested that teachers use these taxonomies as a guide to asking questions at different levels, beginning with low-level recall questions and then moving to higher-level inferential, evaluation, and appreciation questions. Rhodes and Dudley-Marling (1988), however, have pointed out that these taxonomies are based on false assumptions, i.e., that comprehension occurs in discrete categories or levels which are sequential and hierarchical. We have come to understand that levels of comprehension are artificial categories just as are specific skills.

Pearson and Johnson (1978) have formulated a taxonomy of questions based on our more recent understanding of the reading process. This taxonomy takes into account the way in which the reader uses background knowledge, as well as text information, in answering questions about the text. Hence Pearson and Johnson refer to it as a taxonomy of question/answer relationships rather than a taxonomy of questions. They identify three categories:

1. Textually Explicit—The student answers the question with information found in one sentence in the text.
2. Textually Implicit—The student answers the question by integrating information across sentences in the text. In order to connect the information, the student has to make inferences about relationships between different pieces of information in the text.
3. Scriptually Implicit—The student uses his or her own prior knowledge in a way that is relevant to the text.

Rhodes and Dudley-Marling (1988) point out that in this taxonomy questions can fit more than one category depending on the nature of the student's response. One child might find the information in the text and another might use his or her prior knowledge. Both can come up with plausible answers to the question. Thus the source of the answer, the cues in the text, and their interaction with the reader's prior knowledge, become important for the teacher to understand. As mentioned previously, children should be asked to explain the reasoning behind their answers even when their answers are the expected ones.

The Pearson and Johnson taxonomy of question/answer relationships is helpful in that it takes into account another very important aspect of teachers' questions, i.e., whether or not they are text related. Often questions that teachers consider to be higher-level questions do not focus children's attention on obtaining information from the text. These questions can be answered without understanding the text or even without reading it (Rhodes and Dudley-Marling 1988). Questions like "Have you ever had an accident? What happened?" that ask about the children's experiences without relating these experiences to text information are questions in this category. None of the taxonomies, including the Pearson and Johnson one, makes a distinction between "trivial" and "important" questions. This distinction would be critical if a teacher sees his or her questions as a means of focusing children's attention on important text information. A question that focuses on important explicit information in the text may be far more useful in helping a child understand than an inference question that focuses on trivial information. Failure to categorize questions as text related or text unrelated or as important or trivial may lead to the contradictory research findings noted by Aulls (1982): Classroom observational studies (Rosenshine 1976; Medley 1977) found that with low SES children a higher proportion of lower-level questions resulted in better reading achievement scores while studies in instructional methods (Hansen 1981; Manzo and Leganza 1975; Bisken, Hoskisson, and Modlin 1976) found that a greater proportion of higher-level teacher questions produced better achievement. A number of text-explicit questions concerning details related to the central concept may be necessary with children who fail to meet expectations in comprehension. These questions provide the base of information necessary to answer higher-level questions, which prompt critical thinking (Smith 1989). In asking these higher level questions teachers should use precise language such as "What evidence do you have that these stories have the same theme?" (Costa and Marzano 1987). When teachers' questions are vague and general they do not guide student's thinking (Smith 1989).

As will be described more fully in Chapter 5, the teacher's first step in planning a comprehension lesson for a particular text is to determine a central concept or concepts that will be the focus of instruction. Pre-reading questions should focus on making connections between these central concepts and the children's prior knowledge. During- and post-reading questions should also focus on important text information.

Teacher questions discussed thus far relate only to text content. Since comprehension instruction involves instruction in both process and content, teachers' questions should also focus on process. Lipson et al. (1987) found that children who were asked about the reading strategies they used had better comprehension than those who were asked questions about the content of the text.

Questioning children about their strategies focuses their attention on those strategies and eventually increases achievement.

Guideline 15: *Use question sequences as prompts and supports for children's thinking.*

A sequence of questions by teachers does more than focus children's attention on certain aspects of content or process. Such sequences of related questions, built on one another, help develop cognitive processing. Socrates was one of the first teachers to lead learners to discover knowledge through a careful sequence of questions. The Taba method (Taba 1966), which Aulls (1982) recommends for use with expository material, involves questions presented in the following sequence: (1) questions focusing on concept formation, making sure that explicit text information has been understood, (2) questions for integrating and interpreting this information through *convergent* inquiry (calling for one right response), (3) questions for integrating or applying new knowledge to prior knowledge. This last step involves asking *divergent* questions which allow for a number of responses.

Comprehension instruction using teachers' questions can serve as a means of scaffolding instruction. If a child responds with "I don't know" in answer to a teacher's question, the child may not really be lacking the information necessary to answer the question. Farrar (1984) describes a situation in which a child did not know how to answer the question, "Why does Peter call himself a nothing?" (from *Tales of a Fourth Grade Nothing* by Judy Blume). She suggests that a teacher can ask a series of questions that structure the information needed for the answer:

1. How does Peter feel when his brother gets all the attention?
2. Why, then, does he call himself a nothing?

Another possibility is for the teacher to ask the question in an easier form, such as providing choices or asking a yes/no question. Instead of asking question number 2 above, the teacher can ask, "Does the word *nothing* or the word *something* describe how Peter felt?" or "Does the word *nothing* describe how Peter felt?" Then ask the child to explain his answer. Using follow-up questions as prompts rather than probes, and explaining how the questions are designed to help them think of the answer will help avoid the impression of putting a child on the spot.

Guideline 16: *Plan questions. Try to anticipate possible incorrect responses and ways of dealing with them.*

An important part of asking questions is the teacher's response to children's answers. The teacher should not merely indicate that children's answers are correct or incorrect, but should seek their reasoning. Meyer (1985) categorizes incorrect responses as motor mistakes, lack of information mistakes, confused information mistakes, and rule application mistakes. Questioning children should help teachers determine which type of incorrect response the child gave. Teachers can then structure further questions, explanations, or modeling focusing on cues in the text that can lead the child to a correct response.

According to Meyer, a motor mistake can occur when a child has the information but is unable to express it. Teachers need to be sensitive to the fact that a totally inappropriate response may stem from this type of mistake. In a class of remedial readers we were discussing the meaning of the noun *mate*. One child called out "I know. I know. Skipper and giggling. Skipper and giggling." Probing revealed that what seemed like a random and totally inappropriate response actually indicated that the child knew what *mate* meant; she was referring to the TV show *Gilligan's Island* in which Gilligan is the first mate to the Skipper.

Determining whether a child lacks information, confuses information, or applies a rule incorrectly to a particular situation is important because teachers need to respond differently. Children who read a text comparing the Iroquois Indians to the Plains Indians may say that the Iroquois Indians are nomads like the Plains Indians because:

1. They didn't attend to text information about the Iroquois planting crops.
2. They don't know what a nomad is and the text doesn't say.
3. They have confused the Iroquois Indians with the Plains Indians, thinking that the Plains Indians planted the crops.
4. They think all Indians are nomads and, therefore, Iroquois Indians must be nomads.

Each of these situations would require a different type of clarification.

Decisions about what questions to ask before, during, and after reading should be an integral part of planning a comprehension lesson. Teachers should anticipate problems in the text that may result in incorrect responses. Techniques presented in Chapter 5 will provide help in planning pre-reading questions, and those presented in Chapter 8 will provide help in planning during- and post-reading questions. Examples of generic questions that focus on important aspects of narrative or expository structure presented in Chapter 7 can also serve as guides for this planning. But, no matter how much planning teachers do, they cannot anticipate all students' responses to their questions. They must make decisions in the midst of instruction, thinking on their feet, and be ready to put aside the plan because the children's responses indicate that unanticipated teaching is called for.

Guideline 17: Make children aware that your questions are models of the type of questions they should be asking themselves.
So far our discussion has focused on the teacher as the one who asks the questions. However, since comprehension is an active constructive process and since we aim to make children independent learners, they should learn to ask their own questions rather than continually relying on teachers' questions.

In asking questions teachers should view themselves as models of good questioning behaviors. Teachers inquire about important information in the text because they want children to ask themselves similar questions. When posing questions teachers need to point out how good questions can aid comprehension. Chapter 8 will describe several techniques in which teachers model questioning behavior and students generate their own questions.

EXPLANATIONS

Guideline 18: Make sure that explanations of reading strategies provide declarative, procedural, and conditional knowledge.

Explanation is another traditional tool for teachers. In fact, explanation may be what most people think of when they think of teaching. Since explanation involves the teacher talking and the children listening, it is associated with a passive view of learning. Teachers now are urged not to talk so much, but to involve children in experiential learning, letting them discover explanations. These suggestions have merit because when teachers explain the content of the textbooks rather than showing children how to read, children become passive and dependent on the teacher.

In the mediated model of comprehension instruction the teacher explains process rather than content—how to read the text rather than what the text says. This kind of explanation is important for remedial readers, since many of them do not read for meaning; do not know what strategies to use; and even when they know the strategy to use, do not know how to use it. In the initial stage of mediated learning teachers explain how they use a strategy. During the later stages, when the students begin to take responsibility for the task, explanations of how to use a strategy are provided *when needed*. This can be a crucial support for all readers. Teacher explanations must be used in conjunction with the other tools: teacher and student questions, teacher modeling, and interactive discussion.

When Duffy et al. (1987) taught third grade teachers to modify basal reader instruction so that the emphasis of their explanations was on the "mental processing involving using skills as strategies" (p. 352), children in their low reading groups showed greater awareness of content and made more conscious use of strategies. Their achievement was better than that of children who did not receive explanations concerning strategies. Teachers who were the best explainers focused not only on what strategies to use (declarative knowledge) and how to use them (procedural knowledge), but also on when to use a particular strategy and when not to (conditional knowledge). For example, when Teacher A teaches children how to use context to figure out the meaning of a word, a situation arises in which *sad, lazy,* and *tired* are all possible meanings for *despondent* (Roehler and Duffy 1986). The teacher's explanation quoted from Roehler and Duffy (1986) points out that in this situation context is not useful and goes on to suggest an alternative strategy.

> Well, how are we going to know: Is it "tired," is it "sad," or is this dog "lazy?" Could these clues make us think he is lazy? Or could they make us think he is sad? Or could they make us think he is tired? How are we going to know for sure what the word "despondent" means? This might be one time to turn to the dictionary or the glossary. We're really not sure on this one, so we'll have to check. When you get to that point in your reading (when context clues give several plausible answers) and

you can't figure out which one it is, that is the time to look it up. I just want you to know that when you come to a situation like this you have to look the word up (pp. 188–189).

Teachers who are good explainers also recognize that children do not necessarily understand their first explanation no matter how clear and explicit it is. These teachers check children's understanding of initial explanations through questions. When the answers indicate a lack of understanding, teachers restructure explanations to address the children's particular sources of difficulty. Duffy and Roehler (1986) call this process "responsive elaboration" and suggest that it might be an important aspect of the effectiveness of teacher explanations.

Paris, Cross, and Lipson (1984) developed a program called *Informed Strategies for Learning* which proves to be very effective in providing declarative, procedural, and conditional knowledge about 13 reading strategies. The program also focuses on convincing children of the value of using the strategies. A kit, called *Reading and Thinking Strategies* (Paris 1988), based on this program, is available from the Collamore division of D.C. Heath and Company. The kit includes explanations by the teacher and visual metaphors of the strategies in the form of colorful posters. For example, in the module concerned with the strategy of finding the main idea a poster shows a detective with a magnifying glass looking at animal tracks labeled: Pictures, Topic, Title, How, Why, Where, What, and Who. Explanations by the teacher, questions, and class discussions focus on these posters, which displayed in the classroom, serve to remind children to use the strategies. This program uses the explicit model of comprehension instruction—strategies are introduced and texts provide the means of practicing the strategies. The program can also be used in a combined instructional model where strategies are taught in the context of reading texts not specifically designed for teaching the strategies.

MODELING
Guideline 19: Make yourself aware of your own reading strategies. When modeling for children, try to put yourself in their places.
Berliner (1987b) suggests that effective explanations use examples to provide clarity. When demonstrating how they use strategies, teachers provide examples of effective strategy use. They think aloud, verbalizing the processes they use to understand the text. Collins and Smith (1982) propose a three-stage procedure for demonstrating strategies of prediction and comprehension monitoring using the explicit instruction model. First, the teacher reads a text aloud, interrupting once or twice in each paragraph to make comments about the strategies and cues he or she uses to understand the text. The teacher also encourages student participation and comments. This is followed by guided and independent practice of the strategies by the students.

A lesson I used with a group of third grade remedial readers provides an example of the use of this procedure. I encountered a reading comprehension problem while preparing to use the text *The Little Green Man* (Damjan 1975) from Level 15 of the Macmillan r series in a lesson. The pictures gave the impression that the little green man was in a spaceship, but a sentence on the third page stated, "Little green man went outside and got into his spaceship." I used my own comprehension problem as a starting point for demonstrating how to detect and solve this kind of comprehension problem in which information later in the text contradicts an earlier interpretation.

When the group got to that point in the reading, I pointed out that as I read this, I realized there was a problem; the man couldn't have been in the spaceship already if the text said that he went outside to get in it. I told them how I reread and decided little green man had been in his house.

After completing the text we moved to the second stage in which the children used materials developed by Kimmel and MacGinitie (1984) and verbalized how they found text cues that corrected an erroneous initial interpretation. Cooper (1986) has stated that getting children to verbalize their processing is an important component of the modeling procedure.

Modeling is an effective instructional tool often overlooked in teaching reading but there are problems in using it. The first problem is that for sophisticated readers (e.g., teachers) the processes of comprehension can become so automatic that they become inaccessible to conscious awareness (Afflerbach and Johnston 1986; Garner 1987). Teachers must be aware of their own processes before they can model them. Collins and Smith (1982) suggest that teachers can solve this problem by using a text for modeling that is unfamiliar to them. One solution that I have used in training teachers to become aware of their own comprehension processes is to give them a text that is difficult for them and ask them to think aloud about the strategies they use to understand the text (Maria 1988).

A second problem with modeling arises from the fact that teachers who are expert readers may find it difficult to see the same problems in understanding a text that children who are novices at reading may experience. *The Little Green Man* text was rather unusual in that it posed a problem for me as well as for the children. As the text-based model of comprehension instruction suggests, teachers should read carefully the texts they plan to use with children, searching for possible problems. They need to put themselves in the children's places, trying to think as they do. Knowing about children's cognitive and language development is helpful in this regard; but for the most part, this kind of awareness comes from experience with children, with the texts used, and with practice at looking for the problems.

A third problem with the modeling process is that teachers may get so involved in metacomprehension—in getting children to explain their processes—that they forget the goal of instruction is comprehension, not metacomprehension (Cooper 1986). It is more important for the child to understand than to explain how he or she is understanding. Some children can comprehend effectively without being able to explain how they do so, just as others can use phonics but cannot explain phonics explicitly.

A fourth possible problem occurs when a teacher thinks that his or her way of reading a text or solving a comprehension problem is the only way and communicates this point of view to the children. For children who do not use any reading strategies, teacher modeling offers a solution. For readers who already have effective strategies, however, teacher modeling may present a problem. One way to avoid this danger is to explain that often there are alternative strategies and ask children to verbalize different ones they use.

Teacher modeling can be one of the most effective ways of making comprehension instruction clear and explicit for children, as long as possible problems are kept in mind.

DISCUSSION
Guideline 20: Use the tools of questioning, explanation, and modeling in the context of interactive discussion that includes student-to-student, teacher-to-student, and student-to-teacher dialogues.
Although teachers often indicate that they use discussion as a teaching tool, most classroom discussion is better characterized as recitation in which teachers ask questions that students answer (Gall 1984; Stodolsky, Ferguson, and Wimpelberg 1981). Alvermann, Dillon, and O'Brien (1987) have suggested three criteria for distinguishing discussion from recitation:
1. The discussion should include multiple points of view. Discussants should be ready to change their minds after hearing convincing counter arguments.
2. The students must interact with one another as well as with the teacher.
3. A majority of the verbal interactions, especially those resulting from questions that solicit student opinion, must be longer than the typical two or three word phrases found in recitations (p. 3).

Discussion defined in this way is especially important in comprehension instruction for several reasons. First, since comprehension instruction is an active, constructive process, interpretations of text will differ. Some interpretations will take better account of text cues and/or will be based on more appropriate prior knowledge. It is important for children to hear others' interpretations of the same text, so that they can defend or change their own if they feel another makes better sense. Of course, there will not always be disagreement. At times, one interpretation will be obvious; but discussion in which multiple points of view are possible is important in comprehension instruction.

The mediated model of comprehension instruction is based on the idea that children learn by engaging in dialogue with others. So far we have focused on the value of dialogue between teacher and child with the teacher providing the scaffolding or support the child needs until he or she is ready to complete the task independently. Cazden (1986) notes that the theories of Piaget and Vygotsky both suggest that dialogue between peers may have special motivational and cognitive benefits. Piaget (1950) suggests that social interaction is an essential antidote to egocentrism. In confronting alternative viewpoints the child realizes the limitations of his or her own viewpoint.

Vygotsky (1978) theorizes that inner reflection in children's higher-level thought grows out of experiences with argumentation in social dialogue. Peer dialogue is more valuable for the development of reflection because in peer dialogue children can give and follow directions as well as ask and answer questions.

Encouraging children to say more than a few words in answer to a teacher's question is necessary when instruction focuses on the nature of the child's thinking. When children engage in this kind of discussion before reading, more prior knowledge is available for the group to use in understanding the text.

Palincsar and Brown (1989) suggest that teachers do not use discussion as a teaching tool because it is hard to manage. Maintaining activity flow and holding the attention of the students while engaging in a meaningful dialogue where learning takes place is not easy. Vacca and Vacca (1986) have proposed several guidelines for organizing successful classroom discussions that are also supported by Alvermann, Dillon, and O'Brien (1987) and Johnson et al. (1984).

1. Arrange the room so children can engage in face-to-face interactions and move easily from whole-class to small-group organization. Circular arrangements appear to be best.
2. Encourage a climate in which everyone, including the teacher, is expected to be a good listener. (see Guideline 6)
3. Provide clear directions about the topic of the discussion, the goal of the discussion, and the process of discussion. Palincsar and Brown (1989) state that reciprocal teaching is a successful instructional strategy because it provides the clear structure necessary for successful discussion. Using a cooperative learning approach is another way of providing a clear and organized structure for discussion.
4. Keep the discussion focused on the central topic. Discussion should center on very few teacher statements or questions. Follow-up questions used as probes and prompts are helpful, but teachers must be careful not to turn the discussion into a recitation. Alvermann, Dillon, and O'Brien (1987) point out that it is important to distinguish between discussion and recitation for the students. Time pressure may make recitation a more appropriate instructional strategy in some situations.
5. Allot sufficient time for discussion so that students can explore the topic in some depth.
6. Encourage student-to-student interaction and do not permit behavior that squelches discussion. Prompt students to respond to other students' statements; do not interrupt students and do not let other students interrupt, unless absolutely necessary. Avoid answering your own questions.

Subsequent chapters will present specific techniques that make use of all the instructional tools discussed in this section. More specific guidelines for using the tools with these techniques will be presented there.

TEACHER PLANNING: THE TEACHER AS A PROFESSIONAL
Guideline 21: Integrate knowledge about the reading process, about the children you are teaching, and about the nature of the texts you are using in the long-term and short-term planning for comprehension instruction.

The teacher is a professional who brings together information from many sources in making decisions about instruction. Teacher planning has always been recognized as an important component of instruction. Research on teacher planning documents that teaching can be as complex and cognitively demanding as practicing law or medicine (Clark 1988). Experienced, effective teachers report that they do extensive mental planning that is not reflected in the written plans they submit to administrators. These teachers engage in both long- and short-term planning. Researchers working with teachers have found that leading teachers to reflect on their planning enables them "to see and appreciate what is genuinely professional about their work; to kindle or revive the idealism, freshness, and commitment to self-improvement that we often see in the best first-year teachers, but with the difference that accumulated practical wisdom brings" (Clark 1988, p. 9).

In my own work with teachers I have found that reflecting on the planning process helps them make their implicit beliefs about the nature of the reading process more explicit. Planning also helps teachers reflect on how children learn that process, on the nature of reading disability, and on what materials and approaches are appropriate for comprehension instruction. This mental planning helps them decide if their planning and instruction are congruent with their beliefs.

The intent in these first four chapters is to help teachers ponder their implicit beliefs. Many of the ideas presented here may be challenging to teachers' beliefs and their acceptance may require changing those beliefs.

Just as a change in beliefs will not occur overnight, neither can one expect to change one's way of teaching immediately. Duffy (1982) suggests that outside constraints may prevent a teacher's comprehension instruction from reflecting his or her beliefs. Teachers will have to move slowly, preparing children, parents, administrators, and other teachers for the change. Teachers need to collaborate, meet together to share ideas, and support each other's efforts to take professional responsibility for decisions involving the goals of comprehension instruction, and the methods and materials used in achieving those goals.

TECHNIQUES AND STRATEGIES IN READING COMPREHENSION INSTRUCTION

CHAPTER

5

PRE-READING TECHNIQUES— ACTIVATING PRIOR KNOWLEDGE

The first section of this chapter discusses schema theory which calls our attention to the importance of background knowledge in comprehension instruction. The second section describes specific instructional techniques that have been developed in large part because of schema theory. The teacher can use these techniques as pre-reading activities to help children use their background knowledge in comprehending text.

SCHEMA THEORY

In discussing the factor of background knowledge in Chapter 2, schema theory was mentioned briefly. Recall that schema theory is not a theory of reading, but a theory of knowledge; a theory that tries to explain how we store our knowledge, how we learn and how we remember what we have learned. This theory developed by Rumelhart (1980) and others based on the work of Bartlett (1932) suggests that all knowledge is contained in units, called schemata. There are schemata for concepts like pencil or liberty but there are also schemata for situations, events, actions, and sequences of actions. In addition to the knowledge itself, information about how this knowledge is to be used is embedded in each schema.

Schemata are arranged in hierarchical networks. A schema for going to McDonald's and a schema for going to a Michelin four-star gourmet restaurant might be subschemata for the schema of going to a restaurant. Rumelhart (1980) has compared a schema to a play that contains roles that may change depending upon the particular situation. For example, buying a house and buying a pair of shoes are both examples of a *buy* schema in which the buyer, seller, object bought, and money exchanged are part of both situations. Yet the two situations differ: the roles or slots are variable. A couple may buy a house whereas only one person buys a pair of shoes, which cost less than a house. The schema summarizes what is known about a variety of cases that differ in many particulars.

Anderson (1984) points out that there are two forms of schema theory—the strong and the weak. The strong form of schema theory suggests that "people operate on the basis of general principles extracted from experience" (p. 7). It proposes that in ordinary real-life situations people operate like scientists. Their schemata are like scientific theories and from these abstract theories, they deduce what is happening in a particular situation, "Abstract schemata program individuals to generate concrete scenarios" (Anderson 1977, p. 423). We go to a restaurant and we predict a hostess, a waiter or waitress, a menu, and leaving a tip because we have a theory of going to a restaurant. Although the quotation above indicates that Anderson himself was a proponent of this strong form of schema theory, results of several research studies (e.g., Halff, Ortony, and Anderson 1976) led him to propose a weak form of schema theory. The strong form of the theory does not seem to account for the amount of concrete detail people have in their mental representations when they comprehend something, detail not really necessary to the situation. The strong form also does not take into account that real-life situations are not clearcut like scientific experiments. Real-life situations are messy; they do not conform to a theory of what they should be. For example, the phrase *buying a house* causes me to generate a scenario of a young couple buying a house in the suburbs. According to the weak form of schema theory, I did not deduce that buying a house *must* involve a young couple and a house in the suburbs. I certainly realize that it could be a single man or woman buying a townhouse in the city. The weak form of the theory suggests that people get cues to a schema that causes them to call back specific situations from memory. They use these memories as precedents for tentative predictions. Thus, as Anderson (1984) points out, much of what passes for general knowledge is really based on specific instances.

Whether one subscribes to the strong form or the weak, it is clear that schemata are developed by experience and related to a person's culture. The restaurant schema of a person who has only been to McDonald's will not contain slots for a hostess, a waiter or waitress, or a tip. In a research study (Reynolds et al. 1982) that presented a text about sounding—ritual insults which are part of certain black cultures—to both black and white students the white children interpreted the situation as a fight; the black children as an instance of sounding. When told that the white children thought it was a fight, the black children responded, "What's the matter? Can't they read?"

Because it is a theory of knowledge, schema theory is also a theory of memory. Our background knowledge is stored in our long term memory. This memory consists of memories that are individual to us (episodic memory), and knowledge about concepts and relations between concepts, i.e., knowledge that is shared by others (semantic memory). Knowledge in our long term memory is organized systematically in terms of meaning, with hierarchical networks of schemata. These schemata help us retrieve information and help us reconstruct information that was not learned or was learned and forgotten. Research has shown that memory is a reconstructive process (e.g., Bartlett 1932).

Like Piaget's theory of learning, schema theory involves the processes of assimilation in which new facts are added to a schema and of accommodation in which the schema is changed to fit new facts. Rumelhart and Norman (1978) suggest that there are really three processes: accretion, which is similar to Piagetian assimilation; and two other processes which relate to Piagetian accommodation: fine tuning in which one aspect of a schema is refined or changed and reconstruction which involves a major change in the schema. Fine tuning might involve an adjustment in our schema for cat to include a cat with no tail while reconstruction would involve a change like replacing our primitive intuitive understanding of how objects move with a Newtonian theory of motion.

When schema theory is applied to reading, the result is the interactive theory of the reading process—the recognition that reading, like all learning, is a holistic constructive process that involves making inferences. We use our schemata to make inferences in order to understand text because no author ever includes everything he wants us to understand about the text. Consider the text below:

"May I take your order, sir?" inquired the waiter.

"Yes, I believe so," I said.

"No!" Hilda hissed through clenched teeth. "I won't eat a thing. We're through! Do you hear me?"

"Sir!" said the waiter, drumming his pencil on the pad.

"I know," I interrupted hastily. "Hilda, this is not the place for a scene. We'll talk about it later," I urged in a strained whisper (Gillet and Temple 1982, p. 206).

It is likely that this text activated several schemata—one for an expensive restaurant and one for a fight, but a particular kind of fight that also involves a courtship. The author of this text has given us several cues that activate these schemata: the presence of a waiter who is taking the order plus the fact that "this is not the place for a scene" suggest the expensive restaurant. The fact that Hilda is speaking with clenched teeth using the phrases "We're through!" and "Do you hear me?" suggest the fight and the courtship.

A problem arises when the reader and the author do not have the same schema for a situation. There are several situations in which this might happen (Rumelhart 1984; Pearson and Spiro 1980). First, the reader might not have the appropriate schema. For example, a child reading the narrative text above might not have a courtship schema. In Chapter 2 it is pointed out that low SES children and children from minority cultures often lack certain schemata that are part of middle class American children's culture. However, the variation in children's prior knowledge and the precise knowledge sometimes required to understand a particular text suggest that this problem may occur often with many middle class children.

A lack of appropriate background knowledge is particularly likely when reading expository texts. Rupley (1988) suggests that when dealing with narratives it is only necessary for most children to activate schema. With expository texts, on the other hand, children must *build* schema as they are reading. Interpretations that differ from the author's intention are acceptable in literature, but can cause problems if the text is an informational one and the reader learns something that is, in fact, incorrect.

Saying that a reader does not have the appropriate schema should not imply that the reader does not have any knowledge related to the topic of the text. Langer (1982) reminds us that everybody knows something about almost everything. Anderson (1984) suggests that instead of characterizing a reader as lacking or not lacking a particular schema, we should characterize that reader as having a well- or less well-articulated schema.

The second situation in which a reader may not have the necessary schemata involves incorrect prior knowledge. Learning new information which contradicts information already a part of the reader's schema necessitates fine tuning or restructuring.

In the third situation the reader may have the appropriate schema, but the author has not provided enough cues to activate it. In other words, the text is an inconsiderate text. The clothes washing passage presented in Chapter 2 is an example of this.

In the fourth situation the reader might have the schema and enough cues from the author, but the reader does not attend to those cues or realize their significance. One reason some remedial readers may not attend to cues is that they are not reading for meaning; they are bottom-up readers who view reading as a decoding process and do not seek a consistent interpretation of a text. Pieces of the text are processed separately, and the child does not seek to relate the pieces. Other remedial readers form interpretations early in the text and then hold to those interpretations, ignoring later cues that would lead to one intended by the author (Kimmel and MacGinitie 1984).

Finally, the reader may find a consistent interpretation of the text that is not the one intended by the author. This situation was referred to in Chapter 1: readers in later centuries give interpretations to Shakespeare's plays that he probably never intended. Anderson (1977) quotes Doris Lessing as saying that she receives letters from readers who interpret her book *The Golden Notebook* in three distinctly different ways—all completely different from her intended meaning.

In all these situations the teacher needs to act as a bridge between reader and text in both pre-reading and reading instruction. The teacher can guide children to read for meaning, providing support for building or activating the schema appropriate for a particular text, and helping children develop strategies they can use independently to connect prior knowledge to text information for better comprehension and learning.

PRE-READING INSTRUCTION

The goal of pre-reading instruction should be to build or activate a schema appropriate to a central concept in the text. Thus, the instruction draws on the background knowledge the children possess, but only after a consideration of the ideas in the text. This sequence is important. Considering children's background knowledge should come after consideration of ideas in the text. The teacher needs to be sure that he or she is focusing on a concept that is important to the understanding of the story. In the graduate course on comprehension instruction I teach, I ask my students, most of whom are teachers of low SES children, to select two central concepts for the story *The Raccoon and Mrs. McGinnis* (Clymer 1976). I use this story because it is one of the stories used in the Beck, Omanson, and McKeown (1981) study. In this story Mrs. McGinnis wishes on a star for money to build a barn on her farm. The raccoon, who comes to her doorstep every night for the food she leaves him, frightens some bandits who drop a bag of money they have stolen. The raccoon picks up the money and drops it on Mrs. McGinnis's doorstep. Mrs. McGinnis thinks she got the money because she wished on a star. Using a story map, Beck et al. determined that the major concepts necessary to understand the story were *coincidence* because Mrs. McGinnis gets her wish through a series of coincidences, and *habit* because the raccoon's instinctive habitual behavior allows the coincidences to occur.

Yet my students, when asked to determine two central concepts that should be the focus of pre-reading instruction invariably suggest providing instruction related to farms because Mrs. McGinnis lives on one and the children they teach know nothing about farms. Learning about farms may be a legitimate teaching goal, but it is not a prerequisite for getting the point of this story (Maria 1989).

CHOOSING A CENTRAL CONCEPT

All texts contain many ideas, but only certain ideas are central. Pre-reading development of background knowledge related to central concepts improves comprehension of both narrative (Beck, Omanson, and McKeown 1981; Hansen and Hubbard 1984) and expository text (Johnson, Toms-Bronowski, and Pittelman 1984; Langer 1984). In order to determine the central ideas of both narrative and expository texts the teacher must read the text carefully; summaries and main points given in teacher's editions will not give the teacher the understanding of the text needed to effectively guide the children's comprehension. Choosing an appropriate central concept is not always a clearcut process with narrative text. Developing a story map—a graphic outline of the story including the setting, the characters, the action, the problem, and the resolution of the problem—helps in determining one or two concepts crucial for understanding the story (Cooper 1986). (The use of story maps by both teachers and children is discussed in Chapter 7). Only after the teacher chooses one or two central concepts from the story should the focus shift from the text to consideration of whether or not the children have appropriate knowledge about the central concepts.

In helping teachers select an appropriate central concept for a story I have found that they often have problems in deciding how specific the concept should be. The concept should be specific to a particular story, but it should also be general enough so that it can relate to the children's experiences. For example, in the story *Frog and Toad are Friends* (Lobel 1970), Frog convinces Toad to wake up and enjoy the spring. One group of teachers chose *relationships* as the central concept. This term is so general as to be inappropriate for activating prior knowledge related to this text. *Friendship* or *helping a friend*, concepts chosen by other groups, seem much more fitting. Considering a central concept to be *friendship between a frog and a toad* would be too specific.

Not all stories need pre-reading activities; some stories are just to be enjoyed. However, since remedial readers may have particular problems in reading for meaning, pre-reading instruction that connects prior knowledge with text information is important for them, even if the story does not seem to present any particular problem to us. (However, do not forget the point made in Chapter 3: Remedial readers need time to read for enjoyment also.)

All stories center on characters solving problems, and many of the best stories center on problems that are universal. In previewing stories like this teachers should be alert to situations in which children may miss the point unless the appropriate background knowledge is activated. Beck, Omanson, and McKeown (1981) found that children who did not receive pre-reading instruction missed the point that Mrs. McGinnis got money for her farm because of a coincidence rather than her wish. Teachers should also be alert to situations in which children's cultural background may not provide them with the background knowledge appropriate for a particular story. In this case pre-reading discussion can help these children build the necessary knowledge.

Choosing an appropriate central concept for an expository text involves a somewhat different process. If a teacher uses an entire expository text in a reading lesson, the first step—determining the central concept of the text—is usually easier than with narratives since the topic is easier to determine. It may, in fact, be given in the title. However, selection of central concepts in content area texts should be a first step in both long range and short range planning for comprehension instruction. Teachers usually use a portion of the text in a lesson with content area texts. The teacher should determine the topic of a portion of the text as well as the topic of the entire unit or chapter. If the topic of a unit is the Middle Ages, you may want to plan a pre-reading lesson on this topic before beginning the unit. Later these lessons may include portions of the unit dealing with topics like knights or guilds. The curriculum goals for a particular content area will also affect the topics that a teacher chooses as the focus of instruction.

The second step, i.e., considering the level of prior knowledge that the children may have concerning the central concept of the text, is different with content area text. Children read expository text in order to learn from it. If they already know everything about the topic, there is no point in reading the text. Reading expository text involves building a schema. This does not mean that the children have no knowledge related to the topic. It is likely that at least a few of the children will have some information directly related to the central concept chosen. We know that we can expect variation in prior knowledge in any group of children. If any of the children know something about the topic, activities like brainstorming, in which children come up with all the ideas associated with a particular topic, enable the teacher to use the children's knowledge to build knowledge for others in the group. If the teacher decides it is unlikely that any of the children would have enough useful information related to the central concept, then he or she tries to find some knowledge the children have that can serve as an starting point for building a schema for this concept. Anastasiow, Hanes, and Hanes (1982) describe a situation in which the teacher's choice of *flea market* for a pre-reading discussion helped students understand a text about Middle Eastern bazaars, a topic with which none was familiar.

The better a teacher knows his or her students through careful observation and discussion, the better able he or she is to judge their background knowledge, and the less likely he or she will be to overestimate *or* underestimate their knowledge. Since the variation in children's knowledge makes teacher judgment difficult, it is a good idea to select a fall-back concept related to the central concept of the text should the original concept prove inappropriate as the focus for the discussion. The fall-back concept should be more general than the central concept of the text. Using this fall-back concept, the teacher can build an "advance organizer" with the children through carefully guided discussion. An advance organizer is usually a written set of materials discussing a general topic related to the text. It is read before the text. Jerrolds (1985) provides an example of an advance organizer which discusses motion and life as preparation for a text on life at sea. According to Ausubel (1968), who developed the idea of using advance organizers, they foster a connection of new information to concepts already a part of the reader's cognitive structure. They "bridge the gap between what the learner already knows and what the learner needs to know before he or she can successfully learn the task at hand" (p. 148). Research results are mixed, but there is substantial evidence that advance organizers do help comprehension and learning (Jerrolds 1985).

Textbooks usually do not contain written advance organizers. They are difficult to write because they are supposed to take into account the level of familiarity the reader has with the material to be learned. Since variation in prior knowledge is common, it would be necessary to write different advance organizers for different children. A discussion which allows the teacher to personalize instruction (Cazden 1988), scaffolding it differently for individual children in the group, seems to be a better way of providing an advance organizer. With remedial readers in particular, it seems that an advance organizer constructed through discussion is more motivating than reading an abstract text prior to a more specific one.

I was able to use a fall-back concept in a pre-reading discussion that helped a group of fifth grade remedial readers understand a text about the Texas War of Independence (Fradin 1981). I originally chose the concept *Alamo* as a focus for pre-reading discussion for several reasons:

1. I believed that none of these children would have information directly related to the Texas War of Independence; they were all from an Eastern city and probably did not know much about Texas, let alone the Texas War of Independence.

2. A recent television show had centered on resistance at the Alamo. I hoped that some of the children who saw the program would be able to give the group information that would help in understanding the text.

When I asked the children to tell me what came to mind when I said the word *Alamo*, the only response I got was "A place where they keep old things." It was clear that *Alamo* was not an appropriate concept. I then turned to my fall-back concept, *war*. The children had a great deal of knowledge related to this concept and they were able to use their knowledge of the more general topic to understand a particular war. In discussing war one student volunteered the information that people fight wars for freedom. Later, in reading the text, we were able to connect the Texas War of Independence to this general reason for having a war.

Selecting possible fall-back concepts should be part of planning pre-reading instruction. Yet, no matter how carefully we plan, we cannot always anticipate the condition of children's background knowledge. We may over-estimate the children's prior knowledge and need to change our plans on the spot, moving even further back than anticipated to help children develop concepts we assumed they knew.

Because remedial readers have so many problems in reading, we often underestimate their background knowledge. This was brought home to me in a demonstration lesson with a group of seven low SES minority sixth graders participating in a Chapter I program. The text had been chosen because it was related to the sixth grade social studies curriculum. The lesson was designed to provide a demonstration of the semantic mapping technique (discussed later in this chapter, p. 98).

The first step in this technique is to brainstorm about a concept central to the text. In this case the central concept of the text was *knights* (Riese and LaSalle 1986), a concept that seemed to me and to the children's teachers very far removed from the children's experiences. Based on this judgment, it appeared that the fall-back concept, *soldiers*, would be a better focus for the brainstorming. I decided to be an optimist and try *knights* first. The children knew a great deal about knights; each child contributed a piece of information. Individually their knowledge was rather sparse; together it was extensive. They knew that knights were warriors, were skilled in battle, wore armor, fought with lances and swords, and had entertainments in which they fought with each other. (I found out later that their information came from a popular television cartoon with which I was totally unfamiliar.) Thus, while each child did not have the appropriate background knowledge for the text, the group did, and through semantic mapping and group discussion, appropriate background knowledge was developed for each child in the group. When the children read the text using this knowledge base and the ideas in the text, they learned more about knights and their position and value in medieval society (Maria 1989).

CHOOSING AN INSTRUCTIONAL TECHNIQUE

The teacher's third step is to choose a particular teaching technique or strategy. Traditional pre-reading instructional techniques make use of traditional tools of questioning and explanation while the newer techniques use more modeling and discussion. It seems legitimate for teachers to ask "Which strategies are most effective?" Tierney and Cunningham (1984), in a review of the research on reading comprehension instruction, concluded that there is no definitive evidence that one approach for developing background knowledge is better than another. This chapter will present a variety of pre-reading techniques so that teachers may have a repertoire from which to choose. While teachers will probably be more comfortable using some strategies than others, using the same strategies all the time may be boring for both teacher and children.

Teachers should consider the nature of the text and the ideas in the text before choosing a particular instructional technique. Some techniques are more suitable for expository texts while others are more suitable for narratives. (The type of text suited to each technique will be discussed later in this chapter.) Teachers should also consider the children's background knowledge in choosing a particular pre-reading strategy. In situations where the children's background knowledge is more removed from the text topic it may be necessary for the teacher to provide more information and guidance. In the demonstration lesson described earlier I had a picture of knights ready to show the children because I thought they would not have any information related to knights. Cooper (1986) points out that pictures can be quite helpful in building background knowledge appropriate for a particular text. Teachers need to be sure, however, that the students understand how the pictures relate to the topic. Cooper also points out that due to size and artistic considerations, sometimes pictures can be misleading, so like all pre-reading techniques, they should be chosen carefully.

Teachers are often urged (e.g., Cooper 1986) to provide necessary pre-reading knowledge through direct experiences with objects and through field trips. Certainly direct experiential learning can often be the best way of teaching a concept. For young children it is particularly important. One of my graduate students made soup with a group of kindergarten children before she read them the story *Stone Soup*. After reading this story herself, she felt that the children would not be able to understand the story unless they realized that soup tasted good and was a good food because it was a mixture of many different ingredients. She felt that most of her children would not have this understanding of soup because the soup they ate probably came from cans. She provided them with the direct experience of making soup and found that they could make use of this experience in understanding the story.

Experiential learning is also motivating for children. My daughter, a first-year teacher, read a story about fishing for salmon with a third grade low reading group. She brought a tiny piece of smoked salmon for the children to taste since none of them had ever tasted salmon. In her words, "The children are obsessed by salmon." For days, they brought in pictures and articles about salmon. They looked up salmon in the encyclopedia; they loved reading and writing about salmon.

However, even a good thing like experiential learning can be carried too far. Reading time cannot be spent entirely in activities like making soup. Our job is to help children become literate. We should certainly use experiential learning to accomplish that goal, but we should remember that experiential learning is a means toward that goal. As children mature and become more literate, they will no longer have to rely solely on direct experience for learning. As Pearson and Johnson (1978) have pointed out, "the realities of classroom instruction make it impossible to rely on direct experience as the major vehicle for concept development" (p. 34). Time constraints and management considerations do not allow us to make constant use of direct experience as a pre-reading activity. One less direct but effective way of supplying necessary prior knowledge in a content area like social studies is to read stories to the children about related topics. Television can also be used to build a common pool of prior knowledge, helping teachers cope with the wide variation of knowledge found in their classes.

When there is a gap between children's background knowledge and ideas in the text, there is a temptation to fill it by supplying the information through teacher explanation. At times, a short teacher explanation can be the most effective and efficient way of bridging a gap. For example, in working with the story *The Raccoon and Mrs. McGinnis*, Beck, Omanson, and McKeown (1981) explained to the children that raccoons have black fur around their eyes that looks like a mask so that the children would understand why the bandits were frightened. Teacher explanation that makes use of an analogy between the fall-back concept and the topic of the text can be a helpful component of many of the pre-reading techniques presented in this chapter.

Since comprehension is an active constructive process, it cannot be taught if readers are allowed to be passive. Presenting background knowledge to children who lack it may seem to be more efficient, but, pre-reading techniques should involve interactive group discussion that connects children's knowledge to central ideas of the text. The children must be actively involved in making that connection for effective learning to occur.

PRE-READING INSTRUCTIONAL TECHNIQUES

The techniques presented here have all been proven effective in controlled research studies. In addition, I have used them and have found them to be effective with remedial readers. Scripts, which are excerpts of lessons taught by me or by teachers with whom I worked, are provided with each technique as a means of illustrating the points made in the discussion. Although some of the lessons are better than others, they are all actual lessons so none of them is perfect. Some scripts provide examples of effective techniques; some scripts provide practices to be avoided; and some provide both. Since these lessons were all based on a mediated model of comprehension instruction, the teacher scaffolds the task for the children as they try to understand a text and learn strategies that will eventually help them understand other texts they read independently. Because the children in the lessons are all low SES remedial readers and because they have no previous experience with the techniques, all the scripts illustrate problems in getting the children to participate in the discussion. The teacher provides a great deal of support in the sample lessons, modifying the techniques at times in order to provide extra support. Quite a few lessons using the technique would be necessary before more responsibility could be given to the children, but the goal of making them independent learners should not be forgotten.

PREP

PREP—the Pre-reading Plan—is a diagnostic and instructional pre-reading technique developed by Langer (1982). Its purpose is to structure pre-reading discussion. The discussion is diagnostic in that it allows teachers to assess the levels of the students' prior knowledge. It is instructional in that it allows children access to their prior knowledge and helps them build new knowledge as a result of hearing the ideas of others during group discussion. The technique was originally designed for use with expository text, but can also be used successfully with narratives.

A script of a lesson carried out with a group of fifth graders as preparation for reading the trade book *Ferdinand* (Leaf 1936) is provided as an illustration of this technique. In planning the pre-reading lesson for the book the teacher and I picked *bullfighting* as the central concept for the focus. In this book Ferdinand, a bull who is gentle and loves to smell the flowers, is picked to fight in the bullfight in Madrid. When the men come to pick fierce bulls, Ferdinand acts wild because he was stung by a bee. In the bull ring Ferdinand will not fight so he is sent back home to his pasture to smell the flowers. We picked the concept of *bullfighting* because we felt that some knowledge of bullfighting was necessary in order to understand the story, although the story does provide a lot of details about bullfighting. We thought some of the children might have some knowledge about the concept, but many of the children would not. Since the sample script describes a lesson in which a teacher tries the technique for the first time, there are some errors in the use of the technique. However, the teacher and I were pleased with the lesson. The children were able to use the knowledge discussed in the PREP lesson as an aid to understanding the text.

The PREP technique consists of three steps:

1. Initial association with the concept—The teacher asks the children to brainstorm about the concept by asking "What do you think of when I say . . .?"

2. Reflections on initial associations—After all the children are finished giving their responses, the teacher asks each of them "What made you think of . . .?"

3. Reformulation of knowledge—After all the children have responded in step 2, the teacher asks "Based on our discussion, do you have any new ideas about . . .?"

There are several guidelines that should be followed in initiating and guiding the discussion in Step 1.

1. Ask children more specific questions and model possible responses as prompts for children who do not respond to the general questions.

2. In planning the pre-reading lesson note aspects of the topic that are important to understanding the text. Plan questions about those aspects if children do not mention them in brainstorming.

3. Keep discussion focused on the topic.

PREP Script
(T = Teacher, S = Student)

T: *What do you think of when I say bullfighting? What do I mean by bullfighting?*

(There is a period of silence.)

S1: *Bulls have a fight.*

T: *Where do they have this fight?*

S1: *In a rodeo.*

T: *Well, it's not really in a rodeo. I don't think bulls fight in a rodeo. Cowboys ride bulls. What is a bull like?*

S2: *Mean*

S3: *Sharp horns—he sticks people.*

S4: *He kills.*

T: *Does anybody know what country has bullfighting?*

S5: *Texas*

T: *Texas is not a country. It's a. . . .?*

S6: *State.*

T: *Good. Does anyone know a country?*

S2: *Spain.*

T: *Very good. Here's a really hard question. Does anyone know the capital city of Spain? (Pause) It's Madrid.*

(The teacher takes down the globe and the children find Spain and Madrid on the globe.)

T: *What made you think of mean?*

S2: *Sometimes when a bull sees red, he gets very mean.*

T: *You know a lot about bullfighting. Who said horns? What made you think of that?*

S3: *The horns are sharp. They look like they could stick you. They sharpen their horns to make them sharper.*

T: Good. You know a lot too. (To S4) What made you think of kill?
S4: Sometimes when they use their horns, they stick them in the chest and then they die.
T: Who are they going to kill?
S4: The man with the red cape who fights them.
(The teacher then began to introduce vocabulary that had been selected as possible sources of difficulty in reading the text.)

Note that in the script, the teacher's question is initially greeted with silence. The child who responds rephrases the concept saying that bullfighting means "bulls having a fight." This response suggests a possible misconception that bullfighting is a group of bulls fighting each other. The teacher tries to get the discussion started by using questions asking where bullfights take place, again answered incorrectly. So she asks another question that does get the discussion started: "What is a bull like?" This is a better question for her to ask than her first one because understanding that bulls need to be fierce in a bullfight is crucial in getting the point of the story. In planning the lesson, the teacher and I had decided that this was one point that we wanted to be sure was included in the discussion. Cooper (1986) points out that often pre-reading discussion questions suggested in basal reader manuals are too vague and do not guide the discussion towards the points covered by the text. Teachers need to keep the ideas of the text in mind in planning the questions they will use in prompting and supporting the pre-reading discussion (Nessel 1988). In this case it would also probably help for the children to know that bullfighting is a sport in which a man fights a bull so additional teacher questions might focus on these two points.

Responses of students 3 and 4 suggest that they have some knowledge of bullfighting. However, instead of following up on these responses or asking for related responses from other students, the teacher gets somewhat sidetracked. Instead of keeping the discussion focused, she attempts to find out whether the children are familiar with vocabulary she thought would be unfamiliar, namely, *Spain* and *Madrid*. During this first step, she should have tried for responses from all the students and perhaps asked further questions, e.g., "Why do bulls stick people?" She could also have used modeling by participating in the discussion and telling what bullfighting brings to her mind. However she has to be very careful not to take over the discussion.

Langer (1982) suggests that the second step of the technique, asking children questions about the sources of their ideas, heightens students' awareness of their associations and encourages them to listen to one another. My experience in using PREP with many different groups of children has led me to believe that this second step is the greatest strength of the technique. As the script demonstrates, asking the children to identify the sources of their associations calls forth much more discussion and provides richer and more varied knowledge associated with the central concept. In this step in the script, the children add several ideas, i.e., bulls get mean when they see red; people prepare the bulls for the bullfight; the man with the red cape who fights the bull may get killed. Ideas put forth by one child seem to spark awareness in other children as Student 2 mentions that a bull gets mad when he sees red and subsequently Student 5 mentions the man with the red cape who fights the bull. In this second step, student "experts" on the topic can often be identified. As peers, they can communicate their knowledge to the other children even more effectively than the teacher.

A number of teachers have expressed concern over whether children would be able to remember in the second step the idea or ideas they provided in the first step. Several teachers have tried putting children's initials next to their ideas in the first step. However, I have always found that children remembered their own ideas even if the teacher forgot who said what. Moreover, putting down initials seems to cause the children to focus on who gave the idea rather than on the idea itself.

The teacher's comments in the script suggest her surprise at the knowledge the children possess. This surprise reaction is quite common when teachers begin to use this technique. In this particular case, probably because of her surprise, the teacher neglects to move to the third step and ask children what new information they have learned. At times I have forgotten the third step myself, but it is important because it makes the children aware that they can learn from one another. It also makes them aware of how much knowledge they already possess about the topic of the text. My own experience and that of other teachers is that often children resist this third step. They do not want to admit that they did not know it all to begin with. Teacher modeling of an appropriate answer to the question in terms of something he or she has learned is an effective method of overcoming this resistance. It is at this stage that the teacher should move to reading the text. During-reading questions and discussion should relate to the ideas mentioned in the pre-reading discussion. The teacher should make sure the students realize that their background knowledge helped them understand the story. He or she should also encourage the children to consider the knowledge they have about a topic when they are reading independently.

SEMANTIC MAPPING

This term, which was originally applied to a technique developed by Pearson and Johnson (1978), has come to be used for any technique that provides a visual display of the relationships between a central concept and a number of other ideas that are related to it.

Semantic mapping is suggested as an effective technique for activating and building background knowledge before reading (McNeil 1984; Cooper 1986); and writing (Noyce and Christie 1989); for vocabulary instruction (Hanf 1971; Stahl and Vancil 1986); and as an effective post-reading activity (Johnson, Toms-Bronowski, and Pittleman 1981). It can also help learning disabled children construct a summary of a text they have read (Weisberg and Balathy 1985) and serve as a means of assessing comprehension of a text (Marshall 1987). Although it is particularly effective with content area texts that present a number of concepts related to a central topic, it is also effective with simpler expository texts and narratives. As a pre-reading activity designed to activate and build prior knowledge, it is similar to the PREP method in several ways. The first step in semantic mapping is exactly the same as the first step in PREP. After selecting an appropriate central concept, the teacher asks the children to brainstorm about the central concept and writes their ideas on the board.

In the Pearson and Johnson method of semantic mapping as described by Cooper (1986), the central concept is placed in an oval. A student's idea is written in a box if it describes the central concept in some way. It is written in an oval if it is an example of the central concept or if it is the superordinate classification of the central concept, for example, reptile is the superordinate term for turtle. The box or oval is connected to the central concept in the oval by means of an arrow. The relationship between the idea in the box and the central concept is written above the arrow. The first semantic map of *turtles* (figure 1) follows this format.

In the format I use, which is based on the List-Group-Label lesson originally developed by Taba (1967) and described by McNeil (1987), the first step consists of writing ideas on the board or on a piece of paper until the children run out of ideas even when supported by teacher probing. At first, I attempted to place ideas in the same category together as I wrote them down. However, I found it was too difficult to try to probe for ideas, write them down, and categorize them at the same time so now I write the ideas down in no particular order. In the second step, through interactive discussion, the children and the teacher construct a visual display demonstrating how ideas relate to the central concept and to each other. Ideas that relate to one another are placed in categories and then labeled. Lines connect the categories to the central concept. A script excerpt from the demonstration lesson I conducted with a group of seven sixth-grade remedial readers and the semantic map constructed during that lesson follow.

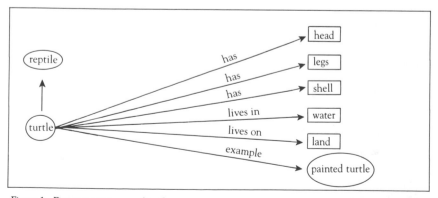

Figure 1. First semantic map of *turtles*.

Semantic Mapping Script

(After explaining that semantic mapping will help the children understand the article about turtles [Morningforest 1978] that they are about to read, I began the technique.)

T (writing the word turtle *in the center of the blackboard): What do you think of when I say the word* turtle?

(A long silence)

Do you remember anything from the story that your teacher read you about turtles? (Their teacher, who was afraid they would not have any knowledge about turtles, had read them a story the previous day.)

(Again, a long silence)

T: Where do turtles live?

S1: Some turtles go in the water.

S2: Sometimes they live on land.

T: Good. What else do you think of when I say turtle?

(Silence)

Have you ever seen a turtle? Think about what it looks like. What does it have?

S2: A shell

T: Good S2.

S3: It looks like a box.

T: Good. Why do you say it looks like a box?

S3: Because the head goes in.

T: The head goes in. Very good. So a turtle has a head. What else does a turtle have?

S4: Legs.

T: Legs, sure. He has a head. He has legs. What about his feet? What are his feet like, S5?

(S5 does not reply).

T: Are they like your feet? Did you see a picture of a turtle's feet? What do they look like?

(S5 still does not reply).

T: Do turtles have toes like you, S6?

S6: They have claws.

T: Yes, their feet do look something like claws. What about the shell, S7: Is it soft? Is it hard?

S7: Hard.

T: Good. Do you know what kind of an animal a turtle is?

All the students: A reptile.

T: Good. I thought maybe you wouldn't know that and you did. Very good. (The teacher points to the words water *and* land.*) These two words go with* turtle. *What would you call this group? What would be a title for this list? What do these two words have to do with* turtle?

(Silence)

T: Are turtles made of water?

All students: No.

T: So the title can't be Things a Turtle is Made Of. What do water and land have to do with a turtle?

S7: Turtles live on land and live in water.

T: That's right. So these are both where...?

S4: Where turtles live.

T: Good (writes title above list, puts box around list and title, connects to turtle with a line.) That was good, S7, but we have to give the list a title.

T (after writing head, legs, claws, and hard shell in a list and pointing to it): What's this?

S2: A turtle's body.

T: So is this all the body? What do we call these? Each one is a . . .?

S5: A part of the body.

T: Good, S5. Parts of the body (Writes this as the title, puts box around it; then makes a list of box and head goes in and points to it) This one is a little harder. What does this have to do with a turtle?

S7: The turtle goes in his shell when he is in danger.

T: Good (writes when he is in danger as title for the list)

T: What does reptile have to do with turtle?

S1: It's what he is.

T: Good. (writes as title) When we read this article, I want you to look for more information that we can add to this map. When we are finished reading, we will make a bigger map and add information that we learned from reading the article (see figure 2).

As the script demonstrates, brainstorming with these children was a very difficult process. I had to ask many questions and restructure my questions to make them easier for the children. The questions focused on what turtles look like, where they live, and what kind of animal they are because the portion of

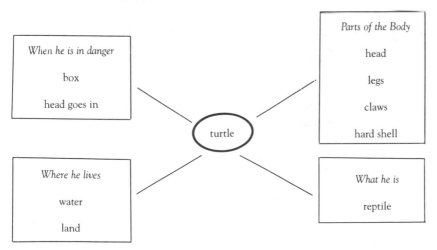

Figure 2. Second semantic map of turtles.

the text that was to be read also focused on these topics. The script appears more like a recitation than a discussion as some children did not volunteer and had to be asked directly for their contributions; later in the lesson those same students began to volunteer (e.g., Student 7). These children had particular difficulty with the technique because they were accustomed to a highly structured comprehension program that emphasized getting the right answer to the teacher's low level questions. After observing the lesson, the children's Chapter I teacher remarked to me that she could see that the children were very anxious because they were asked to think for themselves. She suggested that she would have to change her program so that the children would have more opportunity to think for themselves. (She now uses semantic mapping and other discussion techniques extensively.)

It is clear that a group of children like this will need much scaffolding before they can use these strategies independently. I didn't make any reference to their independent use of the strategy in this first lesson. In addition to rephrasing the questions to make them easier to answer, I framed answers so that the children just needed to provide the end of the sentence.

There are a number of different ways of developing and labeling the categories in the second step:

1. On another board or another piece of paper, the teacher can list some of the original related ideas and then ask the children for the category name. This is the method used in the sample script.
2. When children have had more experience with the technique, they may be able to pick out the related ideas themselves and name the categories.
3. With remedial readers, teachers may need not only to select the related ideas but also to model their thinking about how the ideas are related and how they decide on an appropriate category name. One teacher received many different ideas on the concept of *magic* when she brainstormed with a group of middle class remedial readers. She started to list the names which the children had mentioned—Merlin, Houdini, David Copperfield—then she asked the children if they knew what she was doing. They were able to tell her that the ideas were related and were able to label the category as *Famous Magicians*.

In a variation of semantic mapping, more properly referred to as semantic webbing, lines are drawn from one related idea to another and then to the central idea instead of listing words or phrases in categories. The result, however, is such a confusing visual display that this method is not recommended for remedial readers.

K—W—L (KNOW, WANT TO KNOW, LEARN)

The *Know, Want to Know, Learn* technique was developed by Ogle (1986) as a way of modeling for children the active constructive process that is necessary in reading expository text. It is particularly appropriate to use with content area textbooks, and consists of steps to use before, during, and after reading. It is included here because the first step of the pre-reading segment of the technique is to construct a semantic map of the central concept of the text using the same format used in the lesson on turtles. Once the children become aware of what they already know about the topic, they are asked to anticipate the categories of information they would expect to have included in a text on this topic. The script below illustrates this step of a K—W—L lesson. The central concept was the *Pacific States* since the text to be read was a section of the children's social studies textbook (King, Dennis, and Patter 1980) discussing the surface features of the Pacific states.

In a lesson on the previous day, in an attempt to brainstorm about this topic, it became clear that the children did not understand what a state was. Using a map of the states, along with questioning, explanation, and modeling, I was able to help the children understand that states are divisions of our country. Locating the Pacific states, the children then determined why they were called the Pacific states and identified their physical features. By using these methods, I helped build prior knowledge before the second attempt at brainstorming.

In the second attempt, which took place right before the portion of the lesson contained in the sample script, it was clear that the children had some information about California, Hawaii, and Alaska that could be activated. For Alaska, they gave words like glacier and Eskimo; palm trees, island, volcanoes, and belly dancers for Hawaii; and Hollywood and famous people for California. After brainstorming and discussing, they were able to locate and list related words and label them with the correct state. In the text, however, individual states were mentioned within broader categories like: surface features, climate, industries, cities, and history. I listed ideas related to these categories together (e.g., glacier, island, volcanoes) as a way of helping children organize their knowledge into categories used by the text. The text dealt with groups of states in every chapter and followed the same format in each. Ogle (1986) suggests that anticipating categories in a content area text involves recognizing the more general schema into which a particular topic fits and using past experience with that schema to generate the categories of information. Although Ohlhausen and Roller (1986) warn that headings in textbooks often do not help in building a general schema for a topic like "nation" or "state," the headings of every chapter in this text provided an outline for a general schema into which each group of states could be fitted with appropriate categories. When the children had difficulty in generating anticipated categories, I pointed out how the heading in the text signaled a category of information. I then helped the children anticipate subcategories of information within this general heading. In this way, I helped the children use the structure of the text as well as their prior knowledge to understand the text. The children supposedly had read many chapters previous to the one we read in this lesson; yet they had not noticed that the chapters had the same format. They had no idea of how to use the headings as a way of determining the categories of information to be included. If a K—W—L lesson that focused on the headings as a means of anticipating categories of information had been part of the children's introduction to the book, they could have used this information in reading subsequent chapters. Teachers are urged to look for structural features of the text as well as content knowledge that may help children anticipate information.

K—W—L Script

T: *There are a lot of things that you know about the Pacific states, but there are also a lot of things that you don't know yet. Suppose you were writing a book for fifth grade kids about the Pacific states. What kinds of things would you put in the book?*

S1: *How much water there is.*

T: *The amount of water. (Teacher writes it on the board).*

S2: *Near the ocean.*

T: *So you would tell where they are. (Writes this on the board.)*

S3: *Whether there were islands.*

T: *Yes. Remember when we looked at the map yesterday. We talked about whether there were islands, mountains, or valleys. Let's turn to the book, to page 358. This book can help you. It has headings in heavy print that tell you what it is going to talk about. On page 358, S4, read the heading in heavy print.*

S4: *Surface of the Coastal States.*

T: *What do you think that means?*

S4: *How the ground is.*

T: *Good. How the ground is. (Writes it on the board) What kinds of things will the book talk about when it talks about how the ground is?*

S5: *Dirt.*

S6: *Rocks.*

T: *Yes, it will tell whether the ground is dirt or rocks. (Writes the phrase on the board) What else about the surface? This is the surface of the table.*

S3: *It's flat.*

T: *Yes, it's flat. Is the surface of the ground sometimes flat?*

All students: *Yes.*

T: *So whether it's flat or . . . What could it be besides flat?*

S2: *Bumpy.*

T *(making gesture of bumps with her hand) What do we call bumpy when we are talking about land?*

S5: *Mountains.*

T: *Good for you. Whether it's flat or has mountains. (Writes it on board.) Yesterday we talked about water. What kind of water did we talk about?*

S1: *Streams.*

S4: *Rivers.*

S3: *Ponds.*

S6: *Lakes.*

S7: *Inlets.*

T *(Pointing to the phrases on the board as she says them): So when we read about the surface of the Pacific States we will want to find out:*

the amount of water they have
what the ground is like—whether it is flat or has mountains;
whether there are streams, rivers, ponds, lakes, or inlets.

In the next step of the K—W—L technique, the children are given individual worksheets with three columns headed: What I Know, What I Want to Know, and What I Learned. In the first column children write down things that they know about the topic. In the second column they write down at least three questions whose answers they want to learn from reading the text. At first, it may be necessary for the teacher to work with the whole group and model how to fill out the worksheet. In the lesson of which the script is a part, we used the headings as an aid in making up questions.

Ogle (1986) suggests that children can work in pairs to generate questions about what they want to learn. Cooperative learning groups, like those described in Chapter 4, would also be a good way of providing practice with this strategy. When working in groups, pairs, or individually, remedial readers will continue to need teacher support. When the first two columns are completed, the children read the text or part of the text, writing the answers to their questions in the What I Learned Column. At first this will need to be done in a group with teacher support and modeling. For older students, Ogle suggests post-reading activities such as making a semantic map, making up questions to ask other students, or writing a summary using the information from the What I Learned Column. If a child's question has not been answered in the text, he or she should be given assistance in finding the answer in another source.

INFERENTIAL STRATEGY

The inferential strategy is a pre-reading strategy developed by Hansen (Hansen 1981; Hansen and Hubbard 1984; Hansen and Pearson 1984) designed to encourage children to make spontaneous inferences. This strategy is useful for a reader who answers an inferential question with "I don't know. It doesn't say in the story." Designed for narrative text, this strategy encourages children to compare something from their own lives to something that might happen in the story. It teaches predicting, which is one of the strategies that good readers use spontaneously.

The strategy consists of three steps: the first step is a metacognitive discussion. When introducing the strategy, the teacher should explain why the group will use it in reading. Hansen (1981) introduced the strategy to a group of second graders, explaining that new information could best be understood when it was woven into old information already in our brains. Even when the children have some experience with using the strategy, every lesson should begin with a discussion reminding the children of why they use it. Hansen and Hubbard (1984) suggest that the teacher should question the children, asking them what they do before they read and why. The teacher can then ask the children to imagine that they are going to read a text about a particular topic and ask

105

them what they would think about before reading. Hansen and Hubbard (1984), using the example of reading about schools in Japan, got answers such as: "I might think about our class." "I might think about my old school." "We could be seeing if their school is like ours" (p.587). Often, as in the script below, teachers forget this step when using the strategy. It is important, however, because it provides the focus on process, a necessary component of effective comprehension instruction.

The second step consists of a discussion about three central concepts from a story. Two questions are constructed for each concept. The first question asks the children to relate something they thought or did in a particular situation and the second question asks the children to make predictions about what a character will think or do in a similar situation. For example, in the story, *The Cow Who Fell in the Canal* (Krasilovsky 1957), Hendrika, the cow is bored with the country. One day she falls in the canal and floats down to the city. There she has many adventures. When she comes home she has so much to think about that she is never bored again. In focusing on the concept of boredom the teacher might ask "Have you ever been bored? What did you do to stop being bored?" Immediately after the discussion of this question, the teacher asks the text-related question "Hendrika, the cow in the story we are going to read, is bored. What do you think she will do so that she won't be bored anymore?" As Hansen and Hubbard (1984) point out, these types of questions are not unique to their strategy. Questions relating to the children's experiences and questions requiring predicting are both found in teachers' manuals for basal readers, but they are isolated from each other. The juxtaposition of these two types of questions is unique to this strategy which encourages children to use their experiences to make predictions.

The script describes an inferential strategy discussion that took place before the teacher read the picture book, *Mufaro's Beautiful Daughters* (Steptoe 1987) to a group of second graders. This Caldecott winner is an African folk tale somewhat similar to the Cinderella story. Both sisters are beautiful, but one is mean and jealous of the other because that one is kind and everyone loves her. The prince of the country is seeking a wife and both sisters set out to meet him. The prince marries the kind sister, and the mean sister becomes her servant.

Inferential Strategy Script

T: *Have any of you ever been jealous of someone?*
S1: *My sisters.*
T: *Why are you jealous of your sisters?*
S1: *They take care of this little boy and they always play with him but not with me.*
T: *So you're jealous of the boy because your sisters play with him and not with you. Is that a good feeling?*
S1: *No.*
T: *Who were you jealous of, S2?*

106

S2: *My friend. She has more pretty things than me.*

T: *So you're a little bit envious of her pretty things. Was anybody else jealous? (Silence) No? I've always been jealous of thin people who can eat whatever they want and not get fat. When I eat I get fat, so that makes me jealous of thin people. As S1 told us, jealousy is not a good feeling. Is there anyone else who was ever jealous? No? OK. In the story we are going to read today, there are two sisters, Manyara and Nyasha. Manyara is mean and Nyasha is kind. What problems might arise between the two sisters?*

S3: *Jealousy.*

T: *You think they might be jealous of one another. In what way?*

S2: *The beautiful sister might go to a ball and drop her slipper like Snow White.*

T: *Is that Snow White? Which story is that?*

S4: *It's Cinderella.*

T: *So you think this story is like Cinderella. In what way is it like Cinderella?*

S5: *Her sisters were mean to Cinderella.*

T: *The stepsisters were mean to Cinderella. How did the stepsisters feel toward Cinderella?*

S6: *Sad.*

S2: *Happy.*

T: *Happy?*

S2: *They were happy because Cinderella did all the work. Cinderella was jealous of them.*

(At this point, the teacher decides to start reading the story.)

This script illustrates two problems teachers often have when they begin using this strategy. First, questions that ask children how they feel in certain situations or how a character feels tend to get the answers "sad, mad, or glad," the kinds of answers the teacher in the script received. It is better to ask what happened, what someone did, or what someone thought.

Second, the strategy is supposed to help children use their experiences in making predictions; so the questions about the predictions should relate to the questions about the children's experiences. In the script, the teacher asks the children the reasons they have been jealous. But in talking about the story, she asks what kinds of problems they predict the sisters will have. The appropriate question would have been "In this story, one sister, Manyara, is jealous of her sister Nyasha. Why do you think she is jealous?"

The teacher in this lesson was trying out the technique for the first time; teachers should expect to make errors when trying any technique for the first time. This teacher, like the teacher in the PREP script, was also surprised by the knowledge the children had and the way they related it to the story. The children in this case saw a relationship between this story and Cinderella without any prompting from the teacher and continued to refer to this relationship while reading.

The inferential strategy as it was developed by Hansen is a pre-reading technique. After the pre-reading discussion, the children read the text independently. After reading, they answer teachers' inferential questions about the story, relating them to their predictions and experiences. Hansen (1981) provided second grade children with gray strips of paper and colored strips of paper as an after-reading activity. The children wrote their predictions on the gray strips and the information they got from the text on the colored strips of paper. Then they wove the strips together as a reminder of how their brains connect the new information from the text with what they already know. Once again there was a focus not just on content but also on process. Teachers who use the inferential strategy as a pre-reading technique should be sure that their during-reading and post-reading discussions focus on confirming or refuting the children's predictions and include some discussion of the process of connecting the children's ideas and the ideas presented in the text.

I have also used this inferential strategy successfully with remedial readers during reading. Instead of discussing three concepts before reading the entire story, I break the story into two or three sections and have a strategy discussion before reading each section. (Guidelines for dividing a text into appropriate sections are discussed in Chapter 8.) If teachers find the discussions interrupt the story too much, they might want to use other during-reading techniques focusing on prediction that are described in Chapter 8.

CORRECTING MISCONCEPTIONS

The techniques described in the previous section aid children in comprehending and learning from written text by activating and building knowledge. However, young children not only lack prior knowledge about many topics, they often have inaccurate knowledge. In fact, research indicates that people of all ages, especially children, have misconceptions that affect the understanding of many content area concepts, in science and mathematics (Davis 1981; Larkin et al. 1980; Nussbaum and Novick 1976; Shayer and Wylam 1981), and social studies (Smith 1987). The processes of fine tuning and, particularly, restructuring appear to be more difficult and time-consuming than the process of accretion. Research investigating the relationship between reading and these processes is far less extensive than that investigating the relationship between reading and knowledge accretion. However, it does appear that children can learn new corrected information from a text when it is a considerate refutation text—one that points out and discusses the misconception, and then corrects it by presenting and explaining the new information (Maria 1988). Pre-reading activities that activate the misconception, and post-reading activities in which readers compare their original ideas to the ideas in the text, also appear to be helpful (Alvermann, Smith, and Readence 1985; Alvermann and Hynd 1986, 1987; Dole and Smith 1987; Maria 1988).

The Anticipation Reaction Guide is a technique that is recommended by Readence, Bean, and Baldwin (1985) for use with content area texts where misconceptions are expected. An Anticipation Reaction Guide is a list of about four or five statements related to central text concepts. Some of these statements are expected to challenge students' prior knowledge and beliefs while other statements are designed to be consistent with them. Before reading the text, students are asked to state whether they agree or disagree with certain statements and why—either in writing or in a pre-reading discussion. After reading the text, the students are again asked to react to the statements, providing justification from information in the text.

Dole and Smith (1987) and Maria (1988) found that using think sheets when reading a text also improves learning of scientific information that contradicts common misconceptions. At the top of the think sheet appears a question relating to the new contradictory information. Before reading, the children write their answers to the question on the think sheet based on their everyday ideas. As the children read, they stop at certain points to write down on the think sheet important ideas related to the question. After completing the text, the children choose whether the text information added to their ideas, stayed the same, was contradictory, or confused them.

Often the pre-reading techniques discussed earlier bring out misconceptions not anticipated by the teacher. For example, during the PREP lesson on *bullfighting*, one child suggested that bullfighting meant bulls fighting each other. The fact that these techniques make the teacher aware of the children's misconceptions is another of their strengths. How should these misconceptions be handled? Flood and Lapp (1988) suggest that misconceptions should be corrected during brainstorming. Trivial or irrelevant misconceptions may be effectively corrected in this way. However, correcting inaccuracies during the pre-reading discussion may discourage children from participating in the discussion. Moreover, since research suggests that most misconceptions are not corrected by simply giving the child the correct information, correcting inaccuracies during the pre-reading discussion may not be effective unless they are trivial or irrelevant. Teachers must use their professional judgment. In most cases the preferred procedure is to remind children to look for differences between their pre-reading ideas and the ideas in the text. After-reading discussion should focus on resolving these differences.

CHAPTER

6

TECHNIQUES IN WRITTEN LANGUAGE INSTRUCTION—VOCABULARY

This chapter focuses on vocabulary instruction. Although the term *vocabulary* is used in various ways in the reading field, it always refers to the language units known as words. Thus, somewhat arbitrarily, vocabulary is categorized as a subheading of the factor of linguistic knowledge in the table in Chapter 1. I say somewhat arbitrarily because there are good reasons for categorizing vocabulary as a subheading of background knowledge also; words are labels for concepts and schemata. Since our schemata are built from our experiences, words become symbols for our experiences (Searfoss and Readence 1985).

Some might view the techniques presented in the previous chapter as techniques for vocabulary instruction; however, the purpose of those techniques is not to develop meanings for particular words, but to activate and/or build schemata about the topic of the text. The purpose of the techniques presented in this chapter is to help children learn more about the meanings of words in the text. At times, these two purposes will overlap so that the topic of the text is also a word from the text, but this is not necessarily so. For example, before reading *Patrick Henry* (Sabin 1982), the PREP technique was used to activate and build background knowledge related to the concept of colonial America. The meaning of the word *colony* was also taught as a separate part of the pre-reading lesson by presenting it in a context that could be understood by the children. The overall goal of both activities was to help the children understand the text and to teach them strategies for using both factors while reading independently.

While most reading experts (e.g., Searfoss and Readence 1985; Vacca, Vacca, and Gove 1987) recommend explicit and systematic vocabulary instruction, isolated practice using words other than those found in the reading texts is not recommended. Searfoss and Readence (1985) state that "The use of commercial vocabulary-development materials only imposes additional new words on readers who already have enough new words to master during the course of regular classroom instruction" (p. 189). The burden would be even greater for remedial readers.

The second overall goal of comprehension instruction discussed in Chapter 4 must not be forgotten in helping children understand the meanings of words found in texts they read. Vocabulary instruction that simply teaches children the meanings of words is not effective vocabulary instruction. When dealing with vocabulary, as with any other factor, there should be a focus on process as well as on content. We must teach children strategies that will enable them to determine the meanings of words independently and make connections between new knowledge and their already existing knowledge.

WHAT IS THE RELATIONSHIP BETWEEN VOCABULARY AND COMPREHENSION?

Since the goal of vocabulary instruction is to improve comprehension, the nature of the relationship between vocabulary and comprehension should determine the type of vocabulary instruction. The relationship between word knowledge and comprehension is well established (Davis 1944, 1968; Spearitt 1972; Thurstone 1946). The reader's level of vocabulary is the best predictor of his or her ability to understand text, and the number of difficult words in a text is the best measure of its level of difficulty (Anderson and Freebody 1981).

Three hypotheses about the relationship between vocabulary and comprehension have been proposed (Anderson and Freebody 1981). The aptitude hypothesis holds that vocabulary and comprehension both are the result of intelligence. For some who hold this position, vocabulary instruction would be considered a waste of time since it cannot change the level of a child's intelligence and so will not affect comprehension. Others who subscribe to the aptitude hypothesis agree that vocabulary and comprehension are both a result of intelligence, but also believe that intelligence can be affected by factors in the environment. Those holding this form of the aptitude hypothesis do not recommend explicit vocabulary instruction either; they recommend wide reading and many language enrichment activities in the hope that these types of activities will result in higher intelligence and better vocabulary and comprehension. Conversely, they suggest that remedial readers have low vocabularies and poor reading comprehension because they have less opportunity to read and are not provided with the same opportunities for gaining knowledge as are good readers. The Matthew effect, discussed in Chapter 2, suggests that children who do not meet expectations in reading get worse at reading because of the gap between the amount of reading they do and the amount good readers do. The aptitude hypothesis seems to suggest that this gap affects their reading at least partly by affecting their intelligence.

The knowledge hypothesis suggests that knowledge of word meanings is a good indicator of a high level of knowledge about a topic. The Bransford and Johnson (1972) study that used the Washing Clothes passage, as described in Chapter 2, provided evidence of the importance of background knowledge as a factor in comprehension. This study demonstrated that knowing the meanings of individual words may be necessary, but it is not sufficient for text comprehension. On the other hand, Stahl and Jacobson (1986) found that "knowledge-based pre-teaching improved comprehension but did not overcome the effects of vocabulary difficulty" (p. 316). The instructional implications of the knowledge hypothesis are that vocabulary instruction must involve conceptual learning and the context of a particular subject.

The instrumental hypothesis that holds that the relationship between vocabulary and comprehension is a causal one is supported by research evidence. Although studies which provide traditional kinds of vocabulary instruction are not always successful in improving comprehension, those that provide intensive, in-depth vocabulary instruction are able to facilitate comprehension (e.g., McKeown et al. 1985). Moreover, a meta-analysis of studies that investigated the effect of vocabulary instruction on comprehension found "a significant effect size for the influence of vocabulary instruction upon reading comprehension" (Reutzel and Hollingsworth 1988, p. 361). It appears that direct vocabulary instruction is an important component of comprehension instruction.

Although children can understand a text in which they do not know the meanings of all the words, they may need direct instruction on the meanings of some words. In order to be effective, this instruction must provide many exposures to words and activities in which children make meaningful use of words they are learning. In addition, as suggested by the knowledge hypothesis, this systematic and direct vocabulary instruction must present words in association with each other and in connection with a particular topic. In teachers' zeal to provide effective vocabulary instruction, they must be very careful not to deprive the children of the opportunity to read; wide-range reading is a vital part of vocabulary instruction, providing the integration, repetition, and meaningful use of words that are the hallmarks of effective vocabulary instruction (Nagy 1988).

The volume of free reading is the best predictor of vocabulary growth (Fielding, Wilson, and Anderson 1986). Learning incidental vocabulary by way of independent reading may not seem efficient since children who read grade-level texts have about a one-in-twenty chance of learning the meaning of a particular word from context (Nagy, Anderson, and Herman 1987); yet, over the long term, it can result in a child's learning the meaning of many more words than could be learned through direct instruction. Nagy (1988) points out that children who read twenty-five minutes a day encounter about 20,000 unfamiliar words a year and learn the meanings of about 1000 of those words. Increasing reading time by another twenty-five minutes could result in learning 1000 more words. If children read high-quality texts they could double the number of words learned. Nagy concludes that "Increasing the volume of students' reading is the single most important thing a teacher can do to promote large-scale vocabulary growth" (p. 32). On the other hand, remedial readers who do not have strategies for using context to determine word meaning will not be able to use the opportunities for vocabulary growth through reading independently. Direct vocabulary instruction in strategies and word meanings will be needed.

WHAT IS MEANT BY DIRECT VOCABULARY INSTRUCTION?
You have probably inferred from the discussion in the previous section that the focus of vocabulary instruction in this book will be on teaching children the *meaning* of words. The goal is to provide for both breadth and depth of vocabulary, i.e., teaching meanings of a large number of words and deepening understanding of words already known at some level.

The terms *vocabulary* and *vocabulary instruction* can be confusing because the same terms are used to refer to instruction in word meaning and word recognition. Graves (1984) identifies four types of vocabulary problems: Type 1 words are those whose meanings the children know, words that are part of their oral but not their written vocabulary. Many teachers, especially when they are talking about remedial readers, use the terms *vocabulary* and *vocabulary instruction* to refer to teaching about Type 1 words. For these teachers, the term *vocabulary* is synonymous with sight vocabulary, words that can be instantly recognized. The teachers in the lesson described in Chapter 2 who insisted that vocabulary must be introduced before the children could read *The Best Nest* used the term in this sense. They thought the children would not be able to recognize the word *mattress*, but would understand what a mattress is.

Since teaching Type 1 words involves only word recognition instruction, it will not be considered in this chapter. This does not imply that word recognition instruction is not important particularly for remedial readers. It also does not imply that it never considers word meanings. Usually, however, so much attention is given to word recognition instruction for remedial readers that vocabulary instruction that focuses on word meanings may be neglected.

Vocabulary instruction, as described in this chapter, will be concerned with the other categories of words described by Graves. While some of these categories require word recognition instruction, all of them require instruction about word meaning.

Type 2 words are those that children can recognize. They understand the meaning of the word in one or more context, but not in the particular context in which it is being used. For example, a child knows that a *sound* is a noise. He or she also understands that a *sound* sleep is an uninterrupted sleep. However, he or she does not know that a *sound* is also a body of water connecting two larger bodies of water or between the mainland and an island (as in Long Island Sound). Since many English words have multiple meanings, this situation occurs even when reading narratives. A subgroup of Type 2 words labeled *special words* by Vacca and Vacca (1986) consists of words like *sound* whose special meanings in a particular content area differ from their meaning or meanings in general usage. Type 2 words are quite common in content area texts.

Type 3 words are words that children cannot recognize either orally or in print. Although they may be able to decode the word, they do not have any meaning for it. The meaning is rather easily explained, however, because the children already have the schema the word labels; they just have not been exposed to the particular label for that concept or schema. For example, most children have had the experience of being ecstatic. But very few young children would know that label. Explaining the meaning would involve using synonyms like *very very happy* or *overjoyed.* Many new words encountered in narratives are Type 3 words.

Type 4 words are words children do not recognize and for which they have no meaning. Devine (1986) describes them as words ". . . which cannot be explained through existing or related schemata. For them, schemata must be built 'from the ground up' " (p. 116). In light of the statement in the last chapter that everybody knows something about almost everything, it seems more appropriate to characterize these words as labels for schemata that must be built using anchors remotely related. While such words are found in narrative text, they are quite common in content area expository texts. To master a content area ". . . is to learn its key concepts, that is, its language" (Dale 1975, p. 12). Every content area has its own particular language; and one aspect of that language is the technical vocabulary, such as *photosynthesis,* that is only used in a particular content area (Vacca and Vacca 1986).

In summary, vocabulary instruction, as it is being used here, may involve building new schemata for existing words, providing new words as labels for existing schemata, or building new schemata along with new words to label them. Since variation in children's word knowledge is to be expected, a teacher may be concerned with several different categories of vocabulary problems in teaching a particular word.

WHAT DO WE MEAN WHEN WE SAY WE KNOW THE MEANING OF A WORD?

Characterizing vocabulary instruction as that related to word meanings leads us to this fundamental question that has been answered in many different ways. The Standard Theory of Semantics suggests that we know a word if we are able to define it, i.e., ". . . list the features that capture the essence of the thing (or event or quality) designated by the word" (Anderson and Freebody 1981, p. 90). Many adults, however, would consider that they know words they are unable to define in this sense. For example, I have certainly felt for many years that I knew the meaning of the word *bird.* Yet it was only a few years ago that I learned that what distinguishes a bird from other animals is the fact that it has feathers. While the criteria for a definition is not so stringent in Anderson and Freebody's (1981) description—" . . . for most purposes, a person has a sufficiently deep understanding of a word if it conveys to him or her all of the distinctions that would be understood by an ordinary adult under normal circumstances" (p. 93)—it still retains the idea that to know a word is to know its definition or distinguishing features. Most teachers, too, would probably say that a child knows a word if he is able to define it.

This denotative meaning of a word is the focus of most traditional vocabulary instruction designed to facilitate text comprehension. Typically, before reading a text, children look up the definitions of several words and write them in a sentence. There are several problems with this approach, however (Nagy 1988). While definitions have a place in vocabulary instruction and children should be able to construct a good definition, definitions found in dictionaries or glossaries are often not adequate for any one or more of the following reasons.

1. Words in the definition are less familiar than the word being defined (*annoyed* means *vexed.*) When confronted with a definition like this, children may focus on the fragments of a dictionary entry that they *are* able to understand. An example of the strange ideas that can result from this is provided by Miller and Gildea (1985) cited in Schwartz (1988). A fifth grade girl focused on the phrases *eat out; eat away* found in the definition of *erode* and then used the word *erode* in the following sentence, "Our family erodes a lot."
2. Definitions may be inaccurate.
3. Definitions may be inappropriate for the selection being read. A basic principle that should be conveyed in vocabulary instruction is the fact that word meaning changes according to the context in which the word is found. Definitions are often confusing in this regard. Even when several definitions are given, a child may not be able to select the appropriate definition for the particular situation.
4. Definitions do not contain enough information. They do not tell how a word is used. Also, they do not give enough information to convey new concepts effectively. "Although words are labels for concepts, a single concept represents much more than the meaning of a single word. It might take thousands of words to explain a concept" (Vacca and Vacca 1986, p. 303).

When we think of a word as a label for a schema, we can see that there are other problems with teaching vocabulary through definitions. Considering a word as a label for a schema implies that word meanings constantly change since an individual's experiences constantly change. The question "Do you know this word?" cannot really be answered, then, with a yes or no; a word is known to some degree. That degree is determined by the richness of the word's associations with other words (Readence, Bean, and Baldwin 1985). These associations or connotations of a word are often more important for text comprehension than knowledge of definitions. Vocabulary instruction that seeks to facilitate comprehension cannot rely only on knowledge of word definitions. Effective vocabulary instruction which provides connotational and denotational information about words will require a substantial amount of instructional time; and it will often be impossible to provide direct instruction for all the unfamiliar words in a text.

HOW SHOULD WORDS BE SELECTED FOR VOCABULARY INSTRUCTION?

The first part of this question involves determining *what* words should be selected. The first criterion for selecting words for vocabulary instruction has already been mentioned, i.e., words should be selected from texts that the children are reading. The second criterion is that the words should pose a problem in some way. In using the text-based model of comprehension as a basis for designing pre-reading instruction the teacher should be alert for problems children may have in understanding the meanings of particular words. Since there is not enough time to teach all the words a child does not know in a particular text, how does one choose from among these difficult words?

A third criterion, one for choosing some difficult words over others, is based on how essential those words are to understanding the text. Just as pre-reading lessons designed to build and/or activate background knowledge focus on concepts central to text understanding, so, too, vocabulary instruction should focus on unfamiliar and difficult words essential for understanding the text. For example, when I read *Patrick Henry* (Sabin 1982) in preparing to use it in the lesson mentioned at the outset of this chapter, it was clear that the children would not understand the significance of Patrick Henry's contribution to American history unless they understood that people in a colony do not have the freedom to govern themselves. That is why the word *colony* was selected for direct vocabulary instruction.

A fourth criterion for selecting words for vocabulary instruction is based on the fact that one goal of vocabulary instruction is to teach children the process of determining word meanings independently. Words that may not be essential to understanding the text may be chosen for direct vocabulary instruction because teaching their meanings provides the opportunity for children to learn how to use structural analysis or context as cues to word meaning. For example, in a text on the topic of artificial intelligence that I used with a seventh grade remedial reader I noticed there were several words ending with the suffix *logy*, words like *psychology*, *technology*, and *biology*. This particular text provided a perfect opportunity to introduce this child to the use of structural analysis as a cue to word meaning. Other words not part of the text, such as *biology*, *zoology*, and *archeology*, were used in the lesson because I decided that they would be useful words for this child to know. A fifth criterion for word selection is that words chosen for direct instruction should be useful words. Thus I did not teach *epistemology* or *ecclesiology* even though they were unfamiliar words that shared the same suffix.

A sixth reason for choosing words for vocabulary study is interest. Children must be motivated to use strategies. Teachers who find words interesting and fun will communicate that excitement to children so that teacher attitude may be one of the most important factors in effective vocabulary instruction (Deighton 1970; Manzo and Shirk 1972; Searfoss and Readence 1985; Vacca, Vacca, and Gove 1986). Richek (1988) suggests that direct vocabulary instruction that focuses on interesting words may be helpful in increasing incidental learning of vocabulary, since it makes children more aware of words and their meanings. It should be reiterated, however, that programs which focus on interesting words in isolation from texts and from each other are not recommended because they do not make efficient use of the limited time available for vocabulary instruction.

A second part of selecting words for vocabulary instruction relates to *who* should select them. In the preceding discussion, it was assumed that the teacher would select the words used in vocabulary instruction. Yet the principle of actively involving the children as much as possible suggests that they should play some part in selecting the words they will study.

THE VOCABULARY OVERVIEW GUIDE

The Vocabulary Overview Guide (Carr 1985) is a tool with which children select the words they need to learn. Through explanation and modeling the children are taught to survey the text to see what it is about, to skim for unknown words, and to try to figure out the meanings of the words through context or by using the dictionary. After reading, children fill in the Vocabulary Overview Guide, grouping the new words into categories related to the topic. Good readers may be able to generate and label their own categories; teachers should probably provide the categories for remedial readers (Carr 1986). Beneath each word students write the definition and a clue that will help them connect the word to something they already know or have experienced. Students can use passage and category titles as cues to the words and their meanings. If they are unable to remember a word's meaning, they are taught to use the cues as aids to memory. (An excerpt from a sample Vocabulary Overview Guide can be seen in figure 1.)

I have not used this technique myself, but it seems to have many of the characteristics of effective vocabulary instruction: it teaches words in association with one another and provides a visual display to highlight the associations. Children are actively involved in the process, and the word meanings are made personally meaningful for them. With remedial readers, teachers will probably need to provide extensive instruction in the use of context and the dictionary with this technique. Some of the techniques described later in this chapter will aid children in using the Vocabulary Overview Guide independently. This kind of instruction can also be provided with the teacher taking full responsibility for the process at first, scaffolding the task for the students, then gradually releasing responsibility to them.

THE DISCRIMINATIVE SELF-INVENTORY CHECKLIST

Remedial readers often are not aware of their lack of understanding and might not be adept at selecting unknown words without the teacher's help at first.

117

Example: This excerpt from the Vocabulary Overview Guide for the "Loch Ness Monster" passage was developed by high school students.

Title		Loch Ness Monster	
Categories	People	Monster	Land
Term	credibility	legend	melancholy
Clue	minister	Paul Bunyan	funeral
Definition	believable	a story from the past	sad lonely
	tolerant	extinct	
	mother	dinosaurs	
	open-minded accepting	no longer existing	
	brawny	elusive	
	A. Schwarzenegger	criminals	
	strong	hard to find	
		authentic	
		diamonds	
		real genuine	

Figure 1. Vocabulary overview guide. Reprinted, with permission, from E. Carr, *Vocabulary Overview Guide*, manual accompanying videotape entitled Teaching Reading as Thinking (Association for Supervision and Curriculum Development, Alexandria, 1986).

One technique that I have used with remedial readers, the Discriminative Self-Inventory Checklist (Dale and O'Rourke 1971), appears to provide the kind of scaffolding they need in order to become more aware of their level of understanding of particular word meanings. From the text, the teacher compiles a list of words that are probably unfamiliar to the students, are connected to the topic of the text, and/or are important, useful, or interesting. The children are then asked to rate their understandings of the meanings of the words using a four-level rating system. A Discriminative Self-Inventory Checklist completed by one child in the lesson about knights (see Chapter 5) is illustrated in figure 2.

The Discriminative Self-Inventory Checklist can be thought of as an assessment tool. *Squire, chapel, vow,* and *ceremony* received low ratings from all the students reading the passage, making me aware that these words would require special attention. On the other hand, *equipment, noble,* and *sword* were consistently given high ratings so that they did not need any attention. When the checklist is the subject of an interactive discussion, it can also provide an instructional technique. After the children rated their knowledge of the words, they were asked to explain their ratings. Much information about the words was presented and many associations were made among the words. After completing the discussion, the children decided which words would need special attention including looking for clues to their meaning. Using the Discriminative Self-Inventory Checklist as a first step in the Vocabulary Overview Guide procedure might be helpful for remedial readers since it combines teachers' and students' selections of words.

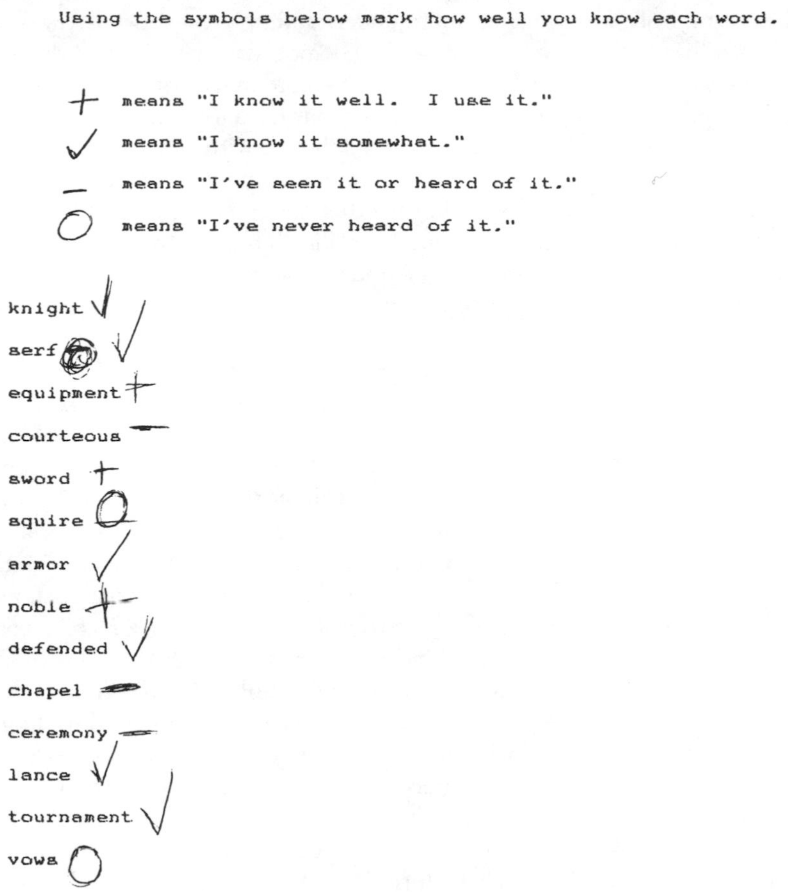

Using the symbols below mark how well you know each word.

+ means "I know it well. I use it."

✓ means "I know it somewhat."

— means "I've seen it or heard of it."

◯ means "I've never heard of it."

knight ✓

serf ◉ ✓

equipment +

courteous —

sword +

squire ◯

armor ✓

noble +—

defended ✓

chapel ◄

ceremony —

lance ✓

tournament ✓

vows ◯

Figure 2. Discriminative self-inventory checklist as completed by a student.

WHEN SHOULD VOCABULARY BE TAUGHT?

Since this chapter takes the position that the program of vocabulary instruction should be related to texts the children are reading, this question relates to whether vocabulary should be taught before, during, or after reading a text. I would suggest that the answer is that vocabulary can and should be taught at all three stages of the reading lesson. When to teach a particular word will depend on the type of vocabulary problem that the word presents, its importance to understanding the text, the manner in which the text presents it, and the teacher's reasons for selecting it for study. The necessity for maintaining a balance between content and process instruction should also influence a teacher's decision about when to teach vocabulary.

Traditionally, in basal reader lessons, vocabulary is presented before reading to help children in word recognition. Because of this, many teachers have come to believe that vocabulary should always be presented before reading. Teaching word meanings before reading aids comprehension (Wixson 1986). If the meaning of a word is important to understanding a text and if this meaning is unfamiliar to the children because they do not have the schemata the word represents and/or because the meaning of the word in the context is unfamiliar (Type 4 or Type 2 words), then the teacher may need to teach the word before the children read the text. This is particularly true with difficult abstract concepts and the special words or technical words common in content area texts and informational trade books. On the other hand, if the teacher always presents the information orally and does not allow children to use text to gain information, the short-term goal of understanding particular texts may be achieved at the expense of the long-term goal of learning how to acquire information from written text.

The amount of context provided by the text is an important factor in deciding whether or not a word should be taught before reading the text. Sometimes it is hard for a teacher to determine whether there is enough context to make the meaning of a word clear. One way of determining whether context is sufficient is to try substituting other words that differ in meaning from the target word and check to see whether the sentence still makes sense, as for example, in the sentence "The choir kept their white robes unsullied." If this sentence was contained in a text discussing how everyone was preparing for the bishop's visit to the church and trying to make everything look nice, it would be possible to guess that unsullied meant unwrinkled rather than clean.

If the text provides enough context for the children to determine meanings for themselves, the teacher needs to consider whether guided reading of the text, in which the teacher supports the children's efforts to make use of the context, might not be a viable alternative to pre-reading instruction. In the final analysis the decision should be based on the difficulty of the word and how important it is to understanding the text. A difficult word that is crucial to understanding should probably be introduced before reading, should be given special attention during reading, and should be the focus of after-reading activities that provide meaningful practice for children. In order to learn word meanings, children will need to be exposed to them many times in many different contexts.

BEFORE READING:
When children first learn to use context to determine word meaning, it may be a good idea to provide the word in context before reading the text. (Attending to the important ideas in the text and using context effectively during reading may be too difficult for them.) When words are presented in context before reading, it is important to be sure that the context is as similar as possible to the context in the text. If the text discusses the missions founded by the Spanish in Texas, the pre-reading sentences or paragraphs should not discuss astronauts going on missions to outer space.

Preview in Context:
When there is sufficient context in the text to determine word meaning and the concepts involved are not difficult ones, the Preview in Context technique

(Readence, Bean, and Baldwin 1985) is a good choice for a pre-reading activity. In this technique the teacher directs the students to the section of the text containing the context for the word (either a sentence or a few sentences). The teacher reads the section containing the target word while the children read along. The teacher then questions the children to guide them toward using the context to determine the meaning of the target word. For example, this section from the text *Knights and Tournaments* can be presented before reading the text.

> At the age of fifteen, a boy became a squire. Then he began to spend time with the knights, who trained him to fight. He practiced with the sword and the lance until he became an expert. With so much time spent in learning to fight, a squire had little time to learn to read and write. When he was twenty-one, the squire was ready to become a knight (Riese and LaSalle 1986, p. 29).

After the teacher reads this section, he or she asks for the definition of a squire. If children have difficulty with the definition, the teacher can ask questions like "Who were the squires?" "What did the squires do?" "How long were boys squires?" "What was the reason for being a squire?" Children should be questioned as to why they give the answers they do so that they can become aware of how the context helps them understand what a squire is. The meaning of the word can be expanded through questioning children as to how the squire's education is different from and similar to their own. *Squire* might also be related to the word *apprentice* if this word is part of the children's vocabulary.

Contextual Redefinition:
Very often texts do not contain enough context for the children to use in determining word meanings (Schatz and Baldwin 1986). In this case, the Contextual Redefinition technique (Readence, Bean, and Baldwin 1985) is useful for presenting words with sufficient context before reading. I used this technique as part of the lesson on the Texas War of Independence discussed in Chapter 5. First, the children's teachers and I selected eight words from the text that would probably be difficult for the children. (If I were doing the lesson again, I would limit myself to five or six words.) I then constructed sentences that would provide context for determining the meanings of these words, as in the examples:

> Americans fighting in the battle at the Alamo would not *surrender*. They chose to keep fighting. The Americans did not have enough *ammunition* for their guns.

First, the words were presented in isolation and the children were asked for their meanings. After some discussion, the children agreed that surrender had something to do with fighting and ammunition had to do with guns. Children were then asked to write their definitions for the words. Like the Discriminative Self Inventory Checklist, this step allows the teacher to assess the children's knowledge of the words being studied. The teacher should not comment as to who is correct, but should move to the next step, presenting the sentences so that the children can be actively involved and check their word meanings against the context provided. After modeling the process with sentences used earlier with other words, I used questioning to guide the children in seeing how the context could help them refine their understanding of *surrender*.

Contextual Redefinition Script
T: *S1, you were right. You said surrender had something to do with fighting. Does surrender mean fighting?*
S1: *No.*
T: *How do you know?*
S1: *It says they kept fighting and they wouldn't surrender.*
T: *That's right. So surrender and fighting can't be the same thing. What do you think surrender means, S2?*
S2: *Stop fighting?*
T: *Why do you think that?*
S2: *Because if you don't keep fighting, you stop fighting.*
T: *That's right. And, in a war, if you stop fighting, you give up.*

The next step in the discussion about each word is for a volunteer to check the dictionary or glossary definition. This definition is compared to the one arrived at after discussion of the context. As a final step, children are asked to check their original definitions and correct them if necessary.

Both Preview in Context and Contextual Redefinition are effective techniques because they attend to both context and definitional knowledge of words, actively involving the children in learning how to determine word meanings. Contextual redefinition is particularly valuable in that it models one appropriate use of the dictionary, i.e., as a check on meaning that one has constructed on the basis of context. Children may need to have some training in how to use the dictionary before they are able to engage in this step efficiently. When this training is presented as a way of enabling them to check their own and others' definitions in the Contextual Redefinition technique, the training has a function.

Concept of Definition

Another approach that focuses on both context and definitional knowledge of words in a manner that I have found effective for remedial readers is the Concept of Definition (Schwartz and Raphael 1985). This technique is particularly effective for use with content area textbooks that present much new terminology because, as its name indicates, it teaches children what types of information are part of a definition. "It provides a general schema or structure for word meaning" (Scwartz and Raphael 1985, p. 199).

The main goal of this technique is much broader than helping children write good definitions. Concept of definition is designed to help children use more strategies in developing and refining their knowledge of word meanings (Schwartz 1988). Since learning the meaning of a word independently often requires children to coordinate different information sources such as word structure, context, and/or the dictionary, children must learn to "orchestrate complex strategies" (Schwartz 1988, p. 111). "Internalizing this 'concept of def-

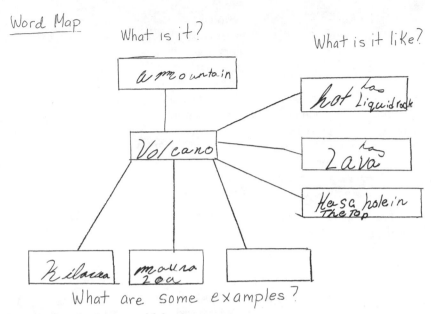

Word Map

What is it?

What is it like?

Figure 3. Completed concept of definition map.

inition' helps students to (1) select and evaluate sources of information for determining the meaning of a new term; (2) combine and organize new information with their prior knowledge about the concept; (3) test their understanding; and (4) recall vocabulary concepts" (Schwartz 1988, p. 109).

This is accomplished through the use of a simplified form of a semantic map developed by Pearson and Johnson (1978), which visually displays the three categories of relationships in a definition: (1) the class to which the concept belongs; (2) the primary properties of the concept that distinguish it from other members of its class; and (3) examples of the concept. The word map demonstrates these three relationships by means of three questions: (1) What is it? (2) What is it like? (3) What are some examples?. A sample word map is presented in figure 3. This map was completed by a fifth grade remedial reader as part of another lesson used in the K—W—L lesson discussed in Chapter 5.

Following the procedure suggested by Schwartz and Raphael (1985), in the first lesson the children were shown blank word maps and told that they would be using them to construct definitions of words. The children were told that other children had found this map very helpful and that understanding the meanings of the new words presented in their social studies text would help them better understand the text. Then in a group discussion children selected the appropriate words from the list below to answer the questions and fill in a group word map for *ice cream*. (Schwartz and Raphael had used soup for their first lesson. I thought ice cream might be more interesting.)

vanilla
dessert

frozen

tastes good

chocolate

strawberry

melts in the sun

As part of the discussion, I explained to the children that to answer the question, "What is it?" you need a very general word that answers the question for many words; while to answer the question, "What is it like?" you need ideas that relate only to ice cream. Using the word map as a guide, I modeled the definition of ice cream.

> Ice cream is a dessert that tastes good. It is frozen and melts in the sun. Some examples are chocolate, vanilla, and strawberry ice cream.

The children then brainstormed about the word *computer* and came up with the following list of ideas.

has a disk drive

smart

has a memory bank

can do your homework with it

has a keyboard

When the group attempted to map *computer*, they realized that they did not have all the necessary information; but as the script excerpts below indicate, they were able to come up with the information.

Concept of Definition Script

T: Which of the ideas we have listed tells what a computer is?

S1: None of them.

T: Well, what is a computer?

S2: A machine.

T: Does everyone agree? Good. A computer is a machine. Let's fill in our map.
(The children correctly identified the ideas on the list as ways of telling what the computer is like.)

T: When we say what a computer is like we should try to fill in things that cannot describe a lot of other things as well as a computer. For example, is a computer the only thing that has a keyboard? What else has a keyboard?

S3: A piano.

S4: An accordion.

T: That's right. Can we do our homework with other things besides a computer?

S2: We can use a pencil or a pen.

After some further discussion, the children decided that the ideas remaining would be appropriate answers for, "What is a computer like?" With my guidance the children were able to identify the properties of a computer which were most important in defining it.

124

Realizing that distinguishing important from unimportant properties is a vital part of learning the meaning of a word, the developers of the concept of a definition word map have added a new element—comparisons (Schwartz 1988). A blank map in this newer version is found in figure 4. In the space for comparisons students fill in terms similar to the word being defined. Teacher and students discuss properties that the defined word shares with the comparison term or terms as well as properties it does not share. Inserting the comparison term into the word map alerts the children to the necessity for determining the most important properties of a word and provides a visual structure to support the process.

When several closely related concepts have been presented using this technique, teachers should supplement the technique with a questioning activity such as that used in the rich vocabulary instruction program developed by Beck et al. (Beck, McCaslin, and McKeown 1980; Beck, McKeown, and Omanson 1987; Beck, Perfetti, and McKeown 1982). In this program relationships among words such as *virtuoso, novice,* and *philanthropist* were probed with questions such as, "Is a virtuoso a novice?" "Could a virtuoso be a philanthropist?" Venn diagrams (Nagy 1988) and Semantic Feature Analysis (McNeil 1984) are two other activities that can clarify distinctions among closely related concepts.

The children were able to come up with many examples of computers: IBM, Apple, Commodore, and Atari. However, this was because the word used was appropriate for the technique. The technique could not be used in the

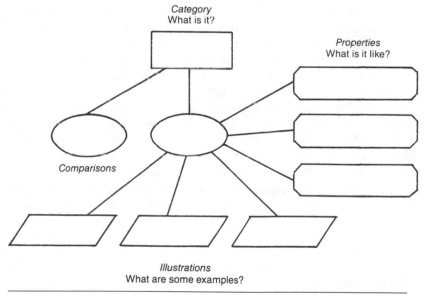

Figure 4. Blank concept of definition map. Reprinted with permission, from R. Schwartz and the International Reading Association, *Learning to Learn Vocabulary in Content Area Textbooks*, Journal of Reading (1988).

same way for the word *squire* in the lesson with the *Knights and Tournaments* (Riese and LaSalle 1986) text discussed earlier; because the text did not contain any examples of squires, the children would not know any, and names of particular squires would not be useful. Schwartz (1988) points out that the technique can and should be used flexibly. In mapping words like *squire* children can provide illustrations of the properties rather than examples of the term. (Note that the newer version of the word map uses *illustrations* as one of the headings.) If the word *squire* were mapped in this way, *helps the knight into his armor* might be given as an illustration of the property *helps the knight*. Schwartz (1988) suggests one way of introducing the word map might be to ask children to map themselves as the concept.

In the next step of the demonstration lesson the children were asked to write a definition of computer using the group word map as a guide. It was gratifying to see how pleased these remedial readers were to accomplish a task easily in which they had previously experienced so much failure. In the second lesson, I read aloud the section of the textbook (King, Dennis, and Patter 1980) that discussed the word *sound* while the children followed along in their own books.

> The Coast Range is quite low in Washington and Oregon. It is broken at two places. These are at Puget Sound, in the north and near the mouth of the Columbia River. A *sound* is a body of water like a large bay extending into the land. There are good harbors on the sound and on the Columbia River (p. 359).

This discussion of *sound* included information that had nothing to do with its definition and information that should be part of the definition. Although all parts of the word map were covered, there were only two properties and one example given in the text; I modeled the process for the children explaining why I chose particular information to fill in the map. I also filled in another example, *Long Island Sound*, explaining that I knew about this example from my own experience. As suggested by Schwartz and Raphael, I also explained to the children that three properties and three examples were not absolutely necessary; they might have more or less than three. I then read aloud another text section that discussed the word *inlet* and the children and I filled in the word map together. After I read aloud a section discussing the word *volcano*, the children filled in the word maps individually. I gave them assistance in finding the information. For example, I pointed out that the names of volcanoes would begin with capital letters so they could skim the section for words with capital letters, but that they would have to read the section carefully to be sure that the word with capital letters was the name of a volcano and not the name of something else. The children then used their maps to write definitions of *volcano*. The girl who filled in the sample word map wrote the following definition:

> A volcano is a mountain that has a hole in the top that hot liquid rock and lava come out of and it erupts every ten years. Some examples are Mauna Loa and Kilauea.

Although it does contain some incorrect information, such as a false generalization based on something this girl had previously learned about a particular volcano, this is a pretty good definition for a remedial ESL reader who is using the technique for the first time. Other children's definitions were also quite good. Note that this child has made use of the word *erupt* which was not used in the text.

Schwartz and Raphael (1985) suggest that the next step would be to present children with texts that contained only partial context, i.e., situations in which information answering one of the questions is not present. In the first lesson our list provided only partial context for the word *computer* and the children were able to handle it quite well, but the word was a familiar one and the use of examples was appropriate. Working with partial contexts for unfamiliar words would be a much more difficult task. Children probably need a great deal of experience with texts that answer all three questions before they can deal with partial contexts. The text the children used was particularly good because the context was complete. Showing children how to use the technique with partial contexts is also important, however, in order to achieve the primary goal of having the children internalize the structure and use it in learning word meanings independently. As discussed by Schwartz and Raphael (1985), this would involve teaching children to locate information in sources other than the text, such as the dictionary and the encyclopedia.

Semantic Mapping

This technique has already been presented in Chapter 5 as an effective one for building and/or activating background knowledge about the topic of the text. Using semantic mapping, the teacher also provides vocabulary instruction. For example, in the pre-reading lesson with the *Knights and Tournaments* (Riese and LaSalle 1986) text, a semantic map was developed for *knights*, the topic of the text. In activating or building prior knowledge related to knights the children deepened their understanding of the meaning of the word *knight*. Semantic mapping helped them build on what they already knew about knights and helped them see the relationships with many other words. The children also learned the meanings of other words such as *armor* and *lance* in a meaningful way, i.e., in the context of a particular subject (knights), and in relation to each other.

In using semantic mapping for vocabulary instruction a teacher may also introduce new words related to the topic as part of the pre-reading discussion. For example, I could have introduced *tournaments* in our pre-reading semantic mapping of knights and asked the children to place it in the proper category related to knights. I decided, instead, to wait until after reading the text. The children, then, were able to add ideas and words from the text to expand the semantic map of *knights*.

When a semantic map is used to activate children's background knowledge before reading, expansion of the semantic map after reading can be effective for vocabulary instruction, as well as a way of connecting text information with prior knowledge. This integration of background knowledge and

127

vocabulary instruction is a particular strength of the semantic mapping technique. A weakness is that unfamiliar words in the text not related to the word being mapped cannot be taught in this way (Nagy 1988).

Although semantic mapping is effective, it takes a substantial amount of time. Therefore, words to be mapped should be chosen carefully to include as much vocabulary from the text as possible, but avoid the temptation to include unfamiliar words that do not really fit into the semantic map. *Semantic Mapping: Classroom Applications* (Heimlich and Pittelman 1986) contains many sample lessons using semantic mapping for vocabulary instruction both before and after reading.

DURING READING

Vocabulary instruction during reading should be less formal than either before or after reading. When children have been made aware of words, they may ask for the meanings of some words when they are reading. If there is sufficient context for children to determine the meanings themselves, they should be encouraged to do so; if not, the teacher should provide a simple explanation during reading. Of course, further instruction and practice should be provided. The teacher can also provide vocabulary instruction during reading by pointing out situations where context is helpful and modeling the thinking processes involved in making effective use of context. This kind of instruction makes children aware of the value of learning how to use context.

The clarifying strategy used in the Reciprocal Teaching technique (Palincsar and Brown 1984) (described in Chapter 8) teaches children to look for words whose meanings they do not understand and to determine the meaning through context or asking for an explanation.

During-reading instruction should not focus on individual word meanings to the extent that children's attention is drawn away from understanding the main ideas of the text or understanding the point of the story.

AFTER READING

After-reading activities can provide practice with words that were the focus of before- and during-reading instruction. Meanings of other words in the text that are interesting, useful, and offer the opportunity to teach children how to use structural analysis or context as cues to word meaning are also appropriately taught after reading. Semantic mapping may also be used successfully at this point.

STRUCTURAL ANALYSIS

While structural analysis aids word recognition, it should also be used as an aid in determining word meanings (Readence, Bean, and Baldwin 1985; Vacca and Vacca 1986). When combined with context, it provides a way of connecting unfamiliar to familiar words and learning new meanings independently. Structural analysis instruction should not involve memorization of lists of roots or affixes, but should consist of teaching students to use their knowledge of word parts in known words to help get some sense of the meanings of unknown words. Readence, Bean, and Baldwin (1985) describe a lesson using the Mor-phemic Analysis Strategy in which children are guided toward the meaning of the unfamiliar word *matricide* by noting its similarity to known words such as *maternity* and *maternal*, *suicide* and *homicide*.

Structural analysis instruction for remedial readers should probably focus on compound words or words with a recognizable stem to which an affix has been added (Vacca and Vacca 1986). Affixes that are taught should have invar-iant meanings such as those found in Vacca and Vacca (1986), or those most commonly found in words (Devine 1986). A list of affixes useful in particular content areas can be found in Burmeister (1978). Dale and O'Rourke (1971) is an excellent source for comprehensive lists of roots, affixes, and word origins; however, many of the words listed are used infrequently so teachers should be selective in using these lists.

CONTEXT

The main goal of the pre-reading techniques that present words in context (Preview in Context, Contextual Redefinition, and Concept of Definition) is to teach children the meanings of words that are necessary for understanding their texts. Teacher modeling and discussions related to the ways in which context signals word meaning make these pre-reading techniques effective in accomplishing a secondary goal—teaching children how to use context for word meanings independently. Providing instruction in the use of context dur-ing reading is also important if students are to see the value of using these techniques independently.

Schatz and Baldwin (1986) define context in terms of the sentence in which the target word appears, and in the sentences immediately preceding and following it. In many cases, however, the entire text may provide a context for the word. Looking back over a text after reading for information that pro-vides near and far context for an unknown word may be more valuable than presenting the words in artificial sentence contexts. Of course, teachers should be sure that there is sufficient context, and especially with remedial readers, they will need to provide modeling and support before children can engage in such activities on their own.

Since a single context gives only limited information, presenting words in multiple contexts is recommended. Gipe's (1978-1979) interactive context method described in McNeil (1984) presents unfamiliar words in three familiar contexts in three sentences, and is an effective method for vocabulary instruc-tion. However, it is somewhat artificial in that words are not studied in the context of complete texts.

In basal readers where there is repetition of words the text may provide multiple contexts for a particular word. For example, in *The Little Green Man* (Damjan 1975), the word *dull* occurs three times and the word *sigh* twice. When I used this text with a group of fourth graders, I did not present the words before reading, as suggested by the manual, because I felt there was sufficient context for the children to determine the meanings on their own. The meaning of the word *dull* was checked during reading right after the second and third times that it occurred. (After Little Green Man watches a mechanical cat chase a mechanical mouse):

> "How *dull*," said Number 737. "If only the mouse would run after the cat once in a while. But the machines don't work that way. If only we had some real animals on this planet—even a bird. Machines are so *dull*" (Damjan and Kenelski 1975, p. 9)

This word was checked during reading because knowing its meaning is important to understanding the story; Little Green Man leaves his own planet and comes to Earth because he is bored. The meaning was checked after the passage above because the first occurrence of *dull* does not provide enough context to determine its meaning. Little Green Man Number 737 pushes a button to get his four green pills for food and says "How easy life is—and how *dull*." If one did not know the meaning of the word *dull*, this sentence would not be helpful. Little Green Man could be happy because he got his food so easily, or he could be unhappy because he doesn't like pills for food.

After reading, we looked for *dull* and *sigh* in the text and checked to make sure that the meanings the children had come up with made sense in every context. *Sigh* was also important to discuss since Little Green Man sighed once because things were dull and once because he was happy. The children were able to make use of the surrounding context to distinguish between the two situations. Discussion focused on how the children had determined word meanings while reading. Instruction like this, which supports children's use of context strategies in texts, is an example of the combined model of comprehension instruction recommended in Chapter 4. (However, note that the text in the lesson just discussed was a narrative and the words were Type 3 words— those for which children already had the concepts.) This type of during-reading instruction, use of the cloze procedure that will be more fully described in Chapter 7, and the Concept of Definition technique, all expose children to realistic situations in which there are a variety of clues to word meanings. These activities often make better sense than programs using artificial texts where context is provided by a particular kind of clue, e.g., comparison/contrast or restatement.

With more difficult pre-reading concepts, artificial contexts, such as those provided by the Contextual Redefinition technique, may be more appropriate. In using these artificial contexts teachers should focus on how the contexts provide clues to word meanings rather than on identifying the particular type of clue.

As suggested earlier, after-reading activities can provide the practice so necessary for learning difficult words. Many activities used in the intensive vocabulary instruction discussed earlier are described in Beck and McKeown (1983) and Nagy (1988). Activities like these can be integrated into other post-reading activities designed for evaluating comprehension as well as enriching and extending students' knowledge of word meanings.

In providing vocabulary instruction just as in providing instruction for building or activating background knowledge in comprehension, teachers should use a variety of techniques. The difficulty of the concept, the level of the reader's word knowledge, the way the text presents the word, and the teacher's long- and short-term goals for vocabulary and comprehension instruction are all factors that should affect choice of a particular technique.

7

TECHNIQUES IN WRITTEN LANGUAGE INSTRUCTION—SENTENCE STRUCTURE, COHESION, AND TEXT STRUCTURE

This chapter continues the discussion of linguistic knowledge as a factor that affects reading comprehension. Here we move beyond the word level so that the focus is on children's ability to understand different types of sentence structure, the relationship of one sentence to another, and the structure of texts. Successful readers use their knowledge of language and text structure, as well as their world knowledge, to help them comprehend written text. Chapter 5 points out that linguistic knowledge is particularly helpful when the topic of the text is unfamiliar. Linguistic knowledge, therefore, is a critical cuing system for older children who have entered the stage of reading to learn and who read in school mainly with expository content area texts.

In Chapter 2, I discuss the fact that many remedial readers have language differences or language disorders and therefore do not have the linguistic knowledge necessary to understand the language used in many texts. Chapter 3 points out that many texts are inconsiderate in their language and structure. The way language is used in these texts causes problems even for children with normal language development, i.e., the structure of the sentences may be far too complex, the relationships between sentences may be unclear, and the text may be poorly organized so that its structure cannot be determined easily. In addition, many middle grade children, at all reading levels, appear to be unaware of different expository text structures; thus they are unable to use structural cues as aids to comprehension (Meyer, Brandt, and Bluth 1980).

Therefore, just as the teacher must be alert to discrepancies between text content and children's background knowledge, so too he or she must be alert to disparities between language used in the text and the language ability of the children. Once again the teacher must serve as a bridge between children and text, using a mediated model of instruction to provide the scaffolding and support children need so they can expand their linguistic knowledge and use it to comprehend text.

This instruction should not attempt to make children into linguists. They do not need conscious knowledge of how language is structured, but they must be able to use it effectively to comprehend written text. Teachers, however, do need explicit knowledge about how English sentences and texts are structured and about the language development of school-age children. Thus the four sections of this chapter—Sentence Structure, Relations Between Sentences (Cohesion), Narrative Text Structure, and Expository Text Structure—contain brief summaries of information in these areas, based on research in the fields of linguistics, language development, text analysis, cognitive psychology, and reading.

In addition, each of the sections presents teaching techniques. Many of the techniques suggested by other authors (e.g., Baumann 1986) are examples of the explicit instruction version of the mediated model of comprehension instruction. Strategies for understanding sentences and the relations between them are introduced at the sentence level using this model. Strategies for using text structure as an aid to comprehension are introduced in short paragraphs that have been especially constructed as ideal examples of particular structures. Only after practice in these artificial and isolated situations does the child learn to use the strategies with the texts used in class. At times, if a child has a real problem with a particular aspect of language or text structure, this type of bottom up approach may be necessary.

However, often children can be alerted to and assisted with problems arising from difficult or unfamiliar language and/or alerted to language and structural cues as they read text for information and/or enjoyment. Most of the techniques presented here suggest ways teachers can provide this type of support, guiding children toward independent use of linguistic cues as they seek to understand written text. These techniques mainly are examples of the text-based version or the combined-approach version of the mediated model of comprehension instruction. Explicit instruction techniques provide practice in the use of linguistic cues.

SENTENCE STRUCTURE

LINGUISTICS

In the past instruction in syntax consisted of learning to analyze sentences in terms of their surface structure. Children were taught to identify the parts of speech and to diagram sentences to show how the parts of speech related to one another. At the outset, describing the surface structure of different languages was also the goal of the science of linguistics.

However, in 1957, Noam Chomsky revolutionized the field by moving beyond this goal (Chomsky 1957). He offered a theory of how people use syntax to understand language. Chomsky suggests that in addition to surface structure, sentences have a deep structure that is universal to all languages and that consists of relationships. Sentences with different surface structures may have the same deep structure as in the two sentences: *Mary hit the ball* and *The ball was hit by Mary*. On the other hand, sentences can have the same surface structure but the relationships signalled by this structure may be totally different, as in the two sentences: *He is eager to please* and *He is easy to please*. In the first sentence *he* is the agent of the action, *he* is doing the pleasing. In the second sentence *he* is the recipient of the action; *he* is being pleased. Comprehension of a sentence involves translation from the surface structure to the deep structure. Simple sentences like *Mary hit the ball* have the same pattern at both levels of structure while a sentence in the passive voice like *The ball was hit by Mary* must be transformed in order to be understood.

Transformational grammar (Chomsky 1965) emphasizes the role syntax plays in determining the meaning of sentences. Case grammar (Fillmore 1968) emphasizes the role of semantics. Fillmore proposed that there is an underlying level of the deep structure which consists of universal concepts that specify all the possible relationships between nouns and verbs. Sentences consist of propositions (noun-verb relationships) and modality which includes such aspects as tense, mood, or negation. Complex sentences may contain many propositions. Readers and listeners must perform special operations before they can make the transformations necessary to make the translation into the deep structure. For example, McNeil (1987) points out that in order to understand the sentence *We elected Mary president*, a reader must insert the idea that *Mary is president* into the basic sentence *We elected Mary*.

Transformational grammar and case grammar focus on the role of structure in determining the meaning of sentences. More recent sociolinguistic theories (Searle 1965; Halliday 1975) emphasize the communicative function of language. They point out that pragmatics, or the way in which language is used, is another factor affecting its meaning. For example, a child in a class might utter the sentence, *It's very hot in here,* not as a comment on the temperature but as a request for the window to be opened. The teacher would probably be more direct if she wanted the window open and say something like *Please open the window.* The point with regard to comprehension is that the same sentence can have different meanings or different sentences may be used to convey the same meaning depending upon who uses the sentence and when and where.

There are two important implications for comprehension instruction arising from these theories:

1. Meaning expressed in the deep structure of the language is not always so readily apparent in the surface structure.
2. Sentences cannot be understood in isolation. Their interpretation depends on the context in which they are presented and the function they serve.

LANGUAGE DEVELOPMENT

Early theorists in the field of language development considered the preschool years the critical years for language development. It was recognized that children's vocabularies expanded significantly throughout the school years, but syntactic development was seen as involving only minor refinements. Children's conversation was described as similar to that of adults in that it contained all the syntactic structures used by adults in normal conversation (Chomsky 1969). Although the preschool years are still viewed as an extremely important period of language development, research demonstrates that there is considerable syntactical development in the school years, but many children still have difficulty understanding certain sentence types in the middle elementary grades (e.g., Bormuth et al. 1970; Chomsky 1969). The sentence types that are difficult for school-age children tend to be those that are exceptions in some way to the common order of information presentation (in English) and are more likely to be found in written English than in oral English. For example, sentences in the passive voice and sentences with relative clauses embedded between the subject and the verb (e.g., *The witch who yelled at the children grabbed the box.*) violate the principle that the noun preceding the verb is the subject of the sentence. When the sentence above was used in a study with fourth and fifth graders, many of them responded "The children" to the question "Who grabbed the box?" (MacGinitie, Katz, and Maria 1980) Other studies (e.g., Maratsos 1974) demonstrate that it is not just the order of the words that make such a sentence difficult to interpret but the interaction of that order and the nature of the words. A sentence like *The boy who broke the window ran away* does not pose a comprehension problem since the child knows that the noun nearest the verb (window) is incapable of running away.

One solution that might come to a teacher's mind is to search for materials with more familiar sentence constructions. Devine (1986) points out that "writers frequently embed several kernel sentences into one many-layered, idea-packed sentence, forgetting that—although they feel comfortable with such constructions—their readers may lose track of the subjects and predicates of the various embedded sentences" (p. 190). Texts with a preponderance of this type of language should certainly be avoided.

On the other hand, we must not forget our obligation to expand children's linguistic knowledge. The salesman referred to in Chapter 3 who told me that the series he sold contained only short sentences also indicated that it did not have any sentences in the passive voice because research had shown that this type of sentence was more difficult to understand. In the long run, as was discussed in Chapter 3, this kind of misguided attempt to help children understand what they read will hinder their comprehension. Children not exposed to more difficult language will never learn to understand it. The passive voice exists because it permits the expression of ideas in a particular way that is not possible in the active voice, i.e., emphasis is on the object or content rather than the actor. Children not exposed to the passive voice probably will never be able to understand or use it.

Sentences that express relationships by using certain conjunctions may also pose problems for children. A sentence like *I did my homework after I played* is more difficult to understand than *After I played, I did my homework* since the child must transform the order of events to understand the first sentence (McNeil 1987). Once again world knowledge is an important factor affecting the interpretation of the first sentence. Part of its difficulty is that the two events described can occur in either order. You can play first and then do your homework or you can do your homework and then play. In addition, comprehension of sentences containing the conjunction *because*, such as *I hurt myself because I fell off my bike*, which also reverse the natural order of events, pose difficulties for school-age children (Emerson 1979). Bormuth et al. (1970) found that 44% of the fourth graders in their study had difficulty understanding a sentence like *As we entered, the curtain rose*. In this sentence one must recognize that the events happened simultaneously even though one is mentioned before the other.

Sentences containing other conjunctions such as *if* (*If you had some money, you would buy some candy*) and *although* (*Although it rained recently, the ground is still dry*) are difficult to understand (Bormuth 1970; Hood and Bloom 1979) because they involve entailment, i.e., the truth of one clause implies the truth of the other. Sentences with *although* are more difficult because they involve negative rather than positive entailment. *Although* allows us to express an exception (Rain usually makes the ground wet, although in this case it is still dry). Owens (1984) points out that conjunctions expressing relationships with negative aspects are more difficult to understand than conjunctions that express positive relationships. Thus *because* is learned first followed by *if, although,* and *unless.*

Even when conjunctions are not involved, negation in a sentence increases its difficulty. In simple sentences the *not* may be missed. However, sentences that are most difficult to interpret are those referred to as semantic inversions, sentences like *Which sentence is less difficult to understand?* or *She is not unattractive*. In order to understand these sentences we must transform them to their opposite (McNeil 1987).

The implication for comprehension instruction that arises from these discoveries in development of children's language is that, just as we cannot assume children's comprehension at the text level, so too we cannot assume it at the sentence level.

COMPREHENSION INSTRUCTION: SENTENCE STRUCTURE

A number of activities can help children understand difficult sentences. Although these activities present sentences in isolation, they all involve construction of sentences so that they are helpful for writing as well as for reading. Weaver (1979) (cited in McNeil 1987) increased comprehension substantially by having children rearrange scrambled words into meaningful sentences by first finding the verb. Then the children were taught to ask *wh* questions (*who, what, where, when,* and *how*) about the verb and to look for words that answer the questions so that the clause makes sense both syntactically and semantically. Once they became proficient with simple sentences, they were timed and urged to increase the speed at which they solved the sentence anagram. Then more complex sentences with more than one clause were introduced. Although Weaver worked with individual children, McNeil (1987) recommended the activity for groups. Sentence combining, an activity in which several simple sentences are combined into one complex sentence, also improves reading comprehension (Straw and Schreiner 1982; White and Karl 1980).

Probably the best means of improving comprehension of difficult sentence structures, however, is to help children understand them in basal reader stories, content area textbooks, and children's literature. Difficult sentence structures are identified here so that teachers can be alert to them as they read texts to use with children. Teachers can point out these difficult sentences, and through modeling can help children to be alert to their occurrence. Modeling the strategy of clarifying as part of the Reciprocal Teaching procedure (which was suggested in Chapter 6 as a way of providing vocabulary instruction during reading) is also an effective way of teaching children to understand complex sentences during reading. (The Reciprocal Teaching technique will be described in Chapter 8.)

Identifying difficult sentences is only the first step. Children will also need help in understanding them. At times, the teacher may need to explain a sentence. However, usually teachers can use *wh* questions appropriate to the particular sentence to help children actively construct the meaning. In some cases questions like "What is the topic is this sentence?" and "What does it say about the topic?" might be appropriate, while in other cases questions like "Who is doing something in this sentence?" "What are they doing?" and "Where are they doing it?" might be more appropriate. Questions like these will help children break the sentence into parts for easier comprehension. The questions should be presented as models of the types of questions children should ask when reading independently. Teachers should urge children to paraphrase sentences, checking with the teacher and with one another to be sure they have captured the meaning of the original sentence. Above all, the sentence should be viewed as part of a text and a context. Teachers should encourage children to use their world knowledge and the information contained in other sentences in the text as aids to understanding a difficult sentence.

FIGURATIVE LANGUAGE

A sentence may have a simple structure and yet be difficult to comprehend because it contains figurative language. Similes and metaphors involve comparisons between a literal element called the *topic* and a figurative element called the *vehicle*. What is common between the topic and the vehicle is referred to as *ground*. A metaphor (That soldier is a lion) may be more difficult to comprehend than a simile (That soldier is as brave as a lion) because the ground must be inferred. There are also aspects of the topic and the vehicle that are dissimilar. These are referred to as *tension*. It is the tension between the topic and the vehicle that give figurative language its freshness and appeal. In the sentence "That soldier was as brave as a lion," the topic is *soldier*, the vehicle is *lion*, the ground is the fact that soldiers and lions are both brave, and the tension involves the fact that the soldier is a person while the lion is an animal (the soldier fights in a war while the lion hunts for food.)

Traditionally, reading instruction involving figurative language focuses on identifying the forms of figurative language and practicing translating it into literal language. This type of instruction assumes that figurative language is inherently difficult for children because they have difficulty distinguishing the literal from the non literal. We have already argued against this assumption in Chapter 4 by pointing out that even young children can make inferences (Frederiksen 1975, 1979; Kintsch 1974; Mandler and Johnson 1977a). Moreover, primary grade children use figurative language extensively (Pearson and Johnson 1978).

Instead of focusing on the form of figurative language or on translating non-literal language to literal language, instruction must focus on the vocabulary used in the metaphor or simile (Pearson and Johnson 1978; Searfoss and Readence 1985). Similes and metaphors can only be comprehended if one has schemata for both the topic and the vehicle and if one's schema for each element contains the element common to both, the ground. The following sentence is an example that is difficult for most of us to understand because, although we may think we know the meaning of the word *cheetah*, our schema for *cheetah* does not contain the common element that is the ground.

> "Martha, we've got to get rid of the cat; he walks across our furniture like a cheetah" (Searfoss and Readence 1985, p. 220).

Most of us would find this sentence difficult to interpret because we think of cheetahs as big and spotted and fast. Yet none of these elements applies to the situation. The sentence says that the cat is walking, so speed can't be the problem. In order to understand the sentence, one needs to know that a cheetah cannot retract his claws, so if a cheetah walked over the furniture, he would scratch it.

If we want to help children understand figurative language, we need to provide the type of vocabulary instruction described in Chapter 6, instruction that focuses on the connotations of words, their relations with other words, and the contexts in which they occur. Context is particularly important in determining whether a sentence should be interpreted literally or figuratively (McNeil 1987). If the sentence "You have egg on your face" was spoken by a mother to her young child who had just finished breakfast, it might well be interpreted literally, while if it was spoken by a football player to another player who had just fumbled the ball, it should be interpreted figuratively. Thus whether sentences are difficult to understand because of difficult structure or figurative language, comprehension instruction on the sentence level must often deal with them in context rather than in isolation.

RELATIONS BETWEEN SENTENCES: COHESION

In the seminal work in linguistics, *Cohesion in English*, Halliday and Hasan (1976) identify the ways in which the English language links sentences in a text. This analysis is important because although text structure had been studied for centuries, no one had ever looked at the ways an author links sentences to establish local coherence—relating adjoining sentences that may be structurally independent. Cohesion is different from global coherence or text structure. Global coherence in text includes other factors such as organization, situational consistency, and cohesion. Cohesion exists in the text while "coherence is both a text-related and a reader-related phenomenon" (Moe and Irwin 1986, p. 5). The reader establishes a coherent mental representation of the text partly by means of cohesion but also by means of other factors such as world knowledge, text structure, and context.

Halliday and Hasan (1976) provide a taxonomy of cohesive ties (the links that establish cohesion). This taxonomy is summarized below. Although all of these cohesive ties can be used to provide links within sentences as well as between sentences, the focus here is on between-sentence cohesive ties. Thus, the examples are all cohesive ties linking sentences. Most of these examples posed problems for some of the middle grade remedial readers whom I taught in my Title I classes.

Cohesive Ties

Reference—A word that cannot be understood in its own right. It must make reference to something else for its interpretation.

Type	Example
Personal Pronouns (*I, he, she, it,* etc.)	Traffic policemen ride around in police boats. *They* even give out traffic tickets (Rauch and Clements 1974, p. 21).
Demonstrative Pronouns (*this, that,* etc.)	Some people prefer the larger, less expensive waterbus. *This* is a motor driven boat (Rauch and Clements 1974, p. 21).
Demonstrative Adverbs (*here, there,* etc.)	On the reservation, not even the winter winds bent his back. *There* he stood as straight as the trunk of the pine tree (Smucker 1976, p. 12).
Comparative Adjectives or Pronouns (*other, same, different,* etc.)	The driver, or gondolier, stands on a deck at the back of the gondola. He rows, or moves, the boat with a long oar. Some people prefer the *larger, less expensive* waterbus (Rauch and Clements 1974, p. 21).

Substitution—A word that is used as a substitute and that sometimes adds an element of contrast.

Type	Example
Noun Substitution (*one, some,* etc.)	There is a city in Europe that does not have a paved street. It does not have *one* made of dirt (Rauch and Clements 1974, p. 21).

Verb Substitution	Traffic policemen ride around in police boats.
(*do*)	When they *do*, they give out traffic tickets
	(Rauch and Clements 1974, p. 21).
Clause Substitution	Is he going to pass the exam? I hope *so*.
(*so*)	

Ellipsis—Words are left out.

Type	Example
Verbal Ellipsis	Jim: Hi, Tony! I see you have to shovel the
Clausal Ellipsis	sidewalk. *Too bad!* I was going to ask you to
	come over and watch TV.
Nominal Ellipsis	Tony: *Sounds like fun.* But the shoveling has
	to get done (A Snow Job, *Sprint*, Feb. 1,
	1979, p. 5).

Lexical Cohesion—The same term, a synonym, or a superordinate term is used.

Type	Example
Same Word	"We want boots James can put on," said
	Mother.
	"We can find some boots for *James*," said the
	man (Clymer and Gates 1969, p. 39).
Synonym	Waterways are the streets of this city. These
	avenues are called canals (Rauch and Clem-
	ents 1974, p. 21).
Superordinate Term	With all these *boats* moving through the busy
	canals, traffic must be regulated (Rauch and
	Clements 1974, p. 21). (This sentence oc-
	curred after a paragraph discussing the gon-
	dola and the waterbus.)

Conjunction—Links are made between two ideas so that the understanding of the second idea is related to the understanding of the first idea.

Type	Example
Additive or Alternative	There are owls and bluebirds and ostriches.
(*and, or, too, also*, etc.)	But bluebirds don't look like owls, and owls
	don't look like ostriches. There were many
	kinds of dinosaurs, *too*.
Adversative	There are owls and bluebirds and ostriches.
(*however, but*, etc.)	*But* bluebirds don't look like owls, and owls
	don't look like ostriches. There were many
	kinds of dinosaurs, too.
Causal or Conditional	If only he could get to be good at some other
(*so, then, therefore,*	sport. *Then* he wouldn't mind looking like
etc.)	such a fool at baseball (Smucker 1976, p. 31).
Temporal	Mr. Clark agreed and walked to the starting
(*then, next*, etc.)	line. He shaded his eyes to survey the run-
	ning area. *Then* he told the boys and girls to
	move back from the line (Smucker 1976,
	p. 31).

The first four categories of cohesive ties described above are similar in that in these, unlike the conjunction category, the cohesive tie replaces the word or words to which it refers (Ellipsis replaces a previous idea with a 0). One idea cannot be understood without reference to the other.

In a few cases the reader may have to read ahead in order to determine the referent for the cohesive tie. This is called cataphoric reference. Cataphoric reference, which reverses the common linguistic order, has been found to be a source of difficulty for school-age children (Barnitz 1980; Chomsky 1969; Monson 1982).

ANAPHORA

In most cases in text, however, the cohesive tie relates back to something that has already been read. This is called anaphoric reference or anaphora. Several reading experts (Baumann 1986; Pearson and Johnson 1978) focus on problems and instruction related to anaphora, using taxonomies categorizing anaphoric cohesive ties in slightly different ways than Halliday and Hasan. For example, Baumann and Stevenson's (1986) Selective Taxonomy of Anaphoric Relationships focuses on the referent for the cohesive tie rather than the cohesive tie itself. The main categories in this taxonomy are noun, verb, and clause substitution.

Anaphora can be a source of comprehension difficulty for children in grades two through grade eight (Gottsdanker-Willekens 1986). Cohesive ties within a sentence are easier to understand than those operating between sentences (Barnitz 1980). This is partly because the closer the cohesive tie is to the referent the easier it is to understand (Barnitz 1986; Moberly 1978). When the referent and cohesive tie are separated by several sentences the situation becomes even more difficult.

Cohesive ties that replace nouns or noun phrases are easier to learn and understand than those that replace verbs or verb phrases, and they in turn are easier than those that replace clauses (Barnitz 1980). Pronouns are the easiest type of anaphora (Moberly 1978; Monson 1982), with personal pronouns easier to understand than demonstrative pronouns (Bormuth et al. 1970). Goodman and Gespass (1983), in a study that used longer passages which provided more context for understanding pronouns, found that children in grades two through six had less difficulty with pronouns than with other elements in text. They argue that children have more understanding of the elements of cohesion than some studies suggest. However, they only considered pronouns. Different studies (Lesgold 1974; Moberly 1978; Monson 1982) found different orders of difficulty for substitution, ellipsis, and lexical cohesion. Lesgold (1974) suggested that this was due to differences in the semantic content of the texts and in the background knowledge of the readers in the different studies.

Comprehension of cohesive ties, like comprehension of difficult sentence structures, rests on factors such as world knowledge, the rest of the text, the context in which the text is read, as well as the specific nature of the cohesive tie. Often world knowledge resolves pronoun ambiguity. However, teachers need to be alert to situations in which world knowledge is not helpful. Part of the reason that the middle-grade children I worked with had difficulty with the cohesive ties in the Venice passage (Rauch and Clements 1974) was that their prior knowledge about cities was not helpful in understanding text about a canal city like Venice.

While children's ability to comprehend anaphora increases with age (Gottsdanker-Willekens 1986), it appears that situations involving cohesive ties that may cause a comprehension problem also increase (Phillips and Zinar 1979). Teachers need to be alert to the occurrence of these situations in a text: the use of many cohesive ties, a substantial distance between a cohesive tie and its referent, and/or a cohesive tie whose referent is a substantial portion of text rather than a word or phrase. An example of the latter situation occurs in a text section designed for third graders (Lauber 1959). One paragraph of the text discusses how rain carries away top soil when the ground is bare. In the first sentence of the next paragraph, "In the forest—or on planted land—*this* does not happen" (Phillips and Zinar 1979, p. 12), it is hard to determine whether the referent for the demonstrative pronoun *this* is the whole first paragraph or only some parts of it.

COMPREHENSION INSTRUCTION: ANAPHORA

Techniques for helping children understand anaphoric relations between sentences are similar to those used to help children understand individual sentences. Teachers need to develop children's awareness of possible sources of difficulty in connecting a cohesive tie with its referent. Teacher's questions that focus on matching cohesive ties with their referents can help children make these matches; in addition they can alert the teacher to possible comprehension problems. For example, when I worked with children on the Venice passage I asked questions like, "It says 'This is a motor-driven boat.' What is a motor-driven boat?" (See example for demonstrative prounouns in taxonomy on page 139) or "It says the waterbus is larger and less expensive. Larger and less expensive than what?" (See example for comparative adjectives in taxonomy on page 139.)

When children have difficulty answering questions like these, teachers can model their own processes in finding the answers. For example "It says 'This is a motor-driven boat.' The *this* tells me that it is something the author has mentioned before. The sentence right before talks about a waterbus. The sentences before that talk about a gondola rowed with a long oar; so the waterbus must be the motor driven boat." Once again, the clarifying strategy in the Reciprocal Teaching procedure is one way of providing this type of instruction.

Useful activities include those in which children match cohesive ties with their referents by drawing an arrow from the cohesive tie to the referent (Baumann and Stevenson 1986). At first the teacher can underline the cohesive tie; as children become more proficient, they can find the cohesive ties themselves. Performing this type of exercise with their own written material may help children write more cohesively; it may also aid in comprehension. Complete texts should be used whenever possible though at times it may be necessary to start with pairs of sentences. Below, a paragraph from the Venice passage demonstrates what part of a completed exercise might look like.

The gondolas hold two to four passengers. The driver, or gondolier, stands on a deck at the back of the gondola. He rows, or moves, the boat with a long oar. Some people prefer the larger, less expensive waterbus. This is a motor driven boat. It makes scheduled stops along the larger canals.

COMPREHENSION INSTRUCTION: CONJUNCTIONS

As the taxonomy on page 140 demonstrates there are many different conjunctions in English that signal several kinds of relationships. Conjunctions can relate ideas within sentences and between sentences. They can also act as signal words to a particular text structure relating large portions of texts to one another.

Although adults and children have more trouble when they must infer a connection than when it is made explicit with a conjunction (Irwin 1980; Irwin and Pulver 1984), school-age children have problems with certain conjunctions even on the sentence level (see previous section on sentence comprehension). Since there are so many conjunctions, deciding which ones to teach and when to teach them becomes a problem similar to that encountered with teaching vocabulary. As with vocabulary, teachers should provide instruction that focuses on conjunctions that cause problems for the children and those that are important for understanding the texts. Since conjunctions often play an important role in content area text, they can be taught as one element that helps children understand this type of text. As with the other types of cohesive ties, teachers can point out conjunctions and use questions and modeling to demonstrate the way in which they signal relationships.

A particular problem with conjunctions is that often the same word can signal different types of relationships. In the taxonomy on page 140 the word *then* is used as a signal for a conditional and for a temporal relationship. A question like, "What would have to happen before he wouldn't mind looking like such a fool at baseball?" along with an explanation of how *if* and *then* often go together would be appropriate in helping children understand how *then* signals the conditional relationship in the example. Questions like, "Which happened first—Mr. Clark walked to the starting line or Mr. Clark told the boys and girls to move back from the line? How do you know?" would be more appropriate for helping children understand how *then* signals a temporal relationship.

Sentence completion activities and sentence cloze activities in which children are asked to fill in a blank or sentence with an appropriate connective

help assess problems that children may have with conjunctions, as well as provide opportunities for modeling strategies for using conjunctions as aids to
comprehension. If the sentences are used for assessment, children should be
familiar with the topics. For example, before beginning a series of lessons on
adversative conjunctions, one group of children was asked to complete sentences like the following (MacGinitie and Maria 1982):

My mother told me to do the dishes but _____.
I ordered a plain hamburger even though _____.
My food looked good yet _____.

Completion of sentences as follows indicated that most of the children had no
problems with *but* but did not understand the use of *yet* and *even though*.

My mother told me to do the dishes but I didn't.
I ordered a plain hamburger even though they put pickles on it.
My food looked good, yet it fell on the floor.

We were particulary interested in teaching children to use adversative
conjunctions as aids in learning new information that contradicted misconceptions they held. Beginning with the more familiar adversative *but*, we moved
from sentences on familiar topics to sentences on topics about which children
had misconceptions, using pairs of function cloze and content cloze sentences
like those listed below to highlight the role of the adversative conjunction.

Movies often show octopuses attacking divers, _____ they really swim away
if a person comes close to them.

   a. and
   b. but

Octopuses are afraid of human beings, _____ they swim away if they see a
person.

   a. and
   b. but

(Function cloze)

Gorillas are timid creatures, and if you met a gorilla in the woods, he would
_____.

   a. run away.
   b. attack you.

It is often thought that camels store water in their hump, but the hump really
contains _____.

   a. fat.
   b. water.

(Content cloze)

Next, we used paragraphs in which *but* signalled a relationship between portions of the text, moving again from paragraphs on familiar topics to those
related to the children's misconceptions. Then, we used sentences and paragraphs in the same order that contained more difficult adversatives like *yet*,
although, and *even though*. Although this bottom-up approach is somewhat successful, it requires more time than most teachers would be able to give.

As suggested at the outset of this chapter, a more realistic approach would be to deal with problems related to conjunctions as they arise when children are reading. I have found that using a conjunction in a familiar situation is an effective way of helping students understand the relationship that a particular conjunction signals when it poses a problem in a content area text. In the script (MacGinitie, unpublished manuscript) below notice how the teacher points out the signal word *though*, using it in a more familiar situation to help children understand how *though* can aid them in understanding the meaning of the phrase *tell little*.

In providing this kind of support teachers help children use their background and linguistic knowledge together as aids to comprehension. This is important because while guide words are aids, especially for poorer readers, teaching only guide words is not *the* answer to the problem of comprehending relationships of ideas in sentences. The background knowledge of the reader affects his or her ability to comprehend a text more than ability to interpret surface clues (McNeil 1987).

Learning the origin of place names is a good way to begin the study of a country. The names are often clues to the ideas and culture of its early explorers and settlers, though they may tell little about the people who live in an area after the names have become fixed (*Canada: A Geographic Study*)

In answer to a question asking for reasons for looking at place names when studying a country, several students write that place names "tell a little" about the people who live in an area after the names have become permanent. The teacher might get these students together and work with them in this way:

Teacher: Read the second sentence again. Why is that word "though" there?
Student: (Doesn't know.)
T: What other word could you use (in the sentence) that would mean the same thing?
S: "But"
T: Good. "but" and "though" both warn you what is coming next is different from what you might expect. After you've read that place names give clues about the ideas of early explorers and settlers, might you expect that they would also give clues to ideas of later settlers?
S: Yes.
T: Sure. But then there's that "though" warning you to watch out, when you read what comes next. What does come next?
S: "They may tell little about the people who live in an area after the names have become fixed."
T: What does "they may tell little" mean?
S: They may tell a little.
T: Would it make sense to say that "The names are often clues to the ideas of early settlers, though they may tell a little about later settlers?"
S: No.
T: So "tell little" is not quite the same as "tell a little." "Tell little"

145

means "tell not very much, maybe nothing;" "tell a little" means to
"tell something." If I said, "He talks all the time, though he says little
worth listening to," how much of what he says would I think is worth
listening to?

S: Not very much.

T: Not very much at all. *Going back to our sentence, how much do*
         place names tell about settlers who arrive after the names have be-
         come fixed?

S: Not very much.

THE CLOZE PROCEDURE

Although the cloze procedure is widely used for assessment it is also recommended for use in comprehension instruction. This procedure forces children
to focus their attention on semantic and syntactic information in the text and
combine this information with their background knowledge. It provides children with the experience of using background knowledge, linguistic knowledge, and other factors in a holistic process in order to understand a piece of
text and the sentences that are part of the text. Thus it is particularly appropriate for developing inferential thinking (Carr, Dewitz, and Patberg 1989).

Teachers should begin with short passages with only one or two deletions
(Carr, Dewitz, and Patberg 1983, 1989). Options can also be provided. Later,
deletions can be increased, and longer selections from basal readers and/or
content area textbooks can be utilized. Insertions that make sense in terms of
the entire text context can be accepted even if they are not exact matches.
Content words or structure words can be deleted depending upon the focus of
instruction. For example, if the teacher wants to increase student awareness of
pronouns and their role in aiding comprehension, he or she can delete only
pronouns. When the focus is on inferential comprehension, Carr, Dewitz, and
Patberg (1989) suggest the following two criteria for deletions:

1.   Delete words that are important in the text.
2.   Delete words which provide children with the opportunity to make use of
     forward and backward text clues as well as their background knowledge. A
     backward clue is one which precedes the blank so that one must look back
     in the text for it. A forward clue follows the blank so that one must look
     ahead in the text to find it. The first blank in the passage below can be
     filled in correctly (skidded) if a backward clue is utilized (the road was very
     slippery). For the second blank, a forward clue (the boat was under the
     bridge) is helpful.

It had been raining for a long time, and the road was very slippery. The car
_____ out of control and crashed through the railing on the _____.
The boat was halfway under the bridge and missed being hit. (Carr, Dewitz, and
Patberg 1983, p. 382)

Forward clues are a particular source of difficulty (Carr, Dewitz, and Patberg 1983). Therefore, after explaining to the children how cloze exercises can
help their comprehension, the teacher should begin by having them read the

entire text without making any attempt to fill in any of the blanks. Children should be informed that this will provide them with some understanding of the entire text, and will help them to use forward and backward syntactic and semantic cues.

Second, the text should be read aloud sentence by sentence with children suggesting words for the blanks. Reasons for the choices must be given based on clues found in the text. When options are available, children should be encouraged to try to supply an appropriate word before looking at the options. Different choices can be discussed, and the most appropriate choice should be agreed upon. With remedial readers, teachers may need to begin by supplying some words for the blanks, modeling the thought processes that led to the choice of the word. One way of doing this effectively is to make a passage available on an overhead projector with deleted words covered with masking tape. Once an insertion has been agreed upon, the tape can be removed and the choice can be compared to the word in the text. One advantage of using this procedure (referred to as Zip Cloze [Aulls 1982]) is that the same passage can be used again with different words deleted. When children have had some experience with the procedure they may work in groups, pairs, or independently and then come together to discuss their choices and compare them with the original text. The focus should be on the reasons for the choice of the insertion. Providing children with a checklist like the one below when they work independently is one way of ensuring this focus on appropriate clues. This checklist is based on one developed by Carr, Dewitz, and Patberg (1983).

SELF MONITORING CHECKLIST

1. Does the answer make sense?
2. Does the answer make sense in the sentence and in the text?
3. Is the answer based upon a combination of knowledge you had before you read the passage and the clues in the passage?
4. Is there a forward clue in the same sentence, paragraph, or passage?
5. Is there a backward clue in the same sentence, paragraph, or passage? (p. 382)

In the Inferential Training Technique developed by Carr, Dewitz, and Patberg (1989) children then move to using the cloze procedure with passages taken from their content area texts and to answering inferential questions about the text. Worksheets provided at this stage continue to focus children's attention on the clues in the text that can be combined with their background knowledge as an aid to answering questions.

NARRATIVE TEXT STRUCTURE

Research on narrative text structure centers around three questions:

1. What type of structure (story grammar) do stories have?
2. Do adults and children use knowledge of this story structure (story schema) as an aid to comprehension?

3. What is the best way of activating and building children's story schema as an aid to story comprehension?

STORY GRAMMAR

Four different descriptions of story structure or story grammar have been developed (Mandler and Johnson 1977; Rumelhart 1975; Stein and Glenn 1979; Thorndyke 1977). These four story grammars confirm that the structure of stories involves a setting, a plot, and a resolution. The folk tale, *Stone Soup*, is used to illustrate these elements in more detail.

1. The setting introduces the main character or characters and gives information about the time and the place in which the story takes place. (Once upon a time a young man was walking down a country road.)
2. The plot contains one or more episodes consisting of:
    A. An initiating event that causes a reaction in the protagonist, i.e., he/she recognizes that there is a problem. (The young man comes to a house. He is hungry.)
    B. An internal response in which the protagonist sets a goal. (The young man decides to try and get some food.)
    C. An attempt or attempts to achieve the goal. (When the young man asks for food, the old lady in the house says she has none. He then tricks the old lady into giving him food by first asking for a stone and then for all the other ingredients necessary for making a delicious soup.)
3. The resolution is the outcome, the success or failure in achieving the goal and the consequences of the actions. (The young man achieves his goal. He and the old lady have a delicious meal. The young man realizes he can use this scheme to feed himself again, so he takes the stone with him as he continues his journey.)
4. The theme, usually unstated in stories that are not fables, relates events in the story to the problems of life in general. (*Stone Soup* is a good story because it can be interpreted in several different ways. For example, one person might say that the theme of this story is that people are gullible and curious and can be easily managed by appealing to these elements in their personality. Another might say that the message of the story is that indirect means can often be successful when direct methods are not.)

While the story grammars have been very helpful in understanding narrative structure, they do have limitations since they are all based on simple folk tales and fairy tales. Stories with complex structures involving several episodes have to be reduced to a simple form in order to fit a story grammar (Carnine and Kinder 1985; Dreher and Singer 1980). Schmitt and O'Brien (1986) point out that sometimes even simple stories that are much loved by children and adults like *Alexander and the Terrible, Horrible, No Good, Very Bad Day* (Viorst 1972) do not fit the story grammars. They suggest that Alexander makes no attempts to solve the many problems that occur during his bad day and there is no resolution. (It may be, however, that Alexander's continually stated comment, "I'm going to go live in Australia," as he is confronted with each problem resolves the problems for him even though it may not seem like a resolution to the adult reader.) Despite these limitations, story grammars have made a valuable contribution since they have made us more aware that stories have both a temporal and a causal structure whose crucial elements include both outside events and the inner feelings and ideas of the characters.

STORY SCHEMA

Schema theory suggests that we have a schema for story just as we have a schema for other concepts. Story structure therefore resides in the mind of the reader as well as in the text (Applebee 1978, 1980; Stein and Glenn 1978). Like other types of linguistic knowledge, this knowledge is intuitive rather than explicit. Even young children exposed to stories can use story structure to help them comprehend what they hear or read, remember and recall stories, and create new stories (Mandler and Johnson 1977b; Stein and Glenn 1979). Children can also use story structure in conjunction with story content as an aid to prediction (Gillet and Temple 1986), but they cannot consciously describe the elements of a story in the way it has been described above.

Some research with folktales and fables (Mandler and Johnson 1977a; McConaughy 1980; Shannon, Kameenui, and Baumann 1988) has suggested that children's story schema differs from that of adults in that children focus on the events of the story more than the underlying causes of the events. In recalling and composing stories children tell what happened in the same way that adults do, but, unlike adults they do not tell why the events occurred, so that the internal motivations and reactions of the characters are missing. Shannon, Kameenui, and Baumann (1988) found that only about 50% of the students in their study could identify explicitly stated motives of characters in fables.

However, another study which used interviews and allowed the children to handle and refer to the books being discussed (Lehr 1988) found that 70% of the kindergarten children in the study mentioned internal thought processes of characters that motivated their actions in the stories. In this study kindergarten children were also able to identify realistic stories with similar themes 80% of the time and folktales with similar themes 35% of the time, indicating that the children's background knowledge played an important part in their ability to identify themes and motives. Amount of exposure to literature was correlated with kindergarten, second-grade, and fourth-grade children's ability to identify and generate themes and to match stories with similar themes, suggesting that children's knowledge about story structure plays a part in their higher level comprehension of stories.

NARRATIVE TEXT STRUCTURE INSTRUCTION

Since young children make use of story schema in understanding stories even though they are unable to state explicitly the parts of a story, some reading experts (Rhodes and Dudley-Marling 1988; Schmitt and O'Brien 1986) caution against the use of explicit instruction in story grammar. Schmitt and

O'Brien (1986) point out that this type of instruction separates story structure from content. When story elements are considered separately, the temporal and causal links between these elements are de-emphasized, yet it is these links that are critically important for story comprehension. Rhodes and Dudley-Marling (1988) concur with Sebesta, Calder, and Cleland (1982), suggesting that teachers, teaching indirectly, should act as intermediaries between the story grammar concept and children's use of it in comprehension.

It must be emphasized once again that the most important thing a teacher can do to aid story comprehension of all children is to read to them. Children develop and fine tune their concept of story schema by exposure to well-formed stories. Teachers who work with remedial readers with little exposure to literature should begin a reading aloud program using folktales and fairy tales whose structure is obvious, and then expand to a wide range of narratives (Rhodes and Dudley-Marling 1988). Stories that children read themselves should be well-written; teachers should screen trade books and basal reader stories carefully, looking for story elements: Is there a stated problem or conflict? Does the main character have a goal? Is there a theme?

Reading predictable books whose rhythmical, repetitious, and/or cumulative patterns are easily discerned can help make children more aware of story structures. Since these patterns are readily emulated by children, reading predictable books is also a way of encouraging children to engage in other types of activities in which they generate stories as a whole: retelling, acting out, summarizing stories they have heard or read, and telling or writing new stories they compose based on the patterns of the books.

Constructing story maps is another way to provide support for these kinds of activities since they are an overt, concrete representation of the story which can help remedial readers construct their internal representation. Since a story map lists the major elements of the story and links them in a graphic form, it teaches children about story elements.

Story maps were first developed to aid teachers in determining the central concepts (Beck, Omanson, and McKeown 1981) and questions they should ask about stories (Beck, Omanson, and McKeown 1981; Pearson 1982). More recently, story maps have been used with remedial readers. Idol-Maestas and Croll (1985) successfully used the story map form (see figure 1) with a group of children identified as learning-disabled. Their technique is strongly recommended; teachers should instruct children to note essential story elements as they appear and then to fill in the appropriate part of the story map. At first, the teacher models how to fill in a story map; then the teacher and student read and fill it in together until the student can do it independently.

Open-ended frames provide another type of support. These frames can be filled in after reading, or while rereading, or can be used as children's plans for composing their own stories. Fowler (1982) developed several frames that focus on single and multiple elements of a story. Teachers can also develop their own frames quite easily. The first frame below focuses on the single element of setting, while the second focuses on multiple story elements. This second frame is

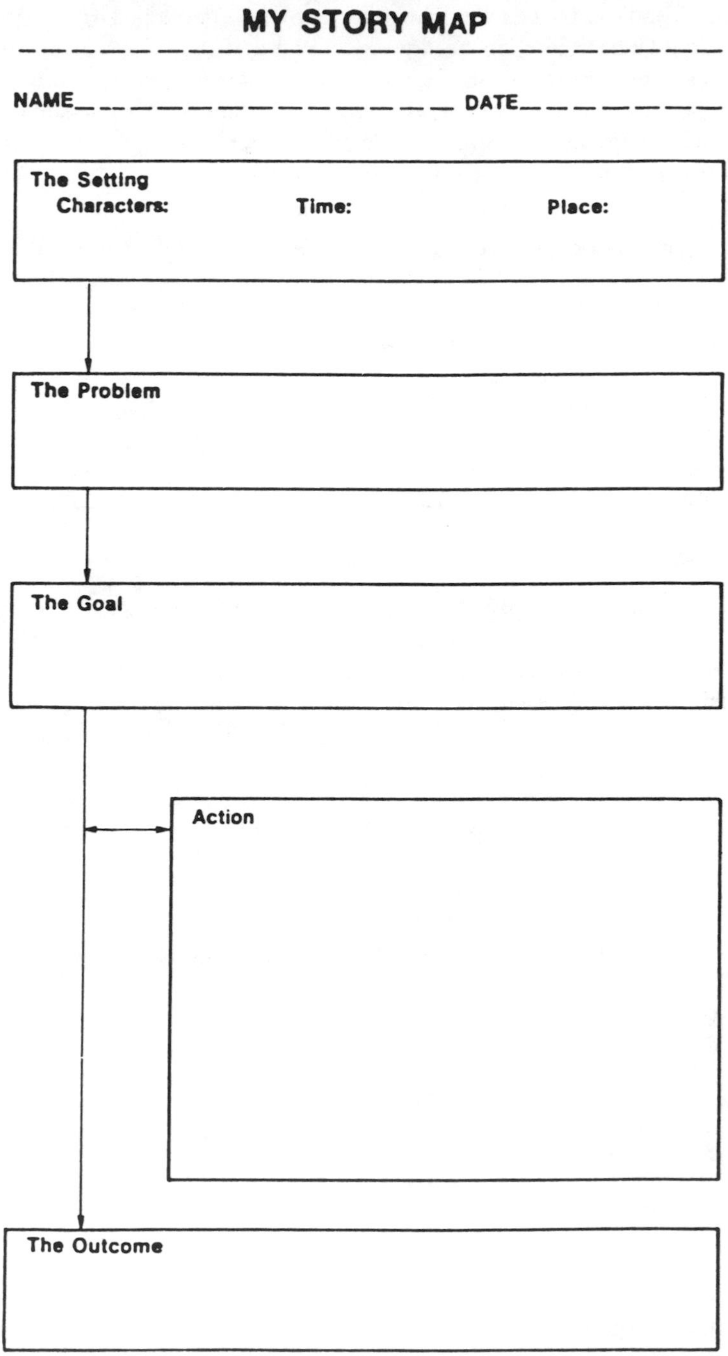

MY STORY MAP

NAME_ _ _ _ _ _ _ _ _ _ _ _ _ _ _ DATE_ _ _ _ _ _ _

The Setting
Characters: Time: Place:

The Problem

The Goal

Action

The Outcome

Figure 1. Blank story map form. Reprinted from I. Idol-Maestas and V. Croll, *The Effects of Training in Story Mapping Procedures on the Reading Comprehension of Poor Readers* (University of Illinois, Urbana, 1985).

based on and can be used with the story map frame developed by Idol-Maestas and Croll (1985). Teachers need to be careful that the frames are appropriate for each story. The story frame below is appropriate for stories containing three attempts at solving a problem, with the third attempt the successful one. Be sure that the spaces in the frames are large enough to spare children the frustration of trying to fit their ideas into spaces that are too small.

SETTING FRAME

This story takes place _____. The main character is _____. Words or clues from the story that tell when and where the story takes place are _____.

STORY FRAME

This story takes place _____. The main character is _____. The problem starts when _____. _____ decides to _____ _____. _____ tries to accomplish his or her goal and solve the problem by _____. Next, _____ _____. The problem is solved when _____. The story ends _____.

In Chapter 4, I suggest that teachers should ask questions that are important to the text. Since questions that are important for story comprehension relate to the critical elements of the story, asking questions based on story grammar indirectly teaches children to use story structure as a comprehension aid. Singer and Donlan (1982) and Marshall (1983) provide schema-general questions that can serve as models for specific questions related to a particular story. Singer and Donlan's list can be found in McNeil (1987). Marshall's (1983) questions are listed below; notice that many are really question frames.

Theme:
    What is the major point of the story?
    What is the moral of the story?
    What did _____learn at the end of the story?

Setting:
    Where did _____ happen?
    When did _____ happen?

Character:
    Who is the main character?
    What is _____ like?

Initiating Event:
    What is _____s problem?
    What does _____ have to try to do?

Attempts:
    What did _____ do about _____?
    What will _____ do now?

Resolution:
    How did _____ solve the problem?
    How did _____ achieve the goal?
    What would you do to solve _____s problem?

Reactions:
    How did _____ feel about the problem?
    What did _____ do _____?
    How did _____ feel at the end?
    Why did _____ feel that way?
    How would you feel about _____?

(Reprinted with permission of N. Marshall and the International Reading Association.)

Story maps can help teachers translate these general questions into specific ones. For example, with the story *Stone Soup*, the teacher can ask, "How did the young man get something to eat?" instead of, "How did the young man solve his problem?"

Teachers should also ask questions that encourage children to compare and contrast different stories they have read, noting that the elements are the same but that they differ in certain particulars. For example, comparing the fable *The Fox and the Grapes* and the folktale *Stone Soup*, the teacher can ask, "What is the problem in both stories?" "How does the fox solve the problem?" "How does the young man solve the problem?" "Which is the best solution?" "Why?"

Asking questions that relate to the particular aspects of a genre (Butler and Turbill 1984) and comparing stories of a similar type such as fables, myths, or mysteries can help children discover the elements that compose that classification of literature. The students then develop schemata for particular genres, as well as a generalized story schema. The use of Venn diagrams (see figure 2) provides a type of visual support when comparing several stories; the story map can diagram only one story at a time.

The inferential strategy described in Chapter 5 suggests a way of connect-

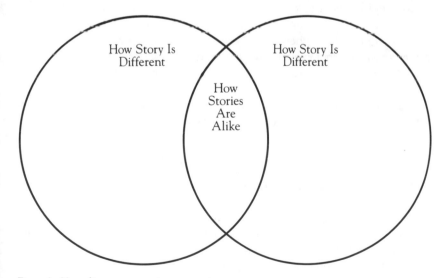

Figure 2. Venn diagram comparing two stories.

ing children's experiences to the content of a story. This technique also focuses children's attention on certain structural elements, most often character's motivation or internal responses. In the script of the inferential strategy found in Chapter 5, for example, the lesson focuses on jealousy as a motivation for uncharitable actions by a story character. Research cited earlier indicates that internal response or motivation is an aspect that may be lacking in children's story schema. Since the inferential strategy technique can be particularly effective in helping children see connections between their own motivations and those of story characters, it may be effective in improving their comprehension; they become more aware of this aspect of structure as well as central concepts of story content. The inferential strategy technique can help build and/or activate the type of social inference schema described by McNeil (1987, p. 23) who writes, " . . . the social inference schema includes the goal of the character and the internal responses, thoughts and subgoals that lead the character to action."

Direct, explicit instruction concerning the elements of story structure is effective in improving the story comprehension of school-age children according to some studies (e.g., Gordon and Braun 1982, 1983; Fitzgerald and Spiegel 1983; Whaley and Spiegel 1982). Other studies (e.g., Dreher and Singer 1980; Sebesta, Calder, and Cleland 1982) found that direct instruction of story structure did not improve comprehension, but Fitzgerald (1989) points out that knowledge of story structure was not pretested in any of the studies. The difference in results may be due to the fact that in those studies that showed no improvement, the children already had a well-structured story schema. Remedial readers who have language differences or language problems and/or have not had much exposure to stories may not have a well-structured story schema; they might benefit from direct instruction in story grammar. Nelson-Herber and Johnson (1989) suggest that "Even children who already have a sense of story structure can benefit from being given labels for their knowledge" (p. 264). However, teachers should remember that teaching labels is not their primary goal and that explicit instruction in narrative structure should be "designed to complement actual story reading and story writing not serve as a substitute for them" (Gordon 1989, p. 79)

Gordon (1989) describes a method for explicit instruction in story structure that combines reading and writing instruction and is based on the mediated and the writing process models of instruction. "Through 'think alouds' (Davey 1983), the teacher models the reasoning processes during reading and writing, and shows how the knowledge of structure helps in understanding the story being read or in framing the story being written" (Gordon 1989, p. 80). The instruction occurs over an extended period of time, helping children to transfer what they have learned to unfamiliar stories and to their own written stories. Sample lessons found in Gordon (1989) can serve as models for teachers who wish to provide explicit instruction about story structure to remedial readers in intermediate and primary grades.

EXPOSITORY TEXT STRUCTURES
Research on expository text structures has considered the same type of questions addressed by the research on narrative text structure, i.e., questions related to:

1. types of expository text structures. (Several different expository text structures have been identified. Therefore, one additional consideration is whether some structures are easier to understand than others.)
2. children's awareness of them.
3. methods of training children to recognize these text structures and use them in comprehension (Horowitz 1987).

TYPES OF EXPOSITORY TEXT STRUCTURES
There is some variation in the way that expository structures are categorized and labeled. Most experts, however, use a taxonomy consisting of five main types of expository text structure (Horowitz 1987; Meyer and Freedle 1984). The list below uses the categories and labels suggested by Horowitz (1988). Each category is defined and an example is given in parentheses.

1. The comparison-contrast structure which organizes ideas in the text according to their similarities and differences.
   (*Stone Soup* and *The Fox and the Grapes* are both narrative texts; they both contain the elements of story grammar. However, *Stone Soup* is a folktale while *The Fox and the Grapes* is a fable. The moral is unstated in *Stone Soup* but is explicitly stated in *The Fox and the Grapes*.)
2. The cause-effect structure which, as its name makes clear, organizes text ideas according to causes and their results.
   (Early researchers in the area of reading disability were doctors who used a medical model, treating poor reading as a symptom of some type of defect in the child. The use of this medical model has persisted so that external factors like quality of instruction are given too little attention in the field of reading disabilities.)
3. The problem-solution structure in which a problem is posed and an answer is suggested.
   (Many children do not have the background knowledge necessary to understand particular texts. Teachers can help these children by making use of the pre-reading techniques suggested in Chapter 5.)
4. The list structure which describes attributes of an object or idea or list examples. The order of the attributes or examples is not significant.
   (Children read three types of texts in school. Basal readers, containing mostly narrative texts, teach word recognition and comprehension skills. Content area textbooks are provided to help children learn important concepts in science, social studies, etc. Since these books are often difficult for children to read, reading instruction should teach children how to read them. Trade books, books written mainly to entertain rather than

for either reading or content area instruction, can be very effective in reading instruction.)

5. Time order which presents events in a time sequence.

    (In the fifties and early sixties many teachers used trade books to teach reading through an individualized reading model. In the seventies there was a return to the basals. Now, in the eighties, many teachers use trade books again as part of the whole language movement.)

In order to answer the question of which expository text structure is most effective, Meyer and Freedle (1984) presented graduate students with texts on the same topic written in the comparison-contrast, cause-effect, problem-solution, and list structures. They found that comprehension was better with the comparison-contrast structure and the cause-effect structure than it was with the list structure. Comprehension of the problem-solution structure did not differ from that of the list structure. Horowitz (1987) replicated their study with college freshman and ninth graders using their passages on one topic along with passages on a new topic. She found that comparison-contrast, cause-effect, and problem-solution structures were not more effective than the list structure, or for a passage with no structure for one topic, but were more effective for the other topic.

Horowitz (1987) explained her results by suggesting that the search for the most effective type of expository structure is misguided. Like narrative structure, expository structure should not be considered in isolation but in relation to the content of the text, its purpose, and its audience. Certain structures are more suitable for certain content, situations, and readers than they are for others.

The content of particular domains of knowledge has its own structure (Beck and McKeown 1988; Roller and Ohlhausen 1986). For example, history has a narrative causal structure; however, in order to understand history, one needs to know more than the sequence of events in which one event causes subsequent events. One must understand "why a certain action caused some event and why that event led to subsequent events" (Beck and McKeown 1988, p. 33).

Thus the content and language of a text have a structure. A text that is "user friendly" should interweave content and language structures (Calfee and Chambliss 1988). Beck and McKeown (1988) suggest that history should be written in a causal explanatory style. Depending on the author's purpose, the list, problem-solution, or comparison-contrast structure may add explanation to the overall causal structure. Most texts in history and other content areas are a mixture of the types of text structures listed above. Slater and Graves (1989) suggest that good expository text also often contains elements of narrative. Telling a story can be a way of providing a cogent explanation as well as a way of varying style.

On the other hand, Calfee and Chambliss (1988) believe that "while any subject matter is amenable to several organizational approaches, the writer owes it to the reader to pick a lens, communicate this decision and remain true to the contract" (p. 246). They suggest that structures may shift within this overall lens just as one may take motion pictures and still pictures of the same topic. However, when a writer shifts from one structure to another he should provide signals of this shift to the reader.

CHILDREN'S AWARENESS OF EXPOSITORY TEXT STRUCTURES

Another factor to consider in choosing the structure for an expository text, when children are the audience, is whether they will be aware of a particular structure so they can make use of it in comprehension. Are certain text structures inappropriate for expository text to be read by children because they may be unaware of these structures? On the other hand, how will children ever become aware of these structures if they are not exposed to them?

Children have very little exposure to expository text structure outside of school. Even in school, in the early school years, most reading instruction uses narrative texts taken from basal readers. Thus it is not surprising that very few children are aware of expository text structures (Englert and Hiebert 1984; Richgels et al. 1987). By fifth and sixth grade some students do have awareness of these structures (McGee 1982; Richgels et al. 1987), but even in ninth grade, there are many students who do not demonstrate awareness of some expository text structures (Meyer, Brandt, and Bluth 1980).

Studies that use different measures of awareness of text structure have had contradictory results regarding children's awareness of particular types of expository text structure. For example, Meyer, Brandt, and Bluth (1980) found that ninth graders were least aware of the comparison-contrast structure while Richgels et al. (1987) found that sixth graders were more aware of this structure than the problem-solution, cause-effect, or list structure. These contradictory results support Horowitz's (1987) contention that the search for the most effective text structure, i.e., the one of which children are most aware, is a misguided one because it ignores other factors like text content and purpose. What the research tells us is that some middle grade children who are aware of text structure also understand expository text better (e.g., Meyer, Brandt, and Bluth 1980). The next question then becomes whether those children who are unaware of text structure can be taught to be more aware of it and to use this awareness to help their comprehension.

COMPREHENSION INSTRUCTION: EXPOSITORY TEXT STRUCTURE

Because children usually have so little exposure to expository text structures and because so many children appear to have no awareness of them, it may be more necessary to teach these structures directly than it is with narrative structures. Although all reading experts agree that it is important to teach expository text structures directly, there is controversy over whether one should begin this instruction using short texts that are models of the different structures or work directly with content area texts that children use. Those who recommend using short passages (e.g., Richgels, McGee, and Slaton 1989) believe that they allow the structures to be perceived more easily. However, others (e.g.,

Vacca and Vacca 1986) believe that teachers should guide students to recognize the predominant pattern of a long passage from the content area textbooks. That there is usually a mixture of structures within this predominating pattern should also be recognized.

Since research has not provided any answer to settle the controversy, teachers of remedial readers are urged to use short ideal passages to build children's awareness of text structure along with providing the support they need to understand the content area texts they are expected to read. Richgels, McGee, and Slaton (1989) suggest that teachers look for passages within children's content area textbooks that are examples of good structure and use them for instruction whenever possible. They provide a list of well structured passages from current science and social studies textbooks.

The first step in direct teaching of expository text structure is to teach children the meaning of structure as an element that can be considered separate from content. Have children build towers using two different materials with the same number of levels and shapes to point out the difference between materials (content) and structure (McGee and Richgels 1985). Another possibility is to show children pictures of buildings with identical structures made of two different materials (Cooper 1986). Still another is to give children lists of names or objects and ask them to arrange them in different orders such as comparison-contrast or time order (Niles 1964).

Activities recommended for teaching the different expository text structures using short model passages are similar to those recommended for teaching narrative structure. As with narrative structures, expository text structure instruction should include both reading and writing.

A study by Horowitz (1985) found that a group that was given reading and writing instruction with the cause-effect pattern did significantly better than a group who received only reading instruction. Some suggest that children should be taught to recognize the patterns and use them in reading before using them in writing (Devine 1986; Readence, Bean, and Baldwin 1985). Others (e.g., Armbruster, Anderson, and Ostertag 1987) suggest teaching children to write summaries of short well structured passages as an aid to understanding them. Still others (Piccolo 1987; Richgels and McGee 1988) believe that teaching children to write paragraphs with a particular structure is the best way to make them aware of how writers organize texts. Although Piccolo suggests a particular order for introducing the structures, Horowitz's work suggests that such an order is premature. Teachers should begin with those patterns that are most evident in the content area texts that the children use.

Piccolo (1987) suggests the following instructional steps in teaching children how to construct each type of expository text structure:

1. Introduce a text structure, label it, and explain that it answers a particular need. For example, "We are going to study the comparison-contrast structure. It is a good structure to use if you want to show similarities or differences between the topic you are writing about and other topics."

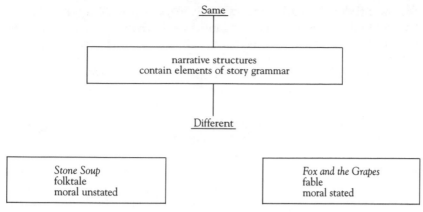

Figure 3. Graphic organizer.

2. Present a graphic organizer that you have constructed to fit a text that is a well-structured model. The graphic organizer above was constructed to fit the sample comparison-contrast text found on p. 155.[1]
3. Read the paragraph upon which the graphic organizer was based. Call attention to words and phrases that signal the organization. Also call attention to the topic sentence.
4. Present another completed graphic organizer with the same structure. This graphic organizer should also contain a topic sentence. Show how to write a paragraph that fits this graphic organizer using appropriate signal words.
5. Help children choose an appropriate topic for the structure under consideration, jot down notes about the topic, organize these notes in a graphic organizer, and finally, compose a paragraph based on the graphic organizer.
6. Present examples of well-written paragraphs by the children as models. Work together as a group to revise paragraphs that are not as good.

After the children have learned to construct paragraphs using a particular structure, they read short paragraphs with that structure and take notes with a graphic organizer. The final step is to practice locating and labeling the structures in content area texts, encyclopedias, etc., distinguishing between the different structures. During both these steps, teacher modeling and teacher questions which focus on signals to the structure are extremely important.

Instructional methods that teach expository text structure, like those used to teach narrative structure, have often relied on the use of frames (Armbruster, Anderson, and Ostertag 1987; Cudd and Roberts 1989) and graphic organizers, as in Piccolo's (1987) method above and those in studies by

---

[1]Teachers who wish to try the Piccolo method can find samples of other graphic organizers appropriate for the different structures in her article, in Jones, Pierce, and Hunter (1988–1989), and Readence, Bean, and Baldwin (1985).

Berkowitz (1986), Richgels and McGee (1988), and Slater, Graves, and Piche (1985). While frames and graphic organizers both function as supports for summarization and construction of texts with a particular structure, graphic organizers are particularly valuable because "A good graphic representation can show at a glance the key parts of a whole and their relations, thereby allowing a holistic understanding that words alone cannot convey" (Jones, Pierce, and Hunter 1988–1989, p. 21).

In the Piccolo method the teacher takes responsibility at first for constructing and completing the graphic organizers. Later, children construct their own graphic organizers to fit the particular pattern, which is an important step since they are actively involved in the process. Berkowitz (1986) found that sixth-graders who constructed their own graphic organizers had better comprehension than those who studied ones constructed by the teacher. An intermediate step that might be helpful to remedial readers would be to provide them with partially completed graphic organizers (Readence, Bean, and Baldwin 1985).

However, learning to connect certain graphic organizer patterns to certain structures should not become an end in itself. Teachers should not adhere rigidly to particular graphic organizer patterns. This type of instruction will be detrimental if it leads the children to believe that every expository text they read will fit neatly into one of these patterns. It is important to relate this instruction to the content area texts that children are reading, i.e., search for the structures being studied in the texts that children are reading in social studies, science, etc.

When Weisberg and Balajthy (1988) reviewed the literature to determine which type of instruction provided the best transfer from understanding short texts constructed to serve as models of a particular text structure to understanding real-world texts, they found that strategies which engaged children actively were the most successful. The most productive activities involved some type of restatement of the information in the text such as constructing graphic organizers and writing summaries. Children were also taught to ask themselves questions about what they read. The strategies were fully explained and time was provided for practice and feedback.

While building awareness of different expository text structures using short passages constructed for that purpose, teachers can help children understand content area texts by providing them with pattern guides (Readence, Bean, and Baldwin 1985; Vacca and Vacca 1986) or graphic organizers that fit the predominant pattern of the text. Of course, if a text is inconsiderate and has no predominant pattern, it is not suitable for instruction about expository text structures. Pattern guides are exercises that pull apart the text organization and require students to attend to this organization and piece it together. For example, if children are reading a section of a history book related to the beginning of the Revolutionary War, written predominantly in a cause-effect pattern, a pattern guide like the one below might be useful.

Why the Thirteen Colonies Decided
to Declare Their Independence

Cause: Patriots take up arms against England in 1775.

Effect in the Colonies_____

Effect in England_____

Cause: The King hires Hessians to serve in the armies in America.

Effect in the Colonies_____

Cause: Thomas Paine writes *Common Sense*

Effect in the Colonies_____

The Second Continental Congress proclaims the Declaration of Independence.

Once children acquire a repertoire of possible graphic organizers using short passages, the teacher can model the process of constructing graphic organizers with content area textbooks using the following steps (Jones, Pierce, and Hunter 1988–1989):

1. Survey the title, headings, illustrations, text objectives, and text summaries to form a hypothesis about the content and structure of the text. While surveying the text, ask questions like, "Is the author comparing things?" "Does there seem to be a time line?" "Does the focus seem to be on causes and effects?" "Do I see any signal words of particular structures?"
2. Choose a particular type of graphic organizer pattern to be constructed if there is enough evidence for such a choice.
3. Read the text carefully with different structures in mind, checking the appropriateness of the graphic organizer pattern chosen, if one has been chosen, or continuing to ask questions about the structure in order to choose an appropriate graphic organizer pattern. It may be necessary to summarize sections of the text as an aid to this process.
4. During and after careful reading of the text, consider the overall pattern and make adjustments in the choice of the graphic organizer pattern or in the number and arrangement of its elements.
5. Construct a graphic organizer.
6. Write a summary of the text based on the graphic organizer.

Since reading content area textbooks is the most difficult reading task that children face in school, remedial readers will need support for a long time before they are able to engage independently in the above process. In addition to helping them with graphic organizers and frames, teachers should ask questions during and after reading which focus on the structure as well as the content, such as "What signal words does the author use to tell us how his ideas are organized?" "How are they organized?" "Is the author comparing ideas here or telling us about causes and their results?" Techniques like Know—Want to Know—Learn (Ogle 1986, 1989) described in Chapter 5 and those discussed in the next chapter attend to both content and structure while actively involving the children in the reading process.

CHAPTER

8

STRATEGIES FOR TEACHING DURING READING

In some ways this chapter is the heart of this book, for here I discuss how to teach children to understand what they read while they read: how to provide them with during-reading instruction that encourages the use of active, effective, generalizable strategies. The first section of this chapter deals with general issues related to instruction that takes place during the reading of a text, the second section suggests strategies that should be taught and specific techniques for teaching them. Descriptions of sample lessons and script excerpts from these lessons are provided once again to clarify how teachers can use these techniques.

GENERAL ISSUES

HOW CAN A TEACHER PROVIDE DURING-READING INSTRUCTION SINCE IT IS NOT POSSIBLE TO GET INSIDE A CHILD'S HEAD WHEN HE OR SHE IS READING?

Of course, during-reading instruction cannot take place as the child is engaged in the act of reading. The term *during-reading instruction* means that reading of a text will be interrupted, that the text needs to be "chunked" into appropriate sections, and that the instruction takes place before and after reading of these sections.

SHOULD CHILDREN BE INTERRUPTED WHILE THEY ARE READING A TEXT?

Not always! Once again it seems necessary to repeat: comprehension instruction is only part of the total reading program. Children need time to read books they enjoy, books that are easy enough so that comprehension instruction is not necessary. But some children have trouble understanding many texts without guidance by the teacher. With these children, interrupting reading to remind them to use the strategies taught and to monitor the way they are using them often may be necessary. Other children may only require this type of guidance with difficult texts.

How Often And When Should Reading Be Interrupted—In Other Words, How Should A Text Be Chunked?

There is no simple answer to this question. It depends on many factors, the first of which is the nature of the text. Stories have less lexical density and therefore may require fewer interruptions than expository text. But some expository texts are less difficult for some children than some stories. A text with much new vocabulary, whether it is narrative or expository material, may require more guidance and therefore, more interruption. In general, the harder the text, the shorter the chunks and the more the interruptions.

The second factor is the age and reading ability of the children. Young children and remedial readers often cannot deal with long texts. These readers need to be interrupted more often in order to make sure they understand what they read.

The third factor relates to the strategy being taught and the technique used to teach it. For example, if predicting is being taught, text reading should be interrupted at points when predictions can be made and when they can be confirmed or rejected. As each individual technique is discussed later in the chapter specific ways of chunking text will be discussed.

The fourth factor is the level of the children's familiarity with a technique and/or strategy. When children first learn to use specific strategies, the text should be chunked into short sections. For example, Palincsar, Brown, and David (work in progress) suggest that when teachers begin using reciprocal teaching they should interrupt reading after each paragraph.

Should Children Read Orally Or Silently In Periods Of During-Reading Comprehension Instruction?

Teaching reading can be frustrating because reading is a process that goes on inside the reader's head, and thus is not visible. Chunking text and interrupting reading are attempts to compensate for this—attempts to make the process "visible." Another approach is to have children read aloud. Although most experts caution against reliance on round-robin reading groups and although research has demonstrated that oral and silent reading involve different task demands, reading instruction with young children and with remedial readers usually involves oral reading (Allington 1984). This is probably because the focus of reading instruction with these two groups is generally on word recognition. Having children read aloud enables the teacher to correct oral miscues and guide children's word recognition strategies.

When the focus of instruction is comprehension, oral reading can sometimes be helpful because it is the only way of determining whether word recognition problems are affecting comprehension and it enables teachers to correct miscues that may interfere with comprehension. Some children are more comfortable with oral reading because they have not had much experience with silent reading. Oral reading can be used at times, but in general children should be encouraged to read silently for several reasons:

1. When children read orally they tend to focus on getting the words right and not on comprehension. In Chapter 2 the point was made that a few miscues will not necessarily interfere with comprehension. However, comprehension cannot be taught if word recognition is a real problem. If children make so many miscues that they need teacher guidance, it is better to give them easier texts so that they can read silently.
2. When one child reads orally in a group, the others often are not attending. All the children can read at their own pace when they read silently. Teachers will need to circulate and monitor children's attention and reading, and provide help with unknown words for those who request it. Teachers need to be sensitive to when children are finished reading and are ready to engage in discussion. Children who are not comfortable with silent reading can be introduced to it gradually and allowed to whisper the words if need be. They will never be comfortable with silent reading if they do not get some experience with it. Shared reading in which the teacher reads aloud while the children read along silently is another way of helping the children make the transition.
3. The goal of comprehension instruction is to provide children with strategies that they may use independently to understand the texts that they read. When children read independently, they read silently. During-reading comprehension instruction should provide guided practice using the same process that the children will use when reading independently.

COMPREHENSION STRATEGIES

One of the main problems in comprehension instruction (see Chapter 4) is that research does not point to a consistent body of skills and strategies to be taught. However, some researchers (Palincsar and Brown 1984; Jones 1986) are beginning to provide evidence supporting the training of children who fail to meet expectations in reading comprehension in using strategies that good readers use spontaneously. These researchers realize that so many demands are made on teachers that time for training is limited. Thus they focus on the use of strategies that are helpful in specific situations, yet generalizable over a number of situations (Jones et al. 1987). Four strategies that good readers use spontaneously seem to fit this criteria:

1. Asking questions
2. Predicting
3. Summarizing
4. Clarifying

After discussion of issues related to each of these particular strategies, techniques suitable for teaching them will be considered. Since several of the techniques involve both asking questions and predicting, discussion of these two strategies will be combined in one section. Techniques presented in the section entitled "Asking Questions and Making Predictions" are: ReQuest (Reciprocal Questioning procedure), InQuest (Investigative Questioning procedure), Active Comprehension, DRTA (Directed Reading Thinking Activity).

ASKING QUESTIONS AND MAKING PREDICTIONS

In Chapter 4, I point out that while teachers can use questions in comprehension instruction to focus children's attention and guide their thinking, their main goal in questioning should be to serve as a model in teaching children to ask their own questions. Training children to ask questions about content area texts is a feature of study skill methods like SQ3R (Survey, Question, Read, Recite, Review) (Robinson 1946) in which headings are converted to questions. However, children need to ask questions before, during, and after reading whether the text has headings or not. After reviewing the instructional research related to training in the self-questioning strategy, Wong (1985) concludes that studies in which children were taught to ask higher order questions, self-monitoring questions, and questions that relate the text to their prior knowledge, show that these strategies improve their comprehension.

However, Wong (1985) also points out that more attention needs to be paid to the types of questions that different groups of children are taught to ask. She suggests that remedial readers might benefit from training in asking questions that monitor their comprehension, while good readers would not need this type of training and would benefit more from learning to ask critical evaluative questions.

All the techniques presented in this chapter (except the visual imagery technique) in some way involve training children to ask their own questions about what they have read, are reading, and are about to read. These techniques also encourage children to make predictions about what they are reading.

Three of the techniques (ReQuest, InQuest, and Reciprocal Teaching) focus on teaching children to ask questions about important information in material they have already read. In order to ask questions about important information, children have to be able to determine what is important. Teachers need to help children use their prior knowledge about the content and structure of texts to determine importance when using these techniques. Like summarizing, learning to ask questions about important information in the text enables children to focus on what is important and to get the gist of the text. When children ask questions about what they are reading they are also testing their comprehension and becoming more aware of comprehension problems. Thus techniques that teach children to ask higher level questions about important text information also help them monitor their comprehension (Palincsar and Brown 1985). Since some readers have difficulty getting the gist of what they have read and monitoring their comprehension, techniques with this focus are particularly appropriate for use with this group.

In using these approaches teachers should keep in mind that their purpose is to train children to ask good questions, not necessarily to ask a lot of questions. Trivial questions should not be encouraged.

Good questions are those that relate to important information in the text; questions that relate to children's own purposes in reading can also be good ones because the answers are important to the children. While the ReQuest, InQuest, and Reciprocal Teaching techniques focus on teaching children to ask about important text information, they also encourage children to ask questions related to their own purposes by training them to ask questions and make predictions about upcoming text. Questioning and predicting are the main focus of the other two techniques: Active Comprehension and DRTA. These two latter techniques foster reading and learning from text with emphasis on the reader's purposes and "the dynamic interaction between the reader and the printed page" (Singer 1978, p. 904).

When good readers make predictions about the text, they may set their own purposes for reading and engage in a dialogue with the author, and thus become active readers. Reading is a problem solving situation that involves taking all text cues and information from prior knowledge into account. Children need to become active readers by solving problems if they are truly to understand the texts. Stauffer (1975) and Nessel (1987) both suggest that the traditional type of reading lesson in which teachers ask questions and children answer them after reading does not encourage them to be active readers. Even when children correctly answer higher level and literal questions, their answers "do not necessarily reflect either good comprehension or careful thinking . . . A student may accurately recall details or appropriately interpret them without understanding the significance of this information in context— and without even considering the many implications" (Nessel 1987, p. 444).

On the other hand, when children are encouraged to: (1) ask questions and make predictions about upcoming text; (2) justify those predictions with evidence from the text, and/or their own experience, and/or knowledge about language and text structure; (3) confirm or reject their predictions after further reading, they can learn to set their own purposes for reading. They can also learn to take account of how different pieces of information from the text and their own experience relate to each other. Making good predictions and confirming or rejecting them based on later text information requires readers to take account of information from all sources. In order to make a good prediction, a reader must fit this information together so that the significance of each piece is considered in relation to his or her background knowledge, the information in the text, and the situation in which the text is read (Nessel 1987).

Training in predicting (which always also involves training in evaluating predictions) is best provided in a group situation. When predictions are discussed in a group, children can become aware of discrepancies between their own interpretations and those of others. This awareness of a discrepancy will be a powerful motivation to look for further evidence and to weigh the evidence—to read and think more carefully (Stauffer 1975). Predictive reading in this way develops "the capacity for self-correcting thought such as we find for instance in scientific inquiry" (Garrison and Hoskisson 1989, p. 482). Focusing on predictions in a group discussion of a text improves the group interaction, for children no longer simply respond to the teacher but react to one another's predictions and argue the merits of the predictions based on text evidence. Curiosity and the urge to settle the argument are also powerful motives to read further. The children's motivation becomes internal rather than external (Nessel 1987).

PREDICTING WITH NARRATIVE TEXT

Making predictions about narrative text is easier for children than making predictions about expository text. As is pointed out in Chapter 7, they are usually more familiar with the content and structure of stories. In Chapter 5 I describe the inferential strategy technique (Hansen and Hubbard 1984), which takes advantage of this familiarity by activating children's experiences related to central concepts in the story and then asking them to use those experiences in making predictions. At times I have used the inferential strategy successfully as a during-reading technique, breaking the text to discuss children's experiences and to make a prediction. However, engaging in this type of discussion may take too much time and attention away from the story.

One problem that teachers have when using stories to teach the predicting strategy is that children will read ahead to get the right answer. Since most of them are used to a classroom climate in which getting the right answer is the goal of instruction, it is not surprising that children would try to read ahead. This means, however, that they are not learning to predict. Changing the focus of instruction to clear thinking rather than the right answer, encouraging risk taking, and explaining to the children that making predictions will help them understand the text better are all ways to discourage reading ahead. Another more concrete way of discouraging reading ahead is to mark the text in chunks for the children, and to use blank sheets of paper (cover sheets) to cover upcoming portions of the text while making predictions (Ruddell and Haggard 1986). *Thinking About Reading* (Ruddell and Haggard 1986) attempts to help teachers with this problem by providing cover sheets, chunking the texts, and inserting graphic cues that signal the children to use the cover sheets and make predictions about the upcoming portion of the covered text.

PREDICTING WITH EXPOSITORY TEXT

In my own experience reading ahead is less of a problem when using expository text. Perhaps this is because the particular expository texts I used were less interesting to the children than the stories. When training children to make predictions about expository text, teachers will often need to help children build schemata about the topics and structures. Schemata can be built by activating and building prior knowledge about the content and by guiding children to attend to text cues like headings and structural cue words.

Like the pre-reading techniques discussed in Chapter 5, the techniques discussed in this chapter are similar to one another. However, like the pre-reading techniques they differ in that some techniques are more suitable for use with narrative text, while others are more suitable for expository text or can be used with both types of text.

REQUEST

This technique developed by Manzo (1968) and described by Tierney, Readence, and Dishner (1985) was originally designed for one-to-one instruction. However, it has also been used effectively in small groups. Tierney, Readence, and Dishner (1985) suggest that it can be used with students from kindergarten to college. The technique is a structured one that focuses on questions about what has been read. One child, or a group of children, and the teacher begin reading a selection sentence by sentence. In a one-to-one situation they read the sentences silently and after each sentence, the child, then the teacher, asks questions about the sentence. In a small group situation the children can take turns as questioner and respondent, or different children can alternate with the teacher. Tierney, Readence, and Dishner (1985) also suggest alternating the role of questioner after each question. In the script that illustrates the technique, different students ask the teacher questions about what has been read, then the teacher asks questions of different students (see script for ReQuest technique).

This technique can be helpful in situations in which sentence constructions are difficult for children to understand. ReQuest is a better way of teaching sentence understanding than activities that consider sentences in isolation; even though the technique focuses on individual sentences, the relationship of one sentence to another is taken into consideration. Reading a text sentence by sentence may also be appropriate with expository text that contains many new concepts. It would not be appropriate to read much of the text in this way because the procedure would become tedious. It also would not be appropriate to read sections of most stories sentence by sentence.

However, on one occasion, I used the ReQuest technique to help fifth grade remedial readers understand one section of a narrative text in a basal reader. This story, *The Mystery of the Moon Guitar* (Niemeyer 1976), was an excerpt from a book. The part of the book that preceded the excerpt was summarized on the first page. If the children did not understand the background information found on this page, they would not understand the excerpt. Since the first page was a summary, it was more lexically dense than a regular story and thus more like expository text. Reading this page sentence by sentence and asking questions about each sentence was helpful to the children in this situation.

In the lesson on which the script below is based, one of my graduate students decided to use the ReQuest technique with a narrative text. She was working in a Basic English course with a group of adult readers who were reading approximately at the fifth grade level. She decided that the text, *The Bet*, a short story by Anton Chekov (Sloan and Capaccio 1983), would be more difficult for her students to understand than other stories that they had been reading. She wanted to teach the students the strategy of asking questions about literature they were reading, and she felt that this particular technique would provide the kind of support these students needed. As suggested by Tierney, Readence, and Dishner (1985), she used the technique flexibly; she started by having the students read one paragraph at a time, then extended sections on which questions were based to a page, and finally to several pages.

The script excerpt is a transcription of the teacher-student dialogue based on the first three paragraphs of the short story. The teacher interrupted the text twice in this short section of text because it presents two important story elements.

In the script you will notice that the teacher models the use of story schema as a way of constructing important questions about the story. In previous lessons the students learned to map stories and became familiar with the elements of story grammar. The first paragraph of the story contains the setting (a group of young men having a discussion about which is more cruel: capital punishment or life imprisonment), while the second paragraph sets the stage for the main event of the story (the banker argues that life imprisonment is more cruel).

This script begins after the teacher explains how to use this technique and how it will help the students' comprehension. The students read the first paragraph below.

> The guests at dinner, all clever young men, were a little drunk. The conversation was loud and lively. Among the things they talked about was capital punishment, or the death penalty. The majority of the guests thought it should be replaced by life imprisonment (Sloan and Capaccio 1983, p. 148).

ReQuest Technique Script

S1: *What kind of people were they?*

T: *Rich young men.*

S: *That's wrong.*

T: *Let's look back. I'm mistaken. They were clever young men. (This mistake illustrates one problem teachers may have in using this technique. Later information in the story made it clear that the young men are rich. However, the information in the first paragraph did not show they are rich.)*

S2: *How was the conversation?*

T: *The conversation was lively and active.*

S3: *What were they talking about?*

T: *That's a good question. They were talking about life imprisonment versus the death penalty.*

S4: *Why were they so loud?*

T: *They were drinking and some were a little drunk. I'm thinking of story schema. Where were they or what were they doing?*

S5: *They were having dinner, maybe at a party.*

T: *How did you know that?*

S5: It says they were guests, and there were a lot of them, so maybe it was a party.

T: You did a good job of backing up your answer. What was the consensus about capital punishment? Consensus means how did most of the guests feel.

S1: Some of them believed in that and some in life imprisonment.

T: Look back at the paragraph to find out how most of the guests felt.

S1: (reading the sentence) The majority of the guests thought it should be replaced by life imprisonment.

T: Read to the end of the next two paragraphs.

> "I don't agree," said the banker, the man who was giving the dinner. "Putting a person to death seems much kinder than shutting him up for life and killing him slowly. Which man is worse—the one who kills at one blow, or the one who makes a life into a nightmare of wasted years?"
>
> "Both ways are wrong," one guest said, "because both are taking life away. The methods are different; the results are the same" (Sloan and Cappacio 1983, p. 149).

S4: Who was giving the party?

T: The banker.

S3: Which man is worse—the one who kills or the one who makes life into a nightmare?

T: That's a good question that you might be thinking about as you read this story. But it can't be answered from this paragraph. We only know from this paragraph how people feel. The question you asked is an opinion question. We might all have a different opinion just as the people in the story had different opinions. Maybe you could ask about how a specific person felt about this question.

S3: How did the banker feel?

T: He felt that capital punishment was better. What was meant by the phrase "killing him slowly"?

S2: If you're in for life, there are days on end with nothing to do and nothing to look forward to and that's the same as a slow death.

T: That was a good answer.

In this excerpt the teacher provides feedback to the student about the quality of the questions—praising questions that focus on important information and explaining that questions should be text related. In one case she suggests a question for a student to ask. She continued this focus on text relatedness and importance of questions throughout the lesson. For example, at a later point a student asks a question about a trivial detail.

Dialogue

S5: Who pounded the table?

T: I think the banker, but do you think that is important to understanding the story?

S5: No.

T: Right. I'm glad you asked that question though. We often ask those kinds of questions because they are easy to think of, but we want to ask important questions—ones that ask about the important parts. Remember story schema if you can.

In later portions of the lesson, the teacher also suggests that students avoid yes and no questions, and provides help in phrasing questions more appropriately. In the excerpt and throughout the lesson the teacher models good questions, extending the students' thinking by asking higher level and important questions.

Although the questions are answered from memory, this teacher encourages the students to refer to the text to check or support their answers. She models the behavior herself and praises a student for providing good support for an answer. When the students have read enough to make a prediction about the way the story might turn out, the teacher asks them for a prediction. She also asks them to evaluate their predictions at later points in the story. However, she then returns to the questioning.

Manzo (1969) suggests using the Reciprocal Questioning procedure up to the point where the students can make a reasonable prediction. He then suggests that after predicting the students should read the rest of the text silently in order to determine whether their predictions are confirmed or refuted. Evaluation of the predictions is the focus of the post-reading discussion. This teacher was probably able to return to the more difficult questioning technique because she was working with well motivated adults. When working with children, it is probably better to follow Manzo's suggestion.

InQuest (Investigative Questioning Procedure)

Like ReQuest, the InQuest technique is designed to teach children to ask questions about material they have read and also to ask questions and make predictions about upcoming material. However, this technique provides a very different context for asking questions and thus the type of questions asked are also different. In this technique developed by Shoop (1986), the children and the teacher do not engage in reciprocal questioning. Drama and role playing are used to encourage children to ask each other questions and to elicit predictions from the point of view of different characters in a story. At critical points in the story, reading is interrupted and children role play a news conference taking place at the scene of the story event. One student assumes the role of a major character, while others are investigative reporters who question the student playing the character about story events as well as ask for predictions of future story events from this character's point of view. After the news conference, the children continue reading.

This technique is most appropriate for use with narratives, since it trains children to interview story characters. Interviewing involves questions that move "beyond the facts and between the lines" (Shoop 1986, p. 674); in using InQuest children are trained to ask high level questions about a character's motivation and answer them from the character's point of view. Thus the technique is designed to enable children to move beyond the surface events of a story and to understand its underlying meaning and theme. Some of the research presented in Chapter 7 suggests that children have difficulty with these aspects of a story. Some children may have particular difficulty because they do not understand that different reading tasks have different purposes. Others may not understand that story events may have an underlying meaning and so may fail to search for this meaning.

The teacher has a different role in InQuest than in ReQuest; the teacher does not join in questioning the character once the children become familiar with the interviewing situation, although he or she provides prompts and feedback for their questions. However, before the children engage in role playing with the story, the teacher prepares them by providing explicit training in interviewing. Shoop suggests that one of the best ways of doing this is to have children view a videotape of reporters conducting an interview. A videotape that contains both good and poor questions would be best. Before viewing the videotape, the teacher directs the children to notice the different kinds of questions reporters ask and how the type of question affects the type of answer. After viewing, the children decide which questions were better and why. Rules for asking good questions can be established and displayed on charts. Interviewing each other and the teacher are also good activities for training children to ask good questions. The first few times InQuest is used with stories, the teacher models the roles of the character and/or the reporters.

I have not had the opportunity to use this technique myself, but several of my graduate students have used it with their middle grade classes and have found that the children love it, and that it helps them to understand stories. The script below demonstrates a lesson by one of my students with a group of eight children. Six of the children were fourth graders reading on grade level and two of them were fifth graders whose standardized test scores indicated that they were reading at the fourth grade level. However, these fifth graders had worked on their class newspaper and had acted as reporters and conducted interviews as part of that experience. In this situation the "below level" readers became the experts who shared their insights about interviewing with the rest of the group. Several weeks before participating in this lesson, the children had viewed a videotape of young people interviewing authorities about a drug program. The group discussed techniques the young people used in the way suggested by Shoop (1986). Guidelines for interviewing that came out of that discussion were:

1. Questions should be worded so that they will get people to give a lot of information.
2. Longer responses are better than shorter responses.
3. A yes or no question will get a better response if the interviewer follows up with question words like *why, when, where, what,* or *how.*
4. A good reporter should ask a variety of questions.

The children in this group and in the other reading groups taught by this teacher also participated in several InQuest lessons with other texts in which the teacher modeled the roles of characters and reporters. As a result of problems in maintaining point of view in these lessons, the groups came up with another rule for asking questions, "You can only ask a character a question that is appropriate for the story and the time in which he or she is living." Rules were displayed on a chart hanging in the classroom. The children and the teacher had also evolved other methods for keeping their roles straight. The teacher provided nametags for children who were playing characters, and the reporters wore hats and used microphones made by attaching sponges to rulers. The hats and the microphones were the children's idea. While at first glance these props may seem like additions made just for fun, the teacher felt that these concrete materials acted as reminders for the children, helping them to keep to their roles.

The basal reader story the children read in this lesson, *Dream Dancer* (Bolton 1985), was suitable for use with the InQuest technique because characters' motivations for their actions were complex. Caroline, the girl in the story, uses an old horse to show her grandfather's boss, Mr. Judd, that he should not waste good talent and not make her grandfather retire. Often inferencing was required in order to understand why a character said or did something.

The script below begins after the children have read 2½ pages of the story. The teacher stops them at the point in the story where Caroline finds out that her grandfather has to retire.

InQuest Script

T: E and B, since you have both had experience with interviewing I would like you to think of some questions you would like to ask Caroline. Remember your goals: acquiring as much information as you can, having the character think back over the events that have taken place so far, and making the character tell how she feels and what she thinks might happen next. A, I would like you to be Caroline in this interview. I think you will be able to handle the questions very well. Remember you are not A, you are Caroline. The answers that you give to the reporters have to come from what we have read in the story. While the reporters are thinking of questions, you might want to read over the pages again so you will be able to answer their questions very well.

Reporter 1: Caroline, why did you go to visit your grandfather every summer?

Caroline: Well, I'm off from school during the summer. My parents like me to visit Grandpa because I get a chance to be in the country. I can help to take care of the horses, and I get to sleep over at grandfather's house. It's different from what I do most of the time. I really love taking care of the horses.

Reporter 2: How did you feel when your grandfather told you he had to retire?

Caroline: I felt surprised and mad.

T: B, add something extra to your question so that Caroline will have to tell you more.

Reporter 2: Why did you feel surprised and mad when your grandfather told you he had to retire?

Caroline: Well, you don't know my grandfather like I do. He's almost like my father. I mean I know that he's kind of old, but he likes to joke with me and stuff. He gets up early in the morning all the time. He's almost never sick, and he's always busy. My grandfather really likes doing things, even going to work.

Reporter 1: What kinds of things does your grandfather do at work? Does he do hard things?

Caroline: My grandfather is an expert furniture maker. His work is kind of hard because he works with wood and nails. But he's very, very good at it. He makes all different kind of furniture. He never takes days off because he likes what he is doing. He makes chairs and furniture all by himself.

Reporter 2: What can you do to stop your grandfather from retiring?

Caroline: Well, I'm going to talk more to my grandfather. Maybe I can talk him out of it. Or maybe I will talk to his boss. I'm not exactly sure.

T: Good questions, E and B. I hope all of you noticed how E and B worded their questions so that A couldn't just give one word answers. A, you did a fine job, too. You answered from what the story told you. Now we're going to read on a little bit and have another interview in a few pages. As you read, think about some questions you might want to ask.

The teacher broke the text reading at two more points in the story to interview Grandpa and Caroline once again. At the end of the story Mr. Judd was interviewed. The teacher continued to prompt the reporters to ask questions that elicited an abundance of information, and the children playing the characters gave a lot of information. Like the girl who had the role of Caroline, they elaborated on the information contained in the text, integrating background knowledge with text information to give full and interesting answers. When necessary, the teacher also prompted the reporters to ask the characters for predictions. The following day, the teacher and the children discussed the questions that had been asked and talked about how asking the questions helped them to understand the story better.

Although in this lesson the teacher only picked certain children to be reporters, in later lessons she moved to a format where all the children who were not playing a character planned the questions together in a group. One child wrote down the questions while others were designated to ask them.

Breaking into the story for such long periods of time is disruptive to the story. Many teachers feel that this is a weakness of the technique and suggest that children should read the story first and then use this InQuest technique as an after-reading activity. However, if the technique is used after reading, there can be no predicting. My students who have used the technique have not found the disruption of the story to be a problem. The questions and answers review text information so effectively that children do not lose track of the story, and they enjoy the role playing so that they are motivated to continue the story. The only way to find out the best way to use the technique with your children is to try it.

ACTIVE COMPREHENSION

This technique, developed by Singer (1978), is supposed to train children to ask questions before, during, and after reading. However, the sample lessons and questions found in descriptions of the technique (McNeil 1987; Nolte and Singer 1985; Singer 1978) focus on training them to ask questions about up-coming information—information that they have not read yet. As in the K - W - L technique described in Chapter 5, the teacher asks the children what they want to know. The children respond to the teacher's question with their own questions. Thus many questions asked in this technique actually resemble predictions, especially when children ask yes/no questions as they do in the script below. In using this technique the teacher should interrupt the text at points where the children can ask questions, and/or at points when their questions are answered by the text.

When integrated with instruction in story grammar as in the Nolte and Singer (1985) study, Active Comprehension is only suitable for use with narrative text. On the first day of the Nolte and Singer study, the teacher reviewed story grammar first. For half the reading period, the children read a paragraph or two at a time while the teacher modeled good questions based on story grammar that were related to central concepts of the story. Children then read the rest of the story and asked their own questions for the rest of the period. The next three days were the central phase of the technique; instead of asking questions that the children answered, the teacher asked questions that required children to provide questions rather than answers, e.g., "What would you like to know about what happens next?" For the next six days the children practiced asking questions under the teacher's supervision. First, they worked in groups in which one child was chosen to ask questions and the other children answered the questions. Then the students worked in pairs, asking each other questions, and finally they worked independently. Nolte and Singer found that the group of fourth and fifth graders they trained in active comprehension understood stories better than a control group after a ten-day period. However, teachers of remedial readers would probably need to spend much more time in the modeling stage and in the central phase with the teacher asking questions that prompt the children to ask questions.

The script below is an excerpt from a lesson I conducted with a group of eight low SES remedial readers. In this lesson the children and I read the first chapter of *Sarah Plain and Tall* (McLachlan 1985). The language in this book is beautiful, but ideas are often implicit rather than explicit. I asked questions and gave explanations to help the children appreciate the beauty of the language and understand its meaning; in addition, I encouraged the children to ask their own questions.

Active Comprehension Script

T: Today I'm going to ask you to do something different. I am going to ask you questions about what you read, and I want you to notice the kinds of questions I ask. But I am also going to ask you to ask questions. You may find asking questions a little harder than answering them at first, but asking questions about what you are reading will help you to understand it better.

(The children and I read the title and discussed the meaning of the word plain *in the title. Since they had just discussed the meaning of* plains *and* prairie *in preparation for reading the book, I pointed out that the meaning of* plain *is not the same in the title. I asked them to describe a plain dress and then made the analogy to a plain person since none of the children had ever heard the word* plain *used to describe a person.)*

Let's look at the picture on the cover. (The picture shows a boy and a girl sitting on the front steps of a farmhouse. A woman is cutting the boy's hair.) What questions do you have about this picture? What would you like to find out?

(Silence from all the children - I wrote question words on the board, such as who, what, where, when, why, *and* how.*) Here are question words to help you.*

S1: Who are these people?

T: OK Good.

S2: Who's cutting the person's hair?

T: Ok S1, you said "Who are these people?" and S2, you are particularly interested in this person who is cutting the hair. Do we already know where they are?.

S3: They are on a farm.

T: Where is the farm?

S3: On the plains.

T: Right. (I read the first two pages aloud to the children while they followed along in their own books.)

Do we know who the people are yet?

S4: First person singular (At first I was stunned by this response. But then I realized someone had been teaching this ESL student English grammar.)

T: Oh, you mean I. Yes, someone is telling the story in the first person singular. We don't know I's name. Who is the boy in the picture do you think?

S5: Caleb.

T: Yes, Caleb is a boy's name. So I might be the girl or the woman. Do we know who is cutting the boy's hair?

All S: No.

T: Do you have any more questions? Do you have any questions about Mama?

S3: Is she dead or alive?

T: What makes you ask that question?

(S3 looks uncomfortable.)

T: That was a good question. I'm not asking you why because you are wrong. I am asking you why so that you can tell the other kids about the clues in the text that made you ask that question. Why do you think S3 thought Mama might be dead?

S4: Because of the way that they talked in the story.

T: What did they say that made you think that?

S6: They said he was asking the question for years.

T: Yes, Caleb was asking about Mama for years. We get the feeling Mama isn't there anymore. But we don't know if she is alive or dead. (I then asked one of the children to read the next section aloud to see if we could find the answers to our questions:

> *Who is cutting the boy's hair?*
>
> *Who is I?*
>
> *Is Mama dead or alive?*

We continued in the same manner to the end of the chapter.)

I began this lesson by encouraging the children to ask questions about the picture on the cover of the book. Although on this occasion showing the picture only generated a few questions, in other lessons children have asked many questions about a cover picture, giving them a good purpose for reading the text. Singer (1978) suggests that asking questions about a picture is a good way to introduce the Active Comprehension technique to children. I have found, when reading picture books with younger children, it often works well to have them ask questions about the pictures and then read to answer their questions. Using pictures as a basis for predicting can also be part of the DRTA technique.

DRTA (DIRECTED READING THINKING ACTIVITY)

The Directed Reading Thinking Activity developed by Stauffer (1975) was one of the first techniques that attempted to teach children *how* to understand what they were reading by encouraging them in the active processing of text. Active Comprehension and DRTA are very similar in that in both techniques teachers ask questions that encourage children to ask questions and make predictions about upcoming text, draw conclusions from the text regarding the validity of those predictions after reading, and provide support from the text regarding the validity of their predictions.

However, DRTA and Active Comprehension are different in that Active Comprehension emphasizes asking questions while DRTA emphasizes predicting. As was described in the previous section, using Active Comprehension, I asked the children what questions they had about a picture. If I were using DRTA, I would ask them a questions like "What do you think the story might tell us about these people?" Children may give predictions in an Active Comprehension lesson because questions that can be answered with a yes or no are just like predictions. They may also ask questions in a DRTA lesson but the focus is on making predictions.

Like Active Comprehension, DRTA is normally used with narrative text and is particularly appropriate to use as a during-reading activity when the inferential strategy activity has been used as a pre-reading activity. In using

DRTA teachers should interrupt the text for discussion at points where the children can make predictions, and/or at points where their predictions are confirmed or refuted by the text, and where children can provide support for this confirmation or refutation.

The script below is an excerpt from a DRTA lesson conducted by one of my graduate students with a group of fifth graders. The story they were reading was *The Mountain of Tears* (Mandel 1979). This story is a Japanese folktale that describes an ancient practice of bringing old people up the mountain to die.

The teacher in this excerpt asks four kinds of questions basic to the DRTA technique:

1. What did you think a story with a title like this might be about?
2. What do you think now? (Is your prediction confirmed or refuted?)
3. What in the story makes you think that?
4. What do you think will happen next?

Like the generic questions related to narrative and expository structure presented in Chapter 7, these basic questions can and should be made specific to the story as the teacher does in this lesson. For example, she asks a specific question calling for a prediction based on the title "What do you think they might do on this mountain to make it a sad or a happy place?" Later she encourages the children to evaluate their predictions with another specific question, "So were any of your predictions right about this being a sad mountain?"

DRTA Lesson Script

(The teacher directs the children to read only the title of the story.)
T: From this title, what do you think the story is going to be about?
S1: A mountain.
T: What makes you say that?
S1: Because it has it right in the title.
T: Okay. What kind of story is this going to be?
S2: A sad one.
T: Why?
S2: Because the title says tears.
T: When you think of tears, what do you think of?
S2: Something sad happening.
S3: Or you could be crying because you're so happy.
T: From the title you've told me it's going to be about a mountain and that it could be either a sad or happy story. What do you think they might do on this mountain to make it a sad or happy place?
S4: They might go hiking.
S5: They might leave somebody there.
T: I think you read the first part of the story. That is not predicting. Guessing what will happen will help you to read it more carefully and understand it better. Please don't read ahead.

(The students read the first paragraph silently. This paragraph described the custom of leaving old people on the mountain to die.)

T: Now that you have read the beginning of the story, do you know why they call it the Mountain of Tears?

S3: Yes, because when old people reached the age of sixty, they were taken to the top of the mountain and left there to die.

T: So were any of your predictions right about this being a sad mountain?

S2: Yes.

T: What in this paragraph tells you that?

S2: It says it was a cruel custom and made the people sad.

T: Good. Why do you think they would take the people to the mountain to die at the age of sixty?

S1: Because they figured they were going to die anyway.

S4: Because they thought they were old and helpless.

T: Okay. Let's find out if your predictions are right.

(The teacher then directs the children to read the next two pages.)

Although most reading experts would encourage the use of the DRTA technique, some questions have been raised about certain of its aspects. First, some authors (e.g., Lynch 1988) believe that asking children to make a prediction based on the title is not a good idea because the title does not provide enough information to make a good prediction. They suggest that this practice encourages wild guessing. In the script one child predicts that the story will be a sad one while another child uses the same evidence to predict that the story will be a happy one. On the other hand, children may have certain expectations based on a title even when the teacher does not ask about these expectations. As with the misconceptions discussed in Chapter 5, a better practice probably would be to bring these expectations out into the open so that they can be discussed and later checked against text information.

Garrison and Hoskisson (1989) have raised a second objection to DRTA as it is normally used. They point out that the emphasis in most DRTA lessons is on reading to see if the predictions are right and then proving them with evidence from the text. This practice may reinforce confirmation bias, "...the psychological tendency to consider only evidence that will confirm the prediction being tested while either ignoring or not seeking evidence that might refute it" (Garrison and Hoskisson 1989, p. 482). (The discussion in Chapter 5 on refuting misconceptions also deals with this issue of confirmation bias.) Since the combination of confirmation bias and the DRTA emphasis on confirmation of predictions may foster poor patterns of thinking, Garrison and Hoskisson suggest a change of emphasis in using the DRTA technique— children should be directed to search for evidence refuting their predictions. In the script if the teacher focused on refutation of predictions instead of saying "Were any of your predictions right about this being a sad mountain?", she would say something like "There were two predictions: the mountain was happy and the mountain was sad. Did you find any evidence to contradict one of those predictions?" This change of emphasis makes sense from the point of view of logic. However, I wonder what the effect would be on the children's motivation. It seems intuitively more motivating to prove yourself right than to prove yourself wrong. This type of emphasis might be appropriate for older children but not for younger ones. These are questions that need to be tested by research. In the meantime, teachers should be on the alert for confirmation bias and should realize that a prediction that is not refuted is not necessarily confirmed. Some predictions must be held tentatively since later evidence may refute them.

RECIPROCAL TEACHING

The Reciprocal Teaching technique (briefly described in Chapter 4 as an exemplar of the combined model of comprehension instruction) was developed by Palincsar and Brown (1984) and has proved successful in a large number of their studies with remedial readers in junior high school (Palincsar and Brown 1984; Palincsar 1985, 1987a) who fail to meet expectations in reading comprehension. They have also used the method successfully in a study that provided listening comprehension instruction for first graders whose test scores indicated that they were at-risk for reading problems (Palincsar 1986a, 1986b, 1987b). At first, Palincsar and Brown used the method in one-to-one instruction and with pairs of students (1982). Later, the researchers, classroom teachers, and reading teachers whom they had trained used it with groups of 7 to 17 (Palincsar 1985, 1987a) composed of children who met expectations in word recognition but not in comprehension. Although I have not had the opportunity to use Reciprocal Teaching for the recommended minimum time of 20 days, I have been very impressed by the way in which groups of 8 to 12 remedial readers respond to the technique even in a single demonstration lesson. I have introduced the technique in staff development sessions to many classroom teachers, who have used it over extended periods of time with remedial readers at many different grade levels. Without exception, they are enthusiastic about the success that the children have experienced. The careful research of Palincsar and Brown, my own experience, and the experience of the teachers with whom I work leads me to recommend this method as the most effective one for use in comprehension instruction of children who have not met comprehension expectations. If you cannot decide which technique to try, try this one.

The script below is an excerpt from a demonstration lesson that I conducted using this technique with a group of six third grade remedial readers. The text that we used was *The Best Nest* (Eastman 1968). Chapter 2 discusses why this text was chosen. It is a simple story, but it contains information about where and how birds build their nests. At the beginning of the story, Mr. Bird is happy with his nest in the birdhouse, but Mrs. Bird is not. She wants to move. The birds try to build their nest in several places—a tree and a mailbox —but they are always chased away. Mrs. Bird disappears; Mr. Bird goes to look for her and sees a cat with feathers next to her mouth and a smile on her face and thinks that she has eaten Mrs. Bird. But he finds Mrs. Bird in their old nest in the birdhouse. She has decided that it is the best nest.

Reciprocal Teaching Script

T: *When we read we have to think about what we read. The first thing you can do is ask yourself questions about what you are reading. (The teacher points to a chart that lists four strategies). This will help you to think about whether you understand it and it will also help you to think about the important parts. What is the second thing you should do S1?*

S1: *Tell the important parts.*

T: *Yes, good. You tell the important parts in your own words and that will help you to remember.*

T: *What is the third thing you should do S2?*

S2: *Guess what is going to happen.*

T: *Yes, if you predict or guess what is going to happen you need to use clues in what you are reading to help you guess. Number 4 says "Explain the hard parts." The teacher needs to explain anything that is hard to understand, and when you are reading you need to be looking for parts that you don't understand so that you can ask for help. We are going to do all four of these things to help us understand what we read.*

(A child is directed to read the first page aloud.)

T: *I am the teacher so the first thing I'm going to do is ask questions. Why is Mr. Bird singing?*

S3: *Because he was happy.*

T: *Because he was happy. Very good. Why was he happy S4?*

S4: *Because he had a nice nest.*

T: *Very good. Now I'm going to tell the important parts of what we just read. Mr. Bird is happy with his nest. He thinks it's the best nest. Okay, now the next thing I'm going to do is guess what's going to happen on the next page. Now I am looking at this picture. Who do you think that is down in the hole there?*

S5: *Mrs. Bird.*

T: *Yes, Mrs. Bird. Does she look very happy?*

S5: *No.*

T: *No, so you know what I think is going to happen? I think ... (S3 raises hand) What do you think?*

S3: *That she's going to get a headache.*

T: *Yes, she looks like she might get a headache. I think maybe she has a headache because she doesn't like the nest. What do you think? Let's see. You read for us S5.*

S5 reads: *"Mrs. Bird came out of her house. 'It's not the best nest,' she said."*

T: *I guessed right, didn't I?*

(For these three pages and the next section of five pages, I continued to model the strategies. The children read the next section silently. In this book, several pages was not a lot of reading. Palincsar, Brown, and David [work in progress]

181

suggest that when working with expository text, at first dialogue should take place after each paragraph. Since I was working with a simple narrative text, I chunked the text in somewhat longer sections. When we came to the fourth section, I asked a child to play the role of teacher.)

T: We are going to do something different. I'm not going to be the teacher anymore. I'm going to let S3 be the teacher. And after she is the teacher, everybody is going to get a turn to be the teacher. What will you have to do, S3, when you are the teacher?

S3 *(looks at chart)*: Ask questions.

T: Good.

S3: Tell the important parts.

T: Yes, tell the important parts and guess what's going to happen. If any of us have anything we don't understand we should ask S3 about it because she's the teacher.

(After the reading)

T: S3, you are the teacher. Ask the questions the teacher should ask.

S3 *(Points to picture of mailbox with the bird on top)*: What is this?

T: Okay. Raise your hands and S3 will call on you.

S5: It's a mailbox.

S3: Good.

T: Any other questions? Okay. That's a question I would have asked, but I would say "Where does Mrs. Bird want to build a nest now?" S3, now you must tell the important parts. Tell us what happened.

S3: They're going to put mail in the mailbox. *(S3 is stating information that is not provided until the next page.)*

T: No, that's guessing what is going to happen. It didn't say that in what we read. We have to tell the important parts of what we read. The birds are going to make a nest. . . .

S3: Inside

T: Inside what?

S3: Inside the mailbox.

T: Okay. Now put that all together. Say the whole thing.

S3: The birds went inside to make a nest in the mailbox.

T: Good. Now you have to guess what's going to happen. You already did. What did you say people were going to do?

S3: Put mail in the mailbox.

(The teacher selects another child to be "teacher." The children read the next section, and the lesson continues until the book is finished.)

As the script demonstrates, the first step in the Reciprocal Teaching procedure is to introduce it to the children. The teacher discusses reasons that text may be difficult to understand and the necessity for learning strategies so that they can comprehend. The children are told that the Reciprocal Teaching procedure will help them learn the strategies that they need. Palincsar, Brown, and David (work in progress) suggest that the teacher should then describe the technique: Children and teacher will participate in a dialogue in which children will take turns playing the role of "teacher." After the children and the teacher read a section of text together, the "teacher" asks questions about important information in the text section read, calls on other students to answer, summarizes that section, points out anything that is unclear, leads the group in clarifying, and makes a prediction about upcoming text. In the script you can see that I did not describe the technique fully until I chose a child to be the "teacher." Since I would only see the children once (I was doing one demonstration lesson to introduce the Reciprocal Teaching technique to a group of classroom teachers and reading teachers), I also did not do the preparatory activities that Palincsar and Brown (1985) recommend. Instead I introduced the strategies by means of a chart which was kept in the children's view throughout the lesson. As the script demonstrates, this chart helped the children keep track of the strategies they were supposed to use in the lesson. Because the text in this particular lesson did not have difficult vocabulary or complex sentence structures, there were no opportunities to use the clarifying strategy. I did remind the children about it at several points during part of the lesson not included in the script. Palincsar, Brown, and David (work in progress) recommend having the children ask questions and summarize after every text section read; predicting and clarifying are used only when they are appropriate.

Although I did not have the opportunity to prepare these children for Reciprocal Teaching, I would use the recommended preparatory activities if I worked with the children consistently. After the introduction and overview of the technique, children should be introduced to each strategy at a very fundamental level. Introduce each strategy on a separate day, and provide practice in the following ways:

I. Preparatory Activities: Questions
   A. Students generate information-seeking questions
      "You want to see the movie 'The Empire Strikes Back' but don't know when the show begins. You call the movie theatre and ask _____ _____?"
   B. Discussion regarding the importance of questioning
   C. Review of question words
   D. Question generating from text
      1. Brief, clear sentence with question word provided
        The falcon is a female hunting bird.
        What _____?
      2. Brief, clear sentence with question word phased out
        Scientists study animal communications through experiments and observations.
        _____ _____?
      3. Provided with a short segment of text, students select main idea question

Deaths from snakebites have been cut down in recent years by the use of antivenins—medicine that work against the snake poisons. There are now few deaths from snakebite in the United States and Canada.

    a. Why do snakes bite people?
    b. In what countries do few people die from snakebite?
    c. Why do fewer people die from snakebite these days?

4. Provided a short segment of text, students generate main idea question

There have been many prominent women in America's history who have done much good for humankind. One of these women was Dr. Alice Hamilton. Dr. Hamilton was very concerned about the health of industrial workers. Through her research and leadership, she was responsible for many changes that improved working conditions for laborers.

_____

_____ ?

II. Preparatory Activities: Summarizing
  A. Students generate summaries about a favorite TV show, movie or story
  B. Discussion of importance of summarizing
  C. Applying summary rules
    1. Identify the topic sentence.

In the fall, wild animals begin to stock food and grow long coats of hair. Many birds fly south. The leaves turn beautiful colors, then die and fall to the ground. The days become shorter and the weather gets cooler. Many signs tell us winter is coming.

What is the topic of the paragraph? _____
What is the topic sentence? _____

    2. Invent a topic sentence if there isn't one.

When a volcano erupts, melted rock, steam, and ashes are forced through the top of the mountain. The area around the volcano is sprayed with ashes and boiling liquid called lava. Trees and buildings in its path are destroyed. Wildlife and people are killed.

What is the topic of the paragraph? _____
Write a summary statement that includes the main ideas of the paragraph. _____

_____

    3. Leave out unimportant information.

Amelia has three pairs of Levis. One pair is navy blue. One pair is light blue (to match her eyes). The third pair is green. She likes them all.

What is the topic of this selection? (Amelia's Levis)
What is the most important thing the author is saying about the Levis?

    4. Give steps or lists a title.

It's always great fun to watch a pizza being made. The pizza maker first grabs a lump of dough and pats it into a flat cake. Then she slips it on her closed fist and twirls it around in the air until it becomes a large pancake. After that, the pancake is tenderly placed on a baker's shovel and covered with cheeses and meats and tomato sauce. Finally, the pizza maker slides the shovel into a special hot oven. In five minutes, the pizza becomes bubbly hot and brown crusted.

This paragraph told _____.

(how a pizza maker makes pizza)

    5. Cross out information that is redundant.

The North Pole is one of the coldest regions on earth. The temperature often drops below 0 degrees. Weather forecasters often report freezing temperatures there. The winds are very strong at the North Pole, gusting up to 60 miles per hour. It is quite windy at the North Pole.

What are the two important characteristics of the North Pole? (coldness, windiness)

Cross out redundant sentences.

III. Preparatory Activities: Predicting

    A. Use of background knowledge relating to predicting

What do you predict you will see when you visit a pet store?

_____

    B. Predicting from a title

Animals in the Postal Service

I predict this story will be about _____

_____

    C. Using headings to predict

Title: _____

        1. caterpillar
        2. cocoon
        3. butterfly

    D. Text questions as predictors

We frequently read about fires that do extensive damage. Many are caused by careless smokers or electrical shorts. Did you know that legend says a *cow* was responsible for the worst fire in Chicago?

I predict the author will next discuss: _____

IV. Preparatory Activities: Clarifying

    A. Discussion regarding why students do not understand the text they are reading.

    B. Unclear referents

There are animals called lemmings that have some very unusual behaviors. Every couple of years, *they* are observed to throw *themselves* into the ocean, commiting what appears to be suicide.

What is the subject of the first sentence? (animals called lemmings)

What does "they" refer to in the second sentence? (the lemmings)

What does "themselves" refer to in the second sentence? (the lemmings again)

    C. Difficult or unfamiliar vocabulary, concepts, or imagery

People who are bilingual—that is, people who speak two languages—are in ever increasing demand. Their services are needed by airlines, schools and the government.

What does the word "bilingual" mean? _____

D. Context clues to discover the meaning of a word
    The speaker did not pay attention to the *heckler* who kept yelling rude comments from the back of the room.
    What is a heckler? _____

After the four days spent introducing the strategies, the teacher and children engage in a dialogue using all four strategies: asking questions, then summarizing, clarifying whenever necessary, and ending a dialogue episode by making a prediction about upcoming text when appropriate. If children have difficulty asking questions, it is sometimes helpful to have them summarize first (Palincsar, Brown, and David work in progress). At first, the teacher models the strategies as I did at the beginning of the lesson in the script. Each teacher will need to decide when it is time to begin having the children take the role of "teacher." At first, the teacher should choose children who he or she thinks will be relatively successful with the process so that these children can also serve as models for the other children in the group. In the script I chose Student 3 because she had given several appropriate answers and raised her hand to answer at times when I called on others to answer; she seemed more verbal than the others and was eager to participate. Nevertheless, as the script demonstrates, she needed a great deal of support in phrasing her questions and summary. All children should be given the opportunity to participate in the dialogue at their own level. In the demonstration lesson each child had the opportunity to play the role of "teacher." Teachers should prompt and support each student according to his or her particular needs. Most of the students in the script needed the same kind of support that I gave Student 3; I had to start them off with questions and summaries. However, the last student to play the role of "teacher" (perhaps as a result of all the modeling to which she had been exposed) asked an excellent inferential question with no prompting from me. I provided positive feedback and suggested a follow-up question.

Reading

Then he (Mr. Bird) saw a big fat cat.
There was a big fat smile on the fat cat's face.
There were some pretty brown feathers near the fat cat's mouth (Eastman 1968, p. 50).

Dialogue

S6: *What did Mr. Bird think had happened to Mrs. Bird?*
T: *That's a great question. That's exactly the question I would ask. You're a wonderful teacher, S6. Please call on somebody to answer the question.*
(One student gives the wrong answer. S6 calls on another student.)
S5: *The big cat ate Mrs. Bird.*
T: *Is that the right answer, S6?*
S6: *Yes.*
T: *Now what should you ask?*
(S6 looks puzzled.)

T: I would ask why. You know what I would ask next? I would say "Why did he think that?" Try that question S6 and call on somebody to answer it.

Because this was the first lesson using the Reciprocal Teaching technique with this group of children, I played a major role in the dialogue by modeling, asking questions, giving explanations, and providing feedback. The dialogue was also very structured. When I acted as teacher modeling the strategies, I presented all four strategies. The children who played the role of "teacher" also used all four strategies. However, as children acquire more practice with the technique, the teacher's role changes; he or she becomes more like a coach providing feedback as needed and challenging children to use the strategies at higher levels, e.g., asking more complex questions or summarizing more concisely. The dialogue structure also becomes more flexible and more like discussion with less teacher-student interaction because the other students provide feedback to the student playing the role of "teacher." Even on the first day of using the technique in the demonstration lesson, children began to interact with the "teacher" independently of me, offering alternative predictions and suggesting rephrasing of questions and information that should be added to summaries.

In introducing Reciprocal Teaching at the beginning of this section I indicated that it had proved to be a successful technique for use with children who were not meeting comprehension expectations. At this point, I would like to explain what is meant by "successful" and consider aspects of the technique that are responsible for this success.

Palincsar (1985) succinctly describes what is meant by referring to Reciprocal Teaching as a successful technique by indicating that (1) the dialogue during intervention improved substantially over time; (2) there was substantial improvement on measures of comprehension including standardized tests; (3) the effects of intervention were durable—they were still evident up to six months after training; and (4) improvement transferred to classroom tasks that were similar to but distinct from the instructed strategies.

These kinds of results were found in a large number of studies with groups ranging from 1 to 18 students. One of the most important aspects of this technique's success is that children apparently use it independently once they are taught it. In the 1984 study by Palincsar and Brown seventh-graders who received instruction in Reciprocal Teaching improved not only on tests used in the experimental setting, but they also showed substantial improvement on social studies and science tests. "This is an impressive finding, particularly given the difficulty investigators have experienced getting generalizable effects of training across task settings (Meichenbaum and Asarnow 1978; Stokes and Baer 1977)" (Palincsar and Brown 1984, p. 147).

Collins, Brown, and Newman (1987) suggest that the effectiveness of the Reciprocal Teaching technique depends on the co-occurrence of a number of factors. Through use of this method children:

1. form a new conception of reading;
2. learn to use independently four strategies that good readers use spontaneously;
3. learn to use these strategies while reading real texts for real purposes;
4. receive instruction in metacomprehension—children are told why they are receiving instruction in these particular strategies;
5. receive scaffolded instruction—children play the role of "cognitive apprentices" and teachers gradually release responsibility to them;
6. act as both producers and critics in using the strategies through engaging in a dialogue that involves student-student interaction as well as student-teacher interaction.

A NEW CONCEPTION OF READING

In Chapter 2, I present research evidence that many children have a conception of reading as decoding and word recognition rather than as a construction of meaning. By using Reciprocal Teaching and the techniques presented previously that focus on comprehension, children come to realize that reading for meaning requires the use of constructive and evaluative strategies. Since engaging in these activities requires them to review the text repeatedly, they also come to realize that reading is not always a "one pass operation" (Collins, Brown, and Newman 1987). Palincsar and Brown have been able to maintain this focus on comprehension in Reciprocal Teaching partly because they have only used the method with subjects exhibiting adequate decoding and inadequate comprehension. Thus, in the studies conducted with seventh graders (Palincsar and Prown 1984; Palincsar 1985, 1987a) subjects had to:

1. read seventh grade level material at 80 words per minute with two or fewer errors per minute;
2. fail to score above 50% on a criterion-referenced measure of comprehension.

Classroom teachers and special reading teachers do not usually teach groups that are homogeneous in this way. Moreover, Chapter 4 suggests grouping children in heterogeneous groups for comprehension instruction, with good readers and remedial readers working together in cooperative groups. From one point of view, Reciprocal Teaching seems suited for use with heterogeneous cooperative groups although the way in which roles are assigned in this type of situation remains to be explored (Palincsar 1987a). On the other hand "If there is too much diversity, it is difficult to identify reading material that is equally challenging to all members and difficult to maintain a pace to the dialogue satisfactory to all" (Palincsar and Brown in press). If Reciprocal Teaching is to be used more extensively in classrooms, this concern about the diversity of the groups will have to be addressed. In the meantime, teachers should explore different groupings when using this technique to determine which type is most beneficial with their students.

LEARNING FOUR STRATEGIES: ASKING QUESTIONS, SUMMARIZING, MAKING PREDICTIONS, CLARIFYING

The other during-reading techniques discussed in this chapter are used to teach the strategies of asking questions and making predictions. The value of these two strategies has already been discussed. Since Reciprocal Teaching combines instruction in these two strategies with instruction in summarizing and clarifying, the rationale for providing instruction in these latter two strategies is presented here.

SUMMARIZING

As with asking questions about important information that has been read, summarizing helps children focus on important text information. However, summarizing also helps them integrate this important information; it is a means of self review, enabling children to monitor their comprehension. Children who are not able to summarize what they have read come to realize that they do not really understand it. Getting the main idea or summarizing is often synonymous with comprehension. Moreover, paraphrasing the gist of the text in their own words enables children not only to comprehend text better but also to process the material more deeply. Thus they learn it better. Summarization is considered one of the most important strategies for comprehension and recall of text since it is helpful in a variety of situations and with all types of texts (Jones et al. 1987).

In order to teach this strategy successfully, teachers need to be clear about what is meant by summarizing. Palincsar, Brown, and David (work in progress) and Maria (1987, 1988) find great variability in what teachers consider a good summary. Often summarizing is confused with retelling, in which the reader tells everything he or she can remember from the text. A summary is different from a retelling in two ways: (1) a summary contains the important ideas in a text, and (2) a summary is brief—the important ideas are condensed. Constructing a summary involves both a selection process, i.e., deciding what information in a text is important and a reduction process, i.e., condensing information by substituting general ideas for more detailed ones (Anderson and Hidi 1988-1989).

In Chapter 7, I discuss the fact that determining important ideas in a text depends upon knowledge of both content and structure. Determining what is important in stories is easier than in expository material because children usually have more knowledge about story content and structure. Content schemata and structural cues used by children can help determine important ideas in expository text. For the most part, Palincsar and Brown have used Reciprocal Teaching with expository text.

However, as the script illustrates, it can also be used with narrative text. Story schema can serve as a guide to both summarizing and generating questions when Reciprocal Teaching is used with narrative text. However, if teachers use Reciprocal Teaching with both narrative and expository text, they will need to make it clear to the children that determining importance depends on different cues in the different types of texts.

Teachers who model the summarization strategy also need to be sure that their summaries are not too detailed. One way of teaching children to condense information is to teach them guidelines for summarization (Palincsar, Brown, and David work in progress). The guidelines below are based on rules identified by Brown and Day (1983) and Guido and Colwell (1987).

1. Summarize using your own words.
2. Include no unnecessary detail.
3. Collapse lists. Use a general term for a list of specific items. Use one word to describe a list of actions that may be in several sentences.
4. Use a topic sentence. Use the topic sentence in the text but say it in your own words or make up your own topic sentence.
5. Don't repeat anything.

These guidelines can be taught as they become necessary when using the Reciprocal Teaching procedure. As they are discussed the teacher adds the guidelines to a chart that can be displayed as an aid for the children. For example, at one point in the demonstration lesson, one of the children tried to summarize by reading information to me from the text. I explained to her that she would learn it better if she said it in her own words; I had her close her book and look at me as she summarized the ideas. At another point in the story, there was an opportunity to teach Rule 2. One section of the text listed all the things that the birds used to build their nest.

Dialogue

(After asking questions about what the birds used to build their nest, S2 attempts to summarize. He looks in the book as he tries to list all the things they used.)

T: Now, you don't want to tell everything they used. Would you say they used a lot of things or a few things to build their nest?

S2: A lot of things.

T: Okay. Say that in a sentence.

S2: They used a lot of things . . .

T: To

S2: They used

T: A lot of things . . . Go ahead.

S2: They used a lot of things to build their nests.

T: Very good. He said the important thing "They used a lot of things to build their nests." He doesn't have to say every single thing because he is telling what is important. He can just say they used a lot of things.

Summarizing is a very difficult skill for children and adults to learn, particularly when working with expository texts. Reciprocal Teaching will probably need to be supplemented by more direct instruction if children are to learn how to determine the main idea and summarize. Following the explicit instruction model in which the teacher gradually releases responsibility to the students, children can be taught to identify the main ideas in pictures, paragraphs, and finally longer texts (Moore and Readence 1980).

When working with expository paragraphs and longer texts, main idea instruction should follow a sequence in which children learn to:

1. identify the topic of a text,
2. distinguish main ideas from topics (a main idea makes a statement about a topic),
3. identify topic sentences at the beginning and end of paragraphs, and
4. construct topic sentences for paragraphs that have no topic sentences.

Since determining the main idea of texts depends on both the content and structure, this kind of main idea instruction should involve teaching children to use both kinds of cues. Teaching different expository text structures as described in Chapter 7 and content schemata like the concept of nation schema (Ohlhausen and Roller 1986) is an integral part of main idea instruction. A more detailed description of this explicit type of main idea instruction can be found in Pearson and Johnson (1978) and Baumann (1986).

Instructional techniques designed to teach children to write summaries are another excellent way to provide direct instruction (see Chapter 9). However, Reciprocal Teaching is also a very good method for providing instruction in summarization; it teaches children to summarize short sections of text at first. As sections of text read become longer and children become more proficient at summarizing, they learn to integrate paragraphs as well as sentences in constructing summaries (Palincsar 1986c).

CLARIFYING

Asking questions and summarizing are strategies that foster comprehension monitoring at the text level. They help children think about whether they have understood what the text is saying. Clarifying, on the other hand, focuses on comprehension monitoring at lower levels: the word, the sentence, and relationships between sentences. Children are taught to be alert for problems at this level and then are taught strategies that will help them solve comprehension problems they encounter. The most usual problems addressed by the clarifying strategy are: (1) difficult or unfamiliar vocabulary, including unusual and metaphorical expressions and idioms, (2) unclear referents, (3) disorganized text, and (4) incomplete information (Palincsar, Brown, and David work in progress).

As I point out in Chapter 7, the clarifying strategy can also be used to alert children to complex sentence structures that may pose comprehension problems. Like predicting, clarifying is not necessary after every text section. When the teacher sees a possible problem, he or she asks if there is anything that was not understood. Many children, like many adults, do not want to admit that there is something that they don't understand so Palincsar, Brown, and David (work in progress) suggest asking them if they think there is anything a younger child might not understand. However, in other lessons in which I used Reciprocal Teaching, children did begin to ask about words and phrases. A section in a text about turtles (Morningforest 1978) contained the following sentence "Then one night she left the pond and moved slowly up into a nearby meadow." I reminded the "teacher" to ask the other children if there were any words or phrases that they did not understand.

Dialogue
T: S1, is there any word you think they don't understand or any word that you don't understand?
S3 (interrupts): Meadow.
T: You read my mind. I wondered if you people understood that word. S1, do you know what it means? Does anyone?
T: Well, a meadow is a field. The turtle left the pond and went to a field.

On another occasion, when reading *Stone Soup* (McGovern 1986), a child interrupted to ask about the sentence, "The pot bubbled and bubbled." The child who was playing the role of "teacher" explained that this meant that the water in the pot was boiling.

If children do not indicate a problem, the teacher can point out the problem and ask the children to explain it as I did at another point in the lesson with the text on turtles. The children were reading about how a turtle gets oxygen. When they were asked if there was anything they did not understand, they did not reply. Although the word oxygen had been introduced before reading, I knew that the children would need many exposures to the word before they could get the concept, so we talked about it again.

Dialogue
T: Do you know what oxygen is?
S1: It's air.
T: Not exactly. It is something that is in the air but it is also in the water. The turtle gets oxygen from the air and the water.
(Of course, the children will need extensive vocabulary instruction of the type described in Chapter 6 before they are comfortable with this concept.)

COMBINING THE FOUR STRATEGIES
Other techniques described in this chapter focus on one or two strategies: asking questions and/or making predictions. Reciprocal Teaching adds two other strategies. After every section of text, children ask questions and summarize. They predict and clarify only when these strategies are appropriate. When Palincsar (1985) did a study to determine whether instruction in using all four strategies was necessary, she found that students who were instructed in simultaneous use of all four strategies responded more quickly and made greater gains than students who were introduced to either asking questions or sum-

marizing alone over a period of several days followed by practice with all four strategies. However, Palincsar noted that children with language problems might benefit more from introduction to each strategy separately. One might begin with ReQuest or DRTA and then move to Reciprocal Teaching. This is an issue that needs to be investigated. In the meantime, teachers can try different combinations with their particular groups.

READING TEXTS WRITTEN FOR
PURPOSES OTHER THAN FOR LEARNING TO READ

Like all the techniques presented in this chapter, Reciprocal Teaching provides strategy instruction in the context of reading texts written for purposes other than learning how to read. In fact, initial discussion of Reciprocal Teaching in Chapter 4 focuses on this aspect of the technique. Learning the strategies in this way may influence children to use them independently, since it demonstrates that they are useful in understanding the type of texts read in situations when reading is not being directly taught. Palincsar and Brown (in press) suggest that with remedial readers it may be beneficial to begin with more considerate texts that lend themselves well to using the four strategies. Although doing this may make using the strategies easier for the children, it may have a negative effect on motivation to use them independently—another issue that needs to be investigated. In the meantime, when using Reciprocal Teaching, teachers should be careful not to use texts that are so contrived that they are unlike the texts children have to read in other contexts.

METACOMPREHENSION INSTRUCTION

An important aspect of all the pre-reading and during-reading techniques presented in this book is that they provide instruction not only in comprehension but also in metacomprehension. When teachers introduce these techniques they explain to the children, as I did in the script excerpt, that they provide strategy instruction because it will help them read independently. Teacher modeling and explanation of the techniques provides awareness of comprehension problems, knowledge of different strategies available (declarative knowledge), knowledge of how to use the strategies (procedural knowledge), and knowledge of when and where to use them (conditional knowledge). However, the particular strengths of Reciprocal Teaching are:

1. the focus on comprehension problems provided by instruction in the clarifying strategy,
2. the integration of instruction providing declarative and procedural knowledge of strategies—children learn a repertoire of strategies from which to choose since instruction is provided in four strategies simultaneously, and
3. the conditional knowledge acquired—as noted in the previous section, children learn that the strategies can be used for reading real texts for real purposes. Clarifying and predicting are used only when appropriate.

SCAFFOLDED INSTRUCTION

The importance of scaffolding comprehension instruction for all children—particularly for remedial readers—is discussed in depth in Chapter 4. All the techniques presented in these last few chapters provide this type of instruction. However, Reciprocal Teaching provides scaffolded instruction in a unique way. The teacher releases responsibility for strategy use to the children by giving them more control over a structured dialogue.

THE RECIPROCAL TEACHING DIALOGUE

The value of using dialogue as a teaching tool is discussed in Chapter 4. Re-Quest, InQuest, Active Comprehension, and DRTA all make more use of dialogue than traditional types of instruction. Encouraging children to respond more actively to the text encourages more student-student interaction. When children offer alternate questions, predictions, and explanations, dialogue in which multiple viewpoints are considered is a natural occurrence.

The Reciprocal Teaching dialogue however, offers the opportunity for much more student-student interaction. In a study in which Reciprocal Teaching was used to provide listening comprehension instruction for first graders, Palincsar and Brown (in press) found that by day 18 of using the technique, some groups had as many as ten exchanges independent of the teacher.

This student-student interaction takes place in a manageable format that provides clear directions about the topic, goal, and process of the discussion, and keeps discussion focused on the central topic—understanding a particular text through the use of four strategies. Results of a study reported by Palincsar (1985) suggests that this dialogue format for teaching the four strategies is superior to demonstrations by the teacher, to direct instruction in the strategies using worksheets, and to independent student practice of the strategies with the teacher giving individual feedback. Teachers who have tried the technique have reported that behavior problems tend to disappear in the groups in which Reciprocal Teaching is used, and this is good evidence for the manageability of the format.

In the Reciprocal Teaching dialogue children take turns playing the role of "teacher." In my own experience with the technique I have been particularly struck by the way in which playing the role of "teacher" motivates remedial readers. I have followed Palincsar and Brown's (1985) advice and have encouraged "students to reinforce one another for a job well done, to select the next teacher, to ask for further information from one another, and to take responsibility for the transition from one section of the text to the next" (p. 154). Playing the role of "teacher" in this way gives children an appreciation of the difficulty of the teacher's job. In addition, it empowers them, giving them a sense of control so that even their body language and tone of voice demonstrate a new sense of pride. At the end of the demonstration lesson from which the script excerpt was taken, the children provided me with an example of their pride. The remedial readers who had participated in the lesson wore name tags so that I could remember their names. When they were leaving the room, I asked them if they wanted to remove the tags. These third graders who normally didn't want anyone to even know that they participated in the Chapter I program said that they wanted to leave the tags on because they wanted to tell the other children in their class that they had been "teachers."

Since the dialogue takes place in a problem solving context in which all participants share responsibility for solving the problem (i.e., understanding a text), taking turns being the "teacher" enables children to play the role of critic as well as producer of the strategies. When students act as critics they must think about what makes a good question, prediction, or summary. They can then apply this metacognitive knowledge to their own summaries and questions in many different contexts (Collins, Brown, and Newman 1987).

Even when teachers are given extensive and similar training in how to implement Reciprocal Teaching dialogues, their use of the technique varies in several respects. Palincsar (1986b) reported that some of the first grade teachers in the listening comprehension study:

1. made the point of the instruction more explicit;
2. conducted dialogues that had more focus and direction;
3. supported children's contributions to the dialogue at the idea level rather than the word level and linked student ideas to new knowledge;
4. made constructive rather than negative comments about student contributions.

Groups whose teachers behaved in this fashion were operating more independently during the final days of instruction and showed better achievement gains. Thus teachers who attempt to implement Reciprocal Teaching should be alert to these aspects of using the technique.

Teachers also need to consider the size of the group and the behavior of the group members in deciding how much structure the dialogue should have. Larger groups may require more structure. For example, teachers who worked with groups that were larger, in a study reported by Palincsar (1987a), made a check mark each time a child participated in the dialogue in order to be sure that all students participated. In this study, which used non-volunteer teachers and seventh grade students, some teachers used procedures that seemed too structured while others were not structured enough.

In the following script, which is an excerpt from a dialogue with a group of first graders on Day 15 (Palincsar 1987b, pp. 16-17), it is not clear who is the discussion leader.

Glow Worms Script

T (reading): *Some glow worms live in caves. They hang from the ceilings of caves.*

K: *I have a good question. Where do they live?*

Ss: *In the ceilings of caves.*

K: *That's right.*

T: *(reading) And, they spin sticky fishing nets.*
What else do we know that spins a net?

M: *A spider.*

T: *That's right.*
(reading) These nets are like spider webs. Some insects that live in these caves see the bright lights.
Oh, what do you think they do?

I: *Die.*

T: *O.K. The glow worm will spin a little net. And another insect sees the little light. And, what's it going to do? (pause) What do insects do when they are near the light? (pause) It's dark out and you're at a ball game and you look up at the lights. What do you see?*

Ss: *Bugs.*

O: *Bugs like the light.*

T: *So, we're back at the cave. Are you back in the cave?*

Ss: *Yeah.*

T: *The insects are outside, they look in the cave and see the lights . . .*

O: *They go in there to get under the lights . . .*

O: *And they get caught in the nets.*

T: *That's right and then what happens?*

O: *The glow worms come out and pull them in and eat them.*

T: *Let's see what it says. (reading) "Small insects that live in the caves see the bright lights and fly up to them. On the way they are caught in the glow worm's fishing lines.*

T: *What does it mean, fishing lines?*

Ss: *The net*

T: *Yes, the net. (reading) The successful glow worms pull in their sticky threads and gobble up the insects. Then they lower their fishing lines again to catch another insect.*
Let's summarize the story so far. We are learning about insects that glow and the last past told us about . . .

J: *glow worms*

A: *They are lightening bugs without wings.*

T: *Yes, without wings. And where do they live?*

M: *In caves.*

T: *Where?*

A: *In New Zealand.*

T: *And how do they catch their food?*

J: *They hang from the ceilings of the caves.*

I: *And they get the bugs under the . . .*

A: *light*

K: *The bugs try to get in and then they get caught.*

T: *And then what happens?*

Ss: *They get eaten by the glow worms.*

Yet in both classrooms children interjected questions as they identified important information and they generated joint summaries at appropriate points in the text. In both dialogues it is clear that the construction of meaning has become a collaborative process involving the children and the teacher.

Variation in the structure of the Reciprocal Teaching dialogue is to be expected. However, since some of this variation may affect student achievement, Reciprocal Teaching should be implemented in a careful and reflective manner in collaboration with other teachers who can provide feedback regarding different aspects of the dialogue.

VISUAL IMAGERY

Although the during-reading techniques discussed thus far in this chapter have moved away from the traditional classroom pattern of teacher questions and student answers to a pattern of student self questioning, student predicting, and student-led discussion, the pattern remains one in which verbal information is processed in a linear, sequential manner.

Visual imagery, constructing pictures with "the mind's eye," has been proposed by a number of experts (Fredericks 1986; Wilson and Gambrell 1988; McNeil 1987) as an alternate and effective way of aiding children's comprehension and recall of text information. Yet imagery is very rarely mentioned in instructional materials for children (Gambrell and Bales 1986). This may be because visual imagery is viewed as a form of daydreaming or fantasy and thus often has negative connotations for teachers (Richardson 1982). Richardson proposes that instead of reprimanding children for daydreaming, we should "capture that imagination" and use it as a teaching method.

Research of the last few years (e.g., Gambrell and Bales 1986; Pressley 1977; Sadoski 1983, 1985) supports the use of visual imagery as a comprehension strategy. Sadoski (1983, 1985) found that third and fifth grade children who reported imaging about the climax of a story had better recall of the story than those who did not report imaging. Constructing visual images is particularly helpful for older children, remedial readers, and children who do not spontaneously integrate text (Pressley 1977). Using visual imagery may also help remedial readers monitor their comprehension of text more effectively. Fourth and fifth grade remedial readers who were told to construct mental images were able to detect text inconsistencies better than those who did not use images (Gambrell and Bales 1986). It seems worthwhile to inform children that using visual imagery is another way in which they may increase their comprehension.

Telling them it is a good idea to use the strategy is not enough, however. As with the other strategies, teachers must provide procedural and declarative knowledge about the strategy. Procedural knowledge involves more than telling children to make a picture in their minds. Bagley and Hess (1982) suggest a model of guided imagery instruction that proceeds in the following steps. Children are trained (1) to relax and concentrate, (2) form images of concrete objects, (3) form images of pictures, (4) form images using all their senses based on listening to guided imagery instruction, and (5) form images from text that they read.

In a demonstration lesson I conducted with a fourth grade class, the children constructed images of an Iroquois Indian village and the interior of an Iroquois longhouse as part of a unit about New York State Indians. First they were directed to look at a picture of an Iroquois village in their social studies book for 10 seconds. This picture contained a wealth of detail (stockade fence, longhouses, people, crops, etc.). Then the children were told to close their eyes and see the picture in their mind's eye for 10 seconds. Images were then discussed with attention to the fact that everyone had a slightly different image of the picture. Next, the children were asked to look at the picture again and concentrate on the details for 15 seconds, then to close their eyes again and see the picture in their mind's eye for 30 seconds. Discussion of images followed with the variety of images again noted.

Next, the children closed their eyes as I slowly read the imagery exercise below that was modeled on an imagery exercise on Navaho Indians developed by Bagley and Hess (1982).

Sit comfortably and relax.
You are at an Iroquois Indian village in New York State about the year 1650.
It is winter. Feel how cold you are.
Feel the snow crunch under your feet.
The wind is blowing. You can hear it and feel it right through your clothes.
See yourself walk through the gate into the village. See the tall fence all around the village.
Feel the roughness of the fence.
See the two rows of longhouses ahead of you.
Smell the smoke coming from the holes in the roofs of the longhouses.
Hear the sounds. There are many people of all ages in the village. But everybody is inside in the many longhouses of the village. The sounds of the people are muffled. Hear the faraway sound of a baby crying. Someone shouts at another person. He yells back.
You are stooping down and pushing aside the skin over the door of the nearest longhouse.
Feel the greasiness of the skin.
Smell the skin. It is wet from the snow.
You go inside the longhouse.
What do you see?
What do you hear?
What do you feel?

Teachers should begin imagery instruction by asking children to visualize familiar scenes before using imagery with content area concepts. The children in the demonstration lesson were able to include detail in their images because they had discussed the Iroquois Indians in class and had looked at the picture in their textbooks. However, some of the images indicated misconceptions about the Iroquois. For example, one child pictured the Indian with a big feather bonnet like those worn by the Plains Indians.

One very interesting aspect of the images constructed by both children and adults who have participated in this exercise is that the emotions evoked by the images are different. Some children and adults reported thinking of themselves as Indians coming home, so they felt happy and warm when they pictured themselves walking into the longhouse. Others pictured themselves as strangers in the village and felt cold and fearful. Since the emotions evoked by images can often be quite powerful, teachers should be careful not to encourage images that can be upsetting.

In the final activity of the lesson the children read a three paragraph section of their social studies book describing life in a longhouse. Children were directed to read the section one paragraph at a time, stopping after each paragraph to make an image of what the paragraph said in their mind's eye. After 15 seconds of imaging, we discussed their images and compared them to the images they had constructed before reading. Images constructed after reading later paragraphs were compared to images constructed earlier. Although some studies (e.g., Clark et al. 1984) have asked remedial readers to make images after reading single sentences, constructing images paragraph by paragraph rather than sentence by sentence seems necessary if we wish to encourage children to make connections between sentences.

Once again the children gave detailed images that indicated that they were making connections between the different details in the text. Teachers who watched the lesson noted that many of those who were most verbal in discussing their images were children who did not usually volunteer responses in class discussions. However, if I taught the lesson again, I would ask each child to draw a stick cartoon of his or her image before discussing it; this would permit the children to have a tangible record of their images before they were influenced by the images reported by others (Cooke and Haipt 1986; Aulls 1978). Just as with asking questions and summarizing, constructing images will only be an effective aid to comprehension if children focus on the important aspects of the text. Through questioning and modeling, teachers can provide guidance in imaging about important text elements. For example, in the demonstration lesson, after children read the paragraph and spent several seconds imaging, I asked questions that focused on the important information questions like:

> How many people did you see?
> What did they look like?
> What were they doing?

As the children become more familiar with imaging and build schemata for text content and structure, teacher guidance can be phased out and children can be encouraged to make use of the imagery strategy independently. In order to use the strategy appropriately, remedial readers will need teacher support for a long time. Children will also need to understand that the imagery strategy is only useful with text that is easy to visualize. Thus teachers will also need to provide them with conditional knowledge about the strategy, i.e., knowledge about when the strategy will be useful, and guide them in making decisions about which texts are easy to visualize.

PLANNING LESSONS UTILIZING THE DURING-READING TECHNIQUES

Although these techniques focus on getting the children to ask questions, make predictions, summarize, etc., teachers will still need to plan appropriate questions, predictions, and summaries so that they can model the strategies and provide feedback to the children about their use of the strategies. They will need to read the texts carefully so that they can choose appropriate strategies to teach and problems that need to be clarified.

The teachers with whom I have worked feel that the result is well worth the effort. Generally, they report that students at all levels enjoy these activities because they enjoy thinking. One junior high student in a prison school who used active comprehension for the first time said to the teacher who was one of my students, "You know Miss M., I think we should ask questions about what we read all the time. I never remembered anything like I remember what we read today."

As with the pre-reading techniques, the differences in emphasis and focus among the during-reading techniques can provide the teacher with some variety, i.e., with a repertoire of techniques to use. However, because many of these techniques are so similar, teachers probably will not want to use all of them. With both pre-reading and during-reading techniques, the best policy is to choose a technique that appeals to you and seems suitable for your students and the materials available. Then spend several weeks using this technique along with other activities with which you and the children are more familiar. Do not introduce another new technique until you and the students are comfortable with the first one.

The best way for teachers to acquire expertise in using any of these techniques is to collaborate with other teachers: planning lessons together, demonstrating techniques for one another, and providing feedback to one another. Staff development programs that seek to encourage teachers to use new techniques for comprehension instruction should provide for this collaboration using the same type of scaffolded instruction that they encourage the teachers to use.

Remember that change is not easy. Risk-taking involves making mistakes for you as well as for the children. Don't be too hard on yourself; you are establishing a climate that focuses on thinking and reflection for yourself as well as for the children. You and the children will be learning together. Enjoy it!

INTEGRATION AND ASSESSMENT

9

READING COMPREHENSION INSTRUCTION IN THE TOTAL LANGUAGE ARTS PROGRAM

While focusing on reading comprehension instruction I do not wish to give the impression that other elements of reading, such as word recognition, are not important. In order to avoid giving such a message, I have repeatedly emphasized that reading comprehension is only one element of a total reading program.

Another danger that arises from the narrower focus is that attention to reading alone will be interpreted incorrectly as advocating that reading be taught as a subject separate from instruction in the other language processes of listening, speaking, and writing. The purpose of this chapter is to provide a wider view that recognizes the relationship of reading comprehension instruction to other language processes.

Just as reading comprehension instruction is only one element of a total reading program, so too is it only one element of a total language arts program in which each of the language processes is learned in terms of the others (Wagner 1985). Reading comprehension provides the unifying thread for the integration of instruction in all the language processes. This integration is particularly necessary for remedial readers for two reasons:

1. Remedial readers are likely to have difficulties with the other language processes. (Chapter 2 discussed the oral language problems that many remedial readers experience.) Extensive reviews of research by Loban (1976), Stotsky (1983), and Tierney and Leys (1986) document the fact that although there are exceptions, most remedial readers also have difficulty with writing.

2. Because many of them have difficulty with the other language processes as well as with reading, remedial readers have more difficulty than other students in integrating instruction presented in isolation.

READING COMPREHENSION INSTRUCTION AND ORAL LANGUAGE

Oral language comprehension is the base upon which written language comprehension is built. Children learn through listening for a long time before they come to school. Their greater facility in listening and the similarities between this process and reading, especially in the primary grades, make listening a process that can be a powerful part of reading comprehension instruction in several ways. First, one of the best ways children can learn about written language is by listening to it. Teachers and parents are urged to read aloud to children of all ages.

Second, children learn to be active constructors of meaning in reading by learning to be active constructors of meaning in listening. One of the premises of this book is that young children and remedial readers for whom decoding is a problem should receive listening comprehension instruction along with instruction in word recognition. This will help them realize that reading, like listening, is a communication process that involves a search for meaning. Although the cognitive demands of listening and reading are different, the fact that they are both "language comprehension processes that have available to them the same set of strategies to accomplish the task of comprehension" (Danks and End 1987) is justification for this approach.

Third, the listening process supports reading comprehension instruction whether children are listening to the text or reading it themselves. Explanations, modeling, questions, and dialogue—the four teacher tools that have been recommended for use in reading comprehension instruction—depend on children listening to the teacher's oral language rather than to a written text read aloud.

Speaking is an important part of comprehension instruction also. The teacher is not the only one who talks; children do learn by listening, but they need to put their ideas into their own words and talk about them in order to really understand. In encouraging children to be active processors and constructors of meaning, the teacher makes sure that the children talk too. Children ask questions, make predictions, and discuss what they already know about the topic of a text before and during reading. They also talk about the processes that they use to understand the text when they "think aloud." They use vocabulary and sentence structures contained in the text while talking not only to the teacher but also to each other. Explaining what the text means to other children helps them to understand better, and listening to other children's questions and explanations allows them to compare their interpretations to those of others.

Previous chapters describe the use of oral language in pre-reading and during-reading activities. Here we will focus on post-reading oral language activities:

1. Discussion
2. Oral retelling
3. Interviewing
4. Drama.

The traditional after-reading activity in which the teacher asks questions and the children answer still has a place; but as I stated in Chapters 4 and 8, discussion in which children interact more with one another is a better format for the kind of active processing necessary for comprehension and learning. Discussion that takes place after reading should focus on the same topics that were the focus of pre-reading and during-reading instruction. If an inferential strategy was used before reading to call up children's experiences about a particular problem experienced by a character in a story, post-reading discussion can center on the similarities and differences between the ways in which the character in the story and the children themselves solved the problem. For example, discussion after reading *The Cow Who Fell in the Canal* (Krasilovsky 1957) compared the way in which the cow solved the problem of her boredom with the ways in which the children solved theirs. The cow, after her one adventure in the city, is content to stay in the field. She is not bored because she can think about her adventures. In discussing this conclusion, the children decided that they would not be contented like the cow. They would want to have further adventures. If semantic mapping was used as a pre-reading activity, information and categories acquired during reading should be discussed and added to the map after reading. After-reading discussion should also focus on the strategies taught during reading. If the focus was on predicting, after-reading discussion can center on why certain predictions were better than others, why some predictions were confirmed and some were not, and whether all predictions were confirmed or refuted. If the focus was on asking questions, after-reading discussion can center on determining which questions were not answered and deciding whether these questions are important enough to warrant further study.

After-reading discussion does not have to be limited to topics already covered. Although the discussion before reading *Ferdinand* (Leaf 1936) centered on the concept of bullfighting, after-reading discussion moved from why fierce bulls were necessary in bullfighting to the way in which Ferdinand differed from the other bulls, and whether or not this difference was good. Children often find ideas in the text that they want to talk about, and these personal responses should be encouraged. The heterogeneous peer-response groups developed by Graves (1984) and Hansen (1984) and the literature-response groups developed by Strickland (Strickland 1988; Strickland et al. 1989), described in Chapter 4, provide a way of structuring this type of after-reading discussion. In all types of post-reading discussion the teacher's job is to support the integrating process, and to help children see ways in which text information relates to their prior knowledge and experience.

Previously, it was suggested that when children put ideas in their own words they understand them better. Thus, retelling a story orally can be a valuable experience for a child (Morrow 1989). Since having each child retell the story would be too much like a test, Rhodes and Dudley-Marling (1988) suggest using one child's oral retelling as a way of initiating a post-reading discussion where the other children and the teacher ask questions about the retelling. The questions require the student who retold the story to expand and reflect on his or her feelings or attitudes about some aspect of the story. This student is also free to turn the question back to the questioner, e.g., "I think the cow should try to get away from the field again. What do you think?" Relating the story to other stories previously read is another activity that helps children move beyond just retelling to comparing and contrasting several texts and giving personal reactions and responses to them.

This format in which members of a group question one member is really a type of interviewing. Interviewing is widely recommended as a pre-writing activity (e.g., Calkins 1986; Noyce and Christie 1989). It can also serve as a post-reading activity either as preparation for a written response to the text or as an end in itself. Since effective interviewing involves asking good questions, this activity is particularly appropriate when during-reading instruction has focused on having children ask questions about the text. The general guidelines for interviewing included as part of the discussion of the InQuest method in Chapter 8 can also be applied to after-reading interviews. In addition to interviewing other children about their understanding of and reactions to narrative and expository text, children can interview each other as they play the parts of characters from stories (as in the InQuest method), from history, science, and social studies. For example, after having read an expository text about photosynthesis, teachers can use visual imagery to help children play the roles of plants making their own food. Then other children can interview the "plants" in order to find out how they make food.

When children role play, they engage in a drama. Informally acting out stories, as well as more formal drama activities, such as Reader's Theatre (described in detail in Noyce and Christie 1989), can be valuable tools in comprehension instruction. "Reader's Theatre is the oral reading of any form of literature or text adapted into script for a play and read aloud in a dramatic manner. Costumes are usually not used" (Aulls 1982, p. 244). Rereading the story from a different perspective for the purpose of creating an effective Reader's Theatre presentation helps children process the story more deeply and clarify concepts. Although children are supposed to write the scripts for Reader's Theatre themselves, this may be too difficult for remedial readers. Aulls (1982) suggests providing purchased or teacher-developed scripts at first. However, the process suggested by Noyce and Christie (1989), in which the teacher and the children work together to develop a script, allows children to be more actively involved in the process while providing them with the scaffolding they need to be successful.

Although oral language activities described here and in the previous chapters have been suggested as a support for reading comprehension instruction, they can serve another purpose at the same time, i.e., providing instruction in listening and speaking. Instruction in oral language is important for all children because it is still developing during the school years. Oral language instruction is particularly important for remedial readers because many have difficulty with oral as well as written language due to language differences and/ or disorders (See Chapter 2). Moreover, oral language in school is very different from the oral language children use outside of school. Similarly, the listening process that children engage in when they participate in reading comprehension instruction is not the same as the process they use when they listen to oral language in more informal social situations at home or in school. This kind of instructional school listening is an active, holistic, constructive process that requires selective attention and comprehension monitoring, and is "oriented toward propositions and argument processing, analysis and synthesis" (Horowitz and Samuels 1987). Because it is so different, Sticht and James (1984) suggest that it should not be called listening at all, and so introduced the term *auding* to refer to this specialized school listening.

One big problem with the traditional pattern of classroom language is that children are provided with so little opportunity to talk. Although children are encouraged to talk during the comprehension instruction described here, the kind of talking they do is very different from the talking they engage in outside of school. In the dialogues described in previous chapters, the participants shift back and forth from reading written language to oral interpretation of the written text. There is very little research that focuses on oral language used in these types of dialogues or on how reading instruction relates to oral language growth. Strickland et al. (1989) did find evidence that children who participated in literature-response groups showed development in a set of linguistic tasks required in classroom dialogue (Lee and Rubin 1979). These tasks were:

1. ordering information, when giving directions, so that listeners could follow;
2. taking account of the discrepancy between their own informational position, background, and experience and those of their listeners;
3. shifting their style of speech according to their listeners or their purposes;
4. being aware of consistent points of view, changing only by intention; and
5. analyzing their information in relation to the problem to be solved (p. 198).

School dialogue focuses on ideas. It involves the explicit context-independent language with which many low SES children have had little experience. Modeling appropriate oral language is an essential part of teachers' instructional techniques described in the previous chapters. For example, in the sample script of the demonstration lesson on Reciprocal Teaching, there are several examples in which I framed oral responses for children. The dialogues given as samples in the discussion on Reciprocal Teaching (Palincsar 1986b,

1987b) provide some documentation that teacher modeling and practice in participating in a dialogue gives children the support they need to grow, not only in their comprehension ability, but also in their oral language ability.

THE READING-WRITING CONNECTION

Stotsky (1987) suggests that there are two basic theories that attempt to explain the relationships between oral and written language and between reading and writing. The first position—represented by theorists such as Moffett (1983), Goodman (1970, 1982), and Smith (1971)—suggests a uni-directional relationship between the language processes, holding that written language knowledge is always dependent on oral language knowledge. Readers cannot understand written texts that are more complex than those they can understand by listening; and writers cannot produce texts that are more complex than their level of oral language. According to this theory, which emphasizes the similarities between oral and written language, oral language activities are the essential tools of reading and writing instruction because growth occurs in reading and writing through growth in listening and speaking (Stotsky 1987).

The second theory described by Stotsky (1987), represented by theorists such as Vygotsky (1962, 1978), Bruner, Olver, and Greenfield (1966), and Simon (1970) acknowledges the differences between oral and written language, and suggests reciprocal and multi-directional relationships among the four language processes. "Oral language may influence written language; written language may influence oral language, and reading and writing may each enhance the other directly in different but equally profound ways" (Stotsky 1987, p. 384). This second theory, like the first, holds that in the beginning stages of literacy, oral language knowledge provides the basis for the construction of meaning in written language. However, through continuous experience and instruction in reading and writing, the reader is eventually able to move directly from print to meaning without the mediation of sound. Vygotsky (1978, p. 116) states this view clearly in a quotation found in Stotsky (1987, p. 380).

> As second order symbols, written symbols function as designations for verbal ones. Understanding of written language is first effected through spoken language, but gradually this path is curtailed and spoken language disappears as the intermediate link. To judge from all the available evidence, written language becomes direct symbolism that is perceived in the same way as spoken language.

Smith (1971), whom Stotsky characterizes as a proponent of the first theory, also suggests that readers move directly from print to meaning even in the beginning stages of reading by making predictions based on sampling distinctive features of the text. However, since predictions in Smith's theory are based on semantic and syntactic features of oral language, the level of reading comprehension is still based on the level of oral language comprehension. Proponents of the second theory, on the other hand, postulate that this ability to move directly from print to meaning enables the child to read and write texts of greater complexity than he or she is able to use or understand orally.

Stotsky does not deny the importance of oral language activities for their own sake and for reading and writing instruction. Studies that provide training in oral language activities (Sticht et al. 1974; Gatlin 1974 cited in Stotsky 1987) found that in some cases this training results in improved reading and writing.

Other studies provide strong evidence that children's reading and writing is influenced by sources other than speech. For example, investigations cited in Stotsky (1987) that compare the speech and writing of middle grade children (Lull 1929; Harrell 1957; O'Donnell, Griffin, and Norris 1967; Loban 1976; Golub and Frederick 1971) consistently find that children's writing is more syntactically complex than their speech. There is evidence that at least some older readers can understand texts by reading that they cannot understand by listening. In summarizing the results of 31 studies comparing auding (listening) and reading, Sticht and James (1984) found that children below seventh grade are able to understand better by listening, whereas at the seventh grade and above, one is equally likely to understand better by listening, or reading, or to have equal understanding regardless of the process used.

Traditionally, the reading-writing relationship has been described in a "mirror" metaphor. According to this view, reading is a passive bottom-up process that moves from text features to meaning, while writing is an active top-down process that moves from meaning to text features (Birnbaum and Emig 1983 cited in Noyce and Christie 1989).

Schema theory and the interactive model combined with more research about the nature of the reading and writing processes (Flower 1981; Graves 1983) have caused a revision in the description of the reading-writing relationship. The composing model of the reading process (Tierney and Pearson 1983) is one way of describing this relationship. This model describes the way in which reading and writing share the five basic processes of planning, aligning, drafting, monitoring, and revising. Readers and writers both plan; they set goals and mobilize prior knowledge schemata in support of their goals. "In order to write about a topic, authors must access their prior knowledge (schemata) of that topic. These schemata serve as the source of the content of the writing. Without schemata, writers would have nothing to write about" (Noyce and Christie 1989, p. 8).

Aligning refers to the way in which readers approach the existing text and writers approach the blank page. Readers make assumptions about the author's purposes. These assumptions affect their own purposes in reading and their interpretations of the text. Writers make assumptions about their audience and decide how their purposes can best be achieved with this audience by adopting a particular "voice."

It is obvious that writers draft their ideas, monitor them constantly by reading to determine whether they are getting their ideas across appropriately, and revise when their monitoring suggests it is needed. The way readers draft is not so obvious, but Tierney and Pearson (1983) point out that readers draft when they construct a tentative model of the text; they monitor both their own comprehension and the way their tentative model fits subsequent facts. When the tentative model does not fit, they too must revise. Although some very real differences must be acknowledged between the two processes in that the writer starts with a blank page and the reader starts with a text from which he or she must construct meaning (Rosenblatt 1989), the similarity between the two processes provides a basis for integrating reading and writing instruction.

Another reason for integrating reading and writing instruction is that reading and writing are mutually supportive processes. Indirect evidence for a relationship between reading and writing is provided by studies indicating a strong positive correlation between reading and writing ability (Stotsky 1983; Tierney and Leys 1986). Studies also found that what children read influences their writing (DeFord 1981; Eckoff 1983; Maya 1979; Stotsky 1983) and that using reading activities to improve writing is generally successful (Noyce and Christie 1983; Stotsky 1983). The reciprocal nature of the reading-writing relationship is supported by studies that found that using writing activities to improve reading is also generally successful (Marino, Gould, and Haas 1985; Noyce and Christie 1983; Stotsky 1983).

A number of writing educators (Hansen 1987) suggest that when children write frequently, a whole new dimension is added to their reading, i.e., they read like authors. They realize that people, not machines, write texts so they are more conscious that reading is a communicative process between a reader and a writer. Moreover, they notice not only what the text says but also how the author says it, i.e., they become more conscious of the language and structure the author uses. It seems likely, however, that while some children may make these connections on their own, teachers need to make overt connections between the two processes for many children.

Writing can be an important support for reading comprehension instruction since it aids recall. When our ideas are written down, we can refer to them at a later time. Notes taken before, during, and after reading can serve as external aids to memory. In addition, writing provides us with an internal aid to memory as well as an external one. When we write about the ideas we have acquired through reading, we must organize and process them to a deeper extent than when we just read about them or just read and discuss them. This deeper processing leads to better recall.

Writing is helpful to comprehension as well as recall. Although discussion is a valuable support for thinking, writing about what we think requires us to be more organized and precise. Writing our response to a text and our reflections about it helps us to know what we really think; our comprehension is deepened. Tierney et al. (1989) found that while reading helped college students acquire multiple perspectives on a topic, writing helped them clarify their own thinking about the topic so that they were able to choose from among these multiple perspectives. The researchers conclude that reading and writing in combination foster critical thinking more so than does reading alone. Along the same line, Vacca and Vacca (1986, p. 206) quote C. Day Lewis as saying "We do not write in order to be understood; we write in order to understand."

Writing is a process that should be taught as an end in itself; literacy involves competence in both reading and writing. However, if writing is to support comprehension instruction effectively, writing activities must be related to what is being read and designed to support text comprehension. Stotsky (1983) found that most studies that used writing in this way, providing instruction in activities like notetaking, outlining, and/or summarizing (Doctorow, Wittrock, and Marks 1978; Dynes 1932; Taylor 1978), improved reading comprehension. On the other hand, studies that focused on teaching writing alone and then measured the effects on reading did not show significant effects on reading comprehension (Stotsky 1983). Although writing instruction can support reading comprehension instruction, it cannot substitute for it.

Another caution about the use of writing as a tool for reading comprehension instruction with remedial readers is that ". . . reading activities based directly on writing activities are only as profitable as the writing skills of the students" (Blanchard 1988, p. 63). Since remedial readers may have as much or even more difficulty with writing than they do with reading, they will require teacher support, modeling, and guidance for a long time before they are able to do most of the following activities independently.

WRITING ACTIVITIES AS SUPPORTS
FOR READING COMPREHENSION INSTRUCTION

Writing can be a tool for helping children activate and build world knowledge and linguistic knowledge before reading. It can help children respond to what they read and move beyond understanding what the text says to thinking critically and reacting to it. In using writing activities after reading, teachers must be careful not to fall into the trap of using it only as a tool for assessing comprehension rather than as a tool for teaching. One way to avoid the trap is to make sure that when children write about what they have read, the audience for their writing is not just the teacher (Rhodes and Dudley-Marling 1988). Writing about what they have read should be a way for children to share their ideas about texts and their enjoyment of them with one another. It can also provide additional independent practice in strategies employed during reading.

ACTIVATING WORLD KNOWLEDGE:
WRITING AS A PRE-READING ACTIVITY

The pre-reading techniques described in Chapter 5 were designed to stimulate discussion that would activate and build world knowledge schemata related to the central concepts in a text. Many of the techniques use writing only as a memory aid. For example, in using both PREP (Langer 1982) and Semantic Mapping (McNeil 1987), the children contribute ideas which the teachers write on the board.

However, there are ways of encouraging children's writing as part of these techniques. Students can be encouraged to write using variations of brainstorming. One way of doing this is to have them work together in pairs writing down their ideas about the topic and then coming together with the group to discuss the different ideas generated. "Brainwriting," developed by Rodrigues (1983) and described by Noyce and Christie (1989), suggests another way of structuring brainstorming in small groups. In brainwriting, each student in a group of four or five writes down his or her ideas about a topic. When several ideas have been written, students exchange lists and add to each other's lists. This exchange continues until the teacher decides the children have generated a sufficient number of ideas. Then the children in each group share the individual lists and compile a combined group list to share with the class. Rodrigues feels that this format gives children more time to think about and react to one another's ideas and is better than discussion, particularly for shy students who often hesitate to participate.

Brainwriting, however, poses a problem with spelling for some children. While teachers should emphasize that the focus of the activity is generation of ideas rather than correct spelling, if the other children are not able to read one child's list because of poor spelling, they will not be able to use his or her ideas. This activity would probably work best in cooperative heterogeneous groups so that students with greater spelling abilities can serve as resources for the other members of the group. Remedial readers should probably use brainwriting only after they have had substantial experience with brainstorming through discussion. However, participating in an activity like this, which involves less teacher direction than the brainstorming described in Chapter 5, is important for remedial readers because it moves them toward independent use of the pre-reading strategy of activating ideas about a topic.

In using the inferential strategy (Hansen and Hubbard 1984) described in Chapter 5, children recall their own experiences and relate them to a central story concept and make predictions about the story based on those experiences. Other techniques use writing activities for the same purpose. Teachers who use the Plausible Stories technique (Blanchard 1988) provide children with key words from a story they are about to read and ask them to compose a plausible story using these key words. Probable Passages (Wood 1984) is a similar activity although it is more structured than Plausible Stories. In using Probable Passages the teacher selects words related to each of the elements of story grammar, then guides the children in placing these words in the appropriate section of a story "frame." As you can see by looking at the story "frame" found in Wood (1984), what Wood refers to as a story frame is really more like the story map described in Chapter 7 (see figure 1).

After completing this first story frame, the teacher and children then insert the words in the appropriate blanks of another frame. The completed story frame below is the probable passage for *The Doughnut Machine That Wouldn't Stop* (Sedgwick 1978).

Probable passage

The story takes place *in a doughnut shop.* Mr. *Tucker* is a character in the story who *owns the store.* A problem occurs when *Tomas, a little boy, pushes the start-button.* After that, *the machine goes whirr, buzz, and clunk and a huge doughnut pops out.* Next, *a customer comes in.* The problem is solved when *they are given a bank*

Setting	Character(s)	Problem	Problem-solution	Ending

Figure 1. Incomplete story frame. Reprinted from K. Wood and the International Reading Association, *Techniques for Assessing Children's Potential for Learning*, The Reading Teacher (1984).

loan and Mr. Tucker and Tomas invent a way to stop the machine. The story ends when *Tomas eats a delicious jelly-cinnamon-honey doughnut (Wood 1984).*

After reading the story, the teacher and children modify the probable passage to fit the events described in the text. In addition to providing children with experience in predicting, this activity also requires them to put story vocabulary in an appropriate context and provides further instruction in story grammar. The support provided by the story maps and frames and teacher guidance seem to make this activity suitable for remedial readers. As Wood suggests, after extensive experience composing probable passages with teacher guidance, children can construct them in pairs or small groups.

When Marino, Gould, and Haas (1985) used the following writing assignment as a pre-reading activity, fourth graders had better recall of a passage about pioneers.

Pretend you are a young person in 1845. You are a pioneer heading for the Oregon country. You and your family have stopped to make camp for the night on the Snake River when you meet a group of young orphans. The oldest is a 13-year-old boy who tells you of his determination to carry on with his father's plan to take the family to Oregon. John, you learn, is a very brave and clever boy, who has just saved his sister from drowning. Write a letter home to your grandparents describing this boy and the story he has told you (p. 204).

While this activity does not really use predicting in the same way as the inferential strategy, it is similar in that it focuses on central story concepts and involves children personally in the story as a preparation for reading. In using an activity like this with remedial readers, the teacher and the students will probably have to write the story together in a group before the children will be able to write in groups, pairs, or individually.

Some of the techniques described in Chapter 5 make more extensive use of writing. For example, the think sheets developed by Dole and Smith (1987) and Maria (1988) as a technique for helping children correct misconceptions, require children to write down their ideas and what the text says about the same question and then compare the two. In the Know—Want to Know—Learn (K—W—L) technique (Ogle 1986a, 1986b), after having constructed a semantic map through discussion with the teacher, the children write what they know and what they want to know in a notetaking format on a worksheet. Using the worksheet forces children to select ideas that they already have about the topic and to construct several questions about what they want to know. Writing on the worksheet serves as a support for organizing their knowledge, a way of setting a purpose for their reading, and a memory aid so that children can keep track of the questions they want to answer through their reading.

Noyce and Christie (1989) suggest adding writing tasks after constructing a semantic map, just as does the K—W—L method. Before reading, rather than taking notes on a worksheet, they suggest that children write a composition using the semantic map as an outline. After reading the text and adding information to their pre-reading semantic map, the children write another composition based on the revised semantic map. These compositions are really summaries of prior knowledge in the case of the pre-reading composition and summaries of prior knowledge and text information in the case of the post-reading composition. As discussed in Chapter 8, summarizing is one of the most valuable comprehension strategies. Ogle (1986b) also suggests that adding summaries to semantic maps provides children with valuable experience in summarizing in a situation in which a graphic organizer provides support for writing the summary. Research by Weisberg and Balajthy (1985) suggests that semantic maps assist remedial readers to summarize text information.

BUILDING LINGUISTIC KNOWLEDGE THROUGH INTEGRATED INSTRUCTION IN READING AND WRITING.

While children often write as part of the techniques for teaching word meanings, they only write definitions as in the Concept of Definition technique; or they write sentences when learning how to use context as clues to word meaning in enriched vocabulary instruction. Writing complete texts should also be a part of vocabulary instruction. Writing texts provides the opportunities for children to use the words they have acquired through reading, thereby helping them understand and retain their meanings. Moreover, children develop a sensitivity to differences in word meanings as they use them in their writing. "Every time a decision is made by a student-writer as to which word is 'best' in a piece of writing, vocabulary learning takes place" (Vacca, Vacca, and Gove 1987, p. 175).

Teachers can support the integration of vocabulary learning by structuring activities in which children write sentences or compositions using the words they have learned in reading. A good post-reading writing activity similar to the Probable Passages pre-reading activity is to give children a list of words that have been taught as part of comprehension instruction. The children should be asked to create a new text with the words. For example, children who read the *Knights and Tournaments* passage (described in Chapters 5 and 6) could be given the words *knight, sword, lance, tournament, squire, ceremony, serf,* and *noble* and asked to write a story that included these words. Teachers will need to model this activity at first. When children are able to write stories independently, they can then be shared. Part of the fun is seeing how many different stories can be developed using the same words.

Chapter 7 suggests the use of writing activities at the sentence level, such as sentence completion exercises and sentence combining, as a way of helping children learn complex sentence structures. The Integrated Sentence Modeling Cycle (Noyce and Christie 1989) is an instructional technique designed to teach children complex sentence patterns. This technique uses writing activities at the text level as well as activities in listening, speaking, and reading. Use of the Integrated Sentence Modeling Cycle led to significant gains in third graders' use of the complex patterns taught and increased writing fluency (Noyce and Christie 1983). It consists of the following steps:

Step 1.   Listening. The children listen while the teacher reads children's stories containing instances of a particular sentence pattern.
Step 2.   Speaking. The children engage in oral games and activities that repeat this pattern.
Step 3.   Writing. Children write stories in which they are encouraged to use the pattern.
Step 4.   Reading. The children read trade books (from Step 1) and books written by children (from Step 3) that contain repeated examples of the target sentence pattern (Noyce and Christie 1989).

An example of the Integrated Sentence Modeling Cycle focusing on sentences containing subordinate clauses beginning with *when* can be found in Noyce and Christie (1989).

Chapter 7 describes instruction in narrative and expository text structure that integrates reading and writing instruction both at the sentence level and text level. Story maps, story frames, graphic organizers, and expository text frames serve as supports for children's construction and comprehension of texts. As Chapter 7 emphasizes, children learn text structures best through writing.

WRITING AS A SUPPORT FOR LEARNING READING STRATEGIES

Chapter 8 describes techniques for teaching children the strategies of asking questions, predicting, and summarizing. These techniques use oral discussion and oral modeling as teaching tools, but writing is needed to supplement oral discussion. When we have to write about ideas, we reflect upon and organize them to a greater extent than when we talk about them.

The lack of opportunity for reflection and planning is a weakness that some teachers see in Reciprocal Teaching. They feel it is unfair to expect children to act as teachers and ask important high-level questions, give good summaries, and make perceptive predictions without giving them the opportunity to plan. "After all," teachers say to me, "you tell us that we should read the text carefully and plan the questions, summaries, predictions, words, and phrases that may need to be clarified." My response to them is that we are asking the children to play the role of teacher so that they can internalize the strategies; we are not training the children to be teachers. To ask children to plan their responses for a dialogue would destroy the value of the dialogue. Yet I recognize the value of the criticism. The during-reading instruction described in Chapter 8 needs to be supplemented by writing activities that give children opportunities to plan and reflect on their use of the strategies.

Asking questions is a difficult strategy, particularly for remedial readers. Oral modeling of questions by the teacher in techniques like Active Comprehension, ReQuest, InQuest, and Reciprocal Teaching can be supplemented by providing opportunities for children to write questions before and after reading. For example, in using any of these techniques, children can write questions they have about the title or about the pictures, before the reading and the dialogue begin. The InQuest demonstration lesson (described in Chapter 8) provides another example. The teacher asks the children playing the roles of reporters to plan and write questions they will ask the child who plays the part of the character from the story.

A graduate student of mine has developed an after-reading activity (Domato 1989) to supplement her use of Reciprocal Teaching in the content areas. Children are given a text segment to read for homework and are told to write several important questions about the text, questions they would ask if they were acting as the teacher. At the outset of class the following day, the children exchange questions with a partner, and the partner answers the questions. Discussion after the children have answered the questions focuses on the quality of the questions rather than on the correctness of the answers. (However, the teacher collects the assignments and uses them to assess how well the children have understood the text.) Exchanging the questions with other students is important because it means that the children are writing the questions for a purpose and for an audience other than the teacher.

Probable Passages (Wood 1984), described in the section on writing as a pre-reading activity, uses writing to help children predict the content of a story, and provide them with a list of words as a basis for the predictions. Another activity in which children write their predictions about a text, and use pictures from the text as a basis for the predictions, was developed by Buckley (1986) and is described by Noyce and Christie (1989). Noyce and Christie also suggest that occasionally children should be asked to write their predictions and the evidence for them when they are engaged in a Directed Reading Thinking Activity. However, if children have a tendency to read ahead, having to write down their predictions may make the waiting time for confirming or refuting the predictions too long.

While summarizing is probably the most valuable comprehension strategy, it is also the most difficult. In Reciprocal Teaching children summarize short text segments orally. However, the rules for summarizing, described in Chapter 8, apply to written summaries as well as to oral ones. Integration of reading and writing instruction is particularly appropriate in instruction in summarizing. Children should also occasionally be asked to write summaries of stories or segments of content area textbooks. Anderson and Hidi (1988-1989) provide the following guidelines for teaching children to write summaries. Children should:

1. Begin writing summaries of short, easy texts. At first, text segments should be used. Stories should be summarized before expository texts. Ideas in the texts should be familiar.
2. Have the text available to refer to when they are writing summaries.
3. Write summaries for themselves (writer-based summaries) before writing summaries for others (reader-based summaries).
4. Learn that a summary should include information important to the author. This involves teaching children to use content and structure of a text as cues to the importance of ideas.

Every effort should be made to provide a purpose for the summary. For example, summarizing a segment from a content area textbook can be used as a way of preparing for a test.

However, for remedial readers, writing a summary of even a short text segment is a difficult task. Remedial readers will have more success if they collaborate with the teacher or with other children in cooperative groups when they are writing summaries. After teaching children the Brown and Day (1983) rules for summarization described in Chapter 8, Guido and Colwell (1987) used the point system below as a way of rating summaries that middle school children constructed in cooperative triads.

EVERY TIME A RULE IS USED IT RATES THIS NUMBER OF POINTS

General idea for a list of items or actions	8 points
Main idea	4 points
Supporting details	1 point
Use of trivia	-4 points
Repeating a fact	-4 points

Points are totaled and become the numerator in a fraction in which the total number of words is the denominator. The ratio score, then, reflects the two crucial aspects of a summary: (1) inclusion of main ideas and (2) brevity. Scoring of the summaries was discussed with the class. The children enjoyed the activity and appeared to benefit from it because they were given definite guidelines for writing an effective summary.

Anderson and Hidi (1988-1989) suggest that children should begin by writing summaries for themselves as an aid to comprehension and recall. Because of their difficulty with the process of summarizing, it may be hard to convince remedial readers of the value of using summaries for this purpose. Avoid having children write summaries for only the teacher to read; activities in which summaries are shared with other students are much more motivating. Writing summaries that are then turned into cloze exercises for use by other children is one way of writing them for a purpose and an audience (Johnson and Louis 1987). At first, teachers and children write the summaries together, deciding which content words should be deleted. Only a few words should be deleted so that the summary has enough context. Deciding what words should be deleted is a valuable activity in itself because it requires attention to the level of importance of each word and the amount of context remaining after word deletion. Nonsense words, partial letter information, and incorrect words can be used instead of blanks to provide variety. Johnson and Louis (1987) suggest that children would be ready to write summaries and turn them into cloze exercises independently after several summary cloze experiences with the teacher. Remedial readers should probably be part of a cooperative learning group when they engage in such a difficult task.

Books read in Sustained Silent Reading time can be shared by children through writing and oral booktalks. Summarizing a book in order to share and encourage other children to read it provides another valid purpose for summarizing (Rhodes and Dudley-Marling 1988). Story maps and story frames, like those presented in Chapter 7, can support children's efforts; but these frames will need to be adapted since giving a complete summary of a story would not encourage a child to read it. Moreover, Rhodes and Dudley-Marling suggest that in writing this type of summary children should include what is important to them as well as what is important to the author. In this way, these summaries are different from more formal summaries that focus on ideas the author considers important. Teachers should make these differences clear to the children.

Summarizing should be only one of many ways that children respond to their reading, and it should not be overused. Asking children to summarize every book they read will be a sure way of discouraging them. Other ways of structuring response to reading through writing will be suggested in the next section.

WRITING AS A RESPONSE TO READING

The value of discussion as a response to reading was emphasized earlier in this chapter. However, if children write their responses to their reading before engaging in discussion, discussions may be better (Kirby and Liner 1981 cited in Rhodes and Dudley-Marling 1988).

One way of encouraging children to reflect on their reading through writing is for them to keep reading journals. The reading journal is a place where children keep track of the trade books they read; but it can be more than that. The journal can be a place where writing about reading begins, a place for trying out ideas. Writing in a journal for about ten minutes a day is an important part of instruction in writing. It provides children with the practice so necessary to their writing growth. In addition, when children write in their journals about what they are reading, it helps them integrate reading and writing and see how each process supports the other. The journal format encourages a personal response to texts so that, at times, directions can be very open-ended. Children can write about something they remember from the text and something it reminds them of as a preparation for participating in a subsequent group discussion (Graves 1984; Hansen 1984). In addition, children can pretend to be one of the characters and write a journal entry taking the role of that character. They can write letters to the author or to one of the characters. *Literacy through Literature* (Johnson and Louis 1987) contains many good suggestions for activities of this kind.

Children can compose new stories in the journals using the same structure as that in a book with a predictable plot they have read. They can also complete a story, give it a different ending, or write it from a different point of view. For example, one of my graduate students gave her high school remedial readers the following assignment after they had read *The Alchemist's Secret* (Gordon 1961). This short story tells about a man who hires an alchemist to poison his wife. The section of the text used in the assignment is the section in which the man gives his reasons for wanting to murder his wife. The alchemist's secret is that the wife has also hired him to murder her husband. The wife does not appear in the text, but the fact that she has also consulted the alchemist is inferred from information given in the story. This story then provides an excellent opportunity to write a story from an alternate point of view. Providing the excerpt from the story in which the husband gives his reasons for wanting to murder his wife gave support to the task for these remedial readers (see figure 2).

In content area classes, journals can be learning logs in which children write about what they learned from the text, what confused them, and the questions they have (Vacca and Vacca 1986). Although teachers should read the journals and provide some kind of feedback to the students about their ideas, they should never make corrections in grammar and spelling. Journal entries are like first drafts. If a teacher and a student decide that a particular journal entry warrants being turned into a finished piece, then either the teacher or the student's peers can help him or her revise and edit it.

Some teachers have formalized the process of responding to journal entries by instituting the use of a dialogue journal. When dialogue journals are used, the teacher becomes the audience for the journal. If the dialogue journal is also a reading journal, then the teacher reacts to the student's response to reading. Since the communication is on a personal level, using dialogue journals provides teacher and student with a way of recreating a pleasant social

---

WORKSHEET

"My wife," said the visitor with a certain agitation, "is a very beautiful woman. Naturally, she has many admirers. She has always ignored them until recently, but now there is one—I don't know which one—a younger man, no doubt. She admits it! She demands that I make some settlement. I will not . . . ."

REWRITE THIS PASSAGE FROM THE WIFE'S POINT OF VIEW

"My husband is a very . . .

Figure 2. Assignment for writing a story from an alternate point of view. Reprinted with permission of P. Tortorella 1989.

environment where they can "talk" about books. Atwell (1987) instituted the use of dialogue journals in her eighth-grade English class as a way of recreating the environment around her dining room table, a place where she and her family and friends talk about the books they read.

The letter (found below) that Atwell (1984) used to introduce the concept of dialogue journals to her students, describes a very open-ended format. At first, remedial readers will probably need directions for more specific activities like those described previously.

> This folder is a place for you and me to talk about books, reading, authors, and writing. You're to write letters to me, and I'll write letters back to you.
>
> In your letters to me, talk with me about what you've read. Tell me what you thought and felt and why. Tell me what you liked and didn't like and why. Tell me what those books meant to you and said to you. Ask me questions or for help, and write back to me about my ideas, feelings and questions.

Dialogue journals provide a situation in which teachers and students communicate meaningfully through writing, so the writing that the children do has a purpose and an audience. The practice helps students' reading and writing, but it also helps teachers know each student in a deeper and more personal way. Because the writing is so personal, teachers should respect the privacy of the journal and never share an entry without the permission of the author. They should try to focus on something good about the student's writing, but they should also be honest with students, for example, telling them when they use language that is not appropriate for teachers to read. They should make specific suggestions in reaction to ideas, but should not make corrections or tell children to make changes unless it is decided to turn the journal entry into a finished piece (Kirby and Liner 1981 cited in Tierney, Readence, and Dishner 1985).

If journals are to be successful, enough time must be alloted for them; but the journal should not become a chore. Taking a break from journal writing may be a good idea (Kirby and Liner 1981 cited in Tierney, Readence, and Dishner 1985). Because dialogue journals make great demands on teachers' time, they have not been used successfully in many classrooms (Noyce and Christie 1989). If teachers attempt to respond to the journals of everyone in their class every day, they will soon be so overwhelmed that they will give up the practice. A better way would be to divide the class so that the teacher responds to the journals of a different group every day. The problem with this format, however, is that it may be a long time before a teacher responds to a student's questions or reactions, and he or she may not want to make another journal entry without receiving a response from the teacher. Another possibility suggested by Gambrell (1985) is to work with one reading group at a time for a period of about three weeks, responding daily to the journals in just this group. Still another possibility is to have students use the journals for communicating with each other as well as with the teacher (Atwell 1987). Cooperative learning groups would be an excellent format for this way of using the dialogue journals.

READING COMPREHENSION INSTRUCTION
—A SUPPORT FOR WRITING INSTRUCTION

Because of the similarities between the reading and writing processes that were described earlier, reading comprehension instruction can support instruction in writing just as writing can support reading comprehension instruction. Reading influences writing because schemata related to world knowledge and linguistic knowledge are acquired to a great extent through reading and thus are an integral part of the knowledge base children draw on when they write. However, a reader interacts with a text to reconstruct meaning; a writer, faced with a blank piece of paper, constructs meaning by constructing a text. Instruction in both reading and writing is necessary, and neither type of instruction can substitute for the other.

Several complaints about traditional writing instruction that writing experts have voiced in recent years are similar to the problems with traditional reading instruction identified at the outset of this book. First, just as traditional reading instruction devoted little time to reading comprehension instruction so too, until recently, little time has been spent on writing instruction. At the beginning of this decade, the research of Graves (1978) and Applebee (1981) and articles in the popular press such as "Why Johnny Can't Write" (*Newsweek* December 8, 1975) documented the lack of writing and writing instruction in American schools and generated concern among educators. At the same time, it was recognized that the little writing instruction that did take place in school did not really teach children *how* to write. In writing instruction, as in reading instruction, the focus was on the product rather than the process. After reviewing the research describing school writing instruction Florio-Ruane and Dunn (1987) provided a summary of its features:

1. Students generally write in response to teacher initiations.
2. Teachers tend to select the purpose and format of student writing.
3. Teacher response to student writing seems to be limited to product evaluation.
4. Product evaluation tends to focus on surface features of language rather than on meaning.
5. Little or no technical support is offered to students during actual writing time.
6. Writing time is limited and considered a private time when peer interaction is discouraged.
7. Little time is spent writing first drafts, and revision is rarely undertaken by student writers.
8. Most school writing never leaves the school or classroom to be read by a wider audience (p. 53).

This description of traditional writing instruction highlights other ways in which it is similar to traditional reading instruction. In traditional writing instruction as in traditional reading instruction, children are not actively involved; they respond to the demands of the teacher. Just as children spend little time reading texts for their own enjoyment so too, they spend very little time writing for their own purposes. Traditional writing instruction focuses on bottom-up skills such as spelling and grammar just as traditional reading instruction focuses on phonics and word identification.

In the past decade researchers and theorists in cognitive psychology and education (Bereiter and Scardamalia 1981; Hayes and Flower 1983; Graves 1978) have begun to explore and describe the nature of the writing process from a new perspective as other researchers and theorists have done with the reading process.

They describe the writing process as consisting of several stages. In the pre-writing stage writers generate ideas; find topics; and plan what they are going to write, deciding on audience, form, and voice. In the drafting stage, writers put their ideas into words and get the words onto the paper. Revising involves reading what is written and changing it to improve meaning and organization. It also involves editing and proofreading for mechanical errors to make the text more suitable for the audience. Finally, publishing means making writing available for others to read. It is important to remember that these are recursive rather than linear stages. Lindemann (1982, p. 23) quoted in Vacca and Vacca (1986, p. 231) describes this aspect of writing very well as

> . . . a messy business, rarely in real life as tidy as textbook descriptions portray it. We don't begin at step one, "find a topic," and follow an orderly sequence of events to "proofreading the paper." Certainly we plan what we want to say before we begin drafting, but the act of writing generates new ideas and shapes new plans. In other words, prewriting and writing occur at the same time. So can writing (drafting) and rewriting, for we never commit words to paper without changing at least one or two here and there.

As a result of this new understanding of writing, the writing process movement (Calkins 1986; Graves 1983), and staff development projects like the South Bay Writing Project (Tiedt et al. 1983), writing instruction has changed. Writing assessments that evaluate writing holistically in terms of ideas and form are now used in at least 22 states (Education Commission of the States 1984). These new types of writing assessment and the whole language movement support the change in writing instruction.

Much more time in school is being devoted to writing. Graves (1983) suggests that children should write every day or at a minimum three times a week, and that the periods devoted to writing should be thirty-five to fifty minutes long. As a result of the whole language movement, writing is taught and practiced even before children learn to read. The time demands of both writing and reading comprehension instruction provide a practical reason for integrating instruction in the two processes as well as integrating both reading and writing with content area instruction. Unless there is this integration, there simply is not enough time.

Writing instruction is beginning to be referred to as writing process instruction. Writing process instruction is similar in many ways to reading comprehension instruction because both focus on meaning and on helping children to think. Many of the guidelines for organizing instruction described in

Chapter 4 can assist writing instruction as well as reading comprehension instruction.

Improving classroom management and creating a literate environment in the classroom, a climate in which risk taking is encouraged and in which the focus is on thinking rather than on the right answer, is as helpful for writing as it is for reading.

Allowing children time to think is also important. In reading instruction this may mean giving children enough time to answer a question. In writing instruction it means that children are not expected to write a finished piece in one session. Writing goes on from session to session and children are expected to write first drafts and revise before publishing. Forming heterogeneous small groups is a good way of organizing children for writing instruction as well as for reading instruction. The writing process approach uses a workshop format in which children help each other with all aspects of writing in peer response groups (Graves 1983; Calkins 1986). Cooperative learning groups in which children collaborate on producing a product is helpful for writing as well as reading (Slavin 1987).

As a result of the writing process movement, teachers have recognized the complexity and difficulty of the process and have begun to provide support to children at all stages. They provide this support using the same tools they use for reading comprehension instruction: they engage in dialogue with children in writing conferences and encourage student-to-student dialogue in peer response groups. They ask questions about process and content so that children themselves will learn to ask the same kinds of questions about their writing; they think aloud; they model; and they write along with the children. This modeling is extremely important in helping children understand that writing is a difficult process for everyone. I will never forget the first time I tried writing along with one remedial reader. He was stunned that my writing didn't just flow, that I had to cross out and rewrite and change focus.

Teachers scaffold tasks for the children by writing collaboratively with them, but more often by helping them find their own voices and focus on ideas without having to meet teacher demands for perfect spelling and grammar simultaneously. These mechanical demands are not ignored; like the reading skills, they are taught in the context of accomplishing a purpose. Children who write for each other recognize the need for spelling, grammar, and punctuation as aids to communication. Published writing must be mechanically correct. In providing this help in writing as in reading, the teacher's overriding purpose is to make the children independent learners.

Many of the same factors that affect reading comprehension instruction also affect writing so that the techniques designed to support these factors are helpful for both. Children's world knowledge provides the content of the texts they write as well as the texts they read. Techniques that activate children's prior knowledge such as PREP (Langer 1982), semantic mapping (McNeil 1987), and the inferential strategy (Hansen and Hubbard 1984) can be used as pre-writing activities also.

Children's level of linguistic knowledge affects their writing as well as their reading. Vocabulary instruction that provides them with new concepts and new labels for old concepts, instruction in sentence structure that provides them with ability to understand and express themselves in complex sentence patterns, and instruction in narrative and expository text structures that makes them aware of the importance of organization and the different ways in which text can be organized make children better writers as well as better readers. The story maps and frames and the graphic organizers using expository text structures support children's writing and reading.

It is as important to their writing as it is to their reading that children be exposed to considerate, interesting texts in a variety of genres. Even for a remedial reader a well-written text, particularly one with a predictable structure, can serve as an impetus to and a model for writing, as well as an aid to comprehension. I read *Fortunately* (Charlip 1964) with a remedial reader whose reading was so poor in sixth grade that he had just about given up hope and seemed totally lacking in motivation. The sigh of contentment he gave after reading the story was followed immediately by "I could write a story like that." And he began to compose on the spot, "Fortunately it was a good day. Unfortunately, it started to rain. Fortunately, I had my umbrella. . . . "

Finally, reading comprehension instruction is an important support for writing instruction because, although reading can take place without writing, there can be no writing without reading. The strategies we teach children in reading comprehension instruction are also helpful in their writing. Teaching children to ask questions about texts that others write can help them ask questions about what they write. Looking for cues that help children make predictions about texts others write will help them see the importance of providing these cues in the texts they write.

Reading comprehension instruction supports growth not only in reading but also in oral language and writing. On the other hand, oral language and writing support growth in reading comprehension. Thus reading comprehension instruction must be provided in the context of a total language arts program where the connections between the language processes are made overt for the children.

C H A P T E R

10

COMPREHENSION ASSESSMENT

WHAT SHOULD BE ASSESSED?

This book on comprehension instruction would not be complete without a consideration of comprehension assessment. Assessment is a necessary component of any type of effective instruction, helping us to answer many questions. Since our goal is to enable our students to comprehend a variety of texts independently, one of the most important questions we need to answer in comprehension assessment is how well they are achieving this goal. Does their comprehension meet our expectations? The answer to this question is very important, but it also leads to a further question, i.e., "How can we help them to comprehend better?" Assessment must not merely tell us about comprehension as a product. It must give us some insight into a child's comprehension process because one of the main goals of assessment is to inform and guide instructional decision making.

Reading is a complex process affected by many factors; children who exhibit problems in comprehension may have problems with one or more of these factors (Schell 1988). Therefore, comprehension assessment which seeks to support instructional decision making must consider how the various factors may be affecting comprehension performance. Previous chapters have discussed these factors—in the reader, in the text, and in the school environment. In assessing the comprehension of remedial readers in particular, teachers need to consider how their word recognition ability, world knowledge, linguistic knowledge, knowledge of appropriate comprehension strategies, and interest and motivation affect their comprehension of texts. Is this child's inability to understand this text largely a result of the fact that he or she cannot recognize the words in it? Does this child have the prior knowledge necessary to understand this text? Is the language used in this text unfamiliar to this child? Does this child know how to combine prior knowledge and text cues in order to make reasonable predictions about what he or she is reading? Is the topic of this text of interest to this child?

The way text factors interact with factors in the reader also needs to be considered as part of comprehension assessment. Is the text this child is reading too difficult for him or her because there are too many words that he or she cannot recognize? Is this child able to comprehend narrative text better than expository text? Is this child having difficulty with this particular text because the text is inconsiderate? Does this child do better with short text than with long?

The effect of different situations also needs to be considered. For example, Burke and Harste (1978) cited in Rhodes and Dudley-Marling (1988) found that retellings that children told to a friend differed from those told to an adult researcher. The place, the purpose for reading, and the task we use to assess reading also affect children's comprehension (Glazer and Searfoss 1988; Niles and Harris 1981; Valencia and Pearson 1988). Is this child more willing to take risks and answer questions in the small comparatively homogeneous Chapter I group than in the classroom? Is this child able to read for details in a text but unable to determine the main idea? Does this child have more success with multiple choice questions than open-ended questions?

An important aspect of the reading situation is the type of instructional support the child receives. Thus another important focus of comprehension assessment should be to determine under what instructional conditions a child comprehends best. Assessment that seeks to answer this question is referred to as dynamic assessment (Valencia and Pearson 1988; Wang 1987; Wood 1988). In dynamic assessment, the teacher presents the child with a reading activity, observes the response, and then introduces modifications to the task (Winograd, Wixson, and Lipson 1989).

This type of focus is particularly important in comprehension assessment that accompanies scaffolded comprehension instruction. Teachers need to know (1) whether the child is benefitting from the instructional support provided by scaffolded instruction, (2) which type of support is most beneficial, and (3) when support is no longer necessary.

Another important focus for comprehension assessment is the function of reading. Comprehension assessment with this focus asks questions like "How do students use reading for learning new information, for personal expression, for gaining new insights, etc.?" (Valencia, McGinley, and Pearson in press).

STRUCTURE OF COMPREHENSION ASSESSMENT MEASURES

Like reading comprehension, reading comprehension assessment is a complex process involving a variety of measures—a portfolio approach to assessment (Winograd, Wixson, and Lipson 1989; Valencia, McGinley, and Pearson in press). Fortunately, many different types of assessment tools are available for teachers to use as part of comprehension assessment. These tests vary not only according to the type of questions that they seek to answer but also according to their structure (Valencia, McGinley, and Pearson in press). Comprehension assessment tools range from the unstructured and spontaneous gathering of information during instruction to structured tests with specifically defined outcomes and directions for administration and scoring (e.g., standardized reading comprehension tests and basal reader tests). In the middle of the continuum are semi-structured measures, informal but planned assessments that require "more input and interpretation from the teacher and/or provide greater latitude in student responses" (Valencia, McGinley, and Pearson in press).

INFORMAL TEACHER-CONTROLLED ASSESSMENT

Since teachers are the only ones who have the opportunity to employ multiple and varied measures over a period of time, classroom assessment using informal measures should play an important role in a complete program of comprehension assessment. Chapter 4 suggests that one of the first things teachers can do to improve comprehension instruction is to provide more time for it. Teachers cannot be expected to test formally all the aspects of comprehension that might help them in making instructional decisions (MacGinitie 1989). If they did, there would be no time left for comprehension instruction. The degree of intrusiveness, i.e., the amount of time it takes away from instruction, is an important consideration (Farr and Beck in press; Valencia, McGinley, and Pearson in press) in choosing a measure of comprehension. It is not the only consideration, however. In-depth assessment of children who fail to meet expectations in comprehension may require a substantial amount of time. However, for the most part, teacher assessment of comprehension should be an integral part of comprehension instruction.

The Test Use in Schools Project funded by the National Institute of Education and conducted from 1979 to 1982 found that teachers rely on information gathered during instruction, i.e., their own observations and their students' classroom work, more than any other source in making decisions about instruction. However, in gathering information to make decisions about reading instruction, teachers generally focus on the social and emotional factors affecting reading performance (Calfee and Hiebert 1987). For information about children's reading performance and about what they need to be taught, teachers rely on externally developed more formal tests like those that accompany the basal readers. Calfee and Hiebert (1987) describe the teacher's current role in classroom reading assessment as that of a "sorter" who classifies and labels children according to directions imposed by others.

Many teachers, administrators, and parents do not consider the information that teachers gather during instruction "real assessment." They view assessment and instruction as separate activities, partly because they think of assessment and formal testing as synonymous terms; they assume that assessment and instruction require different materials, use different methods, and have different goals (Brown and Lytle 1989). Assessment is seen as a burden, "taking time away from instruction" and something we do for "them, the authorities," rather than a necessary component of instruction and a support for ourselves and our students (Valencia, McGinley, and Pearson in press).

The gap between assessment and instruction may be even larger for remedial readers than for other children. Reading assessment of remedial readers is still largely based on a medical model that focuses on a search for causes of the reading problem within the individual. This model of assessment suggests the "need for expertise and specialization beyond the domain of the classroom teacher" (Vacca and Vacca 1986, p. 64). Thus in many cases different people may be responsible for the comprehension assessment and the comprehension instruction of remedial readers. A child may be tested by a school psychologist or learning disabilities specialist during one or two sessions. Input from the classroom teacher based on information gathered during instruction is often not a part of this assessment. Very often too there is no communication between the classroom teacher and the specialist after the assessment. The specialists often have little idea whether the recommendations they gave helped the child or even whether the recommendations were carried out. While support personnel can be helpful in the in-depth reading assessment of remedial readers, if assessment and instruction are to be integrated, comprehension assessment of remedial readers also needs to be conducted by the person or persons who provide them with comprehension instruction. Sharing information gathered with a variety of measures and as part of instruction is an important reason for close communication between specialists and classroom teachers.

Valencia and Pearson (1988) suggest that we must broaden our definition of reading assessment and think of assessment as a help to ourselves and our students. "Assessment should be a natural part of the teaching/learning process—not something added on or imposed as an afterthought" (Valencia, McGinley, and Pearson in press).

One reason information gathered during instruction is not viewed as "real assessment" and more attention is paid to information provided by externally developed tests may be that teachers often do not record the information they gather or organize it systematically. Teachers have very little training in assessment. Calfee and Hiebert (1987) argue that if children's reading comprehension is to be assessed appropriately, teachers will need better training so that they will have more knowledge about assessment strategies and the reading process. They propose a model of assessment in which the teacher's role is that of an applied researcher who:

1. Forms hypotheses about why children are experiencing difficulty in comprehending what they read.
2. Systematically varies factors such as type of text, testing format, and amount of assistance.
3. Collects and records data under these various conditions, exploring hypotheses about particular children.

4. Interprets the data—deciding how particular children can benefit from instruction.
5. Reformulates hypotheses that can then be tested.

The cyclical nature of this model of assessment in which hypotheses are tested and then reformulated is particularly suited to comprehension assessment. Since comprehension is not a subject to be mastered, its assessment must be cyclical and formative rather than summative. If teachers view their roles in assessment as that of researchers, then they will recognize the need for the documentation and organization of the assessment data that they collect. When teachers document and organize the data they collect, others will have more respect for their assessment.

OBSERVATION

Observation is one of the most valuable methods of comprehension assessment. Teachers can observe children as they read in a natural situation in school so observation has good ecological validity, i.e., children's reading comprehension is assessed using the same tasks and texts that are used for instruction. Because observation is integrated with instruction and does not interfere with instruction, it can be used to assess children's reading comprehension in many different situations, with different types of texts, different levels of teacher support, etc. (Valencia, McGinley, and Pearson in press). In addition to answering questions about how well children comprehend what they read, it provides insight on how to help them comprehend better. We can observe children's responses before, during, and after reading a variety of texts to determine what factors affect their comprehension, how well instruction supports their comprehension, and how they integrate skills and strategies when reading in different functional contexts.

Teacher observation has not been viewed as an important part of comprehension assessment because it is often perceived as subjective and unreliable (May 1986). We teachers are human beings and so we are prone to bias. We may give too much weight to some events or observations and too little to others. However, scores on even the most carefully constructed test can also be misleading. A score does not always represent a child's true performance; there is always the element of chance. For example, a child may be distressed emotionally or sick physically on the day of the test; he or she may misinterpret the directions.

Researchers are well aware of the problem of observer bias and take steps to counteract their own biases by (1) training observers in what to look for and how to look, (2) using objective methods of recording observation data, and (3) comparing data collected through a number of different observations (Gay 1987).

Calfee and Hiebert's (1987) model for assessment suggests that in acting like researchers teachers should use the same methods to improve the objectivity and reliability of their observations. Teachers can be ethnographic researchers, observing and documenting children's behavior over a period of time and developing hypotheses about factors affecting children's reading comprehension performance as a result of their observations (Smith 1988). For example, after observing a child over a period of time, a teacher may hypothesize that he or she only exhibits problems in comprehension when not interested in the text topic. The teacher can then test this hypothesis using the more traditional research model, systematically observing the child with texts interesting to him or her and texts of no interest to determine whether the hypothesis has merit. However, when we develop a hypothesis we should be aware that we are prone to the "confirming bias" discussed in Chapter 8. We must try to maintain objectivity to overcome our tendency to see what we expect to see.

In order to follow Calfee and Hiebert's (1987) model of assessment, teachers must have a good understanding of the reading process and the factors that may affect it. Valencia, McGinley, and Pearson (in press) suggest that "the first and most important deterrent to unreliability is knowledge. If we know what to evaluate, we will evaluate more consistently." However, we must also recognize that we don't know everything about reading. It is a very complex process. We should be open-minded in our observations of children. Very often their responses do not fit our theories. More weight should be given to their responses than our theories.

Teachers cannot observe all the children in their class at the same time. Vacca, Vacca, and Gove (1987) recommend focusing on one or two children or one reading group for several days, then shifting the focus to another small group of children or observing and documenting only one behavior such as predicting or summarizing.

Although teachers need to observe children's reading comprehension with different texts and in different contexts, they must observe a child more than once with a particular type of text or in a particular situation. For example, before deciding that a child has difficulty with comparison/contrast text structure, a teacher should observe him or her reading a number of texts with this structure. Decisions made on the basis of one observation are as unreliable as decisions made on the basis of one item on a test.

Documenting observations is necessary for reliable identification of patterns of comprehension difficulty. Some teachers jot notes and place them in the children's reading portfolio. Checklists provide another convenient and objective way of recording children's reading comprehension performance. Checklists that can be used to record observations about the effect of various factors on comprehension will be presented in later sections discussing assessment of these factors. Teachers should also construct their own checklists.

Collecting samples of children's work is another way of documenting classroom observation. While the portfolio is an approach to assessment, it is also a container in which assessment data is stored (Valencia, McGinley, and Pearson in press) so that it is available for teachers' reflection. Records of teacher observations, samples of children's work, and both externally developed and teacher made tests stored in the portfolio provide documentation for teacher's assessment of children's comprehension and allow them to share information more easily with other teachers, parents, and administrators.

If students have access to the reading portfolio, they can use the assessment data to reflect on their work and evaluate their progress. Students should also have input regarding what is included in the portfolio. For example, they can select reading journal entries for the portfolio. As part of the assessment, they can explain why they selected the particular entries.

Although control of assessment traditionally has rested with the teacher, part of training children to be independent learners is teaching them to assess their own learning. Learning is enhanced when students share responsibility for monitoring their own learning (Johnston 1985 cited in Valencia and Pearson 1988). Thus comprehension assessment should be viewed as a collaboration between the teacher and the student. Students need to know teachers' expectations for them and the progress they are making in meeting those expectations (Valencia, McGinley, and Pearson in press). Teachers should explain what they hope students will learn from the various assessments they use and also work with students in developing assessment measures. For example, asking children to construct questions about a text is not only a good way of providing them with practice but also a way of enabling them to collaborate in constructing an assessment of comprehension.

Teachers should also observe their own behavior since the instruction they provide has an important effect on children's reading comprehension. Being objective about one's own behavior is even more difficult than being objective about the behavior of others. Vacca and Vacca (1986) suggest a few general questions that teachers might use as starting points for reflections about their own instruction, questions like "What did I do today in class that was most helpful to the children?" and "Is there anything I wish I could do over? Why?" They also suggest that teachers can respond best to questions like this by keeping a daily journal on their own teaching. Although this may seem like a tremendous burden, if journal writing is part of the class routine, teachers can write in their journals when the students write. This practice allows teachers to serve as models of literacy and document their own ideas about instruction for later reflection.

OPEN-ENDED QUESTIONS AND RETELLINGS

Teachers have traditionally assessed comprehension during instruction by means of open-ended questions, questions in which students construct a response rather than choose one. Questions like this posed orally or in writing can focus on collecting different types of information. We can ask questions to find out if children understand what they read, why they do not understand, and what strategies they are using in different reading tasks. Chapter 4 criticized the practice of using questions solely for assessment and urged teachers to make better use of questions as an instructional tool. However, questions can be used for assessment and instruction simultaneously. The suggestions about teacher questioning made in Chapter 4 can improve assessment as well as instruction.

Although retellings have been used extensively in reading research, they are not widely used in comprehension assessment. Chapter 9 discusses the use of oral and written retellings as an instructional technique. However, a number of authorities (Morrow 1988; Ringler and Weber 1987; Winograd, Wixson, and Lipson 1989) suggest that teachers should make greater use of retellings because they help determine what a student understands about a text when he or she does not have the structure and information provided by the teacher's questions. "Retelling can add immeasurably to our understanding of readers' comprehension, because it allows us to get a view of the quantity, quality and organization of information gleaned during reading" (Winograd, Wixson, and Lipson 1989, p. 123).

Children should be told before they read that they are going to be asked to retell the text. If the teacher is using the retelling for a particular purpose, the children should be told the purpose (Morrow 1988). For example, if the score depends on the number of ideas, children should be told to remember as much as possible.

After the child reads the text, the teacher should initiate the retelling through use of open-ended questions or statements such as:

Tell me what you have read, using your own words.

What is the story all about? (Ringler and Weber 1984, p. 152).

One problem in using retellings to assess comprehension is that recall is not exactly the same as comprehension. A child may understand an idea in the text but not remember it and fail to include it in the retelling. Remedial readers, particularly those classified as learning disabled, may have memory problems. Thus it is important to supplement retellings with questions.

The teacher should not interrupt the retelling, but after it has been completed, he or she may probe for further information with prompts such as:

Tell me more about what you have read.

Tell me more about what happened (Ringler and Weber 1984, p. 152).

After using these general probes, teachers may also use probes that make more specific reference to the text.

Another problem in using retellings is that some children may have difficulty in expressing their ideas. A poor retelling may be a reflection of this difficulty rather than a lack of comprehension. Poorly written retellings are even more likely to be a result of problems in expressing ideas. However, teachers may want to use written retellings with children who have had some practice with the procedure and who do not have problems with writing. The use of written retellings allows testing of a number of children at the same time.

Another problem with retellings is that they are difficult to score. Researchers who use retellings use a text analysis system to divide a text into ideas and assign those ideas to a particular level of importance. They score retellings by determining the number of text ideas they contain giving more weight to ideas at higher levels of importance. Ideas contained in the retelling but not in the text may also be noted. Ringler and Weber (1984) and Morrow (1988) suggest that teachers can score retellings in the same way using their own judgment rather than a text analysis system. There are two problems with this approach. First, because retellings are never in the same words as the text, deciding whether a particular idea in the retelling matches an idea in the text is often very difficult. I have had some training and a great deal of experience scoring retellings, and I still find the process very difficult and time-consuming. Teachers simply do not have enough time or training for this approach. Second, when researchers score retellings in this detailed way, there are always two independent scorers in order to be sure that the scoring is consistent. It is unlikely that teachers would be able get other teachers to help them with such a time-consuming process.

A better approach is to look at recalls qualitatively. Are there any misinterpretations or restructurings in the retelling that indicate a lack of comprehension? Does the child use the structure of the text to structure the retelling? The Retelling Profile below is a good checklist for scoring retellings qualitatively (see figure 1).

TEACHER MADE TESTS

The tests that teachers develop themselves are an important source of information for them (Dorr-Bremme 1983). Previous sections urged teachers to strive for objectivity and reliability when using observation and retellings as measures of comprehension. Teachers should also try to be consistent and objective in scoring the tests they construct.

Formal tests use multiple choice questions with one correct answer because this format is less subjective and thus more reliable. Reliability refers to the consistency of a test. If a child's score on a test depends on who is giving it, then we cannot have confidence in the information that it gives us. Another advantage of multiple choice questions is that since they do not require a child to construct a response, if a child gives an incorrect answer, we can be more confident that it is due to a problem in comprehension rather than a problem with expressing his or her ideas in writing.

However, questions that are easy to score consistently, i.e., short factual, open-ended questions, and multiple choice questions with one correct answer may not be the most appropriate type of assessment for the type of comprehension instruction recommended in this book. We need to be concerned about the instructional validity of our tests as well as their reliability. Does the way that we test children in comprehension match the way that we teach them? If our instruction focuses on getting children to see the relationships between ideas in the text and their own prior knowledge, then our test questions should have this focus, rather than a focus on facts. If we encourage divergent responses during instruction we must also provide children with test formats that allow for divergent responses.

Qualitative: The Retelling Profile

Directions. Indicate with a checkmark the extent to which the reader's retelling includes or provides evidence of the following information.

	none	low degree	moderate degree	high degree
1. Retelling includes information directly stated in text.				
2. Retelling includes information inferred directly or indirectly from text.				
3. Retelling includes what is important to remember from the text.				
4. Retelling provides relevant content and concepts.				
5. Retelling indicates reader's attempt to connect background knowledge to text information.				
6. Retelling indicates reader's attempt to make summary statements or generalizations based on text that can be applied to the real world.				
7. Retelling indicates highly individualistic and creative impressions of or reactions to the text.				
8. Retelling indicates the reader's affective involvement with the text.				
9. Retelling demonstrates appropriate use of language (vocabulary, sentence structure, language conventions).				
10. Retelling indicates reader's ability to organize or compose the retelling.				
11. Retelling demonstrates the reader's sense of audience or purpose.				
12. Retelling indicates the reader's control of the mechanics of speaking or writing.				

Interpretation. Items 1-4 indicate the reader's comprehension of textual information; items 5-8 indicate metacognitive awareness, strategy use, and involvement with text; items 9-12 indicate facility with language and language development.

Figure 1. Qualitative retelling profile. Reprinted, with permission, from J. Mitchell and P. Irwin 1990, *The Reader Retelling Profile: Using Retelling to Make Instructional Decisions.* In preparation.

Open-ended questions that focus on the relationship between concepts rather than on isolated facts are one good format for teacher-constructed tests. Another test format, one that focuses on the relationship between ideas, was developed by Valencia et al. (1989). The test below (see figure 2) is a test that I constructed using the Valencia et al. (1989) format. In this format, children are directed to rate how closely ideas are related to a central concept.

I used this particular test in a research study (Maria 1988) to assess fifth-grade children's prior knowledge before they read a text about seasonal change. I also used it to assess what they had learned from reading the text. Although the children had never seen this format before, they did not seem to find it too

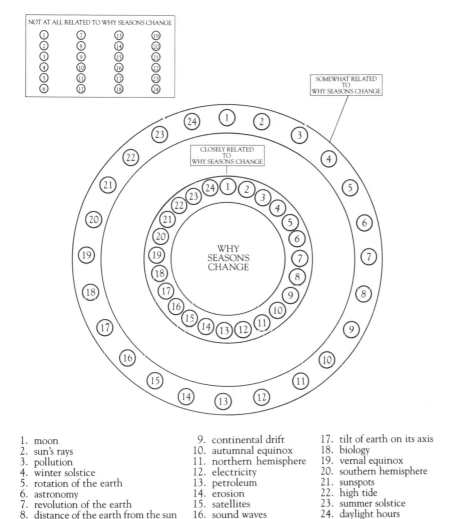

1. moon	9. continental drift	17. tilt of earth on its axis
2. sun's rays	10. autumnal equinox	18. biology
3. pollution	11. northern hemisphere	19. vernal equinox
4. winter solstice	12. electricity	20. southern hemisphere
5. rotation of the earth	13. petroleum	21. sunspots
6. astronomy	14. erosion	22. high tide
7. revolution of the earth	15. satellites	23. summer solstice
8. distance of the earth from the sun	16. sound waves	24. daylight hours

Figure 2. Circle test that helps children determine relationships between ideas.

difficult. Scores on this test were closely correlated with scores on other tests using multiple choice and open-ended questions.

Open-ended questions can also be constructed to allow for divergent responses. A number of other test formats that encourage children to provide divergent answers have been explored by the developers of the new Illinois Test of Reading (Valencia and Pearson 1988). In one format children are directed to choose several alternative answers since there may be more than one correct answer. Students can also be asked to justify their answers or to rate the acceptability of each choice.

When we use alternative testing formats, we collect information about how children's comprehension varies with different tasks. However, further research is needed to determine the best ways of utilizing alternative testing formats like those described above. Teachers acting as researchers can explore the use of these new testing formats.

TESTING READING COMPREHENSION IN THE CONTENT AREAS

When children learn content by reading about it and when reading strategies are taught as part of content area instruction, teacher constructed tests that assess how well the children learned the content can also assess their reading comprehension and their use of strategies. Although at times the purpose of instruction may be retention of facts, the purpose of most content area instruction is the assimilation of facts that "involves making inferences and integrating information for understanding rather than simply remembering" (Jones et al. 1987, p. 40). At other times the teacher's instructional purpose may be to restructure students' ideas, i.e., effect conceptual change. Each of these instructional purposes requires a different type of assessment; teachers must align their assessment with the type of learning they expect as a result of their instruction (Jones et al. 1987). They should plan the culminating activity that they will use for summative evaluation of a content area unit as they are developing the purposes and instructional activities for the unit.

How this can be done through activities that integrate assessment of content and process and the processes of reading and writing is illustrated in an example provided by Jones et al. (1987). In planning a unit on the Jackson presidency Mrs. Sampson decided that she wanted her students to remember three issues that Jackson faced in his presidency: conflicts over the National Bank, the Tariff of 1828, and the extension of voting rights to all white men. However, she also wanted her students to realize how those issues applied to today's society. Her instructional goals in reading were to help her students to become more confident with the problem/solution and the comparison/contrast structures. The culminating assessment task planned by Mrs. Sampson was a project in which students selected one of the three issues, searched for information about current government handling of the issue, and then prepared a short paper comparing Jackson's handling with current treatment of the issue. This activity assesses application of both kinds of knowledge the students gained from instruction: knowledge about social studies content and knowledge about expository text structure.

Mrs. Sampson also involved the students in self-assessment. In a class discussion after the paper was written, she asked them to evaluate what they had learned by comparing the organizational patterns they used in writing the paper with those provided as guides to reading the material in their textbook. The discussion then focused on why these text structures were appropriate for this content.

When we use sophisticated assessments like this that require a substantial amount of writing, there is always the danger that a child will do poorly not because of poor comprehension but because of poor ability to express himself or herself in writing. Every type of test has it strengths and weaknesses, so in constructing tests to measure comprehension, teachers should be sure to include a variety of formats.

INFORMAL READING INVENTORIES

Administration of an informal reading inventory is an important first step in the in-depth assessment of a child who is failing to meet expectations in reading. Informal reading inventories are individually administered tests consisting of graded word lists and graded passages. The word lists are used to determine the grade level passage where testing should begin.

A number of reading textbooks, e.g., Ringler and Weber (1984) and Gillet and Temple (1986) offer directions for teachers in constructing their own informal reading inventories. However, informal reading inventories are often offered as part of a basal reading system and there are also a number of commercially available informal inventories which are not tied to particular basal programs, e.g., the Analytical Reading Inventory (Woods and Moe 1989) and the Basic Reading Inventory (Johns 1988).

Informal reading inventories are criterion-referenced tests. The child's performance is compared to an arbitrary standard rather than to the performance of other children. Percentage of oral accuracy in reading the passages and percentage of oral comprehension questions answered correctly are used to determine the child's independent, instructional, and frustration reading levels. Commonly accepted criteria are:

Independent level–Oral Accuracy: 97% or higher; Comprehension: 90% or higher.

Instructional level–Oral Accuracy: 90–96%; Comprehension: 70–90%.

Frustration level–Oral Accuracy: below 90%; Comprehension: below 70%.

(Detailed information on administration, scoring, and interpretation of informal reading inventories is available in the manuals of the tests and the reading textbooks cited previously, Ringler and Weber [1984] and Gillet and Temple [1986].)

Informal reading inventories traditionally have been used to match children with appropriate level materials. The problems associated with matching children with materials, especially on the basis of one test, have already been discussed in Chapter 3. However, informal reading inventories provide information about comprehension that is not provided by group tests like the standardized reading tests and the basal reader placement tests. Since open-ended comprehension questions are used, students have the opportunity to give more elaborate responses and there is greater latitude in the answers that teachers can accept. Since the test is individually administered, teachers can also probe for answers.

The published informal reading inventories have several forms. Using these different forms allows us to test children's reading under different conditions, e.g., when they read orally or silently, when the text is not available, and when it is available. Thus informal reading inventories can be used diagnostically to help in determining what factors are affecting children's comprehension.

Wixson and Lipson (1984) suggest that the diagnostic value of informal reading inventories can be increased by administering several different inventories that vary other conditions like a child's interest in the text topic. However, such a time-consuming process would probably only be possible in a clinic situation.

Manuals of some commercially published tests (e.g., Woods and Moe 1989) suggest analyzing patterns of responses to the comprehension questions as another way to determine a child's particular area of comprehension difficulty. Questions that assess the comprehension of the graded passages on the commercially available informal reading inventories are labeled in categories such as main idea, vocabulary, fact questions, and inferential questions. The manuals suggest that teachers note the category(ies) with which a child has particular difficulty.

There are several problems with this type of analysis however. The first problem is that students answer so few questions in each category that patterns are hard to determine. If patterns are found, they are unreliable because of the small number of items on which the pattern is based. A second problem has to do with the way the questions are categorized. Test developers use their own judgment in labeling categories and some of these judgments have been criticized. For example, Duffelmeyer and Duffelmeyer (1989) found that 54% of the graded passages on three popular commercially published informal inventories did not have a main idea. Since there was a "main idea" question for each of these passages, 54% of the questions were inappropriately labeled. Another problem with categorization is that the classification system is based on a view of reading as a set of skills rather than a holistic process.

However, the latest editions of some informal reading inventories (e.g., Woods and Moe 1989) use retellings as the measure of comprehension. The questions are used as probes for information not included in the retellings. Questions whose answers have been provided as part of the retelling are omitted. Using retellings as part of an informal reading inventory is a good way for teachers to gain experience with this type of comprehension assessment.

As mentioned previously, informal reading inventories can also be used to determine whether poor memory is a factor affecting a child's comprehension performance. When children cannot answer questions from memory, teachers allow them to look back at the text. The strategies they use in rereading the text can also be observed, e.g., does the child skim for the answer or does he or she read through the entire text?

USING INSTRUCTIONAL TECHNIQUES FOR COMPREHENSION ASSESSMENT

The instructional techniques described in Chapters 5 through 9 provide many opportunities for unintrusive assessment. These techniques can be used for assessing the factors that affect comprehension while also assessing comprehension itself.

In-depth assessment of children who fail to meet expectations in comprehension may require the use of more intrusive measures. While some of these measures may be measures of word recognition, the focus here will be on measures suitable for the in-depth assessment of comprehension.

BACKGROUND KNOWLEDGE

Brainstorming, the first step in PREP, Semantic Mapping, and the K—W—L technique, which asks students to provide their associations with the central concept or concepts of a text about to be read, is an effective way of assessing prior knowledge as well as activating it (Holmes and Roser 1987; Langer 1982). The quality and quantity of students' responses during brainstorming helps teachers determine the level of students' background knowledge about central concepts of the text.

Of course, as was discussed in Chapter 5, in any group of children, there will be a great deal of variation in background knowledge about a particular topic. A pre-reading discussion cannot provide an in-depth probing of the background knowledge of every individual in the group. However, if teachers probe for background knowledge about specific categories of information found in the text and if they try to involve as many students as possible in the discussion, they can get a general idea of the knowledge possessed by the group. Teachers then will need to decide whether the discussion has provided the children with the necessary background knowledge or whether they need to provide the children with additional background knowledge so that they can comprehend the text successfully.

Langer (1982) classifies responses in the PREP technique in three levels. Responses that take the form of superordinate concepts, definitions, analogies, or a linking of the central concept to another concept indicate a high level of integration of ideas and *much* background knowledge about the central concept. For example, in the PREP script found in Chapter 5, with probing from the teacher, Student 4 indicates a higher level of background knowledge about bullfighting than the other students when he describes the bull killing the man with the red cape. Examples, attributes, and defining characteristics indicate *some* background knowledge about the central concept. In the same script Student 3 indicates some knowledge about bullfighting when he provides the response "Sharp horns—he sticks people." Students who have *little* background knowledge about the central concept tend to focus on low level associations trying to figure out the meaning of the concept by using their knowledge of prefixes, suffixes, and other morphemes. Student 1's initial response in the

PREP script, "Bulls have a fight," indicates little background knowledge about bullfighting.

Other responses that indicate little knowledge include making an association based on the sound of the word given by the teacher (the teacher says the word "park," and the child responds "dark") or discussing a first hand experience that does not relate to the central concept. For example, when I demonstrate the PREP technique with my graduate classes, I ask my students for their associations with artificial intelligence because I have found that students tend to have varying levels of knowledge about this concept. In every group that responds to this concept, there is at least one student who analyzes the meaning of the word using a strategy similar to that used by Student 1 with the term *bullfighting*, i.e., he or she gives a response like "fake intelligence." When this response is probed, students talk about people with artificial or fake intelligence, of people they have met, people who pretend to know about something when they really do not. These responses indicate little background knowledge about the artificial intelligence that scientists are attempting to build into computers.

Langer (1982) has provided the checksheet below for teachers to use in rating children's responses when using the PREP technique (see figure 3). Numbers 1 and 3 in this checklist refer to steps 1 and 3 in the technique. Children whose responses indicate little prior knowledge at first may remember more about the concept or even learn more about it during the PREP discussion so that when they discuss their associations or tell what new information they have learned they give a higher level response. In the PREP script in Chapter 5 Student 4's initial response, "kill," was a lower level response than the description of bullfighting which he provided later in the discussion. Comparing students' responses at the beginning and end of the discussion can help teachers assess the effectiveness of the pre-reading instruction.

Although Langer developed the checklist for use with the PREP technique, teachers can use it whenever they ask children to give associations for a concept. Semantic Mapping and Know—Want to Know—Learn do not suggest asking children about the reasons for their responses. However, especially when children give low level responses, teachers can probe the responses briefly during the discussion or in later individual interviews. When using the inferential strategy (Hansen and Hubbard 1984), teachers may also want to question children whose inappropriate responses or lack of response suggest that they do not have experience relevant to the story they are about to read. One or two questions are often enough to determine whether they need more background knowledge about the story.

The semantic maps children construct in groups, pairs, or individually before reading can be analyzed not only for the level of background knowledge but also for the way in which the knowledge is organized. Semantic maps constructed after reading assess children's comprehension of the text. Comparison of semantic maps constructed before reading and revised after reading provides an even better measure of comprehension and learning. Both kinds of semantic

PHASE 1   What comes to mind when . . . ?
PHASE 2   What made you think of . . . ?
PHASE 3   Have you any new ideas about . . . ?

STIMULUS _____ (note word, picture, or phrase)	MUCH superordinate concepts, definitions, analogies, linking		SOME examples, attributes, defining characteristics		LITTLE morphemes, sound alikes, recent experiences	
Student Names	1	3	1	3	1	3
1.						
2.						
3.						
4.						
5.						
6.						
7.						
8.						
9.						
10.						

Figure 3. PREP response checklist. Reprinted, with permission, from J. Langer and the International Reading Association, *Facilitating Text Processing: The Elaboration of Prior Knowledge* (International Reading Association, Newark, DE, 1982).

maps can be placed in the reading portfolio to provide documentation of learning.

Predictions, retellings, summaries, children's questions, and their responses to teachers' questions during reading can also be used to assess how children make use of their background knowledge in comprehending the text. Cloze passages and written retellings, summaries, and answers to questions can be used for the same purpose after reading. Using these measures to compare children's comprehension when pre-reading instruction is provided to their comprehension when it is not helps teachers decide who benefits from this instruction and who no longer needs it. Teachers can also question children to determine whether they activate background knowledge when they read independently.

The Anticipation Reaction Guide is especially suited to assessing children's background knowledge when they may have misconceptions. However, determining the presence of a misconception is often difficult since children may give the correct answer to a question and still hold the misconception (Maria and MacGinitie 1987; McNeil 1987). Research (Alvermann and Hynd 1987, 1988; Maria 1987, 1988) suggests that questions that require adults and children to apply knowledge contradicting the misconception in a problem-solving situation are more effective in determining the presence of a misconception than questions only requiring them to provide the knowledge. Thus, in testing for the presence of a misconception, application questions should be used both before and after reading.

LINGUISTIC KNOWLEDGE: VOCABULARY

The techniques for providing vocabulary instruction before, during, and after reading described in Chapter 6 provide alternatives to the typical multiple choice vocabulary test. Preview in Context, Contextual Redefinition (Readence, Bean, and Baldwin 1985), and Concept of Definition (Schwartz and Raphael 1985) provide teachers with the opportunity to assess not only children's knowledge of word meanings but also their ability to determine word meanings from context; thus these are measures of the process of determining word meaning and word meaning itself.

Teaching children to use partial contexts to determine word meaning is an important part of the Concept of Definition technique. Observing children as they use this technique offers the opportunity to assess how well they use the following three processes which Sternberg (1987) suggests are important for determining word meanings through context:

1. Choosing from context those cues that are useful in learning about a word.
2. Combining the information provided by the relevant cues.
3. Using information one already possesses, including knowledge of word parts.

The word maps used in the Concept of Definition technique provide a durable record of a child's growth in the process of using context and in his or her understanding of what is meant by a definition. Dated maps can be placed in the reading portfolios to provide documentation of this progress. After some experience with the technique, children can write some definitions without the support of the word maps. Children's definitions written with and without the support can be compared in order to determine whether the child still needs the support of a visual organizer.

The Vocabulary Overview Guide (Carr 1985) and the Discriminative Self-Inventory Checklist (Dale and O'Rourke 1971) are examples of the type of collaborative assessment recommended earlier. In using these techniques children collaborate with the teacher in assessing their own knowledge of vocabulary. Use of Reciprocal Teaching during reading provides another example of collaborative assessment of vocabulary knowledge. In using the clarifying strategy as part of this technique, children assess their own understanding of word meanings. Observing children's responses during this step of Reciprocal Teaching allows the teacher to assess their vocabulary knowledge and their ability to monitor their comprehension.

LINGUISTIC KNOWLEDGE:
LANGUAGE WITHIN AND BETWEEN SENTENCES

MacGinitie and MacGinitie (1989) suggest a number of ways to determine whether children have difficulty with particular written language patterns. When children read aloud, teachers should be alert for signs of confusion, e.g., puzzled looks and unsuitable intonation even when there are no problems with word recognition. Teachers should also observe children's writing and comprehension of material read to them for indications of problems.

In previewing text, teachers must be alert for sentence structures and figurative language that may cause problems for the children. They should then ask questions about sentences containing these patterns. For example, in Chapter 7, I stated that many middle grade children had difficulty understanding that the sentence, *As we entered, the curtain rose*, indicated that the two events happened simultaneously (Bormuth et al. 1970). A teacher might ask "Did the curtain rise before they entered, at the same time they entered, or after they entered?"

Teachers can observe children's ability to match cohesive ties with their referents during the activities they use for instruction in this area. Children's responses in cloze passages and the reasons they give for these responses provide information concerning their use of cohesive ties. The clarifying step of the Reciprocal Teaching strategy offers teachers a structure not only for providing instruction in vocabulary and written language but also for continuously assessing these factors and their effect on text comprehension in collaboration with the students.

TEXT STRUCTURE

Retellings are appropriate measures for assessing children's knowledge of text structure. Teachers can use story map forms like the example in Chapter 7 to analyze narrative retellings for the presence of important elements of story grammar. Graphic organizers can serve the same purpose for expository text.

On the other hand, analysis of story maps and graphic organizers completed by children allows teachers to assess their use of text structure when given this kind of supportive context. Samples of these activities, written retellings, and summaries constructed with and without their support should be part of the reading portfolio.

Careful observation of the texts children write and their predictions when using the K—W—L and/or Reciprocal Teaching techniques provide information not only about children's knowledge of text structure but also of how they apply it in understanding texts. For example, the child who predicts that a text which discusses the problem of water pollution will probably then discuss ways of combatting the problem shows a good understanding of the problem/solution text structure.

METACOMPREHENSION: KNOWLEDGE ABOUT
READING, ONESELF AS A READER, AND READING STRATEGIES

Observation of children's oral reading and analysis of their patterns of miscues is an unobtrusive way of gathering information about their perceptions of reading. Consistent patterns of miscues that do not make sense in context suggest that a child perceives reading only as decoding and not as a process of constructing meaning. However, such a pattern might also indicate lack of background knowledge about a topic. It is also important to remember that when children read material that is too difficult, they tend to make errors that fail to take account of context because they cannot recognize enough words to establish a context. Further assessment is necessary before drawing any conclusions about the reasons for a child's failure to use context.

Another way of determining children's perception of reading and themselves as readers is to ask them. The Index of Reading Awareness (Paris, Cross, and Lipson 1984; Paris and Jacobs 1984) is a group test designed to determine children's perceptions of reading goals and tasks by asking questions like "Why do you go back and read things over again?" and "What is the hardest part about reading for you?" Although the test has a multiple choice format, older students who are capable of writing responses can be given the same questions in an open-ended format (Winograd, Wixson, and Lipson 1989).

Interviewing children individually is another way of determining their knowledge about reading, themselves as readers, and the strategies that they use in reading. Kraus (1983 cited in Vacca, Vacca, and Gove [1987]) who interviewed first and second graders, found that even at this age children can verbalize their perceptions about reading and about themselves as readers, and that these perceptions reflect the manner in which they read. The teacher in the Kraus study asked questions like "What would you do to teach someone to read?" and "Who is the best reader you know? What makes him or her the best reader?"

Interviews can be a few questions or an extensive structured interview like the Reading Comprehension Interview (Wixson et al. 1984). The Reading Comprehension Interview, designed for children in grades 3 through 8, asks questions somewhat similar to those asked by Kraus. In this interview, found in figure 4, the teacher probes children's knowledge about different task requirements and the strategies they use in different tasks and settings.

Although this interview is an intrusive measure that requires about half an hour to administer, information gathered about remedial readers can be well worth the time spent. When I used the Reading Comprehension Interview with M, a remedial reader I taught for two years, I discovered that his idea of a good reader was one who "was fast and could sound out hard words." M read very slowly and had problems with decoding, but he did attend to meaning, using background knowledge and linguistic knowledge to such good advantage that his comprehension was often surprising given his low level of word recognition. The interview made clear that while M recognized his weaknesses, he did not recognize the real strength that he had. The interview also indicated that although M felt very uncomfortable with the basal reader, he did not feel threatened by a content area textbook because "That's social studies, not reading." As a result of the interview, M and I began using his social studies textbook for his reading lessons. I pointed out his strength in reading and encouraged him to use context more as an aid to word recognition.

When we interview children, we need to be sure we are not asking leading questions, prompting students to answer in a particular way. Using an interview protocol with questions decided on before the interview is one way of lessening the problem. When interviewing children, we also need to remember that children often tell adults what they think the adults want to hear. Children need to develop trust in us before they are ready to reveal their true beliefs and attitudes.

Helping children recognize that they should read for meaning is an important goal of reading instruction. Teachers might want to administer the Index of Reading Awareness or to interview selected children at the end of the year to determine how well their instruction meets this goal. Place copies of the index and interview protocols in the reading portfolio to provide evidence about children's progress and the value of the instructional program. Another way of making the interview process a more durable record is to ask older children to write answers to questions from the Reading Comprehension Interview in their reading journals (Vacca and Vacca 1986). The children answer only one or two questions a day. Although this format is less time consuming for the teacher and gathers information from a larger number of children, it assumes that students have an adequate level of writing ability.

Using think alouds, i.e., asking children to stop at certain points in their reading and talk about *how* they are reading rather than what they are reading, is another way of gathering information about children's knowledge and use of reading strategies. Wixson and Lipson (1984) and Lipson et al. (1988) report considerable success in using the think aloud procedure to assess how children are making use of various factors in reading.

Name: Date:
Classroom teacher: Reading level:
                                                Grade:

Directions: Introduce the procedure by explaining that you are interested in finding out what children think about various reading activities. Tell the student that he or she will be asked questions about his/her reading, that there are no right or wrong answers, and that you are only interested in knowing what s/he thinks. Tell the student that if s/he does not know how to answer a question s/he should say so and you will go on to the next one.

General probes such as "Can you tell me more about that?" or "Anything else?" may be used. Keep in mind that the interview is an informal diagnostic measure and you should feel free to probe to elicit useful information.

1. What hobbies or interests do you have that you like to read about?
2. a. How often do you read in school?
   b. How often do you read at home?
3. What school subjects do you like to read about?

Introduce reading and social studies books.

Directions: For this section use the child's classroom basal reader and a content area textbook (social studies, science, etc.). Place these texts in front of the student. Ask each question twice, once with reference to the basal reader and once with reference to the content area textbook. Randomly vary the order of presentation (basal, content). As each question is asked, open the appropriate text in front of the student to help provide a point of reference for the question.

4. What is the most important reason for reading this kind of material? Why does your teacher want you to read this book?
5. a. Who's the best reader you know in _____?
   b. What does he/she do that makes him/her such a good reader?
6. a. How good are *you* at reading this kind of material?
   b. How do you know?
7. What do you have to do to get a good grade in _____ in your class?
8. a. If the teacher told you to remember the information in this story/chapter, what would be the best way to do this?
   b. Have you ever tried _____?
9. a. If your teacher told you to find the answers to the questions in this book what would be the best way to do this? Why?
   b. Have you ever tried _____?
10. a. What is the hardest part about answering questions like the ones in this book?
    b. Does that make you do anything differently?

Introduce at least two comprehension worksheets.

Directions: Present the worksheets to the child and ask questions 11 and 12. Ask the child to complete portions of each worksheet. Then ask questions 13 and 14. Next, show the child a worksheet designed to simulate the work of another child. Then ask question 15.

11. Why would your teacher want you to do worksheets like these (for what purpose)?
12. What would your teacher say you must do to get a good mark on worksheets like these? (What does your teacher look for?)

Ask the child to complete portions of at least two worksheets.

13. Did you do this one differently from the way you did that one? How or in what way?
14. Did you have to work harder on one of these worksheets than the other? (Does one make you think more?)

Present the simulated worksheet.

15. a. *Look over this worksheet. If you were the teacher, what kind of mark would you* give the worksheet? Why?
    b. If you were the teacher, what would you ask this person to do differently next time?

Figure 4. Reading comprehension interview. Reprinted, with permission, from K. Wixson et al. and the International Reading Association, *An Interview for Assessing Students: Perceptions of Classroom Reading Tasks,* The Reading Teacher (1984).

Lytle (1982) cited in Bean (1988) has developed a method for analyzing think aloud protocols in which readers' statements are categorized into six kinds of "moves" (verbal responses of the reader to a sentence in the text):

1. Monitoring—statements that indicate the reader does not understand.
2. Signaling—statements that indicate the reader does understand and what he or she understands.
3. Analyzing—the reader comments on features of the text, e.g., text structure. The reader also may paraphrase the text.
4. Elaborating—the reader responds to the text by connecting prior knowledge or indicates that he or she likes or dislikes the text. Wixson and Lipson (1984) provide an example of a child reading the title "When Dinosaurs Lived on Earth" and then talking about the paleontologists who dig up bones, indicating that this topic had been previously discussed in social studies.
5. Judging—statements that indicate the reader evaluates the text.
6. Reasoning—the reader does something to try to comprehend. For example, the child that Wixson and Lipson (1984) describe indicates that he is trying "to figure out what the story is about" after reading the title.

Lytle (1982) defines strategies as patterns of moves. She found that secondary school students tend to use their own preferred patterns of moves, demonstrating a particular reading style, i.e., an overall pattern of moves and strategies used within and across texts (Brown and Lytle 1989). Teachers may wish to consider readers' think aloud responses from this point of view to determine whether they have developed a reading style that interferes with their comprehension. However, detailed analysis of the type conducted by Lytle would probably be too time consuming for teacher use.

Even when detailed analysis is not used, think alouds are intrusive assessments that take a considerable amount of teacher time. Moreover, children with language difficulties should not be assessed with think alouds or with interviews because they do not have sufficient verbal ability to put their thinking into words. However, even children with no language problems will find interviews and think alouds disconcerting at first. Providing practice with the think aloud procedure before using it for assessment purposes is essential.

Despite their drawbacks, interviews and think alouds can often provide insights about children's reading comprehension not available through any other method. For example, in a research study (Maria 1987) I interviewed students regarding the reasons for their answers to questions about a text designed to correct misconceptions in physics. The interviews made it clear that while the children had corrected some of their misconceptions they had also developed new ones as a result of reading the text. I would never have known about these new misconceptions if I had not interviewed the children.

Intrusive methods are not always necessary, however. Careful observation of children's use of strategies is not intrusive and is an important component of effective comprehension instruction. For example, Reciprocal Teaching is an

247

instructional technique, but it is also a means of assessment. Children's questions and answers, their summaries, predictions, requests for clarifications, and replies to others' requests for clarifications in the Reciprocal Teaching dialogue provide a wealth of information about their text comprehension and the strategies they use. This dual focus on children's comprehension and their strategies is important; strategies should be assessed in relation to how effective they are for the child.

Using a form like the Reciprocal Teaching checklist below enables teachers to document this information. They can focus on one or two children in each session and compare checklists gathered at various stages to evaluate children's progress and their own instruction.

Reciprocal Teaching Checklist

Name _____ Date _____

Participation

    Volunteers to be teacher   _____

    Volunteers responses in the discussion   _____

    Elaborates on others' responses   _____

Asking Questions

    Asks important questions   _____

    Questions are worded clearly   _____

    Teacher prompting is not needed   _____

    Giving a summary first helps him or her to ask questions   _____

Summarizing

    Uses his or her own words in summaries   _____

    Summaries are neither too long nor too short   _____

    Does not need to reread text before summarizing   _____

    Teacher prompting is not needed   _____

Predicting

    Uses background information together with text information in making predictions   _____

    Uses text structure in making predictions   _____

    Evaluates predictions   _____

Clarifying

    Asks for clarification when he or she doesn't
understand something   _____

    Is alert to words or sentences that may cause
comprehension problems for others   _____

Summaries, questions, responses, and predictions
indicate good comprehension   _____

Particular Problems Noted (e.g., sentence structures, words, etc.) that required clarification

_____

_____

_____

When using other techniques like Active Comprehension or DRTA, which focus on asking questions and making predictions, the sections of the checklist appropriate for these strategies may be used. Domato (1989) has developed another checklist (see figure 5) that may be used for the qualitative assessment of children's questions.

    A more detailed checklist (see figure 6) has also been developed for assessing children's use of predictions in the DRTA technique (Gillet and Temple 1982).

INTEREST AND MOTIVATION

A number of reading textbooks (e.g., Estes and Vaughan 1985; Vacca and Vacca 1986) recommend the use of published or teacher constructed questionnaires to determine children's reading interests and attitudes toward reading. However, teachers can collect this information in less intrusive ways. When children record the books they have read in their reading logs, the number and types of books read provide information about their reading interests and attitudes. Interests expressed by children in informal conversations with one another and with the teacher are another source of information for the teacher who is a careful listener. During sustained silent reading periods, teachers should be alert for the following behaviors: (1) increased concentration, (2) a reluctance to stop reading, (3) greater spontaneous reactions (laughs, frowns, etc.), (4) selection of reading material of increasing difficulty, and (5) greater impatience with disturbances. These behaviors may indicate a greater interest in reading in general or special interest in a particular text (Hunt 1970 cited in Rhodes and Dudley-Marling 1988).

    When assessing children's comprehension, teachers should make every effort to ensure that texts that are of interest to the child are part of that assessment. Comparing a child's comprehension of texts of interest to him or her to comprehension of texts of less interest allows us to determine whether interest has a strong effect on his or her comprehension.

    Motivation can be assessed by careful observation. Using any excuse not

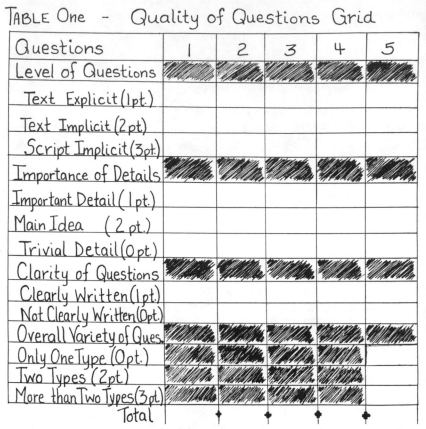

Questions	1	2	3	4	5
Level of Questions	▨	▨	▨	▨	▨
Text Explicit (1pt.)					
Text Implicit (2pt)					
Script Implicit (3pt.)					
Importance of Details	▨	▨	▨	▨	▨
Important Detail (1pt.)					
Main Idea (2pt.)					
Trivial Detail (0pt.)					
Clarity of Questions	▨	▨	▨	▨	▨
Clearly Written (1pt.)					
Not Clearly Written (0pt.)					
Overall Variety of Ques.	▨	▨	▨	▨	▨
Only One Type (0pt.)	▨	▨	▨	▨	▨
Two Types (2pt.)	▨	▨	▨	▨	▨
More than Two Types (3pt)	▨	▨	▨	▨	▨
Total					

TABLE One - Quality of Questions Grid

Figure 5. Checklist for assessing the quality of children's questions. Reprinted, with permission, from C. Domato, Direct Training of Generating Questions with Reciprocal Teaching, unpublished manuscript (1989).

to read, demanding constant guidance or engaging in behaviors that disrupt the reading lesson all indicate a motivation *not* to read. The Stress Reaction Scale (Gentile and Macmillan 1988) is a checklist of behaviors of this kind which can guide teachers' observations.

This section presents many different types of comprehension assessment to provide you with a repertoire of measures from which to choose. As with instructional techniques, you should not expect to try everything at once. Try one type of assessment until you feel comfortable with it. A good idea would be to pick an assessment technique that complements the instructional technique that you have decided to try. For example, after using Reciprocal Teaching for a few weeks, use the checklist as a means of assessing children's use of the strategies. Remember, however, that your ultimate goal is use of a variety of measures so that your assessment and your instruction reflect the interactive nature of the reading process.

DRTA Inventory

Student _____

	USUALLY	OCCASIONALLY	RARELY
Offers spontaneous predictions			
Predicts without coaxing			
Participates from the start			
Makes logical predictions			
Predictions show awareness of story structures			
Changes predictions when necessary			
Refines predictions as DRTA proceeds			
Can explain predictions clearly			
Can justify predictions from text			
Can relocate specific information			
Uses both explicit and implied information			
Shows awareness and tolerance of others' positions			
Uses others' predictions to extend or modify own ideas			
Shows original thinking			
Seeks confirmation of unconfirmed ideas from other sources			
Uses illustrations to get information			
Can effectively scan material before DRTA			
Uses context to analyze new words			

Figure 6. Sample checklist for the Directed Reading Thinking Activity (DRTA). Reprinted, with permission, from J. Gillet and C. Temple, *Understanding Reading Problems: Assessment and Instruction* (Scott, Foresman and Company, Boston, 1982).

EXTERNALLY DEVELOPED TESTS

This section will discuss basal reader tests and standardized reading tests. As part of the description of both types of tests, several types of test validity will be considered: (1) content and construct validity—How well do these tests measure reading comprehension as the process is currently understood? (2) ecological validity—How well does the reading measured by these tests represent the reading that children do in school? (3) instructional validity—How well do these tests measure the comprehension instruction provided to children in school?

BASAL READER TESTS

Two types of group administered silent reading tests are provided as part of basal reader programs. The first type is placement tests, which are designed to match children with the appropriate level basal reader. These placement tests usually use test passages followed by multiple choice questions. The test passages are taken from the basal readers and graded according to readability. Chapter 3 discusses the difficulty in determining the readability of texts. Another difficulty in matching children with appropriate level materials is that children's reading performance varies with different texts and situations. Thus their performance on one basal reader placement test cannot totally represent how they will be able to read other texts. If basal readers are used for reading instruction, then a basal reader placement test can be used to provide a first guess about the appropriate level to use for instruction. However, this decision should be viewed as tentative and should be subject to change if teacher observation suggests that the placement is inappropriate. Moreover, as Chapter 3 suggests, children should be allowed to read a variety of texts and not be limited to reading those at a particular level.

The second type of basal reader tests are "mastery" tests designed to determine whether the children have mastered the skills taught as part of the program. The Harcourt Brace Jovanovich basal reading program (Farr 1989), for example, provides mid-unit tests, unit tests, and end-of-book tests.

Basal reader tests are criterion-referenced tests like the informal reading inventories. The criterion for acceptable performance on these tests is set arbitrarily. For example, test developers may decide that a child demonstrates satisfactory performance in reading comprehension ("mastery") if he or she answers 80% of the questions correctly on the test of reading comprehension. As Farr and Carey (1986, p. 142) point out, a criterion set arbitrarily is as "meaningful as the judgment used to arrive at it is fallible."

Although the basal reader mastery tests use a format similar to that used by standardized reading tests, i.e., multiple choice questions with one right answer, they are not as broadly based as standardized tests. Since they are not usually as long as standardized tests, they may not be as reliable.

Another problem with these tests has to do with calling them "mastery" tests. In Chapter 1 the point was made that comprehension "skills" are not mastered as are word recognition skills. As we grow older, we use these "skills" in understanding more difficult texts under different conditions and for different purposes. Thus a "mastery" test of comprehension "skills" is a contradiction in terms.

Despite their drawbacks the basal reader tests are a pervading influence in comprehension assessment. When teachers are asked how they assess reading comprehension in their classes, they usually reply that they use these tests (Fraatz 1987 cited in Calfee and Hiebert 1987).

There are several reasons teachers rely on basal reader tests (Dorr-Bremme 1983). First, they are immediately accessible. Teachers can give them whenever they choose and can obtain the results immediately. This is an important consideration, for the demands on teacher time can be overwhelming. Second, the texts on the placement tests are taken directly from the basal readers and the skills tested on the "mastery" tests are those recommended for instruction in the basal reader manuals. If the teacher follows the basal reader program in comprehension instruction then these tests appear to have good ecological and instructional validity, i.e., they test what was taught using texts like those used in instruction. This is important to teachers. They want tests that match their instruction and that will help them make practical decisions such as what materials to use with a child and which reading group to place him or her in. Unfortunately, since tests determine to a great extent what and how teachers teach (Farr and Beck in press), the fact that the basal reader tests are based on a view of reading as a set of discrete skills discourages teachers from using comprehension instruction that focuses on teaching strategies. Every time I give a workshop for teachers I hear the comment, "I like the kind of instruction you are suggesting, and I think it would be very valuable for my children. However, I have to teach specific skills because this is what is tested."

The content and construct validity of a test are even more important than instructional and ecological validity. It has been suggested (Anderson et al. 1985; Valencia and Pearson 1988) that basal reader tests do not have good construct validity because they are based on a view of reading as a set of discrete skills. They have instructional validity only because they match a curriculum that also represents an inadequate understanding of the reading process. If the basal readers change their instruction to fit the new understanding of the reading process, then they should also change the way they assess comprehension. While the new concepts of the reading process have begun to affect basal reader instructional suggestions (Pearson 1986), they have not yet had an effect on the way they assess comprehension (Valencia and Pearson 1987, 1988). Although recent editions of basal reader "mastery" tests attempt to assess skills in the context of comprehension rather than in isolation (e.g., Farr 1989), they still claim to assess skills rather than assessing comprehension as a holistic process.

Quite a few years ago a number of researchers (e.g., Davis 1968) found that scores of subtests that claimed to measure separate aspects of comprehension were so closely correlated that it was not justifiable to say that they were measuring different aspects of comprehension (Drahozal and Hanna 1978). Although basal reader tests claim to assess specific skills, they may in fact just be measuring comprehension. Teachers may want to use basal reader tests as tests of comprehension performance because they provide an outside check on their own observations. However, they need to recognize that the tests are subject to error just as are their own observations.

STANDARDIZED TESTS

Standardized reading tests are used more now than ever before (Madaus 1985; Pipho 1985; Salganick 1985; Valencia and Pearson 1987 cited in Valencia and Pearson 1988). The federal government requires standardized testing of children enrolled in Federal programs such as Chapter I. Statewide standardized testing of reading increased tremendously in the 1970s, and the school reform movement of the 1980s accelerated the emphasis on testing. Forty-six states currently mandate testing in reading (Valencia et al. 1989). Half of these states use tests or test items purchased from standardized test publishers (Afflerbach 1987; Selden 1988), and most of the other states that develop their own reading tests model them after existing standardized tests (Valencia et al 1989). However, two states (Michigan and Illinois) have recently developed standardized tests of reading that differ from the traditional tests in a number of ways. Several other states are in the process of developing tests similar to those of Michigan and Illinois (Farr and Beck in press).

Teachers usually administer standardized reading tests as part of a large scale assessment program mandated by the district or state and thus they may not control which tests are given or even how the test results are used. However, it is becoming common for districts to seek teachers' input in text selection by asking them to serve on test selection committees along with administrators (Farr and Carey 1986). Teachers should know more about the nature of standardized tests, the way they relate to the new understanding of the reading process and the way their results should be interpreted. Then teachers can be more helpful in standardized test selection, use their results appropriately as a guide to further assessment and instructional decisions, and be alert to the misuse of their results.

TEST FORMATS

Traditional standardized reading tests use two formats: multiple choice questions placed after the passage or a modified cloze procedure in which choices are given for deletions in a cloze passage. Proponents of multiple choice questions (e.g., MacGinitie 1989) suggest that this format is better because it permits testing certain aspects of comprehension (e.g., determining the main idea), which cannot be tested with the cloze procedure. Proponents of cloze suggest that it is more like story or trade book reading than the multiple choice format. They also point out that cloze passages are easier to construct than multiple choice questions and that scores on the two types of tests are highly correlated (Farr and Carey 1986).

Opponents of cloze criticize it for measuring aspects of comprehension, such as syntactic competency (Farr and Carey 1986) or "special ability for utilizing redundancy in a passage" (Weaver and Kingston 1963; Coleman and Miller 1968 cited in Farr and Carey 1986, p. 37), rather than comprehension itself.

Whether a standardized test uses multiple choice questions or a modified cloze format, there is only one correct answer. This format makes the tests more reliable but eliminates the use of questions that allow for divergent answers. Critics (e.g., Farr and Carey 1986) question the construct validity of tests that require one correct answer, suggesting that they are incompatible with a view of comprehension as a constructive process that may result in different interpretations of a text by different readers. Teachers often have problems with this aspect of the multiple choice format. Every teacher has stories of children who came up with alternate answers to a multiple choice test that made sense based on an alternate understanding of the text or a misunderstanding of the question.

Another problem with a multiple choice format with one correct answer is that reading to answer multiple choice questions about short passages is often a matching exercise rather than a reading process that involves reasoning. However, it has been suggested (Johnston 1983; Wixson and Peters 1987) that this format can be a more valid measure of reading if the distractors (incorrect answers provided as choices) are chosen carefully so that reasoning is necessary to answer the questions correctly.

The new Illinois reading test contains multiple choice questions with 1, 2, or 3 correct answers (Valencia et al. 1989). While this format seems more compatible with the view of reading as a constructive process, it may make deciding on an acceptable answer more difficult. For example, in the first multiple choice question accompanying the practice passage below, I can see four possibly acceptable answers.

> Jane likes cats better than she likes dogs. She has two cats. Her grandmother gave her one of the cats for her birthday. Jane thinks cats seem so much smarter than dogs. They always watch very carefully and seem to know when she wants to pet them or give them some attention. She likes their soft fur. She likes it when they curl up in her lap. And her cats don't run around with their tongues hanging out like her neighbor's dogs. But what Jane likes most about cats is the way they take care of themselves. They don't seem to depend upon people the way dogs do.

Why does Jane like cats much better than dogs?
A. Her grandmother gave her one.
B. Cats seem much smarter to her.
C. Cats don't seem to need people as much as dogs do.
D. Cats watch everything around them.
E. She likes the way their tongues hang out (Illinois State Board of Education 1984, p. 7).

However, the third and sixth graders Valencia and Pearson (1988) interviewed indicated that they preferred a format that permitted several answers to one that had only one correct answer.

TEST PASSAGES

Traditional standardized tests use a number of short passages. Most tests include both narrative and expository passages, different genres, and different content domains appropriate for the age level of the children for whom the test is intended. To provide a variety of passages and keep the test within a reasonable time limit, short passages must be used. A variety of passages is provided as a way of ensuring ecological validity, i.e., providing a representative sample of the kinds of texts children read in school.

However, during instruction children usually are expected to read texts that are longer than the test passages (Valencia and Pearson 1986; Flood and Lapp 1986). Developers of new state reading tests in Michigan and Illinois opted for the use of longer passages (500-2,000 words) that they believe are more representative of the types of texts children read in school (Valencia et al. 1989). Wixson and Peters (1987) suggest that long passages should be used on tests because short passages "do not allow for the complex reasoning that is the essence of comprehension" (p. 1). They also cite Langer's (1987) finding that short test passages are often inconsiderate texts since they do not elaborate on ideas.

While the ideal would be to use a variety of longer passages (Farr and Beck in press), practical considerations of time make this impossible. In using longer test passages the developers of these new tests sacrifice variety. The Michigan test contains only two test passages: a narrative text and an expository text. The Illinois test contains only one test passage, but there are several versions of the test, each using a different test passage.

More questions are asked about the longer passages on the new Illinois and Michigan reading tests than are asked about each of the shorter passages on traditional tests. The purpose of these questions "is to ensure that students are able to construct a holistic representation of the text, rather than to ensure that some predetermined set of skills is represented" (Valencia et al. 1989, p. 60). Explicit and inferential questions used on the Michigan and Illinois tests were developed from text maps, graphic organizers that identify the central concepts, and the important relationships in the texts. For narrative texts, the text maps were story maps similar to those described in Chapter 7. Maps for expository texts were similar to the one presented in figure 7.

The test developers claim that using these text maps as a basis for question development ensures that questions are important for understanding the text as a whole.

However, the use of longer passages also means that the types of questions asked can only be those appropriate to understanding one or two passages. Traditional standardized tests ask a few questions that are appropriate for each short test passage so that the test contains a variety of questions and passages.

Another way the Michigan and Illinois tests attempt to achieve ecological validity is by using texts drawn from children's magazines, trade books, reference books, and textbooks (Valencia et al 1989). It should be noted, however, that these types of texts are also used in some traditional standardized reading comprehension tests such as the Gates-MacGinitie Reading Tests (MacGinitie and MacGinitie 1989).

Developers of the Michigan and Illinois tests chose test passages that were structurally sound and considerate in response to Langer's (1987) finding that a

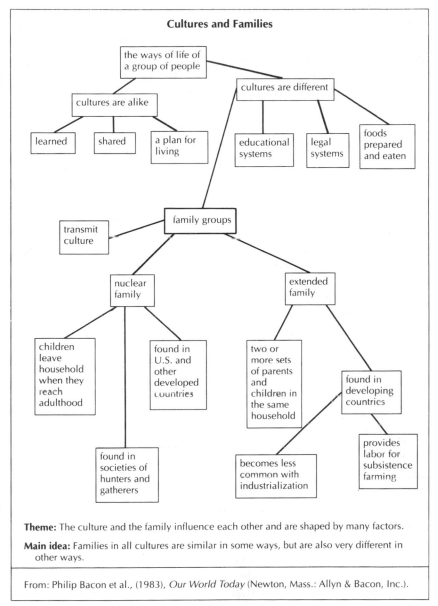

Cultures and Families

Theme: The culture and the family influence each other and are shaped by many factors.

Main idea: Families in all cultures are similar in some ways, but are also very different in other ways.

From: Philip Bacon et al., (1983), *Our World Today* (Newton, Mass.: Allyn & Bacon, Inc.).

Figure 7. Map for expository texts. Reprinted, with permission, from S. Valencia et al., the Michigan State Education Dept. and the Association for Supervision and Curriculum Development. *Theory and Practice in Statewide Reading Assessment: Closing the Gap*, Educational Leadership (1989).

number of passages used in standardized reading comprehension tests did not have ecological validity because they "violated the conceptual and structural patterns typically associated with the genre they were meant to reflect" (Wixson and Peters 1987, p. 2). Langer concludes that children often make incorrect responses to test questions because of the way test passages are composed. It seems that passages used in tests should be structurally sound and reasonably considerate; however, we know that all the texts children read in school are not considerate. MacGinitie (1989) suggests that if the passages on tests are to be representative of the kind of texts children read in school, a few need to be somewhat inconsiderate. Another problem in choosing considerate test passages is that since text "considerateness" is partly determined by factors in the reader—world knowledge and knowledge of structure—a text that is considerate for one child may be inconsiderate for another.

It is clear that the problem of ecological validity is not easily solved. Salinger (1988) points out that in attempting to solve some problems, new tests with different formats may create other problems. Test developers sacrifice one kind of ecological validity and achieve another when they decide whether to use a variety of short passages or one or two long passages. The fact that whether one chooses short or long texts, one cannot completely represent the types of texts children read in school supports the necessity for using a number of different measures of reading comprehension rather than a single standardized test.

It is too early to tell whether these new state tests will be an improvement over the more traditional tests. However, as Farr and Beck (in press) point out, they have alerted test developers and test users to a number of issues in reading assessment that needed to be addressed. Salinger (1988) suggests that children who are instructed in ways consistent with research findings will score well on the new tests—just as they probably would score well on traditional tests. This is an hypothesis that needs to be tested by further research.

THE TESTING SITUATION

Because of their convenience, standardized tests have assumed a disproportionate role in reading assessment. Their results are being used to make some administrative and instructional decisions for which they are totally inappropriate. The books children are allowed to read, the reading group they are placed in, whether or not they are assigned for special instruction in a Chapter I program or a learning disability resource room, and whether or not they are promoted to the next grade may depend on the scores they receive on a single standardized reading test. Administrators and parents may evaluate teachers as well as students in terms of these scores so that a teacher's job may depend upon how well his or her children perform on these tests. In some sections of the country results of standardized reading tests are published in the newspaper with schools and districts ranked according to how well their students perform.

The pressures that this misuse of standardized test results creates for teachers and students are enormous. Teachers "teach to the test," i.e., make decisions about what to teach in reading based on what they believe is tested on standardized tests. For example, many teachers I know hesitate to spend instructional time using children's literature because the Degrees of Reading Power (DRP) test used for state testing of reading in New York State includes only informational passages. Using informational texts on reading tests can have a positive side if it encourages teachers to use more of them in reading instruction, as children have more difficulty with them than with narrative text. However, when teachers feel that they can only provide instruction that is directly related to one test, they are abrogating their role as professionals. As Berlak (1985) points out, when standardized test scores are used as the only valid and reliable measure of achievement "professional testmakers and publishers in effect are making curriculum and pedagogical decisions that properly belong to teachers, principals and others" (p. 17).

In some regions of the country a tremendous amount of instructional time is devoted to "teaching children how to take the test." While this may help children to deal with the test format, it also creates anxiety. The reading done by children in a testing situation that is full of pressure and anxiety is not like most reading done in school. The frustration and real pain that standardized testing causes for many remedial readers is described vividly in Jervis (1989). Although many schools, like the school described by Jervis, try to make the situation less overwhelming by testing remedial readers in small groups with much teacher encouragement, many children refuse to complete the tests rather than continue to struggle with items that are too difficult. The use of longer texts may make standardized testing an even more difficult and discouraging experience for remedial readers. For many of them, the sight of long texts may be overwhelming. If standardized test scores were not given such undue importance by teachers, administrators, and parents, the testing situation would not be quite so anxiety-provoking.

Computerized testing offers a way of making the testing situation more comfortable for both remedial readers and good readers (Johnston 1983; Haney 1985). Many bright students waste time answering questions that are much too easy rather than answering more challenging questions. The computer can provide a child with items at the appropriate difficulty level so that children spend less time on items that are either too hard or too easy (Johnston 1984).

NORM-REFERENCED AND CRITERION-REFERENCED TESTS

Most tests used in large scale assessment are norm-referenced tests. However, many tests like the Degrees of Reading Power (DRP) test, which are currently used for large scale assessment, characterize themselves as both norm-referenced and criterion-referenced. The DRP test, for example, provides DRP scores that are used to determine independent, instructional, and frustration levels. However, it also provides the types of norm-referenced scores that will be discussed in the next section, i.e., grade equivalents, percentile ranks, normal curve equivalents (NCEs), and stanines.

Criterion-referenced tests are supposed to be different from norm-referenced tests because they score children on the basis of an arbitrary criterion rather than comparing their performance to that of other children, as do norm-referenced tests. Criterion-referenced tests used for large scale assessment, however, are really de facto norm-referenced tests. The criterion is based on pilot testing or estimating how average children perform (Farr and Carey 1986).

Interpreting norm-referenced test scores

When we administer a norm-referenced test to a child, the number of items correct, i.e., the raw score he or she receives, has no meaning. These raw scores are converted into other scores that describe the child's performance in relation to that of other children. The norming group comprises the other children that a child's score is compared with: the group given the test during its development. The norming group typically consists of children randomly selected to be representative of all ethnic backgrounds and socioeconomic levels throughout the country.

The most common type of scores used in interpreting the results of standardized tests are grade equivalents (GEs), percentile ranks (PRs), normal curve equivalents (NCEs), and stanines. Grade equivalents compare the child's raw score to the raw scores of children in the norming group from all the grades by identifying the grade group whose median raw score is the same as the student's score. Grade equivalents are expressed in terms of grade and month in decimals, e.g., from 3.0 to 3.9. Since the norming group was not given the test at every month in the school year, test developers interpolate grade equivalent scores from those times they took the test.

In Chapter 3, I referred to the fact that there is so much misinterpretation of grade equivalent scores that the International Reading Association urged test developers to abandon their use (Reading Research Quarterly 1981). If a second grade child tested in May receives a grade equivalent of 4.5, it means that the child scored above average in this kind of testing situation with this kind of reading material. If a second grade child tested at the same time receives a grade equivalent of 1.9 it means that he or she scored below average in this kind of testing situation with this kind of material. It does not mean that the first child is capable of reading fourth grade instructional material or that the second child should only be given first grade reading material. Grade equivalents tell us how children are reading in relation to the norming group. They are not standards of performance; they do not tell us if this is how well this particular child should be reading. It is important to remember that grade equivalents are not equal units of reading achievement when using them as indicators of children's gains in reading achievement. Gains at the beginning grade levels represent greater gains in achievement than those at later grade levels. Average students may be expected to gain a grade level in a year, but students who are above average grow in reading at a greater rate and below average students grow at a slower rate (MacGinitie and MacGinitie 1989).

If a child receives a percentile rank of 60, it means that 60% of the norming group at the child's grade level got raw scores lower than he or she got. Like grade equivalents, percentile ranks do not represent equal units of reading achievement. However, since they are less likely to be misinterpreted than grade equivalent scores, they are becoming the most popular way of reporting test scores.

Like percentile ranks, normal curve equivalent scores (NCEs) and stanines measure achievement by comparing a child's raw score to the raw scores of children from the norming group at the same grade level. Unlike percentile ranks, NCEs and stanines are standard scores with equal units of achievement. Standard scores assume that what is being measured is normally distributed; i.e., most scores are close to the average while only a few are high or low. Like percentile ranks, NCEs have 99 units while stanines have only 9 units. Estes and Vaughan (1985) suggest that teachers should use stanines in interpreting tests because they are the easiest to understand and the safest to use. A stanine of 1 indicates a poor score, stanines of 2 and 3 are below average; stanines of 4, 5, and 6 are average, stanines of 7 and 8 are above average, and a stanine of 9 is superior. (Again these terms should be understood comparatively, not as standards.) Stanines are the safest to use because they are broad categories. They take the error of measurement (the range of scores a student might achieve with repeated testings) into account better than scores with smaller units like PRs and NCEs. Any scores, however, are usually not as reliable at either end of the distribution. A child who scores very high or very low might achieve a different stanine on a different testing.

Estes and Vaughan (1985) suggest that teachers and other test users do not like to use stanines because they do not seem precise enough. However, they caution that "the manner in which results are expressed by stanines is about as precise as most standardized tests can measure" (p. 60).

One of the biggest problems with the way in which standardized test scores are currently interpreted is the same as the problem with readability discussed in Chapter 3. Because grade levels and test scores are expressed in numbers, we view them as precise. Many test users do not read the manuals that explain factors like error of measurement that demonstrate that the scores are not precise. Even those of us who do have some knowledge of terms like *reliability* and *error of measurement* still put more faith in the preciseness of test scores than is justified.

WHAT STANDARDIZED READING COMPREHENSION TESTS MEASURE

Many teachers believe that standardized reading comprehension tests measure separate comprehension skills. A number of reading experts (e.g., Farr and Carey 1986; Valencia et al. 1989) seem to support this position; they criticize standardized reading comprehension tests indicating that most of them are based on outmoded theories of the reading process in which reading is considered a set of discrete skills. Some test publishers highlight the relationship between their tests and the specific skills approach by providing information relating specific items to specific skills. Research cited in the section on basal reader tests has shown, however, that publishers are not justified in providing this type of information. The reading comprehension subtests of standardized reading tests do not test specific skills. They have been characterized as "the most broad-gauged measures of reading proficiency now in general use" (Anderson et al. 1985, p. 100).

Improvement in reading achievement resulting from comprehension instruction that emphasizes instruction in comprehension strategies is evident on standardized tests (Haller, Child, and Walberg 1988). While this is good news for teachers who are held accountable for children's performance on standardized reading tests, it is not justification for using standardized tests as the only measure of reading comprehension. Unlike the informal measures discussed earlier, standardized reading comprehension tests are not designed to provide teachers with information about how to teach reading to a particular child.

However, information provided by these carefully constructed tests is an important component of a complete program of comprehension assessment. They help us answer our first question in comprehension assessment, "Is this child meeting our expectations in reading comprehension?" by comparing the child's performance to that of other children.

USES OF STANDARDIZED TEST SCORES

Because of the comparative nature of the scores that they yield and the relative ease of their administration, standardized tests can be particularly useful to administrators at the district, state, and federal levels, and can help determine how well large groups of children are learning how to read and how successful the schools are in teaching reading. Administrators can make informed decisions about the allocation of funds using standardized test scores together with information from other types of assessment.

Administrators are also responsible for accountability, i.e., they need to let the public, particularly parents, know the performance level of students in the school. Standardized test scores provide a convenient and objective means that can help administrators fulfill this responsibility. However, they should not be the only measures used in making administrative decisions or in describing children's performance. Teacher judgment about the child's level of comprehension based on the informal measures described earlier should also be considered.

Standardized test scores can also be helpful to teachers. Like the basal reader placement tests, they can be used as a first guess in providing children with materials of appropriate difficulty. For example, if a majority of children in a class receive high standardized test scores, a teacher will know that he or she needs some advanced materials. If most students receive low scores, easier materials should be tried (MacGinitie and MacGinitie 1989).

Standardized test scores can also help teachers decide how successfully individual children understand what they read. They should be considered when decisions are being made about grouping or about providing special reading instruction, but they should not be the only criterion used.

Since standardized tests are not dependent on teacher judgment, it can be useful to compare them with teacher assessment of children's progress. In most cases test scores confirm teacher evaluations (Anderson et al. 1985). However, research has shown (Kellaghan, Madaus, and Airasian 1981; Rudman et al. 1980; Salmon-Cox 1981; Stetz and Beck 1981 cited in Farr and Beck in press) that when students do not do as well as expected, teachers discount test scores. When they do better than expected, teachers reconsider their own evaluations to determine whether they have underestimated a child's performance. Although Anderson et al. (1985) endorse this practice, I believe that teachers should reconsider the evidence on which they have based their assessment of children's reading comprehension ability whenever standardized test results are very different from their own judgment. Comparison of standardized test results and our own judgment can remind us of the necessity for objectivity in our assessment of children's reading comprehension.

On the other hand, test scores can also be in error. Differences between teacher assessment and standardized test results do not necessarily mean that the teacher is in error. Teachers assess comprehension with different texts and tasks than those used on standardized tests of reading comprehension. In evaluating children's progress, teachers and administrators must use careful professional judgment, carefully weighing the results from standardized tests and teacher assessment.

Using standardized tests as process measures

Standardized reading comprehension tests usually are considered product measures. Their scores can help us in deciding how well a student understands what he or she reads. But since they do not assess the factors affecting the reading process, they do not help us determine why he or she does not understand.

One of the most important factors affecting reading comprehension performance is the background knowledge of the reader. Developers of traditional standardized reading tests recognize that background knowledge has an effect on comprehension. However, instead of trying to measure its effects, they try to neutralize them. One problem they encounter in this effort is the cultural bias of many passages. A text about going to a restaurant is culturally biased because some children have experience with restaurants while others have not. Children who do not have experience with restaurants are at a disadvantage in reading this passage. Efforts have been directed toward removing texts that are culturally biased, providing text passages on topics that are familiar to most children and providing a variety of topics so that each child will be familiar with the topic of at least some of them.

Another way test developers try to neutralize the effect of background knowledge is by making sure that questions are passage dependent, i.e., the reader cannot answer them without reading the passage. Tuinman (1974)

Last month you read an article about why the seasons change. Think about what you learned from that article. Below you will find several ideas that might or might not have something to do with why the seasons change. For each idea, decide whether or not it is related to why the seasons change.

(YES) = Yes, this idea is related to why the seasons change.
(MAYBE) = I am not sure whether this idea is related to why the seasons change.
(NO) = No, this idea is not related to why the seasons change.

		YES	MAYBE	NO
a.	behavior of animals	(Y)	(M)	(N)
b.	amount of pollution	(Y)	(M)	(N)
c.	spring, summer, winter and fall	(Y)	(M)	(N)
1.	path of comets	(Y)	(M)	(N)
2.	amount of sunlight	(Y)	(M)	(N)
3.	length of day and night	(Y)	(M)	(N)
4.	chlorophyll in plants	(Y)	(M)	(N)
5.	directness of sun's rays	(Y)	(M)	(N)
6.	revolution of the earth around the sun	(Y)	(M)	(N)
7.	eruption of volcanoes	(Y)	(M)	(N)
8.	ocean currents	(Y)	(M)	(N)
9.	cause of earthquakes	(Y)	(M)	(N)
10.	distance of the earth from Mars	(Y)	(M)	(N)
11.	tilt of the earth on its axis	(Y)	(M)	(N)
12.	rotation of the earth	(Y)	(M)	(N)
13.	phases of the moon	(Y)	(M)	(N)
14.	position of the stars	(Y)	(M)	(N)
15.	distance of the earth from the sun	(Y)	(M)	(N)

Figure 8. Prior knowledge test.

pointed out that many of the questions on standardized reading tests were passage independent questions. For example, a question like "Who discovered America?," even if it is asked about a passage that states that Columbus discovered America, is a passage independent question since many children could probably answer it without reading the passage. Tuinman suggested that use of passage independent questions makes a reading test invalid because these questions measure children's knowledge and experience rather than their reading.

Cloze tests have been suggested as formats that neutralize the effects of background knowledge more effectively than short passages followed by multiple choice questions. For example, the developers of the DRP state that all the information necessary to complete the cloze passages on the test is available in the passages so that information from past experience is not needed (Touchstone Applied Science Associates 1980). However, if background knowledge is seen as an integral part of the reading process as the new definitions of reading suggest, then reading assessment cannot avoid the effect of background knowledge and assessment of reading must involve assessing background knowledge to some degree. Yet if test developers do not control the effects of background knowledge, the tests assess children's experience rather than their reading. Currently test developers use their own judgment in balancing the effects of background knowledge rather than using a system validated by research (Johnston 1983).

THE MICHIGAN AND ILLINOIS STATE TESTS
Developers of the Michigan and Illinois reading tests (Valencia et al. 1989) are attempting to measure prior knowledge rather than neutralizing its effects. These tests assess children's familiarity with the topic of the test passage before

they read it. Children identify key attributes and examples of an important text concept or identify important ideas that might be found in a text on this topic. A typical item on the Michigan topic familiarity test asks "Does *brave* help to tell about a hero?" (Roeber and Dutcher 1989, p. 65).

Below is an excerpt of a topic familiarity test that uses the same format as that used in the Illinois test. I used this particular test to measure children's prior knowledge about a text used in the research study discussed in Chapters 5 and 9 (Maria 1988). Students are not penalized for lack of prior knowledge in the Michigan and Illinois tests. The topic familiarity test is used to interpret the *constructing meaning score* (the score children receive on questions that they answer about the content of the passage after they have read it).

Two other components of the tests, *metacognitive knowledge about reading* and *reading attitudes, habits, and self-perceptions,* are designed to measure the effect of these factors on the children's comprehension of the test passages. Multiple choice questions in these areas are related to the test passages and are answered after reading the passages.

In the Michigan test metacognitive knowledge questions can be questions about strategy use, text type, text location, text structure, and text features such as graphs, diagrams, or literary devices. Questions about attitudes and self-perceptions ask about children's interest in the selection, their ability to understand it, and the amount of effort they put into reading the selection and answering questions about it (Roeber and Dutcher 1989). The questions below are samples of items from the Michigan Reading Test. The first question is a sample of a knowledge/text type question; the second is an example of a knowledge/strategies question; and the third is an example of a question that tests a child's attitudes and self-perceptions.

1. What type of text is this?
    A. realistic story
    B. fairy tale
    C. biography
    D. mystery
2. When would it help to summarize this story?
    A. to tell about it in class
    B. to take a vocabulary test
    C. to write a story
    D. to fill in the blanks on a worksheet.
(Wixson et al. 1987, Attachment 2D)
3. It was easy for me to read the words in "Daniel's Duck".
    A. strongly agree
    B. agree
    C. disagree
    D. strongly disagree
(Roeber and Dutcher 1989, p. 66)

The developers of these tests hope that by comparing children's comprehension scores to their scores on the other test components, teachers may gain some insight into the factors which may be interfering with a child's comprehension. However, Farr and Beck (in press) caution that asking children about the strategies they use may result in children telling us about the strategies that they think they are supposed to use rather than those that they actually use.

Test developers who attempt to isolate separate factors like prior knowledge and metacognitive knowledge may encounter the same problems as those who attempted to isolate separate skills, i.e., the subtests may be so closely correlated that we are not justified in considering them as measuring different factors (MacGinitie, personal communication). Future research should address this issue.

ANALYZING RESPONSES ON STANDARDIZED READING COMPREHENSION TESTS: INAPPROPRIATE COMPREHENSION STRATEGIES

In the manuals of the Third Edition of the Gates MacGinitie tests (Levels 3-12) MacGinitie and MacGinitie (1989) take a different approach to using standardized tests as process measures, i.e., using standardized test responses as a source of information about *why* children are having difficulty with reading comprehension. They suggest that comparing children's scores on the Vocabulary and Comprehension subtests and identifying certain patterns of incorrect responses on the Comprehension subtest can be first steps in determining what factors and/or inappropriate comprehension strategies may be affecting their comprehension. Low scores on both the Vocabulary and Comprehension subtests may be the result of difficulties with many factors, especially decoding. However, a child with this pattern of scores may have problems in both decoding and comprehension. For example, this pattern may also indicate a child whose fund of background knowledge is different from that needed for the test. Teachers should administer a test of listening comprehension as the next step in determining the child's area of difficulty. If the child scores well on the test of listening comprehension, he or she may need instruction in decoding rather than comprehension (MacGinitie and MacGinitie 1989).

If a child has a low comprehension score but a good vocabulary score, it is unlikely that the child's poor comprehension is the result of decoding difficulties, poor vocabulary, or limited school-related background knowledge (MacGinitie and MacGinitie 1989). MacGinitie and MacGinitie (1989) suggest that children with this pattern of scores may be unfamiliar with the syntax and text structures of written language. Other possibilities are that they do not interrelate parts of a text or monitor their comprehension.

On the other hand, children with good comprehension scores and low vocabulary scores probably have used a broad range of information and well-developed strategies in order to score so well in comprehension given their limited vocabulary. These children would probably benefit from instruction in word meanings (MacGinitie and MacGinitie 1989).

It is important to note that the difference between the two subtests should be quite large to be considered a real difference. Small differences are to be expected. (MacGinitie and MacGinitie [1989] provide more detailed information about these differences in the test manuals.)

In 1983 Johnston suggested that the multiple choice format could provide insights about factors affecting a child's reading process and be more useful diagnostically if items and distractors (incorrect answers provided as choices) were constructed more systematically so that "patterns of responses across similar types of alternatives might lead to a diagnosis of the kinds of cognitive difficulties" (Johnston 1983, p. 49) a child was experiencing.

The Gates-MacGinitie reading tests (MacGinitie and MacGinitie 1989) provide an example of this kind of analysis of patterns of incorrect responses. The manuals describe a number of inappropriate comprehension strategies, providing tables of incorrect responses on the tests that may indicate children's use of three of these inappropriate strategies.

The first of these strategies is over-reliance on background knowledge. The child assumes the text says what he or she already knows and answers a test question in terms of his or her prior knowledge rather than in terms of the information in the test passage. For example, the distractor (A) in the second question below is the response that fits this pattern. (The following item was used in field testing the Gates MacGinitie test, fourth edition. Permission granted by Walter and Ruth MacGinitie.)

> Flaming Star whinnied loudly and kicked her heels in the air. With confident, graceful movements she trotted over to the gate—just as Jago appeared around the corner from the stable block.
>
> "All right, I'm comin'," he laughed, *fishing* in his pocket for a piece of carrot.
>
> To Flaming Star, Jago was the whole world. From the day she was born, he had fed her, worried over her, cared for her and loved her. As for Jago, he could not have been more proud of her if she had been his own child. He stroked the white star on her face, the only white mark on her silky chestnut coat, and gave her the carrot. Copyright © 1976 by Nicky Millard. Reprinted by permission of Scholastic—TAB Publications, Ltd.
>
> Jago was *fishing* for the carrot so he could
> a. eat it.
> b. cook it.
> c. feed it to Flaming Star.
> d. put it in his pocket.

If a child consistently chooses distractors like (A) which make sense according to common knowledge but are inappropriate for the text read, he or she may be using this inappropriate comprehension strategy.

A child's use of this strategy may be a compensation for poor decoding skill or lack of knowledge of word meanings. A poor score on the Vocabulary subtest would support this diagnostic hypothesis. The child may not have read the passage at all; he or she may have a habit of looking ahead and answering the questions without looking at the text. However, some children apparently use this strategy even when their decoding skill and word meaning knowledge are adequate (Maria and MacGinitie 1982).

A child's use of this strategy may be a compensation for poor decoding skill or lack of knowledge of word meanings. A poor score on the Vocabulary subtest would support this diagnostic hypothesis. The child may not have read the passage at all; he or she may have a habit of looking ahead and answering the questions without looking at the text. However, some children apparently use this strategy even when their decoding skill and word meaning knowledge are adequate (Maria and MacGinitie 1982).

A second inappropriate comprehension strategy is the failure to interrelate textual units. When children answer test questions using one sentence or group of sentences in the test passage and ignoring other sentences that contradict their incorrect answers, they may be using this strategy. In addition to listing incorrect responses the tables in the Gates MacGinitie test manuals provide the phrases from the test passages that may have resulted in incorrect responses. Several children chose distractor (A), "short," in the first question below even though the text upon which the question is based specifically refers to the mustang's long legs. MacGinitie and MacGinitie suggest that these children may have chosen (A) because of the phrase, *when he was born,* and other indications in the text that he is a baby horse.

1. The mustang's legs were
a. short.
b. thin.
c. brown.
d. swiveled.
2. Why did the mustang have to *struggle?*
a. His eyes were blurry.
b. He was sick.
c. He was tied up.
d. He was so young.

A third inappropriate strategy identified by MacGinitie and MacGinitie (1989) is a question-answering strategy rather than a comprehension strategy. Children who use this strategy look for distractors in the questions that match phrases in the text. MacGinitie and MacGinitie (1989, p. 48) suggest that this strategy may be a reflection of the way these children read, i.e., "they think of 'reading' as scanning the text to find satisfactory words and phrases." Children who consistently choose incorrect responses like distractor (A) in the second question above may be using this strategy because the text contains the phrase, *his blurry eyes.*

To determine whether children are using these or other inappropriate comprehension strategies, and if so, why they are using them, MacGinitie and MacGinitie (1989) recommend discussing children's test responses with them in individual interviews at a time after the test has been completed. This interview can provide instruction as well as assessment if the teacher demonstrates that the inappropriate comprehension strategy does not work.

I have also found that questioning a child about *why* he or she chose particular responses for standardized test questions can provide very useful information. Children are grateful for the feedback. Several children with whom I discussed their test results told me they often wondered how they did on the tests—what they got right and what they got wrong—but nobody ever told them.

Concern over test security often makes it impossible for teachers to use standardized tests in this way because they have no access to the tests. However, if the test is available to the teacher and if it will not be used again to test the same children this kind of discussion can be helpful.

One situation in which I found this procedure particularly helpful involved a third grade girl who had made 23 errors on a standardized reading comprehension test. Such a low score was not consistent with her performance in class. Rather than simply discounting the child's test score, her classroom teacher asked me if I would go over the test with her to determine whether the child had a problem. (I was the reading teacher in the school.) The child and I reread the test together and discussed why she had chosen each answer and whether the answer made sense in relation to the test passage. After we had discussed three or four incorrect responses, she suddenly looked up at me and said, "Are the answers supposed to make sense?" In amazement, I replied, "Yes." She then asked me if she could try redoing the test. Instead of 23 errors, she now made only five errors. Her teacher and I could not determine why she had to be told that test answers should make sense; her teacher felt that she had made this point during instruction. Nevertheless, the short session discussing the test seemed to be of real help to this child because she has not had any further problems with standardized tests. Usually, however, discussing children's standardized test responses with them is only a first step in determining the factors that may be affecting their comprehension adversely. This type of discussion needs to be followed by classroom assessment integrated with instruction, described in the first section of this chapter.

Formal standardized testing and informal teacher assessment each have a part to play in a complete program of comprehension assessment. Informal assessment based on the systematic collection and documentation of information gathered during instruction should be given greater attention, but the use of standardized tests cannot and should not be abandoned.

References

Afflerbach, P. 1987, April. The statewide assessment of reading. Paper presented at the annual meeting of the American Educational Research Association, Washington, D.C.

Afflerbach, P. P., and Johnston, P. H. 1986. What do expert readers do when the main idea is not explicit? In *Teaching Main Idea Comprehension*, ed. J. Baumann. Newark, DE: International Reading Association.

Allington, R. L. 1983. The reading instruction provided readers of differing reading ability. *Elementary School Journal* 75:548–59.

Allington, R. L. 1984. Content coverage and contextual reading in reading groups. *Journal of Reading Behavior* 16:85–96.

Allington, R. L. 1988, May. Developing expertise in reading education: What do we know for sure? Paper presented at International Reading Association, Toronto.

Allington, R. L., and Johnston, P. 1989. Coordination, collaboration and consistency: The redesign of compensatory and special educational interventions. In *Preventing School Failure: Effective Programs for At-Risk Learners*, eds. R. Slavin, N. Madden, and N. Karweit. Boston: Allyn and Bacon.

Allington, R. L., and McGill-Franzen, A. 1989. Different programs, different instruction. In *Beyond Separate Education*, eds. A. Gartner and D. Lipsky. Baltimore: Paul H. Brookes Publishing Co.

Allington, R. L., Boxer, N. J., and Broikou, K. A. 1987. Jeremy, remedial reading and subject area classes. *Journal of Reading* 30:643–45.

Alvermann, D. E., and Hynd, C. R. 1986, December. The effects of varying prior knowledge activation modes and text structure on non-science majors' comprehension of physics text. Paper presented at the National Reading Conference, Austin, TX.

Alvermann, D. E., and Hynd, C. R. 1987, December. Overcoming misconceptions in science: An on-line study of prior knowledge activation. Paper presented at the National Reading Conference, St. Petersburg, FL.

Alvermann, D. E., and Hynd, C. R. 1988, December. Study strategies for correcting misconceptions in physics: An intervention. Paper presented at the National Reading Conference, Tucson, AZ.

Alvermann, D. E., Dillon, D. R., and O'Brien, D. G. 1987. *Using Discussion to Promote Reading Comprehension*. Newark, DE: International Reading Association.

Alvermann, D. E., Smith, L. C., and Readence, J. E. 1985. Prior knowledge activation and the comprehension of compatible and incompatible text. *Reading Research Quarterly* 20:420–36.

Anastasiow, N. J., Hanes, M. L., and Hanes, M. L. 1982. *Language and Reading Strategies for Poverty Children*. Baltimore: University Park Press.

Anderson, R. C. 1977. The notion of schemata and the educational enterprise. In *Schooling and the Acquisition of Knowledge*, eds. R. C. Anderson, 1984. Some reflections on the acquisition of knowledge. *Educational Researcher* 13:5–10.

Anderson, R. C., and Freebody, P. 1981. Vocabulary knowledge. In *Comprehension and Teaching: Research Reviews*, ed. J. T. Guthrie. Newark, DE: International Reading Association.

Anderson, R. C., and Pearson, P. D. 1984. A schema-theoretic view of basic processes in reading comprehension. In *Handbook of Reading Research*, ed. P. D. Pearson. New York: Longman.

Anderson, R. C., Hiebert, E. H., Scott, J. A. and Wilkinson, I. A. G. 1985. *Becoming a Nation of Readers: The Report of the Commission on Reading*. Washington, D.C.: National Institute of Education.

Anderson, R. C., Reynolds, R. E., Schallert, D. L., and Goetz, E. T. 1977. Frameworks for comprehending discourse. *American Educational Research Journal* 14:367–82.

Anderson, T. H. 1980. Study strategies and adjunct aids. In *Theoretical Issues in Reading Comprehension*, eds. R. J. Spiro, B. C. Bruce, and W. F. Brewer. Hillsdale NJ: Lawrence Erlbaum and Associates.

Anderson, V., and Hidi, S. 1988–1989. Teaching students to summarize. *Educational Leadership* 46:26–28.

Applebee, A. 1978. *The Child's Concept of Story*. Chicago: University of Chicago Press.

Applebee, A. L. 1981. *Writing in the Secondary School: English and the Content Areas*. Research Report No. 21. Urbana, IL: National Council of Teachers of English.

Applebee, A. N., and Langer, J. A. 1983. Instructional scaffolding: Reading and writing as natural language activities. *Language Arts* 60:168–75.

Arlin, M., and Westbury, I. 1976. The leveling effect of teacher pacing on science achievement. *Journal of Research in Science Teaching* 13:213–19.

Armbruster, B. B. 1984. The problem of "inconsiderate text." In *Comprehension Instruction: Perspectives and Suggestions*, eds. G. G. Duffy, L. R. Roehler, and J. Mason. 202–17. New York: Longman.

Armbruster, B. B., Anderson, T. T., and Ostertag, J. 1987. Does text structure/summarization instruction facilitate learning from expository text? *Reading Research Quarterly* 22:331–46.

Artley, A. S. 1969. The teacher variable in the teaching of reading. *The Reading Teacher* 23:239–48.

Atwell, N. 1984. Writing and reading literature from the inside out. *Language Arts* 61:240–52.

Atwell, N. 1987. *In the Middle: Writing, Reading and Learning with Adolescents*. Portsmouth, NH: Heinemann.

Aulls, M. 1978. *Developmental and Remedial Reading in the Middle Grades*. Boston: Allyn and Bacon.

Aulls, M. W. 1982. *Developing Readers in Today's Elementary School*. Boston: Allyn and Bacon.

Ausubel, D. P. 1968. *Educational Psychology: A Cognitive View*. New York: Holt, Rinehart, and Winston.

Bagley, M. T., and Hess, K. 1982. *200 Ways of Using Imagery in the Classroom*. Woodcliff Lake, NJ: New Dimensions of the 80's.

Baker, L. 1985. How do we know when we don't understand? Standards for evaluating text comprehension. In *Metacognition, Cognition, and Human Performance*, eds. D. L. Forrest-Pressley, G. E. MacKinnon, and T. G. Waller. Vol. 1, 155–205. Orlando, FL: Academic Press.

Baker, L., and Brown, A. L. 1984. Metacognitive skills and reading. In *Handbook of Reading Research*, ed. P. D. Pearson. New York: Longman.

Balow, I. H., and Balow, B. 1964. Lateral dominance and reading achievement. *American Educational Research Journal* 1:139–43.

Baratz, J., and Shuy, R. 1969. *Teaching Black Children to Read*. Washington, DC: Center for Applied Linguistics.

Barnitz, J. G. 1980. Syntactic effects on the reading comprehension of pronoun-referent structures by children in grades two, four and six. *Reading Research Quarterly* 15:268–89.

Barnitz, J. G. 1986. The anaphora jigsaw puzzle in psycholinguistic and reading research. In *Understanding and Teaching Cohesion Comprehension*, ed. J. W. Irwin. Newark, DE: International Reading Association.

Baron, J. 1978. Intelligence and general strategies. In *Strategies in Information Processing*, ed. G. Underwood. 403–450. London: Academic Press.

Barr, R. C. 1973–1974. Instructional pace differences and their effect on reading acquisition. *Reading Research Quarterly* 9: 526–54.

Barr, R. C. 1982. Classroom reading instruction from a sociological perspective. *Journal of Reading Behavior* 14:375–89.

Barrett, T. C. 1976. Taxonomy of reading comprehension. In *Teaching Reading in the Middle Grades*, eds. R. Smith and T. C. Barrett. Reading, MA: Addison-Wesley.

Bartlett, F. C. 1932. *Remembering*. Cambridge: Cambridge University Press.

Bates, E., Bretherton, I., and Snyder, L. 1988. *From First Words to Grammar*. Cambridge, England: Cambridge University Press.

Baumann, J. F. 1983. A generic comprehension instructional strategy. *Reading World* 22:284–94.

Baumann, J. F. 1986. Teaching third-grade students to comprehend anaphoric relationships: The application of the direct instruction model. *Reading Research Quarterly* 21:70–90.

Baumann, J. F. ed. 1986. *Teaching Main Idea Comprehension*. Newark, DE: International Reading Association.

Baumann, J. F. 1988. Direct instruction reconsidered. *Journal of Reading* 31:712–18.

Baumann, J. F., and Stevenson, J. A. 1986. Identifying types of anaphoric relationships. In *Understanding and Teaching Cohesion Comprehension*, ed. J. W. Irwin. Newark: International Reading Association.

Beach, R., and Appleman, D. 1984. Reading strategies for expository and literary text types. In *Becoming Readers in a Complex Society*, eds. A. Purves and O. Niles. Eighty-third yearbook of the National Society for the Study of Education, Part I:115-43. Chicago: University of Chicago Press.

Bean, T. W. 1988. Organizing and retaining information by thinking like an author. In *Reexamining Reading Diagnosis: New Trends and Procedures*, eds. S. M. Glazer, L. W. Searfoss, and L. M. Gentile. Newark, DE: International Reading Association.

Beck, I., and McKeown, M. 1983. Learning words well—A program to enhance vocabulary and comprehension. *The Reading Teacher* 36:622–25.

Beck, I. L., and McKeown, M. G. 1988. Toward meaningful accounts in history texts for young learners. *Educational Researcher* 18:31–39.

Beck, I., McCaslin, M., and McKeown, M. 1980. *The Rationale and Design of a Program to Teach Vocabulary to Fourth-Grade Students*. Pittsburgh: University of Pittsburgh, Learning Research and Development Center.

Beck, I., McKeown, M., and Omanson, R. 1987. The effects and uses of diverse vocabulary instructional techniques. In *The Nature of Vocabulary Acquisition*, eds. M. McKeown and M. Curtis. Hillsdale: Lawrence Erlbaum and Associates.

Beck, I., Perfetti, C., and McKeown, M. 1982. The effects of long-term vocabulary instruction on lexical access and reading comprehension. *Journal of Educational Psychology* 74:506–21.

Beck, I. L., Omanson, R. C., and McKeown, M. G. 1981. An instructional redesign of reading lessons: Effects on comprehension. *Reading Research Quarterly* 16:462–81.

Belmont, L., and Birch, H. G. 1965. Lateral dominance, lateral awareness and reading disability. *Child Development* 36:57–71.

Benton, C. D, and McCann, J. W. 1969. Dyslexia and dominance: Some second thoughts. *Journal of Pediatric Opthamology* 6:220–22.

Bereiter, C., and Scardamalia, M. 1981. From conversation to composition: The role of instruction in a developmental process. In *Advances in Instructional Psychology*, ed. R. Glaser. Vol. 2. Hillsdale, NJ: Lawrence Erlbaum and Associates.

Berger, N. 1978. Why can't John read? Perhaps he's not a good listener. *Journal of Learning Disabilities* 11:633–38.

Berkowitz, S. J. 1986. Effects of instruction in text organization on sixth-grade students' memory for expository reading. *Reading Research Quarterly* 21:150–60.

Berlak, H. 1985. Testing in a democracy. *Educational Leadership* 42:16–17.

Berliner, D. C. 1981. Academic learning time and reading achievement. In *Comprehension and Teaching: Research Reviews*, ed. J. T. Guthrie. Newark, DE: International Reading Association.

Berliner, D. C. 1987a. Simple views of effective teaching and a simple theory of classroom instruction. In *Talks to Teachers*, eds. D. C. Berliner and B. V. Rosenshine. New York: Random House.

Berliner, D. C. 1987b. But do they understand? In *Educators' Handbook: A Research Perspective*, ed. V. Richardson-Koehler. New York: Longman.

Bernstein, B. 1964. Elaborated and restricted codes: Their social origin and some consequences. In *The Ethnography of Communication*, eds. J. J. Gumperz and D. Hymes. 55–69. Menasha WI: American Anthropological Association.

Bettelheim, B., and Zelan, K. 1981. *On Learning to Read*. New York: Alfred A. Knopf.

Binkley, M. R. 1988. New ways of assessing text difficulty. In *Readability: Its Past, Present and Future*, eds. B. L. Zakaluk and S. J. Samuels. Newark, DE: International Reading Association.

Birnbaum, J., and Emig, J. 1983. Creating minds, created texts: Writing and reading. In *Developing Literacy: Young Children's Uses of Language*, eds. R. P. Parker and F. A. Davis. Newark, DE: International Reading Association.

Biskin, D. S., Hoskisson, K., and Modlin, M. 1976. Prediction, reflection and comprehension. *Elementary School Journal* 77:131–39.

Blanchard, J. 1988. Plausible stories: A creative writing and story prediction activity. *Reading Research and Instruction* 28:60–65.

Blume, J. 1981. *The One in the Middle is a Green Kangaroo*. New York: Dell.

Bolton, E. 1985. Dream dancer. In *Ten Times Round*, eds. T. Clymer, R. Indrisano, D. D. Johnson, P. D. Pearson, and R. L. Venezky. Columbus, OH: Ginn and Company.

Bond, G. L., and Dykstra, R. 1967. The cooperative research program in first grade reading. *Reading Research Quarterly* 2:5–142.

Booth, D., Phoenix, J., and Pauli, W. 1988. *Impressions*. Toronto: Holt, Rinehart, and Winston of Canada.

Bormuth, J. R. 1966. Readability: A new approach. *Reading Research Quarterly* 1:79–132.

Bormuth, J. R., Carr, J., Manning, J., and Pearson, P. D. 1970. Children's comprehension of between- and within-sentence syntactic structures. *Journal of Educational Psychology* 61:349–57.

Brandt, R. S. 1986. On the expert teacher: A conversation with David Berliner. *Educational Leadership* 44:4–9.

Bransford, J. D. 1984. Schema activation and schema acquisition. In *Learning to Read in American Schools: Basal Readers and Content Texts*, eds. R. C. Anderson, J. Osborn, and R. J. Tierney. Hillsdale: Lawrence Erlbaum and Associates.

Bransford, J. D., and Johnson, M. K. 1972. Contextual prerequisites for understanding. Some investigations of comprehension and recall. *Journal of Verbal Learning and Verbal Behavior* 11:717–26.

Brook, J. S., Whiteman, M., Peisach, E., and Deutsch, M. 1974. Aspiration levels of and for children: Age, sex, race and socioeconomic correlates. *Journal of Genetic Psychology* 124:3–16.

Brophy, J., and Good, T. L. 1970. Teachers' communications of differential expectations for children's classroom performance: Some behavioral data. *Journal of Educational Psychology* 61:365–74.

Brown, D. A. 1982. *Reading Diagnosis and Remediation*. Englewood Cliffs, NJ: Prentice-Hall.

Brown, A. L. 1980. Metacognitive development and reading. In *Theoretical Issues in Reading Comprehension*, eds. R. J. Spiro, B. C. Bruce, and W. F. Brewer. Hillsdale: Lawrence Erlbaum and Associates.

Brown, A. L., and Campione, J. C. 1978. Memory strategies in learning: Training children to study strategically. In *Psychology: From Research to Practice*, eds. H. L. Pick, H. W. Leibowitz, J. E. Singer, A. Steinschneider, and H. W. Stevenson. New York: Plenum.

Brown, A. L., and Day, J. D. 1983. Macrorules for summarizing texts: The development of experts. *Journal of Verbal Learning and Verbal Behavior* 22:1–14.

Brown, C. S., and Lytle, S. L. 1988. Merging assessment and instruction: Protocols in the classroom. In *Reexamining Reading Diagnosis: New Trends and Procedures*, eds. S. M. Glazer, L. W. Searfoss, and L. M. Gentile. Newark, DE: International Reading Association.

Brown, A. L., and Palincsar, A. S. 1982. *Inducing Strategic Learning from Texts by Means of Informed Self-Control Training*. Tech. Rep. No. 262. Urbana, IL: University of Illinois, Center for the Study of Reading.

Brown, A. L., Palincsar, A. S., and Armbruster, B. B. 1984. Instructing comprehension-fostering activities in interactive learning situations. In *Learning and Comprehension of Text*, eds. H. Mandl, N. L. Stein, and T. Trabasso. Hillsdale, NJ: Lawrence Erlbaum and Associates.

Brown, A. L., Smiley, S. S., Day, J., Townsend, M., and Lawton, S. C. 1977. Intrusion of a thematic idea in children's recall of prose. *Child Development* 48:1454–1466.

Bruce, B. 1984. A new point of view on children's stories. In *Learning to Read in American Schools: Basal Readers and Content Texts*, eds. R. C. Anderson, J. Osborn, and R. J. Tierney. 141–152. NJ: Lawrence Erlbaum and Associates.

Bruck, M., and Tucker, R. 1974. Social class differences in the acquisition of school language. *Merrill Palmer Quarterly* 20:205–219.

Bruner, J., Olver, R., and Greenfield, P. 1966. *Studies in Cognitive Growth*. New York: Wiley.

Buckley, M. H. 1986. When teachers decide to integrate the language arts. *Language Arts* 63:369–77.

Burke, C. L., and Harste, J. C. 1978. Toward a socio-psycholinguistic model of reading comprehension. *Viewpoints in Teaching and Learning* 54:9–34.

Burmeister, L. E. 1978. *Reading Strategies for Middle and Secondary School Teachers.* Second Edition. Reading, MA: Addison-Wesley.

Butkowsky, I. S., and Willows, D. M. 1980. Cognitive-motivational characteristics of children varying in reading ability: Evidence for learned helplessness in poor readers. *Journal of Educational Psychology* 72:408–22.

Butler, A., and Turbill, J. 1984. *Towards a Reading-Writing Classroom.* Rozelle, NSW, Australia: Primary English Teaching Association.

Cadenhead, K. 1987. Reading level: A metaphor that shapes practice. *Phi Delta Kappan* 68:436–41.

Calfee, R., and Chambliss, M. 1988. Beyond decoding: Pictures of expository prose. *Annals of Dyslexia* 38:243–58.

Calfee, R., and Hiebert, E. 1987. The teacher's role in using assessment to improve learning. *Assessment in the Service of Learning.* Proceedings of the Educational Testing Service Invitational Conference. Princeton, NJ: Educational Testing Service.

Calkins, L. M. 1986. *The Art of Teaching Writing.* Portsmouth, NH: Heinemann.

Cambourne, B. 1984. Language, learning and literacy. In *Towards a Reading-Writing Classroom,* A. Butler and J. Turbill. Rozelle, NSW, Australia: Primary English Teaching Association.

Camp, L. W., Winburg, N. E., and Zinna, D. 1981. Strategies for initial reading instruction. *Bulletin of The Orton Society* 31:175–88.

Campione, J. C., and Brown, A. L. 1978. Toward a theory of intelligence: Contributions from research with retarded children. *Intelligence* 2:279–304.

Capobianco, R. J. 1967. Ocular-manual laterality and reading achievement in children with special learning disabilities. *American Educational Research Journal* 2:133–37.

Carbo, M. 1981. *Reading Style Inventory Manual.* Roslyn Heights, NY: Learning Research Associates.

Carbo, M. 1987. Reading style research: "What works" isn't always phonics. *Phi Delta Kappan* 68:431–35.

Carbo, M., Dunn, R., and Dunn, K. 1986. *Teaching Students to Read Through Their Individual Learning Styles.* Reston, VA: Prentice Hall.

Carnine, D., and Kinder, D. 1985. Teaching low-performing students to apply generative and schema strategies to narrative and expository material. *Remedial and Special Education* 6:20–30.

Carr, E. 1985. The Vocabulary Overview Guide: A metacognitive strategy to improve vocabulary comprehension and retention. *Journal of Reading* 21:684–89.

Carr, E. 1986. *Vocabulary Overview Guide* (Manual accompanying videotape entitled *Teaching Reading as Thinking.*) Alexandria, VA: Association for Supervision and Curriculum Development.

Carr, E., Dewitz, P., and Patberg, J. 1983. The effect of inference training on children's comprehension of expository text. *Journal of Reading Behavior* 15:1–18.

Carr, E., Dewitz, P., and Patberg, J. 1989. Using cloze for inference training with expository text. *The Reading Teacher* 42:380–85.

Carver, R. P. 1977–1978. Toward a theory of reading comprehension and rauding. *Reading Research Quarterly* 13:8–63.

Cazden, C. B. 1972. *Child Language and Education.* New York: Holt, Rinehart, and Winston.

Cazden, C. B. 1986. Classroom discourse. In *Handbook of Research on Teaching,* ed. M. C. Wittrock. Third Edition. New York: Macmillan.

Cazden, C. B. 1988. *Interactions Between Maori Students and Pakeha Teachers.* Auckland, NZ: Auckland Reading Council.

Chafe, W., and Danielewicz, J. 1987. Properties of spoken and written language. In *Comprehending Oral and Written Language,* eds. R. Horowitz and S. J. Samuels. San Diego: Academic Press.

Chall, J. 1983. *Stages of Reading Development.* New York: McGraw Hill.

Charlip, R. 1964. *Fortunately.* New York: Parents Magazine Press.

Chekov, A. 1983. The bet. In *Aiming High,* eds. A. Sloan and A. Cappacio. New York: Amsco School Publications.

Chomsky, N. 1957. *Syntactic Structures.* The Hague: Mouton.

Chomsky, N. 1965. *Aspects of Theory of Syntax.* Cambridge: MIT Press.

Chomsky, C. 1969. *The Acquisition of Syntax in Children from 5 to 10.* Cambridge: MIT Press.

Clark, C. M. 1988. Asking the right questions about teacher preparation: Contributions of research on teacher thinking. *Educational Researcher* 17:5–11.

Clark, D. 1988. *Dyslexia: Theory and Practice of Remedial Instruction*. Parkton, MD: York Press.

Clark, F. L., Deshler, D. D., Schumaker, J. B., Alley, G. R., and Warner, M. M. 1984. Visual imagery and self-questioning: Strategies to improve comprehension of written material. *Journal of Learning Disabilities* 17:145–49.

Clay, M. M. 1969. Reading errors and self-correction behavior. *British Journal of Educational Psychology* 39:47–56.

Clay, M. M. 1985. *The Early Detection of Reading Difficulties*. Third Edition. Portsmouth, NH: Heinemann.

Clymer, T. 1976. *Reading 720*. Lexington, MA: Ginn.

Clymer, T., and Gates, D. 1969. New Boots. In *May I Come In?*. Boston: Ginn.

Clymer, T., Stein, R. M., Gatts, D., and McCullough, C. 1976. *Inside Out*. Boston: Ginn.

Cochran, E. D., Coleman, D., Cortright, A., Forman, D., and Reid, E. 1970. Random House Reading Program. New York: Random House.

Coleman, E. B., and Miller, G. R. 1968. A measure of information gained during prose learning. *Reading Research Quarterly* 3:369–86.

Coleman, R. I., and Deutsch, C. P. 1964. Lateral dominance and right-left discrimination: A comparison of normal and retarded readers. *Perceptual Motor Skills* 19:43–50.

Collier, J. L, and Collier, C. 1974. *My Brother Sam is Dead*. New York: Scholastic.

Collins, A., Brown, J. S., and Newman, S. E. 1987. *Cognitive Apprenticeship: Teaching the Craft of Reading, Writing and Mathematics*. (Technical Report No. 403)Urbana, IL: Center for the Study of Reading, University of Illinois.

Collins, A., and Smith, E. E. 1982. Teaching the process of reading comprehension. In *How and How Much Can Intelligence Be Increased?*, eds. D. K. Detterman and R. J. Sternberg. Norwood, NJ: Ablex.

Connor, F. P. 1983. Improving school instruction for learning disabled children. The Teachers College Institute: *Exceptional Education Quarterly* 4:23–44.

Constanzo, P. R., and Shaw, M. E. 1966. Conformity as a function of age level. *Child Development* 37:967–75.

Cooke, J. K., and Haipt, M. 1986. *Thinking With the Whole Brain: An Integrative Teaching/Learning Model (K–8)*. Washington, D.C.: National Education Association.

Cooper, J. D. 1986. *Improving Reading Comprehension*. Boston: Houghton Mifflin.

Costa, A. L., and Marzano, R. 1987. Teaching the language of thinking. *Education L* 45:29–33.

Crowl, T. K., and MacGinitie, W. H. 1974. The influence of students' speech characteristics on teachers' evaluations of oral answers. *Journal of Educational Psychology* 66:304–308.

Cudd, E. T., and Roberts, L. 1989. Using writing to enhance content area learning in the primary grades. *The Reading Teacher* 42:392–404.

Dale, E. 1975. *The Word Game: Improving Communications*. Bloomington, IN: Phi Delta Kappa.

Dale, E., and O'Rourke, J. 1971. *Techniques of Teaching Vocabulary*. Menlo Park, CA: Benjamin Cummings Publishing Co.

Damjan, M., and Kenelski, M. 1975. The Little Green Man. In *Secret Spaces*, eds. C. B. Smith and R. Wardhaugh. (Level 15 of the Macmillan r series.) New York: Macmillan.

Danks, J. H., and End, L. J. 1987. Processing strategies for reading and listening. In *Comprehending Oral and Written Language*, eds. R. Horowitz and S. J. Samuels. San Diego: Academic Press.

Davey, B. 1983. Think aloud—Modeling the cognitive processes of reading comprehension. *Journal of Reading* 27:44–46.

Davis, F. B. 1944. Fundamental factors of comprehension in reading. *Psychometrika* 9:185–97.

Davis, F. B. 1968. Research in comprehension in reading. *Reading Research Quarterly* 3:499–545.

Davis, R. B. 1981. The postularion of certain specific, explicit, commonly-shared frames. *Journal of Mathematical Behavior* 3:167–201.

Davison, A. 1984. Readability formulas and comprehension. In *Comprehension Instruction: Perspectives and Suggestions*, eds. G. G. Duffy, L. R. Roehler, and J. Mason. 202–217. New York: Longman.

Davison, A. 1988. Assigning grade levels without formulas: Some case studies. In *Readability: Its Past, Present and Future*, eds. B. L. Zakaluk and S. J. Samuels. Newark, DE: International Reading Association.

Day, J. D. 1980. Training summarization skills: A comparison of teaching methods. Unpublished doctoral dissertation, University of Illinois.

de Cordova, J. K. 1989. Vocabulary development and ESL and LEP students. In Teachers Response Packet *Dreams Go Far*. (Level M) New York: McGraw Hill.

DeFord, D. E. 1981. Literacy: Reading, writing and other essentials. *Language Arts* 58:652–58.

Deighton, L. 1970. *Vocabulary Development in the Classroom*. New York: Teachers College Press.

Denckla, M. B., and Rudel, R. G. 1976. Rapid "automatized" naming (R.A.N.): Dyslexia differentiated from other learning disabilities. *Neuropsychologia* 14:471–79.

Devine, T. G. 1986. *Teaching Reading Comprehension: From Theory to Practice*. Boston: Allyn and Bacon.

DiVesta, F. J., Hayward, K. G., and Orlando, V. P. 1979. Developmental trends in monitoring text for comprehension. *Child Development* 50:97–105.

Doctorow, M., Wittrock, M. C., and Marks, C. 1978. Generative processes in reading comprehension. *Journal of Educational Psychology* 70:109–118.

Dole, J. A., and Smith, E. L. 1987, December. When prior knowledge is wrong: Reading and learning from science text. Paper presented at the National Reading Conference, St. Petersburg, FL.

Domato, C. 1989. Direct training of generating questions with reciprocal teaching. Unpublished manuscript.

Downing, J. 1980. Learning to read with understanding. In *Persistent Problems in Reading Education*, ed. C. M. McCullough. 163–178. Newark DE: International Reading Association.

Doyle, W. 1983. Academic work. *Review of Educational Research* 53:14–21.

Dreher, M., and Singer, H. 1980. Story grammar instruction unnecessary for intermediate grade students. *The Reading Teacher* 34:261–68.

Duffelmeyer, F. A., and Duffelmeyer, B. B. 1989. Are IRI passages suitable for assessing main idea comprehension? *The Reading Teacher* 42:358–63.

Duffy, G. G. 1982. Fighting off the alligators: What research in real classrooms has to say about reading instruction. *Journal of Reading Behavior* 14:357–74.

Duffy, G. G., and Roehler, L. R. 1986. The subtleties of instructional mediation. *Educational Leadership* 44:23–27.

Duffy, G. G., Roehler, L. R., Sivan, E., Rackliffe, G., Book, C., Meloth, M. S., Vavrus, L. G., Wesselman, R., Putnam, J., and Bassiri, D. 1987. Effects of explaining the reasoning associated with using reading strategies. *Reading Research Quarterly* 22:347–68.

Dunn, J. 1980. Playing in speech. In *The State of the Language*, eds. L. Michaels and C. Ricks. 202–212. Berkeley: University of California Press.

Durkin, D. 1978–1979. What classroom observations reveal about reading comprehension instruction. *Reading Research Quarterly* 16:515–44.

Durkin, D. 1981. Reading comprehension instruction in five basal readers. *Reading Research Quarterly* 16:515–44.

Durkin, D. 1985. Introduction. In *Reading, Thinking and Concept Development*, eds. T. L. Harris and E. J. Cooper. xi–xix. New York: College Entrance Examination Board.

Dynes, J. J. 1932. Comparison of two methods of studying history. *Journal of Experimental Education* 1:42–45.

Eastman, P. D. 1968. *The Best Nest*. New York: Random House.

Eckoff, B. 1983. How reading affects children's writing. *Language Arts* 60:607–16.

Eder, D. 1981. Ability grouping as a self-fulfilling prophecy: Microanalysis of teacher-student interaction. *Sociology of Education* 4:151–61.

Education Commission of the States 1984. *Issuegram Sept. 26*. Denver, CO: Author.

Educational Product Information Exchange. 1977. *Report on a National Survey of the Nature and Quality of Instructional Materials Most used by Teachers and Learners* (Technical Rep. No. 76.) New York: EPIE Institute.

Ehri, L. 1979. Linguistic insight: Threshold of reading acquisition. In *Reading Research: Advances in Research and Theory*, eds. T. Waller and G. MacKinnon. Vol. 1, 63–114. New York: Academic Press.

Emerson, H. 1979. Children's comprehension of *because* in reversible and non-reversible sentences. *Journal of Child Language* 6:279–300.

Englert, C. S., and Hiebert, E. 1984. Children's developing awareness of text structures in expository materials. *Journal of Educational Psychology* 76:65–74.

Entin, E. B., and Klare, G. R. 1978. Factor analyses of three correlation matrices of readability variables. *Journal of Reading Behavior* 10:279–90.

Entwistle, D. R. 1979. The child's social environment and learning to read. In *Reading Research:*

Advances in Theory and Practice, eds. T. Waller and G. MacKinnon. 1:145–69. San Diego: Academic Press.

Estes, T. H., and Vaughan, J. L. 1985. *Reading and Learning in the Content Classroom*. Second Edition. Boston: Allyn and Bacon.

Evertson, C. M. 1987. Managing classrooms: A framework for teachers. In *Talks to Teachers*, eds. D. C. Berliner and B. V. Rosenshine. New York: Random House.

Farr, R. 1989. *HBJ Reading Program Laureate Edition—Testing*. Orlando, FL: Harcourt Brace Jovanovich.

Farr, R., and Beck, M. in press. Evaluating language development: Formal methods. In *Handbook on Teaching the English Language Arts*.

Farr, R., and Carey, R. F. 1986. *Reading: What Can Be Measured?* Newark, DE: International Reading Association.

Farrar, M. T. 1984. Asking better questions. *The Reading Teacher* 38:10–15.

Federal Register, December 29, 1977, 42(163):65083.

Ferguson, C. 1989. Individual differences in language learning. In *Teachability of Language*, eds. M. L. Rice and R. L. Schiefelbusch. Baltimore: Paul H. Brookes Publishing Company.

Fielding, L., Wilson, P. T., and Anderson, R. C. 1984. A new focus on free reading: The role of trade books in reading instruction. In *The Contexts of School-Based Literacy*, ed. T. E. Raphael. 149–159. New York: Random House.

Fillmore, C. 1968. The case for case. In *Universals in Linguistic Theory*, eds. E. Bach and R. Harmas. New York: Holt, Rinehart, and Winston.

Finn, P. J. 1985. *Helping Children Learn to Read*. New York: Random House.

Fitzgerald, J. 1989. Research on stories: Implications for teachers. In *Children's Comprehension of Text*, ed. K. D. Muth. Newark, DE: International Reading Association.

Fitzgerald, J., and Spiegel, D. L. 1983. Enhancing children's reading comprehension through instruction in narrative structure. *Journal of Reading Behavior* 15:1–17.

Fleischner, J. E., and Marzola, E. S. 1988. Arithmetic. In *Handbook of Learning Disabilities Volume II: Methods and Interventions*, eds. K. Kavale, S. Forness, and M. Bender. Boston: College Hill Publications, Little Brown and Company.

Flood, J., and Lapp, D. 1986. Types of texts: The match between what students read in basals and what they encounter in tests. *Reading Research Quarterly* 21:284–97.

Flood, J., and Lapp, D. 1987. Forms of discourse in basal readers. *Elementary School Journal* 87:299–306.

Flood, J., and Lapp, D. 1988. Conceptual mapping strategies for information texts. *The Reading Teacher* 41:780–83.

Florio-Ruane, S., and Dunn, S. 1987. Teaching writing: Some perennial questions and some possible answers. In *Educators' Handbook: A Research Perspective*, ed. V. Richardson-Koler. New York: Longman.

Flower, L. S. 1981. *Problem-Solving Strategies for Writing*. Orlando, FL: Harcourt Brace Jovanovich.

Forrest, D. L., and Waller, T. G. 1979. Cognitive and metacognitive aspects of reading. Paper presented at the meeting of the Society for Research in Child Development, San Francisco.

Fowler, G. 1982. Developing comprehension skills in primary students through the use of story frames. *The Reading Teacher* 35:176–79.

Fraatz, J. M. B. 1987. *The Politics of Reading*. New York: Teachers College Press.

Fradin, D. B. 1981. *Texas in Words and Pictures*. Chicago: Children's Press.

Fredericks, A. D. 1986. Mental imagery activities to improve comprehension. *The Reading Teacher* 39:78–81.

Frederiksen, C. H. 1975. Representing the logical and semantic structure of knowledge acquired from discourse. *Cognitive Psychology* 7:371–458.

Frederiksen, C. H. 1979. Discourse comprehension and early reading. In *Theory and Practice of Early Reading*, eds. L. B. Resnick and P. A. Weaver. Vol. 1. Hillsdale, NJ: Lawrence Erlbaum and Associates.

Frederiksen, N. 1984. Implications of cognitive theory for instruction in problem solving. *Review of Educational Research* 54:363–407.

Fry, E. B. 1969. The readability graph validated at primary levels. *The Reading Teacher* 22:534–38.

Fry, E. B. 1989. Reading formulas—maligned but valid. *Journal of Reading* 42:292–97.

Gabrys, R. E. 1979, April. Training teachers to be businesslike and warm. Paper presented to the annual meeting of the American Educational Research Association, San Francisco.

Gall, M. D. 1984. Synthesis of research on questioning in recitation. *Educational Leadership* 42:40–47.

Gambrell, L. B. 1985. Dialogue journals: Reading-writing interaction. *The Reading Teacher* 38: 512–15.

Gambrell, L. D., and Bales, R. J. 1986. Mental imagery and the comprehension monitoring performance of fourth-and fifth-grade poor readers. *Reading Research Quarterly* 21:454–64.

Garner, R. 1987. *Metacognition and Reading Comprehension.* Norwood, NJ: Ablex.

Garner, R., and Kraus, C. 1981–1982. Good and poor comprehender differences in knowing and regulating reading behaviors. *Educational Research Quarterly* 6:5–12.

Garner, R., Wagoner, S., and Smith, T. 1983. Externalizing question-answering strategies of good and poor comprehenders. *Reading Research Quarterly* 18:439–47.

Garrison, J. W., and Hoskisson, K. 1989. Confirmation bias in predictive reading. *The Reading Teacher* 42:482–86.

Gates, A. I., and Bennett, C. C. 1933. *Reversal Tendencies in Reading: Causes, Diagnosis, Prevention, and Correction.* New York: Bureau of Publications. Teachers College, Columbia University.

Gates, A. I., and Russell, D. H. 1938. Types of materials, vocabulary burden, word analysis and other factors in beginning reading. *Elementary School Journal* 39:27–35, 119–28.

Gatlin, E. 1974. The extent of the relationship between the maturity of oral and written extemporaneous compositions in the language of community college freshman. Doctoral dissertation, University of South Carolina 1974. *Dissertation Abstracts International* 35:6534A.

Gavelek, J. R. 1984. The social contexts of literacy and schooling: A developmental perspective. In *The Contexts of School-Based Literacy,* ed. T. E. Raphael. New York: Random House.

Gay, L. R. 1987. *Educational Research.* Columbus, OH: Merrill.

Gentile, L. M., and McMillan, M. M. 1988. Reexamining the role of emotional maladjustment. In *Reexamining Reading Diagnosis: New Trends and Procedures,* eds. S. M. Glazer, L. W. Searfoss, and L. M. Gentile. Newark, DE: International Reading Association.

Gibson, E. J., and Levin, H. 1975. *The Psychology of Reading.* Cambridge, MA: MIT Press.

Gillet, J. W., and Temple, C. 1982. *Understanding Reading Problems.* Boston: Little, Brown and Company.

Gillet, J. W., and Temple, C. 1986. *Understanding Reading Problems.* Second Edition. Boston: Little, Brown and Company.

Gipe, J. P. 1978–1979. Investigating techniques for teaching word meanings. *Reading Research Quarterly* 14:624–44.

Glazer, S. M., and Searfoss, L. W. 1988. Reexamining reading diagnosis. In *Reexamining Reading Diagnosis: New Trends and Procedures,* eds. S. M. Glazer, L. W. Searfoss, and L. M. Gentile. Newark, DE: International Reading Association.

Goetz, E. T., Schallert, D. L., Reynolds, R. E., and Radin, D. I. 1983. Reading in perspective: What real cops and pretend burglars look for in a story. *Journal of Educational Psychology* 75:500–510.

Golinkoff, R. 1975–1976. Comprehension in good and poor readers. *Reading Research Quarterly* 4:623–59.

Goluh, I., and Frederick, W. C. 1971. *Linguistic Structures in the Discourse of Fourth and Sixth Graders.* Tech. Rep. No. 166. Madison: University of Wisconsin, Wisconsin Research and Development Center for Cognitive Learning.

Good, T. L. 1987. Teacher expectations. In *Talks to Teachers,* eds. D. C. Berliner and B. V. Rosenshine. New York: Random House.

Good, T. L., Grouws, D. A., and Beckerman, T. M. 1978. Curriculum pacing: Some empirical data in mathematics. *Journal of Curriculum Studies* 10:75–82.

Goodman, K. S. 1973. Dialect barriers to reading comprehension. In *Language, Society and Education: A Profile of Black English,* ed. J. S. DeStephano. 265–275. Worthington, OH: Charles A. Jones.

Goodman, K. S. 1976. Reading: A psycholinguistic guessing game. *Journal of the Reading Specialist* 4:126–35.

Goodman, K. S. 1982. Behind the eye: What happens in reading. With O. S. Niles. In *Language and Literacy: The Selected Writings of Kenneth S. Goodman* Vol. 2., ed. F. V. Gollasch. London: Routledge and Kegan Paul. [Originally published in *Reading Process and Program,* eds. K. S. Goodman and O. S. Niles. Urbana: National Council of Teachers of English, Commission on the English Curriculum, 1970.]

Goodman, K. S. 1984. Unity in reading. In *Becoming Readers in a Complex Society,* eds. A. Purves and O. Niles. Eighty-third yearbook of the National Society for the Study of Education Part I, 79–114. Chicago: University of Chicago Press.

Goodman, K. S., and Gespass, S. 1983. *Text Features as They Relate to Miscues: Pronouns.* Research Report No. 7. Program in Language and Literacy. Tucson, AZ: University of Arizona, Arizona Center for Research and Development.

Goodman, K. S., and Goodman, Y. M. 1978. *Reading of American Children Whose Language is a Stable Rural Dialect of English or a Language Other than English.* U.S. Dept. of HEW, Project NIE-C-00-3-0087, Final Report.

Goodman, K. S., Shannon, P., Freeman, Y. S. and Murphy, S. 1988. *Report Card on Basal Readers.* Katonah, NY: Richard C. Owen.

Gordon, A. 1961. The alchemist's secret. *Tactics.* Glenview, IL: Scott Foresman.

Gordon, C. J. 1989. Teaching narrative text structure: A process approach to reading and writing. In *Children's Comprehension of Text*, ed. K. D. Muth. Newark, DE: International Reading Association.

Gordon, C. J., and Braun, C. 1982. Story schemata: Metatextual aid to reading and writing. In *New Inquiries in Reading: Research and Instruction*, eds. J. A. Niles and L. A. Harris. Rochester, NY: National Reading Conference.

Gordon, C., and Braun, C. 1983. Using story schema as an aid to reading and writing. *The Reading Teacher* 37:116–20.

Gordon, C., and Pearson, P. D. 1983. *The Effects of Instruction in Metacomprehension and Inferencing on Children's Comprehension Abilities.* (Tech. Rep. No. 277) Urbana: Center for the Study of Reading, University of Illinois.

Gottsdanker-Willekens, A. E. 1986. Anaphoric reference instruction: Current instructional practices. In *Understanding and Teaching Cohesion Comprehension*, ed. J. W. Irwin. Newark, DE: International Reading Association.

Gough, P. B. 1972. One second of reading. In *Language by Ear and by Eye*, eds. J. F. Kavanagh and I. G. Mattingly. Cambridge, MA: MIT Press.

Gough, P. B., and Hillinger, M. L. 1980. Learning to read: An unnatural act. *Bulletin of The Orton Society* 30:171–76.

Graves, D. H. 1978. *Balance the Basics: Let Them Write.* New York: Ford Foundation.

Graves, D. H. 1983. *Writing: Teachers and Children at Work.* Portsmouth, NH: Heinemann.

Graves, D. H. 1984. A discription of procedures for the study. In *Teacher Change: Reading and Writing*, (chair) J. Hansen. Symposium presented at the National Reading Conference.

Graves, M. F. 1984. Selecting vocabulary to teach in the intermediate and secondary grades. In *Promoting Reading Comprehension*, ed. J. Flood. Newark, DE: International Reading Association.

Guido, B., and Colwell, C. G. 1987. A rationale for direct instruction to teach summary writing following expository text reading. *Reading Research and Instruction* 26:89–98.

Guszak, F. J. 1967. Teacher questioning and reading. *The Reading Teacher* 21:227–34.

Guthrie, J. T. 1973. Reading comprehension and syntactic responses in good and poor readers. *Journal of Educational Psychology* 65:294–99.

Halff, H. M., Ortony, A. and Anderson, R. C. 1976. A context-sensitive representation of word meaning. *Memory and Cognition* 4:378–83.

Haller, E. P., Child, D. A., and Walberg, H. J. 1988. Can comprehension be taught? A quantitative synthesis of "metacognitive" studies. *Educational Researcher* 17:5–8.

Halliday, M. A. K. 1975. *Learning How to Mean: Explorations in the Development of Language.* London: Edward Arnold.

Halliday, M. A. K. 1980. Cohesion and Register. Paper presented at the meeting of the American Educational Research Association, Boston.

Halliday, M. A. K. 1987. Spoken and written modes of meaning. In *Comprehending Oral and Written Language*, eds. R. Horowitz and S. J. Samuels. San Diego: Academic Press.

Halliday, M. A. K., and Hasan, R. 1976. *Cohesion in English.* London: Longman.

Hammill, D., and Bartel, N. 1975. *Teaching Children with Learning and Behavior Problems.* Boston: Allyn and Bacon.

Haney, W. 1985. Making testing more educational. *Educational Leadership* 43:4–13.

Hanf, M. B. 1971. Mapping, a technique for translating reading into thinking. *Journal of Reading* 14:225–30.

Hansen, J. 1981. The effect of inference training and practice on young children's reading comprehension. *Reading Research Quarterly* 16:391–417.

Hansen, J. 1984. Learners work together. In *The Contexts of School-Based Literacy*, ed. T. E. Raphael. New York: Random House.

Hansen, J. 1987. *When Writers Read.* Portsmouth, NH: Heinemann.

Hansen, J., and Hubbard, R. 1984. Poor readers can draw inferences. *The Reading Teacher* 37:586–89.

Hansen, J., and Pearson, P. D. 1983. An instructional study: Improving the inferential comprehension of good and poor fourth-grade readers. *Journal of Educational Psychology* 75:821–29.

Harrell, L. E., Jr. 1957. A comparison of the development of oral and written language in school-age children. *Monographs of the Society for Research in Child Development* 22:5–77.

Harris, A. J., and Jacobson, M. D. 1976. Predicting twelfth-graders' comprehension scores. *Journal of Reading* 20:43–46.

Harris, A. J., and Sipay, E. R. 1985. *How to Increase Reading Ability*. New York: Longman.

Harste, J., and Mickulecky, L. 1984. The content of literacy in our society. In *Becoming Readers in a Complex Society*, eds. A. Purves and O. Niles. Eighty-third yearbook of the National Society for the Study of Education. Chicago: University of Chicago Press.

Hayes, J. R., and Flower, L. S. J. 1983. Uncovering cognitive processes in writing: An introduction to protocol analysis. In *Research on Writing: Principles and Methods*, eds. P. Mosenthal, L. Tamor, and S. A. Walmsley. New York: Longman.

Hayes, M. S., and Jenkins, J. R. 1986. Reading instruction in special education resource rooms. *American Educational Research Journal* 23:161–90.

Heath, S. B. 1983. *Ways With Words*. New York: Cambridge University Press.

Heimlich, J. E., and Pittelman, S. D. 1986. *Semantic Mapping: Classroom Applications*. Newark, DE: International Reading Association.

Hess, R. D., and Shipman, V. 1968. Maternal influences upon early learning. In *Early Education*, eds. R. D. Hess and R. M. Bear. 91–103. Chicago: Aldine.

Hidi, S., and Baird, W. 1983, November. Types of information saliency in school texts and their effects on children's recall. Paper presented at the National Reading Conference, Austin, TX.

Hiebert, E. H. 1983. An examination of ability grouping in reading instruction. *Reading Research Quarterly* 18:231–55.

Hill, P., and Kimbrough, J. 1981. The aggregate effects of federal education programs. The Rand Publications Series. Santa Monica, CA: Rand Corporation.

Hill, C. L., and Hill, K. A. 1982. Achievement attributions of learning-disabled boys. *Psychological Reports* 51:979–82.

Hinshelwood, J. 1917. *Congenital Word Blindness*. London: H. K. Lewis.

Holmes, B. C., and Roser, N. L. 1987. Five ways to assess readers' prior knowledge. *The Reading Teacher* 40:646–49.

Hood, L., and Bloom, L. 1979. What, when and how about why: A longitudinal study of early expressions of causality. *Monographs of the Society for Research in Child Development* 44:1–47.

Hornsby, D., Sukarna, D., and Parry, J. 1986. *Read On: A Conference Approach to Reading*. Portsmouth, NH: Heinemann.

Horowitz, R. 1985. Text patterns: Part I and Part II. *Journal of Reading* 28:448–54, 534–41.

Horowitz, R. 1987. Rhetorical structure in discourse processing. In *Comprehending Oral and Written Language*, eds. R. Horowitz and S. J. Samuels. New York: Academic Press.

Horowitz, R. 1988. Teaching text patterns: Issues, problems and prospects. Paper presented at the National Reading Conference, Tucson, AZ.

Horowitz, R., and Samuels, S. J. 1987. Comprehending oral and written language: Critical contrasts for literacy and schooling. In *Comprehending Oral and Written Language*, eds. R. Horowitz and S. J. Samuels. San Diego: Academic Press.

Huey, E. B. 1908. *The Psychology and Pedagogy of Reading*. New York: Macmillan (Reprinted Cambridge, MA: The MIT Press, 1968.)

Hunt, L. 1970. The effect of self-selection, interest, and motivation upon independent, instructional and frustrational levels. *The Reading Teacher* 24:146–51.

Idol-Maestas, I., and Croll, V. J. 1985. *The Effects of Training in Story Mapping Procedures on the Reading Comprehension of Poor Readers*. (Technical Report Number 352) Urbana: Center for the Study of Reading, University of Illinois.

Irwin, J. W. 1980. The effects of explicitness and clause order on the comprehension of reversible causal relationships. *Reading Research Quarterly* 15:477–88.

Irwin, J. W., and Pulver, C. 1984. The effects of explicitness, clause order and reversibility on children's comprehension of causal relationships. *Journal of Educational Psychology* 76:399–407.

Irwin, P. A., and Mitchell. *The Reader Retelling Profile: Using Retellings to Make Instructional Decisions*. in preparation.

Jarvella, R. J. 1971. Syntactic processing of connected speech. *Journal of Verbal Learning and Verbal Behavior* 10:409–16.

Jerrolds, R. W. 1985. The advance organizer: Its nature and use. In *Reading, Thinking and Concept Development*, eds. T. L. Harris and E. J. Cooper. New York: College Entrance Examination Board.

Jervis, K. 1989. Daryl takes a test. *Educational Leadership* 46:10–15.

Johns, J. L. 1988. *Basic Reading Inventory*, 4th ed. Dubuque, IA: Kendall Hunt.

Johnson, D., and Myklebust, H. R. 1967. *Learning Disabilities: Educational Principles and Practices.* New York: Grune and Stratton.

Johnson, D. D., Toms-Bronowski, S., and Pittelman, S. D. 1984. *An Investigation of the Effectiveness of Semantic Mapping and Semantic Feature Analysis with Intermediate Grade Level Children* (Program Report 83.3) Madison, WI: Wisconsin Center for Educational Research, University of Wisconsin.

Johnson, D. W., Johnson, R. T., Holubec, E. J., and Roy, P. 1984. *Circles of Learning: Cooperation in the Classroom.* Alexandria, VA: Association for Supervision and Curriculum Development.

Johnson, R. H. 1965. Individualized and basal primary reading programs. *Elementary English* 42:902–904.

Johnson, T. D., and Louis, D. R. 1987. *Literacy Through Literature.* Portsmouth, NH: Heinemann.

Johnston, P. H. 1983. *Reading Comprehension Assessment: A Cognitive Basis.* Newark, DE: International Reading Association.

Johnston, P. H. 1984. Assessment in reading. In *Handbook of Reading Research*, ed. P. D. Pearson. New York: Longman.

Johnston, P. H. 1985. Understanding reading disability: A case study approach. *Harvard Educational Review* 58:153–77.

Johnston, P. H., and Winograd, P. N. 1985. Passive failure in reading. *Journal of Reading Behavior* 17:279–99.

Jones, B. F. 1986. Quality and equality through cognitive instruction. *Educational Leadership* 44: 5–9.

Jones, B. F., Palincsar, A. S., Ogle, D. S., and Carr, E. G. 1987. *Strategic Teaching and Learning: Cognitive Instruction in the Content Areas.* Alexandria, VA: Association for Supervision and Curriculum Development.

Jones, B. F., Pierce, J., and Hunter, B. 1988–1989. Teaching children to construct graphic representations. *Educational Leadership* 46:20–25.

Keenan, D. 1982. An evaluation of the effectiveness of selected readability formulas applied to secondary texts. *Reading Horizons* 22:123–28.

Kierstead, J. 1986. How teachers manage individual and small-group work in active classrooms. *Educational Leadership* 44:22–25.

Kimmel, S., and MacGinitie, W. H. 1984. Identifying children who use a perseverative text processing strategy. *Reading Research Quarterly* 19:162–72.

King, A. V., Dennis, I., and Patter, F. 1980. *The United States and the Other Americas, senior authors N. Marshall and J. Jarolimek.* New York: Macmillan.

Kintsch, W. 1974. *The Representation of Meaning in Memory.* Hillsdale, NJ: Lawrence Erlbaum and Associates.

Kintsch, W. 1979. On modeling comprehension. *Educational Psychologist* 14:3–14.

Kintsch, W. 1986. Learning from text. *Cognition and Instruction* 3:87–108.

Kintsch, W., and Miller, J. R. 1984. Readability: A view from cognitive psychology. In *Understanding Reading Comprehension*, ed. J. Flood. Newark: DE: International Reading Association.

Kintsch, W., and van Dijk, T. 1978. Toward a model of text comprehension and production. *Psychological Review* 85:363–94.

Kintsch, W., and Vipond, D. 1979. Reading comprehension and readability in educational practice and psychological theory. In *Perspectives on Memory Research*, ed. L. G. Nilsson. Hillsdale, NJ: Lawrence Erlbaum and Associates.

Kintsch, W., and Yarbrough, J. C. 1982. Role of rhetorical structure in text comprehension. *Journal of Educational Psychology* 74:828–34.

Kirby, D., and Liner, T. 1981. *Inside Out.* New York: Boynton-Cook.

Klare, G. R. 1984. Readability. In *Handbook of Reading Research*, ed. P. D. Pearson. New York: Longman.

Klare, G. R. 1985. Matching reading material to readers: The role of readability estimates in conjunction with other information about comprehensibility. In *Reading, Thinking and Concept*

Development, eds. T. L. Harris and E. J. Cooper. 233–56. New York: College Entrance Examination Board.

Klare, G. R. 1988. The formative years. In *Readability: Its Past, Present and Future*, eds. B. L. Zakaluk and S. J. Samuels. Newark, DE: International Reading Association.

Kounin, J. S. 1970. *Discipline and Group Management in Classrooms*. New York: Holt, Rinehart, and Winston.

Krasilovsky, P. 1957. *The Cow Who Fell in the Canal*. New York: Harper and Row.

Kraus, C. 1983. The influence of first-grade teachers' conceptual frameworks of reading on their students' perceptions of reading and reading behavior. Ph.D. dissertation, Kent State University.

La Berge, D., and Samuels, S. J. 1974. Toward a theory of automatic information processing. *Cognitive Psychology* 6:293–323.

Lambert, W. E., and Macnamara, J. 1969. Some cognitive consequences of following a first-grade curriculum in a second language. *Journal of Educational Psychology* 60:86–96.

Lambert, W. E., and Tucker, G. R. 1972. *The St. Lambert Program of Home-School Language Switch, Grades K through 5*. Montreal: McGill University.

Lambert, W. E., Just, M., and Segalowitz, N. 1970. Some cognitive consequences of following the curricula of the early school grades in a foreign language. In *21st Annual Roundtable*, ed. J. Alatis. Washington, DC: Georgetown University Press.

Langer, J. A. 1982. Facilitating text processing: The elaboration of prior knowledge. In *Reader Meets Author: Bridging the Gap*, eds. J. A. Langer and M. Smith-Burke. Newark, DE: International Reading Association.

Langer, J. A. 1984. Examining background knowledge and text comprehension. *Reading Research Quarterly* 4:468–81.

Langer, J. A. 1987. The construction of meaning and the assessment of comprehension: An analysis of reader performance on standardized test items. In *Cognition and Linguistic Analyses of Standardized Test Items*, ed. R. Freedle. Norwood, NJ: Ablex.

Language Arts, Dec. 1984. NCTE and IRA presidents take stand on misuse of readability formulas. 61:883–4.

Larkin, J. 1983. Research on science education. In *Computers in Education: Realizing the Potential*, eds. A. M. Lesgold and F. Reif. Washington, D.C.: Office of the Assistant Secretary for Educational Research and Improvement.

Larkin, J. H., McDermott, J., Simon, D. P., and Simon, H. A. 1980. Models of competence in solving physics problems. *Cognitive Science* 4:317–45.

Lauber, P. 1959. *Our Friend the Forest*. New York: Doubleday.

La Shell, L. 1986. Matching reading styles triples reading achievement of learning disabled students. *The Clearinghouse Bulletin on Learning/Teaching Styles and Brain Behavior* 1(i):4.

Leaf, M. 1936. *Ferdinand*. New York: Puffin Books.

Lee, D. M., and Rubin, J. B. 1979. *Children and Language*. Belmont, CA: Wadsworth.

Lehr, S. 1988. The child's developing sense of theme as a response to literature. *Reading Research Quarterly* 23:337–57.

Lerner, J. 1985. *Learning Disabilities*. Fourth Edition. Boston: Houghton Mifflin.

Lesgold, A. M. 1974. Variability in children's comprehension of syntactic structures. *Journal of Educational Psychology* 3:333–38.

Liberman, A. M., Cooper, F. S., Shankweiler, D., and Studdert-Kennedy, M. 1967. Perception of the speech code. *Psychological Review* 74:431–61.

Liberman, I. Y., Shankweiler, D., Camp, L., Heifetz, B., and Werfelman, M. 1980. Steps toward literacy. *Auditory Processing and Language: Clinical and Research Perspectives*, eds. P. Levinson and C. H. Sloan. New York: Grune and Stratton.

Lindemann, E. 1982. *A Rhetoric for Writing Teachers*. New York: Oxford University Press.

Lipson, M. Y., Bigler, M., Poth, L., and Wixkizer, B. A. 1987, December. Instructional applications of a verbal report methodology: The effects of thinking aloud on comprehension ability. Paper presented at the National Reading Conference, St. Petersburg, FL.

Loban, W. 1976. *Language Development: Kindergarten Through Grade Twelve*. Urbana, IL: National Council of Teachers of English.

Lobel, A. 1970. *Frog and Toad are Friends*. New York: Harper and Row.

Lull, H. G. 1929. The speaking and writing abilities of intermediate-grade pupils. *Journal of Educational Research* 20:73–77.

Lundeberg, M. A. 1987. Metacognitive aspects of reading comprehension. Studying understanding in legal case analysis. *Reading Research Quarterly* 22:407–32.

Lynch, P. 1988, September. Workshop presented to Chapter I teachers in New York City District 3, New York.

Lytle, S. 1982. *Exploring Comprehension Style: A Study of Twelfth-Grade Readers' Transactions with Text.* Ann Arbor, MI: University Microfilm.

MacGinitie, W. H. 1979. What do published comprehension lessons teach. *Proceedings, Reading '79.* Toronto: York University.

MacGinitie, W. H. 1984. Readability as a solution adds to the problem. In *Learning to Read in American Schools: Basal Readers and Content Texts,* eds. R. C. Anderson, J. Osborn, and R. J. Tierney. Hillsdale NJ: Lawrence Erlbaum and Associates.

MacGinitie, W. H. 1989, March. Reading: What should be assessed? Paper presented to the meeting of the Washington Educational Research Association. Bellevue, WA.

MacGinitie, W. H., and MacGinitie, R. K. 1989. *Gates-MacGinitie Reading Tests: Manual for Scoring and Interpretation—Level 4.* Third Edition. Chicago, IL: The Riverside Publishing Company.

MacGinitie, W. H., Katz, S., and Maria, K. 1980. Report of the Reading Comprehension task force Section I. Progress report of the research institute for the study of learning disabilities. New York: Teachers College, Columbia University.

Madaus, G. F. 1985. Test scores as administrative mechanisms in educational policy. *Phi Delta Kappan* 66:611–18.

Mandel, P. D. 1979. The mountain of tears. In *The Spirit of the Wind,* ed. Z. Sutherland. LaSalle, IL: Open Court Publishing Company.

Mandler, J. M., and Johnson, N. S. 1977a. The use of a child's own language to test reading achievement in first grade. Unpublished master's thesis. Monterey Institute of Foreign Studies.

Mandler, J., and Johnson, N. 1977b. Remembrance of things passed: Story structure and recall. *Cognitive Psychology* 9:111–51.

Manzo, A. V. 1968. Improving reading comprehension through reciprocal questioning. Unpublished doctoral dissertation, Syracuse University.

Manzo, A. V. 1969. The ReQuest procedure. *Journal of Reading* 2:123–26.

Manzo, A. V., and Legenza, A. 1975. Inquiry training for kindergarten children. *Educational Leadership* 32:479–83.

Manzo, A. V., and Shirk, J. K. 1972. Some generalizations and strategies for guiding vocabulary learning. *Journal of Reading Behavior* 4:78–89.

Maratsos, M. 1974. When is a high thing the big one? *Developmental Psychology* 10:367–75.

Maria, K. 1987, October. Reading and summarizing difficult texts: Are teachers experts? Paper presented at the meeting of the College Reading Association, Baltimore.

Maria, K. 1988, May. Metacognitive training for teachers. Paper presented at the conference of the International Reading Association, Toronto.

Maria, K. 1988, October. Length, constraint and purpose as factors in teacher summaries. Paper presented at the meeting of the College Reading Association, Atlanta.

Maria, K. 1988, December. Helping fifth graders learn with science text. Paper presented at the National Reading Conference, Tucson, AZ.

Maria, K. 1989. Developing disadvantaged children's background knowledge interactively. *The Reading Teacher* 42:296–300.

Maria, K., and MacGinitie, W. H. 1982a. Progress report of the research institute for the study of learning disabilities. New York: Teachers College, Columbia University, 1980.

Maria, K., and MacGinitie, W. H. 1982b. Reading comprehension disabilities: Knowledge structures and non-accommodating text processing strategies. *Annals of Dyslexia* 32:33–59.

Maria, K., and MacGinitie, W. H. 1987. Learning from texts that refute the reader's prior knowledge. *Reading Research and Instruction* 26:222–38.

Marino, J. L., Gould, S. M., and Haas, L. W. 1985. The effects of writing as a prereading activity on delayed recall of narrative text. *Elementary School Journal* 86:199–205.

Markham, E. M. 1981. Comprehension monitoring. In *Children's Oral Communication Skills,* ed. W. P. Dickson. New York: Academic Press.

Marshall, N. 1983. Using story grammar to assess reading comprehension. *The Reading Teacher* 36:176–79.

Marshall, N. 1987, December. When text fails to meet reader expectations... Paper presented at the National Reading Conference, St. Petersburg, FL.

Mattingly, I. 1972. Reading, the linguistic process and linguistic awareness. In *Language by Ear and Eye,* eds. J. Kavanagh and I. Mattingly. Cambridge, MA: MIT Press.

REFERENCES

May, F. B. 1986. *Reading as Communication: An Interactive Approach.* Second edition. Columbus, OH: Merrill.

Maya, A. Y. 1979. Write to read: Improving reading through creative writing. *The Reading Teacher* 32:813–17.

Mazar, B. W. 1986. *Primary phonics.* Cambridge, MA: Educators Publishing Company.

McCall, W. A., and Crabbs, L. M. 1925, revised 1950, revised 1961. *Standard Test Lessons in Reading.* New York: Bureau of Publications, Teachers College, Columbia University.

McConaughy, S. H. 1980. Using story structure in the classroom. *Language Arts* 57:157–65.

McCormick, S. 1987. *Remedial and Clinical Reading Instruction.* Columbus, OH: Merrill.

McDonnell, T. R. 1963. Suggestibility in children as a function of chronological age. *Journal of Abnormal and Social Psychology* 67:286–89.

McGee, L. M. 1982. Awareness of text structure: Effects on children's recall of expository text. *Reading Research Quarterly* 17:581–90.

McGee, L. M., and Richgels, D. J. 1985. Teaching expository text structures to elementary students. *The Reading Teacher* 38:739–48.

McGill-Franzen, A., and Allington, R. L. in press. Comprehension and coherence: Neglected elements of literacy instruction in remedial and resource room services. *Journal of Reading, Writing and Learning Disability.*

McGovern, A. 1986. *Stone Soup.* New York: Scholastic.

McKeown, M., Beck, I., Omanson, R., and Pople, M. 1985. Some effects of the nature and frequency of vocabulary instruction on the knowledge and use of words. *Reading Research Quarterly* 20:222–35.

McLachlan, P. 1985. *Sarah Plain and Tall.* New York: Harper and Row.

McNeil, J. D. 1984. *Reading Comprehension: New Directions in Classroom Practice.* Glenview, IL: Scott Foresman.

McNeil, J. D. 1987. *Reading Comprehension: New Directions for Classroom Practice.* Glenview, IL: Scott Foresman.

Medley, D. 1977. *Teacher Competence and Teacher Effectiveness.* Washington, DC: American Association of Colleges for Teacher Education EO 143 629.

Meichenbaum, D., and Asarnow, J. 1978. Cognitive behavioral modification and metacognitive development: Implications for the classroom. In *Cognitive Behavioral Interventions: Theory, Research and Procedure,* eds P. Kendall and S. Hollon. New York: Academic Press.

Menyuk, P., and Flood, J. 1981. Linguistic competence, reading, writing problems and remediation. *Bulletin of The Orton Society* 31:13–29.

Meyer, L. 1985. *Strategies for Correcting Students' Wrong Responses.* (Tech. Rep. No. 354) Urbana: Center for the Study of Reading, University of Illinois.

Meyer, B. J. F., and Freedle, R. O. 1984. Effects of discourse type on recall. *American Educational Research Journal* 21:121–43.

Meyer, B. J. F., Brandt, D. M., and Bluth, G. J. 1980. Use of top level structure in text: Key for reading comprehension of ninth-grade students. *Reading Research Quarterly* 16:72–103.

Meyers, J., and Zinar, S. 1979. Cognitive styles in reading comprehension and picture interpretation. Unpublished manuscript.

Miller, G. A., and Gildea, P. M. 1985. How to misread a dictionary. Unpublished manuscript. Princeton, NJ: Princeton University.

Moberly, P. C. 1978. Elementary children's understanding of anaphoric relationships in connected discourse. Unpublished doctoral dissertation, Northwestern University.

Moe, A. J., and Irwin, J. W. 1986. Cohesion, coherence and comprehension. In *Understanding and Teaching Cohesion Comprehension,* ed. J. W. Irwin. Newark, DE: International Reading Association.

Moffett, J., and Wagner, B. 1983. *Student-Centered Language Arts and Reading: K–13,* 3rd Edition. Boston: Houghton Mifflin.

Monson, D. 1982. Effect of type and direction on comprehension of anaphoric relationships. Paper presented at the International Reading Association WORD Research Conference, Seattle, WA.

Moore, D. W., and Readence, J. E. 1980. Processing main ideas through parallel lesson transfer. *Journal of Reading* 23:589–93.

Morine-Dershimer, G., and Beyerbach, B. 1987. Moving right along... In *Educators' Handbook: A Research Perspective,* ed. V. Richardson-Koehler. New York: Longman.

Morningforest, C. 1978. Turtle tale. *Ranger Rick* 12:4–6.

Morrow, L. M. 1987. Promoting intercity children's recreational reading. *The Reading Teacher* 41:266–75.

Morrow, L. M. 1988. Retelling stories as a diagnostic tool. In *Reexamining Reading Diagnosis: New Trends and Procedures*, eds. S. M. Glazer, L. W. Searfoss, and L. M. Gentile. Newark, DE: International Reading Association.

Morrow, L. M. 1989. Using story retelling to develop comprehension. In *Children's Comprehension of Text*, ed. K. D. Muth. Newark, DE: International Reading Association.

Myers, M., and Paris, S. G. 1978. Children's metacognitive knowledge about reading. *Journal of Educational Psychology* 70:680–90.

Nagy, W. E. 1988. *Teaching Vocabulary to Improve Reading Comprehension*. Newark, DE: International Reading Association.

Nagy, W. E., and Anderson, R. C. 1984. How many words are there in printed school English? *Reading Research Quarterly* 19:304–30.

Nagy, W. E., Anderson, R. C., and Herman, P. 1987. Learning word meanings from context during normal reading. *American Educational Research Journal* 24:237–70.

National Joint Committee on Learning Disabilities. 1981. Learning disabilities: Issues on definition. Unpublished manuscript. The Orton Dyslexia Society, Towson, MD.

National Joint Committee on Learning Disabilities and the Preschool Child. 1986. A position paper of the National Joint Committee on Learning Disabilities. *Learning Disability Quarterly* 9:156–63.

Nelson-Herber, J., and Johnston, C. S. 1989. Questions and concerns about teaching narrative and expository text. In *Children's Comprehension of Text*, ed. K. D. Muth. Newark, DE: International Reading Association.

Nessel, D. 1987. Reading comprehension: Asking the right questions. *Phi Delta Kappan* 68:442–45.

Nessel, D. 1988. Channeling knowledge for reading expository text. *Journal of Reading* 41:231–35.

Newcomer, P., and Magee, P. 1977. The performance of learning (reading) disabled children on a test of spoken language. *The Reading Teacher* 30:896–900.

Newsweek December 8, 1975. Why Johnny Can't Write.

Niemeyer, M. 1976. The mystery of the moon guitar. In *Medley*, eds. W. K. Durr, V. O. Windley, and A. A. McCourt. Boston: Houghton Mifflin.

Niles, J. A., and Harris, L. A. 1981. The context of comprehension. *Reading Horizons* 22:33–42.

Niles, O. 1964. Organization perceived. In *Developing Study Skills in Secondary Schools*, ed. H. Herber. Newark, DE: International Reading Association.

Nix, D. 1981. Links: A method for teaching reading comprehension. In *Comprehension and the Competent Reader*, eds. D. F. Fisher and C. W. Peters. New York: Praeger.

Nolte, R. Y., and Singer, H. 1985. Active comprehension: Teaching a process of reading comprehension and its effects on reading achievement. *The Reading Teacher* 39:24–31.

Noyce, R. M., and Christie, J. F. 1983. Effects of an integrated approach to grammar instruction on third graders' reading and writing. *Elementary School Journal* 84:63–69.

Noyce, R. M., and Christie, J. F. 1989. *Integrating Reading and Writing Instruction in Grades K–8*. Boston: Allyn and Bacon.

Nussbaum, J., and Novick, S. 1976. An assessment of children's conceptions of the earth using structured interviews. *Science Education* 60:535–50.

O'Donnell, R., Griffin, W. J., and Norris, R. C. 1967. *Syntax of Kindergarten and Elementary School Children: A Transformational Analysis*. Research Rep. No. 8. Urbana, IL: National Council of Teachers of English.

Ogle, D. M. 1986a. K—W—L: A teaching model that develops active reading of expository text. *The Reading Teacher* 39:564–70.

Ogle, D. M. 1986b. *Know—Want—Learn K—W—L*. (Manual accompanying videotape entitled *Teaching Reading as Thinking*.) Alexandria, VA: Association for Supervision and Curriculum Development.

Ogle, D. M. 1989. The know—want to know—learn strategy. In *Children's Comprehension of Text*, ed. K. D. Muth. Newark, DE: International Reading Association.

Ohlhausen, M. M., and Roller, C. M. 1986. Teaching students to use a nation schema to learn about countries. *Journal of Reading* 30:212–17.

Olshavsky, J. E. 1976–1977. Reading as problem solving: An investigation of strategies. *Reading Research Quarterly* 12:654–75.

Olson, D. R. 1977. From utterance to text: The bias of language in speech and writing. *Harvard Educational Review* 47:257–81.

Orton, S. T. 1928. Specific reading disability—Strephosymbolia. *Journal of the American Medical Association* 90:1095–1099.

Osborn, J. H., Jones, B. F., and Stein, M. 1985. The case for improving textbooks. *Educational Leadership* 42:9–16.

Owens, R. E. 1984. *Language Development*. Columbus, OH: Merrill.

Palincsar, A. S. 1984, April. Reciprocal teaching: Working within the zone of proximal development. Paper presented at the annual meeting of the American Educational Research Association, New Orleans.

Palincsar, A. S. 1985. The unpacking of a multi-component, metacognitive training package. Paper presented at the annual conference of the American Educational Research Association, Chicago.

Palincsar, A. S. 1986a, April. Interactive cognition to promote listening comprehension. Paper presented at the annual conference of the American Educational Research Association, San Francisco.

Palincsar, A. S. 1986b. The role of dialogue in providing scaffolded instruction. *Educational Psychologist* 21:73–98.

Palincsar, A. S. 1986c. *Reciprocal Teaching*. (Manual accompanying videotape entitled *Teaching Reading as Thinking*.) Alexandria, VA: Association for Supervision and Curriculum Development.

Palincsar, A. S. 1987a, April. Collaborating for collaborative learning of text comprehension. Paper presented at the annual conference of the American Educational Research Association, Washington, DC.

Palincsar, A. S. 1987b, April. An apprenticeship approach to the instruction of comprehension skills. Paper presented as part of the symposium *Perspectives on Expert Learning: An Integrative Examination of Theoretical and Empirical Issues*, Washington, DC.

Palincsar, A. S., and Brown, A. L. 1982. *Reciprocal Teaching of Comprehension—Monitoring Activities*. (Tech. Rep. 269). Urbana, IL: University of Illinois Center for the Study of Reading.

Palincsar, A. S., and Brown, A. L. 1984. Reciprocal teaching of comprehension-fostering and comprehension-monitoring activities. *Cognition and Instruction* 1:117–75.

Palincsar, A. S., and Brown, A. L. 1985. Reciprocal teaching: Activities to promote "reading with your mind." In *Reading, Thinking and Concept Development*, eds. T. L. Harris and E. J. Cooper. New York: College Entrance Examination Board.

Palincsar, A. S., and Brown, A. L. 1989. Classroom dialogues to promote self-regulated comprehension. In *Teaching for Understanding and Self-Regulated Learning*, ed. J. Brophy. JAI Press.

Palincsar, A. S., Brown, A. L., and David, Y. M. (work in progress.) *Reciprocal Teaching: A Guide to Implementation*.

Paolo, M. F. 1977. A comparison of readability graph scores and oral reading errors on trade books for beginning reading. Unpublished master's thesis, New Brunswick, NJ: Rutgers—The State University of New Jersey.

Paris, S. G. 1978. Coordination of means and goals in the development of mnemonic skills. In *Memory Development in Children*, ed. P. A. Ornstein. Hillsdale, NJ: Lawrence Erlbaum and Associates.

Paris, S. G. 1988. *Reading and Thinking Strategies*. Lexington, MA: D. C. Heath.

Paris, S. G., and Jacobs, J. E. 1984. The benefits of informed instruction for children's reading awareness and comprehension skills. *Child Development* 55:2083–2093.

Paris, S. G., and Myers, M. 1981. Comprehension monitoring, memory and study strategies of good and poor readers. *Journal of Reading Behavior* 13:5–22.

Paris, S. G., Cross, D. R., and Lipson, M. Y. 1984. Informed strategies for learning: A program to improve children's reading awareness and comprehension. *Journal of Educational Psychology* 67:1239–1252.

Paris, S. G., Lipson, M. Y., and Wixson, K. K. 1983. Becoming a strategic reader. *Contemporary Educational Psychology* 8:293–316.

Paterson, K. 1977. *Bridge to Terabithia*. New York: Thomas J. Crowell.

Pearl, R., Bryan, T., and Donohue, M. 1980. Learning disabled children's attributions for success and failure. *Learning Disabilities Quarterly* 3:3–9.

Pearson, P. D. 1974–1975. The effects of grammatical complexity on children's comprehension, recall, and conception of certain semantic relations. *Reading Research Quarterly* 10:155–92.

Pearson, P. D. 1982. *Asking Questions About Stories*. Boston: Ginn.

Pearson, P. D. 1985. Changing the face of reading comprehension instruction. *The Reading Teacher* 38:724–38.

Pearson, P. D., and Gallagher, M. C. 1983. The instruction of reading comprehension. *Contemporary Educational Psychology* 8: 317–44.

Pearson, P. D., and Johnson, D. D. 1978. *Teaching Reading Comprehension.* New York: Holt, Rinehart, and Winston.

Pearson, P. D., and Spiro, R. J. 1981. Toward a theory of reading comprehension instruction. In *Reading Comprehension: Trends in Research and Teaching*, eds. L. J. Campbell and S. M. Grist. New Brunswick, NJ: The State University of New Jersey-New Brunswick.

Pearson, P. D., Hansen, J., and Gordon, C. 1979. The effect of background knowledge on young children's comprehension of explicit and implicit information. *Journal of Reading Behavior* 11:201–209.

Perfetti, C. A., Beck, I., and Hughes, C. 1981. Phonemic knowledge and learning to read. Paper presented at the meeting of the Society for Research in Child Development, Boston.

Phillips, J. M., and Zinar, S. 1979. Cohesion and readability: Cohesive ties in a basal reading series, grades 1–6. Unpublished manuscript.

Piaget, J. 1950. *The Psychology of Intelligence.* London: Routledge and Kegan Paul.

Piccolo, J. A. 1987. Expository text structure: Teaching and learning strategies. *The Reading Teacher* 40:838–47.

Pichert, J. W., and Anderson, R. C. 1977. Taking different perspectives on a story. *Journal of Educational Psychology* 69:309–15.

Pipho, C. 1985, May. Tracking the reforms, part 5: Testing—can it measure the success of the reform movement? *Education Week* 19.

Poeten, J. 1988. Workshop on whole language. Presented for the Furnace Woods School District, Peekskill, N.Y.

Pressley, M. 1977. Imagery and children's learning: Putting the picture in developmental perspective. *Review of Educational Research* 47:585–622.

Rauch, S., and Clements, Z. 1974. A city without roads. In *World of Vocabulary*. New York: Learning Trends.

Readence, J. E., Bean, T. W., and Baldwin, R. S. 1985. *Content Area Reading: An Integrated Approach.* Second Edition. Dubuque, Iowa: Kendall Hunt.

Reading Research Quarterly. 1981. Resolutions passed by Delegates Assembly-April 1981. 16:following 613.

Resnick, L. B., and Robinson, B. H. 1975. Motivational aspects of the literacy problem. In *Towards a Literate Society*, ed. J. B. Carroll. New York: McGraw-Hill.

Reutzel, D. R., and Hollingsworth, P. M. 1988. Highlighting key vocabulary: A generative reciprocal procedure for teaching selected inference types. *Reading Research Quarterly* 23: 358–78.

Reynolds, R. E., and Anderson, R. C. 1982. Influence of questions on the allocation of attention during reading. *Journal of Educational Psychology* 74:623–32.

Reynolds, R. E., Taylor, M. A., Steffensen, M. S., Shirey, L. L., and Anderson, R. C. 1982. Cultural schemata and reading comprehension. *Reading Research Quarterly* 17:353–66.

Rhodes, L. K., and Dudley-Marling, C. 1988. *Readers and Writers with a Difference.* Portsmouth, NH: Heinemann.

Richardson, G. E. 1982. *Educational Imagery.* Springfield, IL: Charles C Thomas.

Richek, M. A. 1988. Relating vocabulary learning to world knowledge. *Journal of Reading* 32:262–67.

Richgels, D. J., and McGee, L. M. 1988. Measurement and instruction in awareness of causation and comparison/contrast text structures. Paper presented at the National Reading Conference, Tucson, AZ.

Richgels, D. J., McGee, L. M., and Slaton, E. A. 1989. Teaching expository text structure in reading and writing. In *Children's Comprehension of Text*, ed. D. K. Muth. Newark, DE: International Reading Association.

Richgels, D. J., McGee, L. M., Lomax, R. G., and Sheard, C. 1987. Awareness of four text structures: Effects on recall of expository text. *Reading Research Quarterly* 22:177–96.

Rieck, B. J. 1977. How content teachers telegraph messages against reading. *Journal of Reading* 20:646–48.

Riese, A. W., and LaSalle, H. J. 1986. *The Middle Ages.* Cambridge, MA: Educators Publishing Service.

Ringler, L. H., and Weber, C. K. 1984. *A Language-Thinking Approach to Reading: Diagnosis and Teaching.* New York: Harcourt Brace Jovanovich.

Rist, R. C. 1970. Student social class and teacher expectations: The self-fulfilling prophecy in ghetto education. *Harvard Educational Review* 40:411–51.

Robinson, F. P. 1946. *Effective Study*. New York: Harper and Row.

Robinson, R., and Good, T. L. 1987. *Becoming an Effective Reading Teacher*. New York: Harper and Row.

Rockwell, T. 1973. *How to Eat Fried Worms*. New York: Dell.

Rodrigues, R. J. 1983. Tools for developing prewriting skills. *English Journal* 72:58–60.

Roeber, E., and Dutcher, P. 1989. Michigan's innovative assessment of reading. *Educational Leadership* 46:64–69.

Roehler, L. R., and Duffy, G. G. 1986. Studying qualitative dimensions of instructional effectiveness. In *The Effective Teacher of Reading: Research into Practice*, ed. J. Hoffman. Newark, DE: International Reading Association.

Roehler, L. R., Duffy, G. G., and Meloth, M. B. 1984. What to be direct about in direct instruction in reading: Content-only versus process-into-content. In *The Contexts of School-Based Literacy*, ed. T. E. Raphael. New York: Random House.

Rohwer, W. D. Jr. 1971. Prime time for education: Early childhood or adolescence? *Harvard Educational Review* 41:316–41.

Rosenblatt, L. M. 1989. Writing and reading: The transactional theory. In *Reading and Writing Connections*, ed. J. M. Mason. Boston: Allyn and Bacon.

Rosenshine, B. V. 1976. Classroom instruction. In *The Psychology of Teaching Methods*, ed. W. L. Gage. Chicago: University of Chicago Press.

Rosenshine, B. V. 1979. Content, time and direct instruction. In *Research on Teaching: Concepts, Findings and Implications*, eds. H. J. Walberg and P. L. Peterson. Berkeley, CA: McCutchan.

Rosenshine, B. V. 1987. Explicit teaching. In *Talks to Teachers*, eds. D. C. Berliner and B. V. Rosenshine. New York: Random House.

Rosenshine, B. V., and Stevens, R. 1984. Classroom instruction in reading. In *Handbook of Reading Research*, ed. P. D. Pearson. New York: Longman.

Rubin, H., and Liberman, I. Y. 1983. Exploring the oral and written language errors made by language disabled children. *Annals of Dyslexia* 23:111–20.

Ruddell, R., and Haggard, M. R. 1986. *Thinking About Reading*. Cleveland, OH: Modern Curriculum Press.

Rumelhart, D. E. 1975. Notes on a schema for stories. In *Representation and Understanding: Studies in Cognitive Science*, eds. D. G. Bobrow and A. M. Collins. New York: Academic Press.

Rumelhart, D. D. 1977. Toward an interactive model of reading. In *Attention and Performance*, ed. S. Dornic. Vol. 6. Hillsdale, NJ: Lawrence Erlbaum and Associates.

Rumelhart, D. E. 1980. Schemata: The building blocks of cognition. In *Theoretical Issues in Reading Comprehension*, eds. R. J. Spiro, B. C. Bruce, and W. F. Brewer. Hillsdale, NJ: Lawrence Erlbaum and Associates.

Rumelhart, D. E. 1984. Understanding understanding. In *Understanding Reading Comprehension*, ed. J. Flood. Newark DE: International Reading Association.

Rumelhart, D. E., and Norman, D. A. 1978. Accretion, tuning and restructuring: Three modes of learning. In *Semantic Factors in Cognition*, eds. J. W. Cotton and R. L. Klatzky. Hillsdale, NJ: Lawrence Erlbaum and Associates.

Rupley, W. H. 1988, October. Process oriented assessment of reading comprehension. Paper presented at the College Reading Association Conference, Atlanta, GA.

Sabin, L. 1982. *Patrick Henry*. Mahwah, NJ: Troll.

Sadoski, M. 1983. An exploratory study of the relationships between reported imagery and the comprehension and recall of a story. *Reading Research Quarterly* 19:110–23.

Sadoski, M. 1985. The natural use of imagery in story comprehension and recall: Replication and extension. *Reading Research Quarterly* 20:658–67.

Safford, A. L. 1960. Evaluation of an individualized reading program. *The Reading Teacher* 13:266–70.

Salganick, L. H. 1985. Why testing reforms are so popular and how they are changing education. *Phi Delta Kappan* 66:607–610.

Salinger, T. 1988, December. New directions in reading assessment: Some reflections on our progress. Paper presented at the National Reading Conference, Tucson, AZ.

Samuels, S. J., and Kamil, M. L. 1984. Models of the reading process. In *Handbook of Reading Research*, ed. P. D. Pearson. 185–224. New York: Longman.

Sanders, N. M. 1966. *Classroom Questions: What Kinds?* New York: Harper and Row.

Sarason, S. B., and Doris, J. 1979. *Educational Handicap, Public Policy, and Social History*. New York: Free Press.

Schank, R. C. 1982. *Reading and Understanding: Teaching from the Perspective of Artificial Intelligence*. Hillsdale, NJ: Lawrence Erlbaum and Associates.

Schatz, E. K., and Baldwin, R. S. 1986. Context clues are unreliable predictors of word meanings. *Reading Research Quarterly* 21:429–53.

Schell, L. M. 1988. Dilemmas in assessing reading comprehension. *The Reading Teacher* 42:12–16.

Schmitt, M. C., and O'Brien, D. G. 1986. Story grammars: Some cautions about the translation of research into practice. *Reading Research and Instruction* 26:1–8.

Schwartz, R. M. 1988. Learning to learn vocabulary in content area textbooks. *Journal of Reading* 38:108–18.

Schwartz, R. M., and Raphael, T. E. 1985. Concept of definition: A key to improving students' vocabulary. *The Reading Teacher* 38:198–205.

Searfoss, L. W., and Readence, J. E. 1985. *Helping Children Learn to Read*. Englewood Cliffs, NJ: Prentice-Hall.

Searfoss, L. W. 1987, October. Workshop on children's literature. Presented at the meeting of the Westchester Reading Council, White Plains, N.Y.

Searle, J. 1965. What is a speech act? In *Philosophy in America*, ed. M. Black. New York: Allen and Unwin; Cornell University Press.

Sebesta, S., Calder, J., and Cleland, L. 1982. A story grammar for the classroom. *The Reading Teacher* 36:180–84.

Sedgwick, B. 1978. The doughnut machine that wouldn't stop. In *Scott Foresman Basics in Reading*, eds. I. E. Aaron, D. Jackson, C. Riggs, R. C. Smith, and R. J. Tierney. Glenview, IL: Scott Foresman.

Selden, R. 1988, May. Teacher assessment. Paper presented at the conference of the International Reading Association, Toronto.

Shafer, S. 1988, 1990. *Bridges I &II*. New York: Scholastic.

Shannon, P. 1983. The use of commercial reading materials in American elementary schools. *Reading Research Quarterly* 19:68–85.

Shannon, P., Kameenui, E. J., and Baumann, J. F. 1988. An investigation of children's ability to comprehend character motives. *American Educational Research Journal* 25:441–62.

Shayer, M., and Wylam, H. 1981. The development of the concepts of heat and temperature in 10–13 year olds. *Journal of Research in Science Teaching* 18:419–35.

Shoop, M. 1986. InQuest: A listening and reading comprehension strategy. *The Reading Teacher* 39:670–74.

Silver, A. A., and Hagin, R. 1960. Specific reading disability: A delineation of the syndrome and relationship to cerebral dominance. *Comprehensive Psychiatry* 1:126–34.

Simon, J. 1970. Evolution genetique de la phrase ecrite chez l'ecolier. Unpublished doctoral dissertation, University of Paris.

Singer, H. 1978. Active comprehension: From answering to asking questions. *The Reading Teacher* 31:901–908.

Singer, H., and Donlan, D. 1982. Active comprehension: Problem-solving schema with question generation for comprehension of complex short stories. *Reading Research Quarterly* 17:166–87.

Slater, W. H., and Graves, M. F. 1989. Research on expository text: Implications for teachers. In *Children's Comprehension of Text*, ed. K. D. Muth. Newark, DE: International Reading Association.

Slater, W. H., Graves, M. F., and Piche, G. L. 1985. Effects of structural organizers on ninth-grade students' comprehension and recall of four patterns of expository text. *Reading Research Quarterly* 20:189–202.

Slavin, R. E. 1987. Cooperative learning and the cooperative school. *Educational Leadership* 45:7–13.

Slavin, R. E. 1988. Cooperative learning and student achievement. In *School and Classroom Organization*, ed. R. E. Slavin. Hillsdale, NJ: Lawrence Erlbaum and Associates.

Sloan, A., and Cappacio, A. 1983. *Aiming High: Stirring Tales and Poems*. New York: Amsco School Publications.

Smiley, S., Oakley, D., Worthen, D., Campione, J., and Brown, A. 1977. Recall of thematically relevant material of adolescent good and poor readers as a function of written vs. oral presentation. *Journal of Educational Psychology* 69:381–87.

Smith, B. S. 1987, December. Examining students' underlining of text: An on-line look at confidence ratings. Paper presented at the National Reading Conference, St. Petersburg, FL.

Smith, C. B. 1989. Prompting critical thinking. *The Reading Teacher* 42:424.

Smith, F. 1971. *Understanding Reading.* New York: Holt, Rinehart, and Winston.

Smith, F. 1978. *Understanding Reading.* Second edition. New York: Holt, Rinehart, and Winston.

Smith, G. B. 1988. Physical arrangements, grouping and ethnographic notetaking. In *Reexamining Reading Diagnosis: New Trends and Procedures*, eds. S. M. Glazer, L. W. Searfoss, and L. M. Gentil. Newark, DE: International Reading Association.

Smith, H. K. 1967. The responses of good and poor readers when asked to read for different purposes. *Reading Research Quarterly* 3:53–84.

Smitherman, G. 1980. White English in blackface, or who do I be? In *The State of the Language*, eds. L. Michaels and C. Ricks. 158–168. Berkeley: University of California Press.

Smucker, B. C. 1976. A time for courage. In *Tell Me How the Sun Rose*, eds. T. Clymer, R. M. Stein, D. Gates, and C. McCullough. Boston: Ginn.

Spearitt, D. 1972. Identification of subskills of reading comprehension by maximum likelihood factor analysis. *Reading Research Quarterly* 8:92–111.

Stahl, S. A., and Jacobson, M. G. 1986. Vocabulary difficulty, prior knowledge, and text comprehension. *Journal of Reading Behavior* 18:309–23.

Stahl, S. A., and Vancil, S. J. 1986. Discussion is what makes semantic maps work in vocabulary instruction. *The Reading Teacher* 39:62–67.

Stanovich, K. E. 1980. Toward an interactive-compensatory model of individual differences in the development of reading fluency. *Reading Research Quarterly* 16:32–71.

Stanovich, K. E. 1986. Matthew effects in reading: Some consequences of individual differences in the acquisition of literacy. *Reading Research Quarterly* 21:360–407.

Stauffer, R. 1969. *Directing Reading Maturity as a Cognitive Process.* New York: Harper and Row.

Stauffer, R. G. 1975. *Directing the Reading-Thinking Process.* New York: Harper and Row.

Stein, A. 1971. Strategies for failure. *Harvard Educational Review* 41:158–204.

Stein, N., and Glenn, C. 1979. An analysis of story comprehension in elementary school children. In *New Directions in Discourse Processing*, ed. R. Freedle. Norwood, NJ: Ablex.

Steptoe, J. 1987. *Mufaro's Beautiful Daughters.* New York: Lothrop, Lee and Shepard.

Sternberg, R. 1980. Sketch of a componential subtheory of human intelligence. *Behavioral and Brain Sciences* 3:573–84.

Sternberg, R. 1982. Introduction: Some common themes in contemporary approaches to the training of intelligent performances. In *How and How Much Can Intelligence Be Increased?*, eds. D. Detterman and R. Sternberg. Norwood, NJ: Ablex.

Sternberg, R. 1985. *Beyond IQ: A triarchic theory of human intelligence.* New York: Cambridge University Press.

Stevens, K. C. 1980. Readability formulae and McCall Crabbs Standard test lessons in reading. *The Reading Teacher* 33:413–15.

Sticht, T. G., and James, J. H. 1984. In *Handbook of Reading Research*, ed. P. D. Pearson. New York: Longman.

St. John, N. H. 1970. Desegregation and minority group performance. *Review of Educational Research* 40:111–34.

Stodolsky, S. S., Ferguson, T. L., and Wimpelberg, K. 1981. The recitation persists, but what does it look like? *Journal of Curriculum Studies* 13:121–30.

Stokes, T. F., and Baer, D. M. 1977. An implicit technology of generalization. *Journal of Applied Behavior Analysis* 10:349–67.

Stotsky, S. 1983. Research on reading/writing relationships: A synthesis and suggested directions. *Language Arts* 60:627–42.

Stotsky, S. 1987. A comparison of the two theories about development in written language: Implications for pedagogy and research. In *Comprehending Oral and Written Language*, eds. R. Horowitz and S. J. Samuels. San Diego: Academic Press.

Straw, S. B., and Schriener, R. 1982. The effects of sentence manipulation on subsequent measures of reading and listening. *Reading Research Quarterly* 17:339–52.

Strickland, D. S. 1988, May. Literature: The younger child. Workshop presented at the conference on Literature in the Classroom. Teachers College, Columbia University, New York.

Strickland, D. S., Dillon, R. M., Funkhouser, L., Glick, M., and Rogers, C. 1989. Research currents: Classroom dialogue during literature response groups. *Language Arts* 66:192–200.

Sutherland, Z., and Arbuthnot, M. H. 1986. *Children and Books.* Seventh Edition. Glenview, IL: Scott Foresman.

Swaby, B. E. R. 1989. *Diagnosis and Correction of Reading Difficulties.* Boston: Allyn and Bacon.

Swift, J. N., and Gooding, C. T. 1983. Interaction of wait time, feedback, and questioning

291

instruction on middle school science teaching. *Journal of Research on Science Teaching* 20: 721–30.

Taba, H. 1966. *Teaching Strategies and Cognitive Functioning in Elementary School Children*. Cooperative Research Project No. 2404. San Francisco: San Francisco State College.

Taba, H. 1967. *Teacher's Handbook for Elementary Social Studies*. Reading, MA: Addison-Wesley.

Tannen, D. ed. 1982. *Spoken and Written Language: Exploring Orality and Literacy*. Norwood, NJ: Ablex.

Taylor, K. 1978. *If Not Grammar, What?—Taking Remedial Writing Instruction Seriously*. [ED 159 668].

Television Bureau of Advertising, New York: January, 1984 report.

Templeton, S., and Mowrey, S. 1985. Readability, basal readers and story grammar: What lies beneath the surface? *Reading World* 24:40–47.

Tharp, R. G. 1982. The effective instruction of comprehension: Results and description of the Kamehameha Early Education Program. *Reading Research Quarterly* 17:503–27.

Thompson, R. 1975. Individualizing reading: A summary of research. *Educational Leadership* 33:57–63.

Thorndike, R. L. 1973. Reading as reasoning. *Reading Research Quarterly* 9:135–47.

Thorndyke, P. 1977. Cognitive structures in comprehension and memory of narrative discourse. *Cognitive Psychology* 9:77–110.

Thurstone, L. L. 1946. A note on a reanalysis of Davis' reading tests. *Psychometrika* 11:185–88.

Tiedt, I. M., Bruemmer, S. S., Lane, S., Stelwagon, P., Watanabe, K. O., and Williams, M. Y. 1983. *Teaching Writing in K–8 Classrooms: The Time has Come*. Englewood Cliffs, NJ: Prentice Hall.

Tierney, R. J., and Cunningham, J. W. 1984. Research on teaching reading comprehension. In *Handbook of Reading Research*, ed. P. D. Pearson. 609–656. New York: Longman.

Tierney, R. J., and Leys, M. 1986. What is the value of connecting reading and writing: In *Convergences: Transactions in Reading and Writing*, ed. B. T. Petersen. Urbana, IL: National Council of Teachers of English.

Tierney, R. J., and Pearson, P. D. 1983. Toward a composing model of reading. *Language Arts* 60:568–80.

Tierney, R. J., Readence, J. E., and Dishner, E. K. 1985. *Reading Strategies and Practices*. Boston: Allyn and Bacon.

Tierney, R. J., Soter, A., O'Flavahan, J. F., and McGinley, W. 1989. The effects of reading and writing upon thinking critically. *Reading Research Quarterly* 24:134–73.

Torgesen, J. K. 1975. Problems and prospects in the study of learning disabilities. In *Review of Child Development Research Volume 5*, eds. M. Hetherington and J. Hagen. New York: Russell Sage Foundation.

Touchstone Applied Science Associates. 1980. *Degrees of Reading Power—Users Manual*. New York: The College Board.

Trelease, J. 1985. *The Read-Aloud Handbook*. New York: Penguin Books.

Tuinman, J. J. 1974. Determining the passage-dependency of comprehension questions in 5 major tests. *Reading Research Quarterly* 9:207–223.

Vacca, R. T. 1988. Readers at risk: contextual influences on reading difficulties. Paper presented at the annual conference of the College Reading Association.

Vacca, R. T., and Vacca, J. L. 1986. *Content Area Reading*. Boston: Little, Brown and Company.

Vacca, R. T., Vacca, J. L., and Gove, M. K. 1987. *Reading and Learning to Read*. Boston: Little, Brown and Company.

Valencia, S. W., and Pearson, P. D. 1986. *Reading Assessment Initiative in the State of Illinois—1985–1986*. Springfield, IL: Illinois State Board of Education.

Valencia, S. W., and Pearson, P. D. 1987. Reading assessment: Time for a change. *The Reading Teacher* 40:726–32.

Valencia, S. W., and Pearson, P. D. 1988. Principles for classroom comprehension assessment. *Remedial and Special Education* 9:26–35.

Valencia, S. W., and Pearson, P. D. 1988, May. State-wide assessment. Paper presented at Conference on Reading Research, International Reading Association, Toronto.

Valencia, S. W., McGinley, W., and Pearson, P. D. in press. Assessing reading and writing: Building a more complete picture. In *Reading in the Middle School*, ed. G. Duffy. Second Edition. Newark, DE: International Reading Association.

Valencia, S. W., Pearson, P. D., Peters, C. W., and Wixson, K. K. 1989. Theory and practice in statewide reading assessment: Closing the gap. *Educational Leadership* 46:57–63.

van Allsburgh, C. 1986. *The Stranger.* Boston: Houghton Mifflin.

Veatch, J. 1985, October. Excellence in preparing reading teachers. Paper presented at the conference of the College Reading Association. Memphis, TN.

Veatch, J. 1978. *Reading in the Elementary School.* Second Edition. New York: John Wiley and Sons.

Vellutino, F. R. 1979. *Dyslexia: Theory and Research.* Cambridge, MA: MIT Press.

Viorst, J. 1972. *Alexander and the Terrible, Horrible, No Good Very Bad Day.* New York: Atteneum.

Vite, I. W. 1961. Individualized reading—the scoreboard on control studies. *Education* 81:285–90.

Vogel, S. 1974. Syntactic abilities in normal and dyslexic children. *Journal of Learning Disabilities* 7:103–109.

Vogel, S. 1975. *Syntactic Abilities in Normal and Dyslexic Children.* Baltimore: University Park Press.

Vygotsky, L. 1962. *Thought and Language.* Cambridge, MA: MIT Press.

Vygotsky, L. 1978. *Mind in Society: The Development of Higher Psychological Processes.* Cambridge MA: MIT Press.

Vygotsky, L. S. 1978. *Mind in Society.* M. Cole et al. eds. Cambridge, MA: Harvard University Press.

Wagner, B. J. 1985. Integrating the language arts. *Language Arts* 62:557–60.

Walp, T. P., and Walmsley, S. A. 1989. Instructional and philosophical congruence: Neglected aspects of coordination. *The Reading Teacher* 42:364–68.

Wang, M. C. 1987. The wedding of instruction and assessment in the classroom. *Assessment in the Service of Learning.* Proceedings of the Educational Testing Service Invitational Conference. Princeton, NJ: Educational Testing Service.

Waters, H. F. 1977. What TV does to kids. *Newsweek* February 21, 1977, 63.

Weaver, C. 1988. *Reading, Process and Practice.* Portsmouth, NH: Heinemann.

Weaver, P. A. 1979. Improving reading comprehension: Effects of sentence organization instruction. *Reading Research Quarterly* 15:29–145.

Weaver, W. W., and Kingston, A. J. 1963. A factor analysis of the cloze procedure and other measures of reading and language ability. *Journal of Communication* 13:252–61.

Weiderholt, J. L. 1974. Historical perspectives on the education of the learning disabled. In *The Second Review of Special Education,* eds. L. Mann and D. Sabatino. 103–152. Philadelphia: JSE Press.

Weisberg, R. K., and Balajthy, E. 1985, December. Effects of semantic mapping training on disabled readers' summarizing and recognition of expository text structure. Paper presented at the National Reading Conference, San Diego, CA.

Weisberg, R., and Balajthy, E. 1988. Issues in transferability of training in expository text structure. Paper presented at the National Reading Conference, Tucson, AZ.

Whaley, J. F, and Spiegel, D. L. 1982. Improving children's reading comprehension through instruction in schematic aspects of narratives. Paper presented at the American Educational Research Association, New York.

White, R. S., and Karl, H. 1980. Reading, writing and sentence combining: The track record. *Reading Improvement* 17:226–32.

Whorf, B. L. 1956. *Language, Thought and Reality.* Cambridge, MA: MIT Press.

Wigfield, A, and Asher, S. R. 1984. Social and motivational influences on reading. In *Handbook of Reading Research,* ed. P. D. Pearson. New York: Longman.

Wiig, E. H., Semel, E. M., and Crouse, M. A. B. 1973. The use of morphology by high-risk and learning disabled children. *Journal of Learning Disabilities* 6:457–65.

Wildrer, H. B., Ludlum, R. P., and Brown, H. M. 1981. *This is America's Story.* Fourth Edition. Boston: Houghton Mifflin.

Wilkinson, A. M. 1971. *The Foundation of Language: Talking and Reading in Young Children.* London: Oxford University Press.

Williams, F., and Naremore, R. 1969. On the functional analysis of social class differences in modes of speech. *Speech Monographs* 36:77–102.

Williams, F., Whitehead, J. L., and Miller, L. M. 1971. *Attitudinal Correlates of Children's Speech Characteristics.* Final Report OEG-0-70-2868(508). Austin, TX: Center for Communication Research.

Wilson, R. M., and Gambrell, L. B. 1988. *Reading Comprehension in the Elementary School.* Boston: Allyn and Bacon.

Winne, P. H., and Marx, R. W. 1987. The best tool teachers have—their students' thinking. In *Talks to Teachers,* eds. D. C. Berliner and B. V. Rosenshine. New York: Random House.

Winograd, P. N., Wixson, K. K., and Lipson, M. Y. 1989. *Improving Basal Reading Instruction.* New York: Teachers College Press.

Wixson, K. K. 1983. Questions about a text: What you ask about is what children learn. *The Reading Teacher* 37:287–93.

Wixson, K. K. 1986. Vocabulary instruction and children's comprehension of basal stories. *Reading Research Quarterly* 21:317–29.

Wixson, K. K., and Lipson, M. Y. 1984. Reading (dis)ability: An interactionist perspective. In *The Contexts of School-Based Literacy*, ed. T. Raphael. 131–148. New York: Random House.

Wixson, K. K., and Peters, C. W. 1987. Comprehension assessment: Implementing an interactive view of reading. *Educational Psychologist* 22:333–56.

Wixson, K. K., Bosky, A. B., Yochum, M. N., and Alvermann, D. E. 1984. An interview for assessing students; perceptions of classroom reading tasks. *The Reading Teacher* 37:346–53.

Wixson, K. K., Peters, C. W., Schwartz, S., Pearson, O., Soifer, R., Kirby, C., Roeber, E., Shakrani, S., and Weber, E. 1985. *Michigan Educational Assessment Program Test Blueprint.*

Wolf, M. 1984. Naming, reading and the dyslexias: A longitudinal overview. *Annals of Dyslexia* 34:87–115.

Wolfram, W. 1973. Sociolinguistic alternatives in teaching reading to nonstandard speakers. In *Language, Society and Education: A Profile in Black English*, ed. J. S. DeStephano. Worthington, OH: Charles A. Jones.

Wong, B. Y. L. 1985. Self-questioning instructional research. *Review of Educational Research* 55:227–68.

Wood, K. D. 1984. Probable passages: A writing strategy. *The Reading Teacher* 37:496–99.

Wood, K. D. 1988. Techniques for assessing children's potential for learning. *The Reading Teacher* 41:440–47.

Woods, M. L., and Moe, A. J. 1989. *Analytical Reading Inventory.* 4th ed. Columbus, OH: Merrill.

Yando, R., Seitz, V., and Zigler, E. 1979. *Intellectual and Personality Characteristics of Children: Social-Class and Ethnic-Group Differences.* Hillsdale, NJ: Lawrence Erlbaum and Associates.

Zakaluk, B. L., and Samuels, S. J. 1988. Toward a new approach to predicting text comprehensibility. In *Readability: Its Past, Present and Future*, eds. B. L. Zakaluk and S. J. Samuels. Newark, DE: International Reading Association.

INDEX

Stanines, 260, 261
Stanovitch, K. E., 6
Stories. *See also* Narrative prose
    aiding comprehension of, 150, 152
    in basal readers, 48
    bland, 48
    choosing central concepts in, 89
    comparing children's experiences to, 153–54
    comparing and contrasting different, 153
    conflict in, 48
    just to be enjoyed, 90
    retelling orally by child, 206
    schema of, 149
    in trade books, 48
Story map(s), 89, *151*, 244. *See also* Text maps
    story frame and, 212–13
    teachers' use of, 150, 153
Story structure, 148
    explicit instruction about, 154
Stotsky, S., 208–9, 210
Strategies
    for active learning, 65
    children's use of, 66
    class discussion of, 105–6
    learning four, 189–90
    pointing out usefulness of, 71
    used by good readers, 72
    used in reciprocal teaching, 72
Stress Reaction Scale (Gentile and Macmillan), 251
Success
    expectations of, 35–36, 64–65
    importance of, 58, 65
Summarizing strategy, 189–90, 214, 216–18
Syntax
    development in children, 135
    oral and written, 12
    to understand language, 134

Taba, H., 75, 99
Taba method, 75
Teacher behaviors, amount of engaged time in class and, 56
Teacher-made tests to assess comprehension, 233, 235
Teacher misconceptions about "every teacher should be a teacher of reading," 41
Teacher(s)
    basal reader and inexperienced, 40
    as bridge between children and text, 133
    collaboration between, 54, 55, 200
    communication between specialists and classroom, 228
    demands and pressures on, 52
    effective, 52, 62
    errors when trying new techniques, 107
    expectations of children's reading

readiness and, 28
    information on students used by, 227
    importance of high expectations for remedial readers and, 64–65
    low expectations for children by, 35–36
    maintenance of strong academic focus by effective, 62
    management skills of, 53–61
    planning by, 81–82
    as models of good questioning behavior, 76–77
    reducing ambiguity of actions of, 64–65
    resistance to whole language instruction and, 44
    as a professional, 81–82
    small group instruction by expert, 59
    special reading, 54, 55, 228
    test scores and evaluation of, 259
    who are good explainers, 78
    who read good stories to children, 30
    working together of special and classroom, 54–55
Teacher's manuals, 39
Teacher support groups for whole language instruction, 44
Teacher training and change, transition period for, 44
Teaching. *See also* Instruction; Reading comprehension instruction
    daily journal of, 231
Teaching skill, 66–67
Teaching tools for reading comprehension instruction, 204
Television, 30
Testing situation, 259–60
Testmakers and publishers, role of, 259
Test results, providing children with feedback on, 268
Tests. *See also* Externally developed tests of comprehension assessment; IQ tests; Placement tests; Reading comprehension assessment; Standardized tests; Teacher-made tests
    computerized, 260
    construct validity of, *255*
    cultural bias and, 263
    ecological validity of, 258
    formats of, 255–56
    instructional validity of, 233
    passage-dependent items in, 263
    reliability of, 233
    teachers' input in selection of, 254
    what is measured by standardized reading comprehension, 262
Test scores
    misleading, 229
    most popular way of reporting, 261
    preciseness of, 262
    uses of standardized, 262–64